A Stitch in Time

LEAN RETAILING AND THE TRANSFORMATION
OF MANUFACTURING—LESSONS FROM THE
APPAREL AND TEXTILE INDUSTRIES

FREDERICK H. ABERNATHY
JOHN T. DUNLOP
JANICE H. HAMMOND
DAVID WEIL

New York Oxford
OXFORD UNIVERSITY PRESS
1999

Oxford University Press

Oxford   New York
Athens   Auckland   Bangkok   Bogotá   Buenos Aires
Calcutta   Cape Town   Chennai   Dar es Salaam   Delhi   Florence
Hong Kong   Istanbul   Karachi   Kuala Lumpur   Madrid   Melbourne
Mexico City   Mumbai   Nairobi   Paris   São Paulo   Singapore
Taipei   Tokyo   Toronto   Warsaw

and associated companies
Berlin   Ibadan

Copyright © 1999 by Oxford University Press, Inc.

Published by Oxford University Press, Inc.
198 Madison Avenue, New York, New York 10016

Oxford is a registered trademark of Oxford University Press

All rights reserved. No part of this publication may be reproduced,
stored in a retrieval system, or transmitted, in any form
or by any means, electronic, mechanical, photocopying, recording,
or otherwise, without the prior permission
of Oxford University Press.

Library of Congress Cataloging-in-Publication Data

A stitch in time : lean retailing and the transformation
of manufacturing—lessons from the apparel and textile industries /
Frederick H. Abernathy . . . [et al.].
p.   cm.
Includes bibliographical references and index.
ISBN 0-19-512615-7
1. Clothing trade—United States—Management. 2. Manufacturing
industries—United States—Management—Data processing.
3. Retail trade—United States—Management.
I. Abernathy, Frederick H.
HD9940.U4 S75   1999   687'.068'8—dc21   98-38224

1 3 5 7 9 8 6 4 2
Printed in the United States of America
on acid-free paper

Contents

	Preface	vii
1.	The New Competitive Advantage in Apparel	1
2.	The Past as Prologue: Historical Background on the U.S. Retail, Apparel, and Textile Industries	21
3.	The Retail Revolution: Traditional Versus Lean Retailing	39
4.	The Building Blocks of Lean Retailing	55
5.	The Impact of Lean Retailing	71
6.	Inventory Management for the Retailer: Demand Forecasting and Stocking Decisions	87
7.	Inventory Management for the Manufacturer: Production Planning and Optimal Sourcing Decisions	107
8.	Apparel Operations: Getting Ready to Sew	129
9.	Apparel Operations: Assembly and the Sewing Room	151
10.	Human Resources in Apparel	165
11.	Textile Operations: Spinning, Weaving, and Finishing Cloth	185
12.	The Economic Viability of Textiles: A Tale of Multiple Channels	203
13.	The Global Marketplace	221
14.	Suppliers in a Lean World: Firm and Industry Performance in an Integrated Channel	243
15.	Information-Integrated Channels: Public Policy Implications and Future Directions	263

Appendix A	List of Acronyms	281
Appendix B	The HCTAR Survey	283
Appendix C	Data Sources	289
Appendix D	Companies Visited or Interviewed by HCTAR	295

Notes	299
Subject Index	347
Name Index	365
Business Index	367

Preface

Retail stores have dramatically increased their use of information technology and systems in the last two decades. Their customers see bar code scanners at checkout counters in their local supermarkets, malls, drugstores, and many shops in the neighborhood, but bar codes and scanning represent just a small part of the changes that are transforming retailing as well as the manufacturing practices of their suppliers. Increasingly, manufacturers must produce their items in an ever-widening offering of styles at competitive prices and then replenish those products for the retailer in a matter of days.

This book details changes in the U.S. apparel and textile industries driven by the demands of modern retailers. What is happening in these industries, two of the oldest sectors of manufacturing, is a microcosm of larger shifts that are affecting a growing diversity of consumer product industries and their upstream suppliers. Understanding the emerging competitive dynamics of what are often considered "sunset" industries sheds a bright light on the fundamental economic changes and challenges facing modern manufacturers.

Advances in information technology have reconfigured American retailing. Retailers can now exchange point-of-sales information—a relatively accurate measure of consumer demand—with their suppliers and accordingly require manufacturers to replenish orders much more quickly than in the past. This has changed the manufacturing rules of the game, particularly in the apparel sector. Garment makers can no longer afford to fill retail orders in months or even weeks; using the cheapest labor generally takes more time—time that many retail replenishment arrangements do not allow. Because "lean" retailing works in an entirely new way, manufacturers have had to reshape their production planning methods, cost models, inventory practices, production operations and workforce utilization, and sourcing strategies. The introduction of time to market as a manufacturing metric has been a "stitch in time" to the U.S.-based manufacturers as they face competition from offshore low wage suppliers located far from our domestic market.

When we began our work seven years ago, we did not appreciate the scope of this transformation. In 1991, the Alfred P. Sloan Foundation approached Fred Abernathy, at Harvard University's Division of Engineering and Applied Sciences, to develop one of its new industry research projects on apparel and textiles. Sloan was planning a series of studies to analyze American manufacturing industries and encourage long-term dialogue between academic researchers and manufacturing companies, as well as with government agencies when appropriate. The Harvard Center for Textile and Apparel Research (HCTAR) was organized with the four of us as principal investigators, a team that encompasses a range of intellectual disciplines and experience. We are grateful for the continued support of the Sloan Foundation and the opportunities it has provided for periodic exchange with other Sloan industry projects. We particularly appreciate the interest and encouragement of Ralph Gomory and Hirsh Cohen of the Foundation.

We then proceeded to develop working relations with executives of the leading organizations in these industries, building on our past associations with major textile firms and apparel producers, leading retailers, and the two national labor organizations represented in the sectors, now merged as the Union of Needletrades, Industrial and Textile Employees (UNITE!). An advisory committee drawn from these executives has proven invaluable in occasional joint discussions and through more frequent individual conversations. We readily acknowledge their counsel and assistance in providing data, opening doors, and reacting to ideas. The members of the advisory committee in the formative stages of our study were: Peter N. Butenhoff of Textile/Clothing Technology Corporation [TC]^2; Alex Dillard of Dillard's Inc.; Paul Gillease of DuPont Fibers; Bernard A. Leventhal of Burlington Menswear; Roger Milliken of Milliken Corporation; Burton B. Ruby of Trans-Apparel Group; and Jack Sheinkman of the Amalgamated Clothing and Textile Workers Union.

One of the proven means in a university of developing ideas, educating, reviewing experience, and reining in intellectual exuberance is a series of seminar sessions with an outside guest, one who makes an initial presentation to advanced students and critical colleagues. We conducted such monthly seminars at the Harvard Business School from 1991 to 1994 when we were starting to gather data and forming our ideas. We recognize the contribution that these sessions and other seminars made to this volume and want to thank the guests and participants.

A continuing research project in a university is also able to attract advanced graduate students at the stage of the Ph.D. dissertation. These young women and men are likely to maintain an interest in a field throughout their careers in research and university teaching or in outside professions. We have drawn such students from two main doctoral programs at Harvard—one in Business Economics, the other in Engineering and Applied Sciences. And we have been fortunate indeed in the high quality of these associates; they have contributed to our work as well as their dissertations. The following have completed their Ph.D. degrees at Harvard in collaboration with this project: Karen Daniels, Peter Fisher, Catherine George, Margaret Hwang, Loo Hay Lee, Zhenyu Li, and Jan Rivkin.

In addition, we appreciate the interest and assistance of a number of university colleagues: Walter Salmon and Robert Buzzell of the Harvard Business School assisted with questions of retail; Y. C. Ho, and Richard Caves of Harvard University and Victor Milenkovic of the University of Miami helped with graduate student recruitment and supervision. Gregory Diehl, Tak Wing Lau, and Z. Bo Tang of the research staff of the Harvard DEAS have made significant contributions to modeling plant production and inventory. Thomas Rawski of the University of Pittsburgh and Gary Jefferson of Brandeis University assisted in our ongoing work in China.

This project has substantially benefited from constructive relations with several federal government departments and agencies. Based on our past associations, a number of government officials have readily discussed the interpretation of data and facilitated our access to regularly available statistics. We are particularly grateful, as are our graduate students, to the Boston Research Data Center of the Department of Commerce, which shared establishment data with us. We have made presentations and led discussions with Commerce Department staff, and senior officials have participated in our seminars and joined in our conferences, creating a fruitful exchange.

In another arena, our numerous visits to textile and apparel companies and large retail organizations have been some of the most instructive experiences of this project. An appreciation of the technology, processes, workplaces, and organizations of these enterprises—and their growing interdependencies—is vital to an understanding of textile, apparel, and retail relationships. Our sessions with senior executives were characterized by unending questions and candid responses; our requests for further data were regularly furnished. In turn, we have assured these participants that no release of any identifiable data would occur without permission. We want to thank the busy executives who shared their time and ideas with us.

In particular, we developed an extensive questionnaire to secure detailed data on apparel business units and their relationships with textile and retail organizations. We learned a great deal from those who helped formulate the sixty pages of questions as well as from those companies that agreed to pre-test the questionnaire before revisions. We are indebted to Alex and William Dillard of Dillard's Inc. and Don Keeble of Kmart, major retailers who asked their suppliers to respond to this voluminous inquiry, and to Jay Mazur of the International Ladies' Garment Workers Union and Jack Sheinkman of the Amalgamated Clothing and Textile Workers Union, the labor organizations that similarly asked companies under collective agreements to respond to us. The results of the survey provided vital measures of the transition in process in the apparel and textile industries from 1988 to 1992.

Three of us have seen firsthand clothing manufacturing operations in mainland China, through the assistance of U.S. retailers that import these products. We have established a research relationship with the Chinese Textile University in Shanghai and have financed a report by Professor Gu on the Chinese textile and apparel industries, along with case studies of particular plants. As for the European perspective, our subcontractor Professor Peter Doeringer of Boston University is preparing a report about developments in these industries in England and France. In an effort to synthesize international competitive forces, we have also met with transportation and logistics specialists, seeking data on air, ocean, and trucking freight rates, time requirements, and customs processes.

The Uniform Code Council, based in Dayton, Ohio, reviewed the paper records of its first fifteen years of experience with Uniform Product Codes (UPC) and made available to us integrated records showing registrations by month for the period 1971–94 and by industrial sector. These data enabled us to relate the development of bar codes for apparel enterprises with the policies of major retailers. We appreciate the cooperation of the late Harold P. Juckett, President of the UCC, and its permission to publish these data. In addition, a history of the development of bar codes has been published in collaboration with HCTAR: Brown, Stephen A., *Revolution at the Checkout Counter: The Explosion of the Bar Code*, Cambridge, MA: Harvard University Press, 1997.

Another distinctive feature of this project has been the development of software to facilitate efficient marker-making, an apparel fabrication process that economizes on cloth. Victor Milenkovic and his students have created software that is now copyrighted, licensed, and in commercial use. We appreciate the cooperation of companies interested in the development of the software and those that have used it. This activity has yielded significant data and helped us to understand an essential step in apparel manufacture.

It almost goes without saying that we acknowledge the assistance over the years of the staff of HCTAR, all those who have arranged our periodic meetings, seminars, conferences, the distribution of reprints, and responses to numerous inquiries. Their efforts in collecting, tabulating, and formatting statistical data, including material from our questionnaire as well as government data, have been invaluable. Heartfelt thanks go to our respective secretaries for working with draft manuscripts, scheduling our meetings and trips, and facilitating the way the four of us have worked together despite our disparate activities and software. The HCTAR staff has included Barbara Cardullo, Igor Choodnovskiy, Scott Garvin, Afroze Mohammed, and Muriel N. Peters; our able secretaries are Rosemary Lombardo, Marie Stroud, Sheila Toomey, and Julie Weigley.

We are particularly grateful to Martha Nichols for helping us take a collection of chapters written in our different pens and, in a humane way, make a book out of them.

The names of all those who have contributed to this volume would be a very large compendium indeed. Nonetheless, the following warrant special mention: William Klopman, Burlington Industries; James Kearns, DuPont; Homi Patel, Hartmarx Corporation; Eugene Gwaltney, Dwight Carlisle, and Fletcher Adamson, Russell Corporation; Peter Jacobi, Levi Strauss; Walter Elisha, Springs Industries; Anton Haake and Hal Snell, J. C. Penney; G. G. Michealson and Tom Cole, Federated Department Stores; Victor Fung, Prudential Asia; William Fung, Li & Fung Limited; Michael Cassidy, Microdynamics; Arthur Gundersheim, UNITE!; Joseph Dixon, Brooks Brothers; Robert Tuttle, Gerber Garment Technology, Inc.; Everett Ehrlich, Rita Hayes, Harvey Monk, and

Joyce Cooper, U.S. Department of Commerce; Jonathon Byrnes, Jonathon Byrnes & Company; Gus Walen, Warren Featherbone Inc.; Bill Mix, Grove Associates.

We value the contribution of all the people and organizations who have assisted our study, as well as the support of our families throughout this intensive project. Understanding the scope of changes in these linked industries and their implications more generally would not have been possible without such cooperation.

Cambridge, Massachusetts FREDERICK H. ABERNATHY
September 1998 JOHN T. DUNLOP
JANICE H. HAMMOND
DAVID WEIL

This book is published as part
of the Alfred P. Sloan Foundation program
on Centers for Study of Industry.

A
Stitch
in
Time

1
The New Competitive Advantage in Apparel

In the late 1940s, Bond Stores, the largest men's clothing chain at the time, created a sensation in New York City by offering a wide selection of suits with two pairs of pants instead of one, reintroducing a level of product choice not seen since before the war.[1] When the line of hopeful buyers at its Times Square store stretched around the block, Bond had to impose a limit of two suits per customer. During World War II, the apparel and textile industries had been converted to supply field jackets, overcoats, and uniforms to the U.S. and Allied Forces. But in the years immediately following the war, returning soldiers, the end of rationing, and pent-up customer demand meant apparel was in short supply.

Fifty years later, it is hard to imagine a retailer—be it a high-end department store, mass merchandiser, or catalog service—limiting an individual customer's clothing purchase. Retailers collect detailed point-of-sales information that reflects the real-time demand for goods by consumers. Through new computer systems, they share this information with suppliers who, in turn, can ship orders within days to automated distribution centers. The contemporary equivalent of Bond Stores now has a much better chance of avoiding stock-outs of popular items and the inventory gluts that lead to costly markdowns. By the same token, the overall risk associated with fickle consumers, numerous selling seasons, and segmented markets—along with fierce overseas competition—has currently made this a tough arena for American retailers and manufacturers.

The most surprising aspect of this story is that today's U.S. apparel and textile industries—left for dead by business commentators and economic analysts in the 1980s—have begun to transform themselves, reaping new competitive advantages. Although Bond Stores' customers were thrilled by a suit with two pairs of pants, contemporary customers want and expect a huge range of choices, and the consumer desire for limitless variety has kept the American apparel industry alive. In 1995, for instance, American consumers purchased 28.7 outerwear garments (all coats, jackets, shirts, dresses, blouses, sweaters, trousers, slacks, and shorts) per capita; in China the estimated number of such garments was only 2 per capita.[2]

The transformation of U.S. clothing and textile manufacturing is very much still in progress and has by no means been successful for every company; but these industries have entered a renaissance of sorts, one that reflects new information technologies and management practices as well as the new economics of international trade. This book describes what has happened since the postwar era in three related industries—retail, apparel, and textiles—and what such companies must do to improve performance. We cover the histories of these industries, including the information technologies that have transformed these enterprises, manufacturing processes, inventory management, the new role of logistics, and global trade implications and policies.

The story is a complex one, involving many individual cases and specifics. This study began with a focus on apparel manufacturing, but we soon concluded that apparel production must be viewed as an integral part of a *channel*. A channel is the set of all firms and relationships that get a product to market, including the original acquisition of raw materials; production of the item at a manufacturing facility; distribution to a retailer; sale of the finished item to the customer; and any installation, repair, or service activities that follow the sale.

A retail-apparel-textile channel typically includes the companies that manufacture synthetic fibers; produce, gather, and refine natural fibers; spin fiber into yarn; weave or knit yarn into fabric; manufacture buttons, zippers, and other garment components; and cut and sew fabric into garments. It also includes the retailers who sell garments to end consumers. The retail link often involves services or instructions to suppliers about fabric and garment design, packaging, distribution, order fulfillment, and transportation. And it is in some of these areas, particularly distribution and order fulfillment, that channel dynamics have undergone substantial change during the last decade.

Supply channels are not new, of course; for centuries, fabric-makers have sold their wares to those who cut and sew garments. But, until recently, most channels in the textile and apparel industries have been characterized by arm's-length relationships among relatively autonomous firms. It is only since the mid-1980s that a number of market and technological changes have encouraged companies to enhance the links among different stages of production and distribution. Indeed, retailers like Wal-Mart Stores, Kmart Corporation, and Dillard's Inc. have been the driving forces behind changes in manufacturing and logistics systems in a way that was unheard of in Bond Stores' time. For instance, entrepreneur Sam Walton built a retail juggernaut that began with thirty-nine Wal-Mart stores in 1971 and grew to almost three thousand by 1996. He did so by insisting that suppliers implement information technologies for exchanging sales data, adopt standards for product labeling, and use modern methods of material handling that assured customers a variety of products at low prices.

We contend that this revolution in retailing practices will determine future competitive outcomes in retail-apparel-textile channels. These new practices—which we call *lean retailing*—have compelled apparel producers to reorganize the manner in which they relate to retail customers, undertake distribution, forecast and plan production, and manage their supplier relations. Lean retailing has also changed the way the textile industry relates to both apparel producers and retailers. Most important, because the apparel industry has been one of the first to face the full brunt of the retail revolution, its story illuminates pervasive changes under way in the entire economy.

In many respects, our findings defy the conventional wisdom. When we began our research, we were advised by American industry participants to establish better performance measures—for example, how many minutes does it take to make a shirt? The traditional view holds that because manufacturing performance is determined by the labor time required to produce an item, then what applies to cars, for example, can also apply to clothing; therefore, U.S. apparel manufacturers might be able to save themselves by improving assembly operations.[3] Yet after years of studying hundreds of American apparel firms, we have found that direct labor content is not the primary issue. The companies that have adopted new information systems and management practices, participating in a well-integrated channel, are the ones with the strongest performance today—not those that have simply improved assembly operations.

The changes we examine in retailing are not only profound but rippling through a growing segment of the American economy. They have already transformed channel relations in such industries as food and grocery, home-building products, personal computers, and office products. The retail revolution is affecting the automobile, health care, and pharmaceutical industries as well. Now that manufacturers of power tools and ball bearings talk about their products as "fashion" items, the apparel industry—always subject to the whims of fashion—has much to say to any industry that involves retailing. Every channel has its particular history, elements, and dynamics, and retail-apparel-textile channels are no exception. *A Stitch in Time* uses the U.S. apparel story to highlight the transformation of retailing and manufacturing across the board.

Five Decades of Change

When Bond Stores had customers lining up around the block to buy suits, "casual wear," as we know it today, did not exist. Even in the 1960s, men wore suits, ties, and hats to the ballpark, and women were clothed in dresses and millinery. As recently as 1969, the dress code at Harvard required undergraduate men to wear a collar, necktie, and jacket in the dining halls; women had to wear a dress or a skirt and blouse. It wasn't until the 1970s that these vestiges of formality gave way to blue jeans and T-shirts—the casual wear uniform. The 1980s ushered in yuppie brands, and in the 1990s history repeated itself as baby boomers' children adopted the bedraggled grunge look. Many business firms have "casual days" for office attire. Now six out of ten U.S. employers now have casual days in their workplaces, all but a few establishing this practice during the 1990s. About seven out of ten organizations with dress-down days permit employees to wear polo shirts, jeans, and sneakers.[4]

The U.S. apparel and textile industries, like the clothing and other products they produce, have undergone tremendous changes over the past half century. From 1950 to 1995, domestic production of apparel doubled, while textile production, less vulnerable to imports, increased almost three times.[5] Yet since World War II, shifting tastes in clothes, rising real incomes, and domestic and foreign competition within the textile and apparel industries have markedly reduced the proportion of consumer budgets expended on apparel and its upkeep (laundry and dry cleaning). In December 1963, apparel's share of the Consumer Price Index was 10.63 percent;[6] by December 1995, that percentage had fallen to 5.52 percent of average household expenditures.[7]

Meanwhile, structural changes in the retail industry have influenced how and where clothing is sold. The growth of the highway system around central cities and the rapid expansion of suburbs created new opportunities for shopping centers, malls, and other outlets closer to a growing number of two wage-earner families. The metropolitan suburbs increased housing units in the 1950s through the 1980s far faster than the inner cities or the rural suburbs.[8] Because inner cities retained a high proportion of lower income families, increased purchasing power for shelter, food, and clothing shifted to the suburbs. That means the large department stores traditionally based in cities, such as Macy's or Marshall Field and Company—served by mass transportation and marketed through newspaper advertisements—suffered from the competition of mass distributors like Wal-Mart and specialty shops in new locations.

The enterprises that compose the apparel and textile industries manufacture a wide variety of products, and the mix has also changed since the postwar era. Over the past thirty-five years in the textile industry, the number of workers employed for carpet and rug production has doubled and is projected to expand further over the next decade. In the apparel industry, more than a quarter of all workers now produce nonclothing items like curtains, draperies, house furnishings, and automotive trimmings; once again, employment since the 1960s in these areas has doubled, while it has dropped off dramatically for actual garment-making.

These changes are related to new technology and foreign competition. Exhortations to buy the "union label" or "Made in the U.S.A." have done relatively little to stem the tide of clothing assembled overseas. For example, the per capita number of outerwear garments purchased in the United States increased from 14.3 to 28.7 in the period from 1967 to 1995.[9] Imports, however, provided half the total in 1995, leaving domestic production with only about the same per capita number of outerwear garments as three decades earlier[10]—all this, even though apparel and textiles in the United States have long been characterized by special import regulation. Tariffs on their imports have remained higher than many other manufactured goods. Since the 1960s, national policymakers have sought to moderate the growth of imports, primarily through agreements with other governments. The Multi-Fiber Arrangement (MFA), a network of bilateral agreements negotiated with participating nations which became effective in 1974, established quotas for imports largely related to estimates of the growth of the U.S. domestic market. The stated purpose of the MFA was to provide for the "orderly" growth of trade in these products among countries on a negotiated basis. Advocates emphasized that "textiles and apparel offer proportionately more jobs, including entry-level positions, to less well educated, more disadvantaged groups in the United States than most other sectors of the economy."[11]

Yet with the signing of the agreements that grew out of the Uruguay Round of international trade negotiations that concluded in 1994, the MFA has now been replaced; textiles and apparel trade are to be integrated into the General Agreement on Tariffs and Trade (GATT) over a ten-year period that ends January 1, 2005. Many American industry participants and policymakers believe these changes could deal a fatal blow to the U.S. apparel industry, which will become even more exposed to global competition. The impact of these trade changes remains uncertain, and national policies that take them into account are still evolving. But if one did not consider the shift in retailing practices that is also recasting the apparel industry—and turned some American companies into unexpected leaders—it might indeed look like "Made in the U.S.A." was a lost cause.

A Dying Industry—or Not?

For many commentators, a book about the future of the U.S. apparel and textile industries is still an oxymoron. The conventional wisdom paints a grim picture of where these industries are headed. Low-cost labor overseas and the increasing penetration of imports have certainly undercut American apparel manufacturers; apparel imports grew rapidly in most categories starting in the mid-1970s. If we measure import penetration in physical units (rather than dollar value),[12] import penetration for men's and boys' suits, for example, went from just 10 percent in 1973 to 43 percent by 1996. A similar expansion in imports occurred for men's and boys' trousers, women's and girls' dresses, and women's slacks and shorts.[13]

As one consequence, the number of business failures among U.S. apparel manufacturers climbed from 227 in 1975 to a high of 567 in 1993.[14] Not surprisingly, employment in the apparel sector during this period declined appreciably. And the U.S. Bureau of Labor Statistics projects a further reduction in the domestic apparel industry during the period 1996 to 2006 from 864,000 workers to just 714,000[15]—this from an industry that employed about 1.2 million employees in 1950 and reached a peak of 1.4 million employees in 1973.[16]

The conventional wisdom explains the industry's decline in this way: Apparel, particularly women's apparel, is driven by price-based competition among generally small manufacturing and contracting establishments.[17] Labor costs represent a significant portion of cost for many garment categories,[18] and U.S. wage levels far exceed those of competitors in countries like the People's Republic of China and Mexico.[19] Although the magnitude of these differences varies as exchange rates fluctuate, under any realistic exchange-rate scenario, the labor cost differential is sufficiently high to put U.S. manufacturers at a very significant competitive disadvantage.

The manufacture of men's shirts provides another illustration. Throughout much of the post-World War II era, the majority of men's shirts sold in the United States were white dress shirts, primarily through department stores. Shirts with stripes, patterns, and uncommon colors constituted less than 30 percent of all dress shirts sold through the 1960s.[20] In this environment, low fashion content and limited product variety made demand for individual shirts relatively predictable. Store buyers succeeded by striking deals with apparel manufacturers for large shipments of white shirts at the lowest possible price and with long delivery lead times. Unlike the women's industry, where style has always mattered more, relatively large men's apparel manufacturers such as Haggar; Hart, Schaffner, and Marx; Fruit of the Loom; Arrow Shirt Company; and Hathaway Shirt emerged, seeking to capture economies of scale.[21]

But hourly compensation levels have increasingly hurt U.S. apparel-makers, if performance is principally determined on a price/cost basis. For example, because of wage differentials between the countries, U.S. apparel-makers would need to be 2.5 times more productive than firms in Hong Kong to be "competitive." As a result, U.S. shirt manufacturers lost enormous market share to offshore producers. And employment in men's and boys' shirts between 1972 and 1996 declined an average of 3 percent a year.[22]

There is just one problem with these accounts. Although the production of basic white dress shirts may lend itself to a price/cost analysis, this "staple" good, like many staple goods, now constitutes only a small proportion of all shirt production: by 1986, little more than 20 percent of men's dress shirts were white.[23] This one-time staple has been replaced by shirts of dizzying diversity in fabric, design, and style, providing the final consumer with a huge assortment of shirts while exposing retailers and manufacturers to increased risk of holding large volumes of unsold goods. Classical economic assumptions about market competition are not directly applicable in this situation, even in a "mature" industry like apparel.

As shown in later chapters, manufacturers that invest in advanced information technologies and use them to change their methods of planning and production can significantly reduce the amount of inventory they hold, thereby reducing the need to mark down or write off unsold products at the end of a season. These manufacturers also earn twice as much in profits than suppliers that continue to operate along traditional lines. Yet the distinguishing feature of such high performers is not their success in shaving off labor costs in the assembly room; it is their effort in changing basic aspects of the way they manage their enterprises.

Although it is true that the American apparel industry could have given up in the early 1990s, with only distribution centers and designers remaining in this country, it did not. Instead, manufacturers have developed, or have been compelled to develop, a competitive service for retailers; best practice American producers can now deliver orders with just a few days' notice, something overseas suppliers have difficulty achieving. These U.S. firms do so through electronic data interchange (EDI), automated distribution centers, and sophisticated inventory management—a triumph of information technology, speed, and flexibility over low labor rates.

The Channel Perspective: Five Propositions

So what has changed the prognosis for American apparel and textiles and provided new opportunities for these industries? The answer is not to be found simply in the clout of a few retailers or the use of bar codes or EDI. To understand why the apparel industry is a prototype for others, we need to look at the underlying dynamics of demand and its impact on manufacturing practice. Consider once again the contemporary customer's appetite for variety. Increased rates of product introduction, product proliferation, and shortened product cycles mean that companies have to respond much faster to rapidly changing markets.

For our purposes, we can represent growing product diversity in the form of a "fashion triangle" (Figure 1.1). Apparel items at the very top of this triangle include dresses from Paris, Milan, and New York runways, which represent a very small share of apparel sold. The majority of fashion products also have a short selling life—usually one season—but are produced for a broader market. At the triangle's bottom are

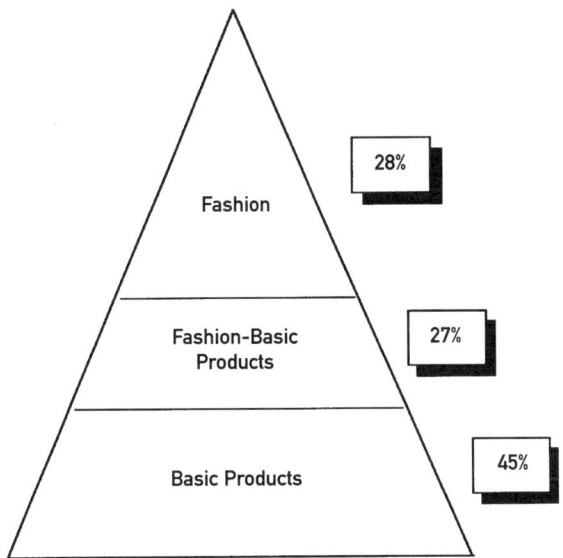

Figure 1.1. The Fashion Triangle

The exhibit shows the breakdown of total dollar volume in the HCTAR sample designated in each category in 1992. (In this exhibit, each business units response is weighted by that business units dollar volume.) The width of the triangle indicates the volume of each product sold.

basic products that remain in a retailer's or manufacturer's collection for several years, such as men's white dress shirts or underwear. Basics historically constituted the majority of apparel products sold. In the middle of the triangle are fashion-basic products, typically variants on a basic item but containing some fashion element (such as stonewashed jeans or khaki pants with pleats or trim). This expanding center of the fashion triangle indicates where the industry is headed. Because a growing percentage of basic apparel items have some fashion content, fashion-basic products are driving product proliferation.

Product proliferation and shorter product cycles, reflected in ever-changing styles and product differentiation, contribute to general demand uncertainty for both retailers and manufacturers, thereby making demand forecasting and production planning harder every day. In a world where manufacturers must supply an increasing number of products with fashion elements, speed and flexibility are crucial capabilities for firms wrestling with product proliferation, whether they are retailers trying to offer a wide range of choices to consumers or manufacturers responding to retail demands for shipments.

To be sure, technological advances in communication and transportation have helped supply channels operate more effectively and efficiently in providing diverse goods. Although these changes have provided strong motivation for increased channel coordination, the development and implementation of key facilitating technologies—like bar codes, the later spread of EDI, and automated distribution centers—have been the real movers here. New channel relationships, in turn, have led to better performance, based on a variety of standards, and enhanced the competitiveness of many sectors of these U.S. industries.

Note that these significant technological, market, and environmental changes largely originated outside the apparel industry itself. As we will make clear, changes that emerge in a market economy in one sphere often have unforeseen consequences in others. Bar codes, for instance, began with the food and grocery industry in the 1970s to lower the labor costs of cashier work and avoid delays to customers.[24] With the commercialization of the laser, automated checkout became more than an industry vision. A committee of CEOs from grocery manufacturers, food chain stores, and other companies met in 1970 to develop a "universal product code" for scanning purposes: the first five digits stand for the manufacturer and the last five identify the item at the stockkeeping unit (SKU) level.[25] All the digits are represented in the now-familiar sequence of light and dark bars of differing widths. By 1975, bar codes had begun to spread throughout food chain stores and grocery manufacturers. But almost another decade passed before the practice was adopted by apparel retailers and manufacturers.

In later chapters about the retail revolution, inventory management, and apparel operations, we provide an in-depth look at how such new technologies have affected the related industries. For now, we present five propositions that arise from the channel perspective of this book. The conventional wisdom can no longer predict future industry dynamics or offer guideposts for private and public policies. The channel perspective, however, indicates why the demand uncertainty and risk associated with today's apparel industry offer new opportunities for U.S. firms.

Proposition 1: The retail, apparel, and textile sectors are increasingly linked as a channel through information and distribution relationships.
In conventional terms, these three sectors are considered distinct industries, separated by traditional market relationships. For example, arm's-length transactions between retail buyers and apparel sellers determine prices and quantities of goods to be delivered. Apparel companies peri-

odically made deliveries based on these contracts and the transaction was then completed. In such a world, coordination problems between the parties were of little concern.

But, as we have already emphasized, this is not the real world of apparel today. At its most fundamental level, the channel perspective reflects a revolution in retail practices. These practices have resulted in the integration of enterprises at all stages of the distribution and production chain, because of the infusion of real-time information on consumer sales. Instead of gearing planning and production decisions to forecasts and guesses made months in advance of a selling season, firms now receive periodic ongoing orders based on actual consumer expenditures. And companies in transformed retail-apparel-textile channels have established a complex web of computer hardware and software, other technologies, and managerial practices that have blurred the traditional boundaries between retailers and suppliers.

Proposition 2: For apparel manufacturers, the key to success is no longer solely price competition but the ability to introduce sophisticated information links, forecasting capabilities, and management systems.

The conventional wisdom holds that the basis of competitive performance for apparel manufacturers is lowest price—period. According to Martin Feldstein, then chairman of President Reagan's Council of Economic Advisers,

> The labor intensive [U.S.] apparel market cannot and should not compete with much lower cost labor elsewhere. The stuff depends on somebody sitting at a sewing machine and stitching sleeves on; it is crazy to hurt American consumers by forcing them to buy that at $4 or $5 an hour of labor. We ought to be out of that business.[26]

Fortunately, clothing production today is more than a simple price/cost game. Successful apparel manufacturers must now focus on their capability to respond accurately and efficiently to the stringent demands placed on them by new retailing practices. This requires establishing systems to handle electronic, real-time orders, as well as creating management and information systems capable of using incoming information to forecast, plan, track production, and manufacture (or source) products in a flexible and efficient manner. Needless to say, these new skills were not part of the management arsenal of traditional apparel firms.

Yet our research indicates that apparel leaders are building these new skills. Analysis of detailed industry data demonstrates that there have been substantial increases in apparel suppliers' investments in information technologies, distribution systems, and other associated services during the same period that new types of retailing practices emerged. In addition, we have found that those firms under greatest pressure by innovative retailers have been the most likely to make such investments, as well as to invest in innovations in other stages of manufacturing. Most important, apparel-makers that have invested in major innovations to collect and use information perform much better than those that have done little to innovate production beyond providing basic information links to retailers.

Proposition 3: The assembly room—the traditional focus of attention for industry competitiveness—can provide competitive benefits only if other more fundamental changes in manufacturing practice have been introduced.

The inputs to garment production are relatively straightforward: fabric, thread, accessories like buttons and zippers, labor, and a modest level of capital investment. The majority of input costs are composed of materials and labor. For example, close to 50 percent of the value of shipments for men's shirts comes from the cost of materials, while 25 percent arises from compensation costs.[27] Reducing textile costs is a viable option for larger apparel manufacturers; they can exert some pressure on suppliers because of the size of their orders. Small manufacturers, however, have few such options. As a result, the conventional method of unit cost reduction revolves, once again, around reducing labor costs. Because the largest labor cost is concentrated in assembly phases, the focus of most productivity efforts has been in the sewing room.[28]

Garment assembly is typically done by "bundle" production, which entails breaking garment-making into a series of worksteps or operations. Each operation is assigned to a single worker, who receives a bundle of unfinished garment parts and undertakes her single operation on each item in the bundle. Completed bundles are then moved forward to the next operator in the production process. To foster productivity (physical output per worker) and constrain supervisory costs, wages are paid on a piece-rate basis, providing incentives for rapid completion of the operation.

Many industry participants have sought to improve assembly productivity, the holy grail for U.S. manufacturers. This generally involves modifications to improve the efficiency of the bundle system, using a variety of methods: "engineering" the assembly process to reduce direct labor requirements for each step, changing the incentive rate to encourage workers to increase their pace, or adopting new technologies to substitute for labor-intensive assembly steps. It is true that through ongoing refinement of apparel assembly processes American manufacturers have been able to achieve some continuous improvements in labor productivity. The International Trade Administration of the U.S. Department of Commerce expressed this view in 1990 that

> The producer who hesitates to employ new strategies will not likely survive, as expected innovations in technology dramatically alter the nature of clothing manufacture. Garment-making in its current labor-intensive form will eventually be phased out in favor of automated, robotized manufacturing, geared for almost instantaneous transition from one style to another. The difficulty of handling cut fabrics by machines may be resolved in the near future, and the quest for higher operating speeds will then receive more attention, taking production levels to new heights.[29]

Yet here the conventional wisdom misses other significant measures of performance. Managers in well-integrated channels pay attention to inventory costs, inventory replenishment practices, information reliability, and time to market rather than the traditional direct costs of labor and materials alone. In fact, competitive performance is already being driven less by how a company manages its assembly operations and more by how it manages the logistics of its operations as a whole. Our study shows that an apparel manufacturer can still be successful with a traditionally organized sewing room; a firm with innovative and productive assembly operations, on the other hand, may not be competitively viable if it has not invested in information links with retailers and other changes in management practices.

Apparel manufacturers are not the only ones learning this lesson the hard way. The emphasis on labor productivity that has preoccupied practitioners and analysts in many industries—such as the total labor minutes required to assemble a car—no longer makes as much sense now that information technology has revolutionized retailing in many product segments. For instance, the current labor costs associated with assembly constitute 40 percent of the final cost of a car. In contrast, distribution-related costs—those associated with the traditional structure of automobile retailing—constitute anywhere between 15 and 34 percent of final cost.[30] It is little wonder that car companies are currently in the throes of radically restructuring their method of automobile distribution.

Proposition 4:   Instead of fashion as the saving grace of the channel, basic and fashion-basic products will prove critical to its long-term survival.
When people consider the U.S. apparel industry, they often think of New York City's Seventh Avenue, which is driven by new design, constantly changing seasonal offerings, and a willingness by consumers to pay a premium for the cutting edge of fashion. New York City and Los Angeles continue to have a competitive advantage in this area because a large number of designers and manufacturers are located in these cities and can respond quickly to changing demands, as well as shape them. This infrastructure allows for "quick response" on the fashion end of the women's and, to a more limited extent, men's markets. Once established, a variety of proponents believe, the experience at the fashion end can be diffused downward to less fashion-oriented products. As a result, some of the fashion-oriented products that had been sourced offshore can then return to the United States.

Those with a pessimistic view of domestic apparel manufacturing often assume that the high fashion end of the industry (the "top" of the fashion triangle in Figure 1.1, page 9) may be its best hope because U.S. firms can capitalize on their proximity to market. The highly acclaimed report by the MIT Commission on Industrial Productivity, *Made in America*, concludes:

> Apparel, textile, and fiber firms and retailers have recently joined to launch the Quick Response Program, designed to improve information flow, standardize recording systems, and improve turnaround time throughout the system.... The program could be an important boon to productivity and competitiveness.... Will Quick Response succeed? According to industry experts, that depends on whether it diffuses down to the high-fashion, quick turnaround segments of the industry or, like much new technology in this industry, is adapted to suit the needs of firms still committed to mass production.[31]

Regardless of where Quick Response has succeeded, however, our research indicates that very different time-based competitive demands have emerged in the industry, driven not by voluntary acceptance of policies but by the changing nature of market competition among retailers. Rather than arising in the fashion, "Seventh Avenue" segment of the industry, the new form of retail competition involves basic and fashion-basic products like jeans, intimate apparel, and T-shirts—the bottom of the fashion triangle.

Basic and fashion-basic apparel categories now constitute the lion's share of industry sales, accounting for approximately 72 percent of all shipments.[32] This implies that a far larger portion of the industry may be viable in the long run than the part that could be saved by "quick response" at the fashion end.[33] Bear in mind, however, that this viability depends on manufacturers using information to plan and execute production in a more sophisticated manner than usual for this and other industries.

Similar dynamics are cropping up in nonclothing areas as well. Grocery stores now stock a profusion of toothbrushes, Home Depot has shelves and shelves of different light bulbs, and Dell offers custom-configured personal computers. The growing presence of fashion-basic elements in myriad consumer products means that all retailers and suppliers may find new competitive opportunities using replenishment.

Proposition 5: Even with full implementation of GATT, a viable apparel industry can remain in North America, drawing on a range of production processes in the United States, Canada, Mexico, the Caribbean, and Latin America.

When it comes to international trade agreements, the conventional wisdom sounds most bleak. It leads to stark conclusions about the long-term viability of the U.S. apparel industry, even with steps taken to improve assembly-room productivity and fashion-oriented quick response. The following comment is typical:

> Among the factors that are expected to have a substantial impact on employment in the textiles and apparel industries, perhaps the most influential will be the trade policy agreed to in the GATT.... The apparel industry, which is far more labor intensive and less competitive internationally than the textile industry, will probably sustain most of the losses from the new trade environment.[34]

Even here, the channel perspective tells a somewhat different story. When domestic channels reduce lead times to market, particularly with basic and fashion-basic products, the comparative advantage of imports declines—despite the lower wage costs of foreign competitors, elimination of quotas on imports, and tariff reductions. This means that the U.S. apparel industry is not necessarily doomed by high direct labor costs, at least for certain products. In fact, we expect a resurgence in certain sectors because of the innovative practices being pursued by some manufacturers and their retailers.

To be sure, the international sourcing arrangements that have been created by retailers and manufacturers over the last twenty years reflect a quest for minimizing unit labor costs. But the long lead times they require will increasingly challenge such arrangements. Manufacturers and retailers that rely on international sourcing will therefore have to reassess the total costs associated with offshore production and revise existing arrangements.

Trade data already suggest a major restructuring in the sources of U.S. apparel imports. The surge in apparel imports in the 1980s came from low-wage countries, primarily the Asian "Big Four"—the People's Republic of China, Hong Kong, Taiwan, and Korea. This group of nations provided 39 percent of all apparel imports in 1964 and 51 percent of all apparel imports by 1988 (measured in square-meter equivalents, a measure of quantity). But by 1996, the Big Four's share of imports had fallen to 26 percent. Their U.S. share has been increasingly displaced by those of Mexico and Caribbean nations.[35] Although these shifts in part reflect changes in U.S. trade policy, such as the North American Free Trade Agreement (NAFTA), they fundamentally arise from new sourcing patterns attributable to channel integration and the consequent need for apparel items that can be delivered in a shorter time to the U.S. market.

The implications of these changes from a private and public policy perspective are enormous. Competing in the transformed retail-apparel-textile channel now requires a set of management practices for both domestic and international sourcing. A successful U.S. apparel-maker, for instance, may assemble basic men's khaki pants in average sizes in Mexico, taking advantage of low labor costs as well as Mexico's proximity to the maker's Texas distribution centers; at the same time, this company can choose to manufacture products with more variable demand, like khaki pants with narrow waists and long inseams, in the United States, providing fast turnaround for retailers and lower exposure to inventory risk.

Going to India or China for low prices alone is no longer the smartest course of action for American manufacturers. Increasingly, they will factor in demand uncertainty and product proliferation when making such sourcing decisions. As we will discuss throughout, many of the capabilities required for this model of competition are new to the apparel industry. The post-GATT competitive arena will be extremely demanding, but, based on the innovations many U.S. manufacturers are making, we believe the American apparel industry has a future.

How This Book Is Organized

Because of our separate academic perspectives and disciplines, the research underlying *A Stitch in Time* comes from a variety of sources. Much of our analysis is based on detailed survey data we collected from 118 business units—a sample representing about one-third of the shipments—in the apparel industry. We supplemented the original survey with microdata collected from a variety of U.S. government and private sources. Our work also draws on numerous case studies of individual enterprises and data gathered at site visits. We have modeled specific channel dynamics in order to understand what optimal practices might look like as the channel develops over time. Finally, we have worked closely with business executives, government officials, labor leaders, and our academic colleagues to exchange views, test ideas, and refine our results on a continuing basis. The appendices present a list of acronyms, a description of the HCTAR survey and other data sources, and a list of companies that we visited or at which we conducted interviews with their executives.

A Stitch in Time is organized into five sections, roughly corresponding to the channel components. The first two chapters provide an overview and historical context. Chapters 3 through 5 analyze developments in the retail sector. Chapters 6 and 7 establish a bridge between retailing and apparel/textile operations through an exploration of the problems of inventory management—a central aspect of emerging channel dynamics. Chapters 8 through 10 focus on the apparel industry; Chapters 11 and 12 look at textiles. Chapters 13 through 15 examine the channel as a whole, from global, private-performance, and public-policy perspectives.

After this introduction, Chapter 2 ("The Past as Prologue") offers a brief history of recent technological and human resource developments in retailing, apparel production—including the role of jobbers, contractors, and manufacturers—and textile enterprises. Here we make clear that the changes wrought by lean retailing echo the last industrial transformation, which occurred in the late nineteenth century with the advent of the railroad and telegraph.

In the retailing section of the book, Chapter 3 ("The Retail Revolution") contrasts traditional practices with the emerging method of lean retailing, starting with a comparison of Wanamaker's, the grandest store of its time, and the companies leading the current wave of retail restructuring. Chapter 4 ("The Building Blocks of Lean Retailing") describes how the essential elements of lean retailing—bar codes, EDI, the modern distribution center, and standards across firms—fit together. Chapter 5 ("The Impact of Lean Retailing") presents some of the key results of our survey, indicating how lean retailers have performed over the last decade and their effects on manufacturers and suppliers.

Next, we move to the inventory "bridge" between retailers and suppliers. Product proliferation has raised the uncertainty of overall demand faced by retailers and suppliers. Chapter 6 ("Inventory Management for the Retailer") looks at formal models of retail inventory management and discusses how they have been modified by lean retailing practices. Chapter 7 ("Inventory Management for the Manufacturer") switches to the supplier's point of view. Because dynamics are shifting in the channel, many suppliers are confronting new inventory challenges in their efforts to replenish items rapidly for retailers. We present two cases that emphasize the importance of using weekly demand variation for different items to help manufacturers set optimal inventory policies. This chapter also describes a new approach to production and sourcing strategies, one that balances traditional and short-cycle production lines.

The next three chapters are devoted to apparel operations and related human resource practices. Chapter 8 ("Getting Ready to Sew") describes the preassembly steps of apparel design, marker-making, and cutting and how they are adapted to new areas like mass customization. Chapter 9 ("Assembly and the Sewing Room") examines the technical aspects of sewing—from different kinds of sewing machines to what sewing operators do—and alternative ways of arranging the flow of assembly operations through an apparel workplace. Chapter 10 ("Human Resources in Apparel") considers the impact of alternative methods of assembly—especially modular, or team-based, production—on firm performance. We also discuss why human resource policies cannot be treated separately from other business decisions regarding rapid replenishment.

In the textile section, Chapter 11 ("Textile Operations") describes the technological processes involved in converting fibers to a vast range of woven and knit products. The textile sector has changed remarkably since World War II, in part because of the capital intensity and technological sophistication of textile equipment, much of which is automated. Chapter 12 ("The Economic Viability of Textiles") places U.S. textiles in an international context, detailing the ways in which the domestic industry has adjusted over the past several decades through dramatic productivity enhancement. Because textile firms are increasingly supplying retailers and industrial users directly, as well as producing fabric for apparel-makers, we also address the multiple channels evolving in this sector.

A Stitch in Time concludes with a look at the many factors shaping today's retail-apparel-textile channel—from the complex management challenges facing suppliers to labor standards and macroeconomic policy. Chapter 13 ("The Global Marketplace") reviews trends in U.S. imports and exports of apparel and textiles, including information on trade by countries and specific products. It then connects these trends to changing trade policies, emphasizing the growing regionalization of trade flows in different parts of the world. Chapter 14 ("Suppliers in a Lean World") examines our survey results from another angle, evaluating firm performance in an integrated channel. Here we highlight the importance of combining information technologies, manufacturing innovations, and new methods of management to respond to lean retailing demands.

Finally, Chapter 15 ("Information-Integrated Channels") touches on a number of public policy issues raised by our findings. These include what can be done about the continuing problem of sweatshops, the new international economics of trade, and the effect of information integration on the business cycle and consumer prices at the macroeconomic level. Last but not least, we take a realistic look at the competitive future of the U.S. retail, apparel, and textile industries.

The information-integrated channel, with its emphasis on time and product perishability, is the basis for our cautiously optimistic—and unconventional—outlook. Even more important, the forces examined in this book provide a glimpse into processes reshaping a considerable portion of the economy. Consumers no longer line up for a special suit at a store like Bond Stores; they also expect an ever more "fashionable" array of cereal products, computers, and automobiles. As the next chapter shows, the changes now under way have their roots in new technologies, just as technical advances in transportation and communication shifted the industrial landscape at the end of the last century.

2

The Past as Prologue: Historical Background on the U.S. Retail, Apparel, and Textile Industries

The emergence of textile, apparel, and retail enterprises in the United States is full of fascinating twists. In 1790, for instance, an act of industrial espionage is said to have launched the domestic textile industry, if not American manufacturing in general. At that time, Samuel Slater, a skilled mechanic, built the first successful water-powered yarn spinning mill in Pawtucket, Rhode Island. Yarn was in short supply in the new country and much in demand in households that did hand weaving as well as in workplaces with looms that produced sheeting, shirting, and stockings for commerce. Some of the American states and improvement societies had even offered generous rewards for the establishment of water-powered combing and spinning, especially those based on state-of-the-art English Arkwright operations. But British law strictly prohibited the export of drawings, plans, or models of these new technologies. It took somebody like Slater—an indentured apprentice for over six years at the Arkwright and Strut's plant in Milford, England—to ferry the plans to America.[1]

Slater was interested in the financial rewards to be had in the new world while still in England. Mindful of British prohibitions, he committed to memory the design and construction of the spinning mill where he worked. Arriving in New York in late 1789, he was referred to Moses Brown in Providence, a prominent merchant who had established a company, Almy and Brown, to develop "frame or water spinning." Brown responded on December 10, 1789, to Slater's initial inquiry, saying Almy and Brown certainly wanted the assistance of a person with Slater's skills because an experimental mill had failed, "no persons being acquainted with the business, and the frames imperfect."[2]

Once in Almy and Brown's Pawtucket plant, Slater found the existing machinery totally unsatisfactory. He entered into a partnership with Almy and Brown to erect "perpetual card and spinning" machines, otherwise known as the Arkwright patents. By 1793, the firm of Almy, Brown and Slater was operating a seventy-two-spindle mill, producing high-quality yarn. From the Pawtucket mill, the American cotton-spinning industry was launched.

The Slater mill not only copied British technology but recreated that country's arrangement of family labor, which included young children, six-day weeks, the minimum twelve-hour day, Sabbath schools, and payment of wages partly in goods and partly in cash. The form of ownership and management also followed British lines—one partner financed the venture, while the other furnished the technical know-how. For these accomplishments, Samuel Slater has been called "the father of American manufactures." His story underscores the international role of textiles and apparel, their impetus in national economic development, and their place in conflicts over domestic production and imports—a theme that recurs throughout U.S. history. For example, from the outset of the new nation, President George Washington and his Secretary of the Treasury Alexander Hamilton wanted to encourage U.S.-based industry. Indeed, Washington wore a dark brown suit, entirely made in America, for his first inaugural on April 30, 1789.[3]

In this chapter, we will concentrate on the past hundred years, outlining major changes in American retail, apparel, and textiles that occurred before the 1980s. The industrial transformation of this earlier period, which affected far more than these three industries, echoes today's enormous shifts in supplier relations, manufacturing operations, and human resource practices. The changes now going on have their analog in the last century, when technological innovations of the day like railroads, telegraph, and steam power—developed for purposes far afield of retail, apparel, or textiles—helped transform the mass distribution of goods and information.

Alfred Chandler described the last industrial transformation in his well-known book *The Visible Hand*. The use of everything from railroads to an improved postal service, according to Chandler, created enterprises with internal administrative structures that coordinated the flow of goods from many individual producers to many more consumers. This administrative coordination reduced "the number of transactions involved in the flow of goods, increased the speed and regularity of that flow, and so lowered costs and improved the productivity of the American distribution system."[4]

The parallels with the information integration now occurring in retail-apparel-textile channels—this time driven by advances in computer and related technologies—are striking. In fact, another industrial transformation is under way, one that rivals the earlier revolution in organizational structure and management. The first three sections of this chapter summarize the emergence of the U.S. retail, apparel, and textile industries over the past century, including a number of human resource issues. The fourth section looks at their channel relations prior to the mid-1980s, before some enterprises started interacting with each other in new ways. This brief historical survey highlights not only the crucial developments that still undergird these industries but also the systems and work practices from an earlier era that no longer match today's competitive requirements.

Retail: From General Stores to Mass Retailers

In urban centers, there have always been small shops with goods for sale. Often the owners of these shops produced the goods themselves, such as the cobblers and silversmiths of old. At farmers' markets, families would display the vegetables they grew or sell eggs from their chickens. At most, a town might have a general store with a motley array of dry goods, based on a limited distribution system—one that relied on local producers and faraway supply houses with extremely long lead times and spotty delivery. The old system didn't begin to shift until the mid-nineteenth century, with the advent of a new kind of middleman. Alfred Chandler writes,

> In the 1850s and the 1860s the modern commodity dealer, who purchased directly from the farmer and sold directly to the processor, took over the distribution of agricultural products. In the same years the full-line, full-service wholesaler began to market consumer goods. Then in the 1870s and 1880s the modern mass retailer—the department store, the mail order house, and the chain store—started to make inroads on the wholesaler's markets.[5]

Until the emergence of mass retail, the wholesaler-jobber dominated the distribution of consumer dry goods to general stores: clothing, upholstered furnishings, hardware, drugs, tobacco, furniture, china, and glassware. Unlike traveling peddlers of the past, who carried everything with them, these salesmen could ride the rails into town with no more than a trunk of samples and catalogs. The new infrastructure created by the railroads and telegraph contributed to the growth of wholesale houses. Retailers no longer needed to carry such large inventories, the risk of losing shipments was reduced, and delivery was more certain on a specified schedule. Increased volume cut unit costs and enhanced cash flow, reducing credit needs. Moreover, these salesmen provided a flow of information to their headquarters on changing demand in various localities as well as the credit ratings of local storekeepers and merchants.

Wholesaler-jobber enterprises of the time, such as Field, Leiter and Company in Chicago (which later became Marshall Field and Company), required both a purchasing organization and an extensive traveling sales force to sell to the scattered general stores in smaller cities and country towns. These buyers and their assistants each handled a major product line like hardware or dry goods. They typically determined the specifications of the goods purchased, the volume purchased, and the price to be charged to customers at retail. These buyers became the most important managers in wholesaler-jobber companies, foreshadowing the key status of the buyer in later retail organizations.

The wholesaler-jobber distribution system peaked in the early 1880s. It was subsequently supplanted by mass retailers in the form of department stores in large urban cities and by mail-order houses focused on smaller communities and rural markets. As Chandler recounts,

> Mass retailers displaced wholesale-jobbers as soon as they were able to exploit a market as large as that covered by the wholesalers. By building comparable purchasing organizations they could buy directly from manufacturers and develop a higher stock-turn than the jobbers. Their administrative networks were more effective because they were in direct contact with the customers and because they eliminated one major set of middlemen.[6]

Other factors drove the development of mass retail as well. The rapid growth of urban cities and access to their downtown areas, initially with horse-drawn streetcars, encouraged mass retailers. Department stores, with a wide range of goods arranged in "departments," provided one-stop shopping, both novel and appealing to consumers of the period. The increase in women seeking ready-made clothing and home furnishings also contributed to the rise of the department store as did newspaper advertising. Although small specialty shops were limited to a few items, such as those found in a traditional dressmaker or milliner's shop, department stores offered fixed prices and the convenience of returning purchases for exchange or cash. They sold goods at a lower markup than specialty stores and, above all, concentrated on achieving a high level of stock-turn (or the number of times products turn over in a given year).

Many of the first department stores have names that are still familiar: Macy's in New York, Marshall Field's in Chicago, John Wanamaker in Philadelphia. Chandler points out that the stores founded in the 1860s and 1870s accounted for almost half of the leading department stores in New York a century later. In addition, he writes, "Because sales were made on the store's premises rather than through traveling salesmen, buyers had an even larger role than they did in the wholesale houses.... They had direct charge of the sales personnel who marketed their lines over the counter."[7]

Then there was the parallel growth of mail-order sales. With the help of new transportation and communications systems, the first company to market a wide variety of consumer goods exclusively by mail and parcel post was Montgomery Ward, formed in 1872. The Grange, the largest organization of farmers, supported the company. By 1887, its catalog of 540 pages listed 24,000 items. But Sears Roebuck and Co. outstripped Montgomery Ward in the 1890s. As with the wholesaler-jobber and the emerging department stores, the buyers at Sears had full autonomy. Chandler notes, "Each merchandise department was a separate dynasty, and the buyer was in complete charge."[8]

Department stores and mail-order houses (and later chain stores in food distribution) dominated mass retailing after 1880 through large volume, high inventory turnover, lower prices, payments in cash that reduced the need for credit and debt, and the crucial role of the buyer. Although wholesaler-jobbers had faded from the scene, the policies, practices, and administrative organizations of many mass distributors were derived from them. Other buying practices came from small shops. Each retail merchandise department, particularly in multi-store organizations, became a separate fiefdom, with the buyer in charge of product selection, scale, timing of orders, and pricing. Up until the mid-1980s, the buyers' personal network of contacts and "feel" for what customers wanted determined marketing policy. And although the wages of nonsupervisory workers in retail have been and still are quite low,[9] the compensation system for buyers provided substantial rewards for favorable results.

Consequently, for decades the decisions of buyers in retail organizations directly affected apparel and textile suppliers. The distribution system that emerged after 1870 would not be challenged until more than a century later. Only in the 1980s, with the development of another system of mass distribution that includes new technology, new management methods, and new links to manufacturing—lean retailing—did the role of the buyer significantly diminish.

Apparel: From Home Work to Modern Manufacture

In colonial days, housewives typically did spinning, weaving, and tailoring for the family. The well-to-do purchased imported cloth and had apparel made by itinerant tailors or those in small shops. The ready-made garment industry grew out of altered rejects and secondhand clothing that were then sold to the poorer classes in the cities. In 1832, a 50 percent import duty curtailed clothing primarily from England and increased the demand for American home industry.[10] By 1850, the U.S. Census reports that there were 4,278 establishments with 97,000 workers—63 percent of them women—in the ready-made clothing industry.[11] Cloth was cut and assembled into bundles in these establishments, given out to workers to take home to sew, and returned for finishing operations.[12]

With the invention of the sewing machine by Howe, and its perfection by Singer in 1851, a new era began in the manufacture of clothing, when more work became concentrated in shops. The Civil War and the consequent need for uniforms stimulated the factory system, and the introduction of standard body-size measurements facilitated ready-to-wear clothing. When Hart, Schaffner, and Marx, for instance, opened its doors in 1879, only 40 percent of men's suits were ready-made. By 1920, most men wore suits that came from a factory. In this period, a number of key technological changes appeared: sewing machines that made many more stitches a minute, long knives instead of shears for cutting, and pressing machines.

From the nineteenth century on, enterprises in the apparel industry have taken one of three general forms: the manufacturer with an inside shop; the jobber; and the contractor with an outside shop, which can supply either manufacturers or jobbers. The jobber, a form characteristic of women's apparel, does not produce in a plant that it owns. Jobbers may purchase cloth and materials; design or purchase design of garments; and cut or contract out cutting of fabrics. They turn over sewing and assembly to contractors, and their main role is to merchandise finished product.

The jobber-contractor system developed to address many of the issues that still concern apparel-makers. It provided great flexibility in coping with fluctuations in style, season, and economic conditions; at the same time, jobbers did not take on the substantial costs of plant, equipment, or employees that "inside shop" manufacturers did. This system also separated and specialized the functions of production from the purchase of materials and the selling of finished products—developments that greatly influence women's and children's apparel today, including the complexity of the regulation of labor conditions.

Regardless, apparel operations in both the men's and women's segments have always been labor intensive; even with continual technological innovation, the work still comes down to cutting cloth and sewing pieces together into a garment. Although union organization has not been so extensive in retail or textiles, unions have been important players in apparel manufacturing. At the same time, apparel manufacturers have pressed for ever greater productivity on the shop floor, hoping to cut labor costs in a variety of ways. These two related historical issues—the ascendancy of a particular system of clothing assembly and the role of unions—have a direct bearing on what is now happening in retail-apparel-textile channels.

Development of the Progressive Bundle System

For the most part, in-plant production methods for apparel have been organized around the way in which cut parts of garments are distributed to operators for sewing and then assembled into the completed garment. From the outset of the factory system in woven apparel, after cloth has been laid out and cut in the configurations of patterns for various sizes, the cut parts have been grouped by parts of the garment—fronts, backs, sleeves, patches for pockets, collars—and tied together into bundles for operators, who sew together individual parts—hence the term "bundle system." Each worker specializes in one, or at most a few, sewing operations.

By the early 1930s, two systems of sewing and assembly emerged in the men's segment of the apparel industry: the progressive bundle system (PBS) and the straight-line system (SLS).[13] The ascendancy of PBS in the men's industry, where it remains by far the dominant system even today, illustrates how product market competition—specifically intense price-based competition—gave rise to distinctive human resource practices.[14]

PBS refined the traditional bundle system by organizing individual sewing tasks in a systematic fashion. It entails better engineering of specific sewing tasks, including some specialized sewing machines, to reduce the amount of time required for each task. A worker receives a bundle of unfinished garments. She performs a single operation on each garment in the bundle. The completed bundle is then placed in a buffer with other bundles that have been completed to that point. Machines are laid out in a manner that speeds up shuttling a bin of garment bundles from operator to operator. With its roots in Taylorism, each PBS task is given a target time or "SAM" (Standard Allocated Minutes). Time-study engineers calculate the SAM for an entire garment for an experienced worker as the sum of the number of minutes required for each operation in the production process, including allowances for worker fatigue, rest periods, personal time, and so on.[15]

The straight-line system (SLS) also attempted to apply Tayloristic notions to apparel but in a way that had more in common with scientific management techniques used in other manufacturing industries. SLS breaks down tasks into simple sewing operations, just as PBS does. Unlike PBS, however, SLS uses the single garment rather than the bundle as the unit of production. As a result, SLS operates essentially without bundles or extensive buffers; operators pass garments directly to the next worker, thus allowing for single or a few apparel items to move through the assembly process rapidly.

In its limited adoptions in the 1930s, the SLS sewing room was organized in short rows of sewing machines based on the sequence of operations for the garment. Even more than under PBS, sewing tasks were broken down in minute detail, both as a means of increasing speed and decreasing skill requirements. Engineers designed operations to take similar lengths of time to achieve line balancing. When a specific task took longer than the surrounding operations, multiple workers were employed on the slower task to achieve balance. Each operator's workstation was connected by a bar or chute that fed the garment directly to the next worker.

Yet line-balancing problems bedeviled SLS operations. Laying out a production line required exact calculation of the number of workers required for a given step to keep single garments moving through the operation continuously—much as a car moves down an assembly line. The lack of buffers for bundles made the system vulnerable to day-to-day fluctuations in the performance of individual operators, whether because of fatigue, health, mood, absenteeism, substitutions, or intentional slowdowns. In a competitive market that placed a premium on price/cost competition and little value on time to market, the small reduction in direct labor cost did not justify the high potential costs and risks that arose from SLS downtime. In contrast, PBS provided apparel manufacturers with a means for improving labor productivity along with adaptability to day-to-day variations in shop-floor conditions.

In 1938, virtually all assembly in the men's shirt industry, for example, was done on the basis of bundle systems of production. By 1956, 41 percent of production workers were classified as operating under the traditional bundle system; 55 percent assembled shirts through PBS, and less than 4 percent used the line system. By 1961, the percentage using traditional bundles had fallen to 26 percent; PBS had risen to 69 percent of all production workers, and line systems remained uncommon at 5 percent. By 1990, PBS had become virtually the only assembly system used in men's and boys' shirt production, with less than 4 percent of production accounted for by SLS and others systems.[16]

The dominance of PBS affects current developments in apparel manufacturing and employee management for two reasons. First, the system depends on buffers between assembly operations to minimize downtime. Standard practice is a one-day buffer between operations.[17] With a pair of pants assembled through roughly forty operations, a large amount of in-process inventory is created. More important, a *given* pair of pants takes about forty days to move from cut pieces to final product. Now that apparel manufacturers face more stringent order-fulfillment requirements and are expected to provide a much wider range of products to retailers, the costs of large amounts of in-process inventory have grown tremendously.

Second, PBS is not set up for large-scale modifications of assembly. Although this system has never had as many problems with line balancing as SLS, creating sufficient buffers between assembly steps to keep everyone in the sewing room occupied remains a challenge. Under PBS, a balanced line is a function of the workers' rate of speed at each of the steps; the total volume moving through the system; the current incentive rates; and such daily uncertainties as turnover and absenteeism. Because introducing changes at any step may unbalance the system as a whole, technological innovations have not easily found their way into the sewing room—which may be out of sync with what an integrated retail-apparel-textile channel requires.

The Role of Labor Organizations

Apparel workplaces have historically been located in major metropolitan areas—New York, Chicago, Philadelphia, Rochester, Baltimore, Cleveland, St. Louis—and drawn on successive waves of immigrants. In the production of both men's and women's clothing, immigrant labor provided a continuing secure labor force that often already had the requisite skills. In 1930, three out of five workers were foreign born, and a large percentage of the native-born were of foreign parentage. The union in the men's clothing field at the time issued official publications in eight different languages. Practically all the manufacturers were first-generation Jewish immigrants.[18] More recently, apparel manufacturers, seeking lower labor costs, have moved to the American South and California. But a disproportionate number of domestic apparel workers are still immigrants.

Given access to a large pool of immigrant labor in urban centers, the jobber-contractor system in women's apparel led to the wide-scale presence and abuses of sweatshops. Sweatshops at the turn of the century encompassed a range of workplaces in which, as one commentator noted, "Congestion, unsanitary quarters, lack of restriction on child labor, absolutely unregulated hours, and miserable pay combine to create a condition which endangers the lives not only of the workers, but of the purchasers of their products."[19] A study in 1893 of the "sweating system" estimated that one-half of the clothing manufactured at that time came from factories, while the other half originated in home work or was subcontracted in small shops often adjoining homes.[20]

Organizing a relatively low-skill immigrant workforce presented great challenges to unions in the garment industry. Employer resistance to unionization, arising from the highly competitive conditions in apparel markets and the significant percentage of total costs arising from labor, further compounded the problem. This difficult environment shaped the organizing and representation strategies of the two major unions—the Amalgamated Clothing Workers of America and the International Ladies' Garment Workers Union (ILGWU)[21]—as well as their relations with employers through collective bargaining arrangements.[22] Both unions established a foothold in the industry because they represented strategic workers in the apparel production process: the skilled cutter working inside manufacturers' plants. Cutters required substantial training, and the withdrawal of their labor could quickly shut down all sewing and pressing operations. Because cutters worked on multiple layers of fabric at one time, their errors were likely to be costly. Not surprisingly, cutters were the highest paid workers receiving day rates.[23]

By organizing cutters first, unions gained the leverage with which they could then organize and represent the much larger, but less skilled, group of sewers who worked in factory settings, particularly in the men's industry, or in the small shops that characterized the women's industry. The principal architects of this approach, Sidney Hillman, founding president of the Amalgamated, and David Dubinsky, long-time president of the ILGWU, were cutters and came out of this craft-group.[24]

Given this union foothold, collective bargaining in apparel focused on the standardization of labor in a market area and a product line. This was done because of the organization of work in clothing shops; the low capital costs and high proportion of labor costs, especially in women's wear for contract shops; the intense product competition among manufacturers within and among geographic markets; and the diversity of products and changing styles. The unions drew on several different methods to standardize wages and conditions within the markets. For the ILGWU, standardizing wages required regulation through collective bargaining of the network of contractors and "submanufacturers" working for jobbers and manufacturers. Emphasizing the potential role of the union in this regard, ILGWU President Dubinsky commented on the difficult conditions of the 1920s:

> The employers in the stable shops with employees whom they were anxious to keep suffered as much as we did because the union was weak. They had to pay decent wages and maintain decent conditions, but they also had to compete with the fly-by-nights and chiselers. They began to recognize that the union was a necessary stabilizing force. They could not meet conditions if their competitors were free to ignore them.[25]

Employers who signed the major collective bargaining agreements with the ILGWU in the women's industry (primarily manufacturers) not only agreed to abide by wage and working conditions for their own employees, they also pledged to use only contractors "designated or registered" with the union and the employer association.[26] These contractors, in turn, agreed to abide by the terms laid out by the collective agreement. The collective bargaining process aimed to control contractors by making the manufacturer responsible in the area-product agreement for its suppliers' behavior and payment of wages and benefits.[27]

Both unions also sought to standardize wages by setting piece rates for assembly work. At the shop level, this was expressed in union involvement in piece-rate setting through union experts.[28] At the manufacturer's level, collective bargaining sought to standardize direct wage and benefit costs for product lines (such as women's coats, suits, dresses, and intimate apparel) through various joint boards. To support these activities, the apparel labor unions created in their national offices industrial engineering departments to seek improvement in work practices and experiences.[29] The unions and their employers also became pioneers in establishing neutral umpires and arbitrators in the handling of labor-management disputes.[30]

Over time, major growth in imports and traditional price/cost competition have reduced the strategic leverage of the apparel unions and their chosen methods of wage stabilization. (The Amalgamated and ILGWU merged in 1995 to form the Union of Needletrades, Industrial and Textile Employees—or UNITE!). On a labor-cost basis alone, U.S. workers cannot compete with foreign apparel assembly operations in developing countries. At the same time, the problem of sweatshops persists, despite government regulation of minimum wages, overtime, child labor, and safety issues. In fact, regulation has increased significantly since the 1930s, and Secretaries of Labor continue to be concerned about sweatshops and violations of labor standards in apparel.

Textiles: From Fiber to Cloth to Finished Product

The basic processes of the textile industry—the spinning of fibers and the weaving of cloth—go back to ancient times. The early phases of the Industrial Revolution in England were closely linked to the mechanization of the textile industry and its transfer from the home to the factory. Textiles have also led the industrialization process in many recently developing countries.

For the United States this brings us back to Samuel Slater, "father of American manufactures." By 1810, the Pawtucket, Rhode Island, enterprise begun with Slater's cunning had spawned a vibrant cotton-spinning industry throughout New England. The next step in developing a U.S.-based industry was to bring the machine that took yarn and transformed it into finished cloth—the power loom—across the Atlantic. This feat was accomplished in much the same way that Slater brought cotton spinning to the United States, through the agency of a crafty Boston merchant, Francis Cabot Lowell. As business historian Robert Dalzell notes,

> [T]he crowning glory of Britain's textile technology ... remained beyond the reach of American manufacturers. Until, that is, Lowell scored his triumph. Leaving the British official who twice searched his luggage none the wiser, he managed by meticulous observation to memorize the principal features of the power loom well enough to produce his own version of it on his return to Boston.[31]

A full-blown textile industry therefore blossomed in New England, fostered by the region's access to abundant water power, capital, mechanical skills, and a hardworking labor force. But the adoption of steam power in New England was delayed until the 1850s and 1860s, at which time most of the significant water-power sites were already in use. The efficiency of steam engines had by then been greatly improved through the use of better materials, and their operating costs reduced by cheaper transportation of coal.[32] Southern manufacturers had already adopted steam engines for textile production, along with newer and more productive technology. As a result, after 1880 the industry began to expand south, particularly in North and South Carolina, Georgia, and Alabama. By 1920, over half of the spinning and weaving capacity was in the South, leading industrialization there. By 1980, little of this basic part of the textile industry remained in New England.

The U.S. textile industry has taken advantage of economies of scale in production to serve large, expanding, and, for much of the century, protected markets for textile products. It has become an industry adept at producing high-quality products in large runs competitively and its strengths and limitations must be understood in this context.

Capital Intensity and Economies of Scale

Primary textile manufacturing includes both the spinning of raw cotton and other fibers into yarn and the weaving of yarn into "greige goods," or unfinished cloth. Although there have been specialized spinning and weaving mills, the great majority of output is produced in enterprises that engage in both operations. In fact, Lowell and his associates established the first incorporated manufacturing operation when they set up an integrated mill, from cotton to finished fabric.[33] The cloth produced in weaving mills requires further finishing—such as bleaching, shrinking, dyeing, and printing—before it is ready for sale to the apparel industry, to retail distributors, or to industrial consumers. To undertake such a comprehensive set of activities, of course, requires significant capital investment. From the outset of the Industrial Revolution, spinning, weaving, and finishing have called for substantial investments in plants, power, and equipment.[34]

Because of this capital intensity, the textile industry has been driven by economies of scale. American plants have largely succeeded through making huge runs of a limited range of products and, since the 1950s, technological changes on the floor—much quieter machinery, for example, or removal of the ubiquitous cotton dust (now required by the Occupational Safety and Health Administration) that used to affect both worker performance and the quality of cloth—have dramatically improved industry performance. Further, the knitting machine has been a key development in manufacturing technology. Knitted goods are an essential and growing segment of the textile industry, a trend that reflects the increasing demand for casual wear. The knitting machine produces cloth as the loom does but uses a different method. The warp knitting machine produces a flat fabric much like woven cloth, while the circular knitting machine creates a tubular fabric. The most important knit goods products are hosiery, knit underwear, and knit outerwear—popular casual wear items like T-shirts, polo shirts, and sweatpants. Knitting mills now account for almost 30 percent of production employees engaged in textile manufacturing.[35]

Continuing integration of the industry also contributed to the rise in productivity. Although small, family-owned and operated companies were the norm in traditional textiles, in the early 1950s leaders like Burlington Industries and Milliken undertook vertical integration to handle textile products from fiber to finishing.[36] Historically, finishing operations were often undertaken by separate firms known as converters, which played a large role in the design of finished goods. Companies like Burlington integrated forward by bringing converting operations in-house, while a number of converters extended their operations backward into primary textiles.

Beyond restructuring for materials flow, the industry has experienced substantial horizontal integration. As a consequence, some segments of textiles, such as spinning, weaving, and knitting, became more concentrated by the late 1970s. The industry underwent another substantial restructuring in the 1980s, and product lines became even more concentrated.[37] Much of this happened because less efficient firms, using older technologies, went under or were absorbed by larger survivors. Between 1977 and 1987, the number of textile establishments declined by 11 percent, from 7,202 to 6,412, and industry employment fell by nearly 25 percent. At present, the four largest firms control about 40 percent of weaving and yarn mills output, although many finishing and dyeing companies and knitting firms remain small.

Human Resources and Productivity Growth

The drive to gain advantage from economies of scale and the role of manufacturing technology in textiles have also affected the people who work in the industry. Ever since garment-making entered the factory system, the textile industry has been much more capital intensive than apparel. Today we estimate capital per worker in apparel at $2,000, while the figure for basic textile operations is several hundred thousand dollars. As a result, human resource practices in the two industries differ considerably.

For one thing, the textile industry's machine operations involve a large number of distinct job classifications defined by the technology and production process; they fall within a narrow range of compensation, with the classifications of loom fixers, weavers, maintenance electricians, and machinists above that range. Because the textile industry has become so capital intensive, there are fewer jobs than in the past—but the people who remain are, on average, paid more than apparel workers; some lower-skill jobs, such as the picker tender opening bales of fiber, have now been automated out of existence. In 1950, average hourly earnings in textiles were $1.23 an hour compared with $1.24 in apparel. By 1980, textile hourly earnings had risen to $5.07 compared with $4.56 in apparel; in 1997, textile workers earned an average of $10.02 an hour, 21.5 percent more than the $8.25 an hour of those in apparel.[38] Currently only 48 percent of textile employees are women, while women constitute 77 percent of apparel workers.

Labor organizations have historically had a small proportion of the textile industry under collective agreements. As the textile industry moved south to the Piedmont states, it drew on a rural and small community workforce, largely made up of native whites.[39] Textile mills at their outset often provided the principal employment in the locality. The first unions were formed among some of the skilled craftspeople, such as loom fixers, weavers, spinners, and slasher tenders, particularly in New England. With the advent of the CIO, industrial unionism sought to organize more workers in the industry, and the Textile Workers Union of America merged with the established Amalgamated Clothing Workers Union in 1976. However, organization met fierce opposition from southern textile employers.[40] Currently, about 15 percent of the textile production and nonsupervisory workforce is organized compared with 25 percent in the apparel industry.[41]

The combined impact of these factors is captured by the following trends. From 1950 to 1996, U.S. production of textiles increased almost threefold. Over the same time period, the number of production workers decreased by almost half. And the rate of textile productivity over this period far outpaced that for the manufacturing sector as a whole. (We discuss the performance of the textile industry extensively in Chapter 13.) Although U.S. apparel firms struggled in the 1980s, competing with foreign producers on labor costs, the domestic textile industry fared much better. Successful exploitation of economies of scale, favorable international trade agreements such as the MFA, and special arrangements for apparel imports made of U.S. textiles—even the clout of certain southern senators, looking after the firms in their states—mean the U.S. textile story has not been determined by import penetration.

Even so, lean retailing practices pose both new opportunities and challenges for the textile industry. Supplier relations in retail-apparel-textile channels are shifting. Textile manufacturers no longer simply supply apparel-makers with cloth; they may also sell a variety of household goods, such as sheets and towels, directly to retailers or serve industrial users with a wide range of products. Because product proliferation is the order of the day in all these markets, textile firms are being asked by their customers to provide many more products in smaller lot sizes and with shorter lead times. In the new competitive arena—where demand uncertainty and time to market have become important factors along with price—textile firms are being forced to adapt to information-integrated channels, rather than just drawing on the economies of scale that led to their success in the past.

Historical Relations Among Retail, Apparel, and Textile Firms

For most of the last century, companies in one of these industries related to those in another through markets as sellers and buyers. The business enterprises that emerged in the American retail, apparel, and textile industries were, for the most part, separated. They weathered diverse competitive conditions; they differed markedly in their capital structures, costs of entry and exit, size and scale of operations, the proportion of direct labor costs, unionization, geographic locations, and so on. There was almost no vertical integration across retail, apparel, and textiles. For example, only a few major manufacturers in men's apparel have also entered into the retail business—Bond Stores in the World War II era, Hart, Schaffner, and Marx more recently—although Levi Strauss, a manufacturer of jeans, has opened some retail operations. As for retailers, most mass distributors have focused on buying and selling rather than manufacturing products.

No textile producer of woven goods has been a significant apparel manufacturer. One company, Burlington Industries, sells directly to organizations that purchase uniforms for airlines, police, and fire personnel. It specifies in the sale that, regardless of the apparel firm used to fabricate uniforms, Burlington's cloth must be used.[42] Another major textile company, Milliken, has a degree of common ownership with a retail business, Mercantile, although these arrangements remain unusual.

Textile firms, however, have been players in multiple supply channels. There are three major categories of sales outlets for these manufacturers: (1) woven goods and some knit goods destined for clothing, in which materials are sold to apparel-makers for fabrication and assembly; (2) home furnishings—such as sheets, bedspreads, towels, and some knit goods—in which the textile firm sells directly to retailers; (3) industrial products, from automobile seat covers and rugs to commercial fishing nets, in which a textile firm sells materials to a car company or other nonapparel manufacturer. Thus, there are at least three kinds of relations among the industries, and multiple textile channels are on the rise. Although apparel uses dominated textile consumption in the past, by the early 1980s apparel's share of fiber consumption was only 37 percent; home furnishings was about 38 percent; and industrial textile products consumed over 20 percent.

Textile companies like Springs have taken advantage of these new outlets—for example, producing Disney-character sheets for retail—but a new dynamic is also developing with apparel-makers, who want shorter runs of materials much more quickly from their textile suppliers. Historically, the textile-apparel relationship involved long lead times or advance commitments to secure the necessary cloth in the right style, texture, and patterns. This occurred not only because of the greater concentration of businesses in the textile industry, but because textile companies generally plan to run their expensive capital equipment at full capacity around the clock. Our research indicates that the relationships between firms in the textile and apparel industries remain underdeveloped, with new competitive forces driving both sides to change.

Even if integration efforts in the past have been uncommon, information flows, transport, and inventory have always been decisive factors in shaping the relations among retail, apparel, and textile firms. As Alfred Chandler and other business historians have made clear, successive changes in information exchange and transport over the last century have reshaped relations among industries, as well as the internal organization of these enterprises. Chandler notes,

> Significantly, it was in several of these [labor-intensive] more fragmented industries—textiles, apparel, furniture, and some food processing—that the mass retailer (the department stores, mail-order houses and chain stores) began to coordinate the flow of goods from manufacturer to consumer. In those industries where substantial economies of scale and scope did not exist in production, high-volume flows through the processes of production and distribution came to be guided—and the resulting cost reductions achieved—by the buying departments of mass retailers, retailers who handled a variety of related products through their facilities.[43]

And so we arrive at the new information technologies of the 1980s. These have begun to create integrated channels among enterprises in the three industries, facilitating even more product proliferation and stimulating changes in merchandising, inventory management, internal production practices, and methods of using human resources. When it comes to the driving force behind the late twentieth-century industrial transformation, lean retailing is at the forefront of that revolution.

3

The Retail Revolution: Traditional Versus Lean Retailing

In 1911, John Wanamaker opened his flagship store in downtown Philadelphia. The twelve-story building, with its forty-five acres of floor space, was the largest of its time devoted to retail merchandising. Its central "Grand Court" had marble arches that rose 150 feet and was capped by a dome. Major physical innovations were hidden behind this visual wonder: sixty-eight state-of-the-art elevators; the latest in fireproofing; a large power plant devoted entirely to the store; and sophisticated heating, ventilating, and sanitation systems.

Wanamaker had been in the forefront of retailing for more than thirty years by the time he opened this store. His goal was to provide the elegant shopping experience of major European boutiques while satisfying the American desire for product diversity. At the same time, he based his retailing system on four fundamental principles: one price for a product (no haggling); prices guaranteed to be "10 percent lower than the lowest elsewhere"; acceptance of cash payments only, in order to keep prices low; and cash refunds or exchanges for unsatisfied customers. With these fundamental principles in hand, he became one of the leading retailers of his day.[1]

Sixty years after the opening of Wanamaker's Philadelphia store, another entrepreneur synthesized a set of existing technologies and, along with a number of other retailers, began another revolution in the industry. Sam Walton started small in the 1970s, but Wal-Mart rapidly became the largest retailer in the United States, with total sales in fiscal year 1995 equaling the combined sales volumes of Kmart, Sears Roebuck and Co., and the supermarket chain The Kroger Co., the next three largest American retail organizations. Walton's successful innovations placed enormous pressure on other mass merchant retailers to alter their practices along similar lines. By the late 1980s, a growing number of retailers had started changing the way they did business.

As we have emphasized, the current retail revolution—involving new information technologies, new product labeling, and new methods of distribution—has driven changes in the apparel and textile industries as well. Yet this revolution didn't happen overnight; nor was it the brainchild of a single entrepreneur. In fact, the retail systems of both Wanamaker and Walton integrated a variety of innovations that had already been pioneered by other retailers. For example, Wanamaker's "one-price" policy was initially adopted by wholesaler Arthur Tappan in the 1820s and experimented with by Lord & Taylor in 1838 and Rowland Macy in the early 1850s. Similarly, bar codes and electronic scanning—key building blocks of new retailing practices—began in the grocery industry. Kmart became the first major nonfood retailer to employ them as a means of tracking inventory in the early 1980s, several years before Walton made this technology a core building block of his distribution system.

This chapter will examine the differences between the traditional retail model and lean retailing. We explore how the set of practices that traditional retailers drew on to merchandise and distribute products became increasingly costly. Then we return to why retailers—Wal-Mart, Kmart, J. C. Penney, Dillard's Inc., Federated Department Stores, and others—adapted technologies and management practices to handle demand uncertainty, product proliferation, and complex sourcing decisions.

The Retail Challenge

Imagine the problems faced by a typical department store. It must cater to a diverse clientele: men, women, and children, with varied tastes, disparate income levels, and a wide range of physical measurements. It must deal with seasonal changes that affect the type of clothes offered—is it winter or summer? The beginning of the school year? The holiday season? If the company operates stores in different geographic regions, its product offerings must also reflect regional differences in style, weather, income, and culture. In addition to these factors, consumer tastes often shift rapidly, sometimes within a single season. These long-standing causes of variation in consumer demand have been further compounded by accelerating product proliferation in all segments of the apparel industry.

The combination of different sizes, colors, styles, fabrics, price lines, and consumer groups means that a retailer must carry an enormous range of different products. The more diverse the consumer base of the retailer, the larger the number of individual products typically measured in stockkeeping units (SKUs).[2] This variety is portrayed in Table 3.1, which shows the number of SKUs provided annually by different types of retailers over the course of a year. The number of SKUs can range from just 10,000 for a discount food store like Costco, which offers a limited number of products sold in large quantities, to more than two million different items in an upscale department store.

Today retailers must manage this profusion of products. At an operational level, this means deciding what types and how many of any one good it should stock to maximize sales per square foot of available space—one of the most critical measures of retail performance. If all goes well, retailers allocate space to different goods efficiently, responding to shifts in consumer tastes (stocking the hits and discontinuing flops); setting pricing policies (markups and markdowns) to deal with both the direct cost of goods and the nature of consumer demand; and controlling inventory to reduce exposure to risk. Further, the contemporary retailer has to keep track of sales and inventory accurately by SKU.

The Elements of Traditional Retailing

The early twentieth-century success of Wanamaker's and other department stores illustrates that the keys to effective retailing are providing customers with a variety of desirable products, procuring those prod-

Table 3.1. Number of SKUs by Retail Segment

Retail Channel	Examples	Estimated Number of Distinct SKUs
Discount food club	Costco; Sam's	10,000
Grocery store	Stop & Shop; Safeway	25–40,000
Super food store	Super Stop & Shop	40–60,000
Category killer	Home Depot; Toys "R" Us	80,000
Mass merchandiser	Wal-Mart; Kmart	100–150,000
Department store	Dillard's; Federated	
Standard		800,000
Flagship		1–2 million

Source: Harvard Center for Textile and Apparel Research.

ucts at a low enough cost to make a profit, marketing them well, and charging prices that reflect customers' willingness to pay. As we discussed in the last chapter, large retailers were able to implement this strategy in the late nineteenth century because the falling distribution costs afforded by a national railway system, as well as new information links arising from the telegraph and later the telephone, provided economies of scale and scope. Other technological innovations, including steel construction, plate glass, and the Otis elevator, allowed retailers to expand multi-story floor space without purchasing more real estate, providing for a more varied collection of products. The creation of a national highway system in the 1950s further fostered the development of mass retailing by opening vast new spaces in suburban malls.

Under the traditional model, retailers ordered desired products far in advance of the selling season because their apparel suppliers charged less for large runs and long lead times with long periods of advance commitment. Retail buyers, assigned to a specific product line, purchased products based on their best guesses of what would sell. They would then apply rules of thumb to allocate volume across styles and sizes. These transactions typically occurred eight to ten months before the goods appeared on the retailer's selling floor. The success of buyers therefore turned on their ability to predict what consumers would want and to obtain those products at the lowest possible cost.[3] Although the order would specify a delivery time far closer to the season, once the buyer placed the order with the apparel manufacturer, it typically remained unchanged until delivery to the retailer's warehouse or individual stores.

As portrayed in Figure 3.1, the typical shipment between an apparel manufacturer and retail customers was large and of low frequency—usually once a season. Once delivered, the retailer held the products in central warehouses or as inventory in individual stores' "back rooms." When the desired time of display and sale arrived, workers stocked the product on the selling floor and replenished from store or warehouse inventories as the selling period progressed. Inventory control relied on painstaking, manual comparisons between sales records (paper receipts) and physical counts of items on the floor, in the back room, and in warehouses.[4] Overstocks at the close of a season were then marked down for clearance, warehoused in inventory for future sales, or sold to a secondary market supplying discount retailers.

Those who could predict, or in some cases create, markets for new products clearly were at an advantage. Not surprisingly, fast tracks in

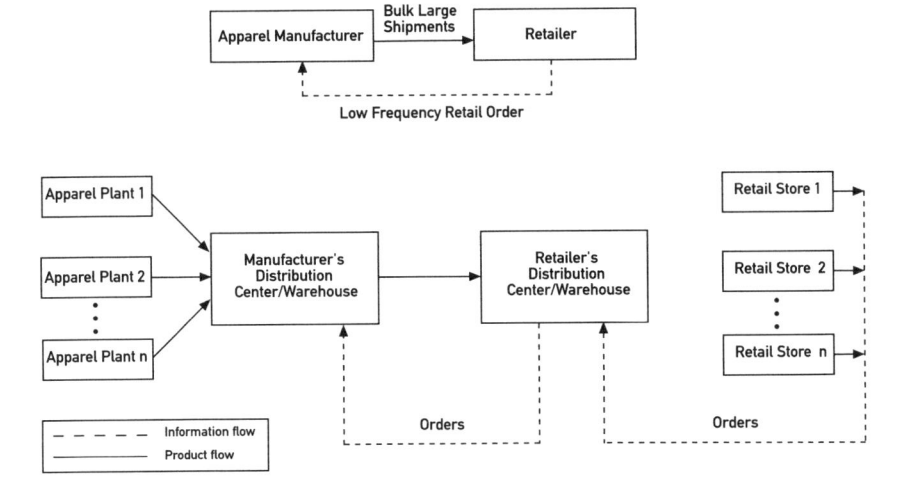

Figure 3.1. Traditional Retailing-Apparel Supplier Relations

the traditional retail world started with buyers, and many apparel CEOs successfully demonstrated their "feel" for the market early in their careers. This list includes John Wanamaker and Marshall Field in the early era of the department store; Stanley Marcus of Nieman Marcus and Millard S. Drexler of The Gap are more recent examples of "buyer" CEOs.[5]

The best traditional retailers were also good at merchandising. Effective merchandising requires matching the retailer's product mix to the tastes and incomes of its targeted customers. Establishing the target customer base is therefore a critical first step in any merchandising strategy. Although this may seem obvious today, Wanamaker shook up the existing retail world in the 1870s by seeking to understand his customers' preferences as a basis for making merchandising choices.[6]

A century later, retailing success is often attributed to combining effective marketing with an understanding of consumer tastes. The growth of private-label programs among retailers in the 1980s exemplifies this trend. In private-label programs, retailers create a distinctive product line under their exclusive name and license. If successful, a retailer's private-label program can capitalize on the same type of strong brand recognition that has yielded profits to companies like Levi Strauss or more recently Tommy Hilfiger. For example, the success of The Gap's jeans, J. C. Penney's Arizona line, and Sears's Canyon River Blue line has led to erosion of the market share held by the two leading jeans manufacturers, Levi Strauss and VF Corporation.[7] According to Standard & Poor's, "In the 1980s the standout performers in retailing developed a sustainable competitive advantage by differentiating themselves in the eyes of the consumer. . . .The winners have either created new markets or revitalized old businesses with a price and product mix geared toward a narrower market."[8]

In addition to effective buyers and merchandising, successful traditional retailers relied on a third element: purchasing products at low costs through buying power (volume or cash position), or via access to the cheapest domestic and international sources for apparel. As we've already noted, international sourcing has become increasingly prevalent. Beginning in the 1970s, retailers expanded their offshore sourcing efforts, especially after quality standards improved, establishing sourcing offices and relationships in low-wage countries, particularly in Asia.

The Growing Costs of Traditional Retailing

Nevertheless, large-scale retailing came with its own risks. Through their buying power, traditional retailers could dramatically lower the direct costs of procurement and, in the process, usurp the role of wholesalers in the apparel distribution system.[9] Purchasing in large quantities for their stores, however, subjected retailers to the attendant risk of selling "perishable" products like apparel. The absence of business systems capable of adjusting to real-time demand information, as well as the lack of information between the time when orders were placed and the actual selling season, meant that early order commitments could not be amended pending new information.[10] In terms of the retail bottom line, this risk appeared in the indirect costs associated with holding inventories of unwanted products and stock-outs of popular items.[11]

Two trends over the past twenty-five years have compounded the problems inherent in the traditional retail model. First, product proliferation has vastly increased the number of products retailers are required to manage in their stores. Second, the total amount of retail space in the United States has expanded dramatically, even while consumer expenditures on apparel items have declined as a share of total expenditures. Some analysts deem this "the overstoring of America." Since the early 1980s, retailers have faced the growing costs associated with holding inventories of a wider variety of goods in a world increasingly characterized by industry overcapacity. Low-cost international suppliers helped fill the gap for a while, but the traditional retail model

Product Proliferation

In Chapter 1, we introduced the fashion triangle, which includes the three types of goods commonly sold by apparel retailers: fashion, fashion-basic, and basic products. Although product variety in apparel has historically been associated with the fashion end of the industry, the number of products available to U.S. consumers in almost every apparel category has grown significantly over the past two decades.

Consider men's shirts. Throughout much of the post–World War II era, the majority of men's shirts sold in the United States were white dress shirts. But today a shirt manufacturer's "basic" collection typically includes solid white, blue, and a white/blue weave, as well as white with color stripes in pure cotton, cotton/polyester blends of various mixtures, and other fabrics like 100-percent cotton oxford, pinpoint oxford, and several qualities of broadcloth.[12] Most of the collection will come with a choice of collar styles, and some will include a French cuff option. There are also common cuts ("silhouettes"), such as regular, athletic, loose fit, and long. In addition to these dimensions, there are quarterly collections of different fabrics. Each shirt corresponding to a combination of these characteristics—for example, a 16–35 blue, button-down, pinpoint oxford shirt with French cuffs cut long—has its own pattern of demand that varies considerably over the course of a year.[13]

For a retailer, a larger number of SKUs raises the level of uncertainty regarding what product will sell or not sell in any period. In practical terms, this means that a retailer carrying a broader array of goods faces increased costs both for carrying goods in inventory that will not sell (overstocks) and running out of a good that sells beyond expectations (stock-outs). The costs associated with demand uncertainty, which were previously connected primarily with fashion products—that is, the problem of selling a highly perishable item—have grown enormously for apparel retailers. Apparel retailers are not alone: The variety of products offered has increased considerably in most consumer product sectors, from most segments of the retail food industry to home building products to personal computers.[14]

Increasing product proliferation was clear among the business units in our survey, as vividly portrayed in Figure 3.2. The average number of SKUs per business unit rose from an average of 3,871 in 1988 to

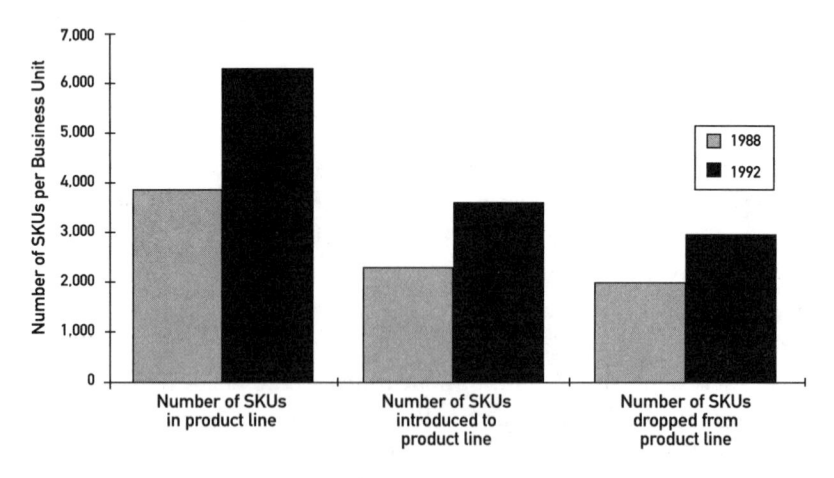

Figure 3.2. Product Proliferation, 1988 and 1992

6,304 in 1992. This overall increase is mirrored by growth in the average number of new SKUs introduced per year by apparel business units, which increased from 2,368 in 1988 to 3,688 in 1992. Meanwhile, the number of discontinued SKUs rose from 2,057 to 3,050. This means that a large portion of each apparel firm's product line consists of new products. The consequent "churning" of products adds further uncertainty to the retailer's or manufacturer's already difficult tasks.

Retail Overcapacity

Construction of retail centers, particularly shopping malls, boomed in the 1980s. Rapid expansion of retail space arose from a simple formula that had traditionally proven successful: Add more stores and revenue growth will follow. The early age of retailing was marked by the expansion of stores within major metropolitan areas, but in the early 1960s, retailers started flocking to large, enclosed suburban malls and non-enclosed "strip malls." As a result, between 1972 and 1992 the annual rate of new shopping-center construction outpaced the growth in population and potential consumers.[15] The size of retail establishments also grew during this period because of two important trends.[16] First, the number of independent department stores—usually a single-site enterprise of relatively moderate size—declined dramatically in the 1980s. Second, many multi-enterprise retailers either built large new stores or expanded the size of existing ones.[17]

Far outpacing the overall growth in population, retail space per capita rose from 5.3 square feet per person in 1964 to 9 square feet in 1974 to 16 square feet in 1988. By 1996, it had grown still further, reaching close to 19 square feet.[18] In comparison, per capita retail space in a developing country like Mexico is estimated at .3 square feet.

The growth in consumer expenditures did not rise commensurately with the boom in retail space. The apparel and upkeep share of household expenditures in the Consumer Price Index fell from 10.6 percent in 1963 to 5.5 percent in 1995. Per capita expenditure for apparel and related services declined from $1,710 in 1992 to $1,698 in 1994 (in current dollars).[19] And these downward expenditure trends occurred in the face of *growth* in the average number of outerwear garments consumed per capita: from 14.3 garments in 1967 to 28.7 garments in 1995.[20] In other words, the amount of money spent by an average consumer per garment fell over this period, reflecting in part more casual workplaces, which allow people to spend less on clothing for work, and intense price competition. Retailers with more and more floor space were chasing fewer and fewer apparel-consumption dollars.[21]

The Retail Fallout

Increasing product proliferation, retail overcapacity, falling relative per capita expenditures on apparel, and the constant pressure to provide lower prices to consumers created an unforgiving competitive environment for retailers. Overall margins for the industry (particularly for specific retail segments like department stores) declined between 1977 and 1987. By the mid-1980s, a number of the most prestigious retailers were faltering, with some filing for bankruptcy or being acquired by other retailers.

Department stores proved to be one of the most adversely affected retail sectors.[22] Their inability to adapt to changing consumer tastes and the emergence of new retail channels that targeted specific consumer segments—specialty stores (especially so-called "category killers"), catalog stores, and mass merchants—led to erosion in market share. Although in the 1960s and 1970s the majority of apparel sales occurred in department stores, by 1990 they accounted for only 29 percent of all sales.[23] Venerable giants like Macy's, Gimbels, Saks Fifth Avenue, Federated, and Wanamaker filed for bankruptcy in the late 1980s and early 1990s.[24]

Product proliferation coupled with industry overcapacity revealed the costs inherent in the traditional model of retailing. Three types of costs were particularly high under the old model: forced markdowns to clear out unsold goods; lost sales from stock-outs; and the costs associated with holding inventory. In 1985, the losses associated with markdowns, stock-outs, and inventory carrying costs for U.S. retail-apparel-textile channels were estimated to be $25 billion.[25] An estimated 56 percent of these losses, $14 billion, arose from the need to mark down unsold products, either through store sales and promotions or through the use of the sizable secondary market for items purchased by discount retailers for sale to other consumer segments. Product stock-outs accounted for 24 percent, $6 billion, of the losses, and the cost of inventory carrying itself constituted the remaining 20 percent, $5 billion.

Price reductions from the beginning to the end of the season also increased dramatically over the period from 1948 to 1988, one in which there was considerable growth in product proliferation. Consequently, the difference between early season and end-of-season prices for women's apparel from the late 1960s to 1988 grew substantially.[26] Although these losses were borne throughout the entire channel to some extent, a disproportionate share, 65 percent, fell on retailers. This is not surprising, given the traditional retailing strategy under which retailers commit to purchases well in advance of the selling season.

Despite its high costs and negative impact on the bottom line, being left with unwanted apparel products—or running out of fashion hits—was viewed by most traditional retailers as a cost of doing business. With neither timely information on the state of sales at the store, nor the capability to use that information, little could be done to resolve this source of uncertainty and excess cost in the channel. This historical constraint only began to change with the advent of the current retail revolution.

The Lean Retailing Alternative

> The whole point is speed and clarity of communications. With this new technology, buying procedures that used to take weeks have now been cut to days—and sometimes even hours. That has greatly enhanced our response to new trends, reduced turnaround times and increased the flexibility of all those involved in the buying process.[27]
>
> —*William Howell, Chairman, J.C. Penney, 1995*

If lack of information provided a regrettable but unavoidable cost of doing business in retailing before the late 1980s, access to information has become crucial to competitive success in the 1990s. The ability to gather, transmit, and use information regarding sales at the cash register has created a new way of offering products to customers. It has created the lean retailer.[28]

The leveraged buyouts, mergers, and corporate restructuring of the 1980s left many of the historic retail powerhouses in a vulnerable condition, with a number of the strongest traditional retailers—Macy's, Saks, Sears—in an extremely weakened state. But this industry landscape also left the field open for the emergence of a new kind of retail competitor, one able to harness information as a central component of its competitive strategy.

A number of retailers filled this role, becoming the vanguard of the lean retailing revolution. Lean retailing represents an amalgam of technologies and management practices adopted and refined by various companies. Although no single retailer pioneered or adopted all the innovations that compose lean retailing, we focus here on those in three segments—mass merchants, national chains, and departments stores—that played important roles in initiating the larger transformation.

Mass Merchants: Wal-Mart

Wal-Mart is the most well known of the early lean retailers.[29] Traditional mass merchants sought cost advantage through economies of purchasing scale. Given limited information on sales, this meant that these retailers purchased large inventories of goods that they would then "push" to consumers, often by means of price reductions and sales promotions. Beginning in the late 1970s, Wal-Mart sought to reduce its costs by using emerging information technologies to track consumer sales at the checkout counter, monitor its inventory of goods within and across stores, and then supply its stores on an ongoing basis via highly efficient, centralized distribution methods. By capitalizing on "real-time" information on sales and inventory position, Wal-Mart increased its ability to let consumer demand "pull" its orders. As a result, it could reduce the amount of inventory it needed to hold for any given product and focus its resources on stocking those goods that were being purchased by consumers.

The Wal-Mart strategy required and fostered the development of a company-wide computer system to track incoming and outgoing shipments to the various stores. Through the use of its own proprietary standard, Wal-Mart gathered and exchanged information among its stores, distribution centers, and the main office in Bentonville, Arkansas, to monitor sales, place orders based on those sales, track shipments to the distribution centers, and coordinate the flow of materials and information throughout the system.[30] By the early 1980s, the company's investments in this information system—including satellite links to handle its immense amount of daily data—totaled more than $700 million.[31]

Wal-Mart reaped the full benefits arising from its extensive information systems when it shifted its focus from internal purposes to a means of interacting with suppliers. In 1987, Wal-Mart began its first major experiment in changing its relationship with a key supplier, Procter & Gamble, by establishing the "Wal-Mart Retail Link" program. This program provided Procter & Gamble with access to Wal-Mart's point-of-sales information, allowing the supplier to track sales of its products on a real-time basis and manage its inventory accordingly. In the words of Lou Pritchett, Procter & Gamble's vice president of sales at the time, "P&G could monitor Wal-Mart's inventory and data and then use that information to make its own production and shipping plans with a great deal more efficiency. We broke new ground by using information technology to manage our business together, instead of just to audit it."[32]

The Wal-Mart/Procter & Gamble partnership has been often cited by the business press. The program began through an informal discussion between Sam Walton and Procter & Gamble's Pritchett. Although the effort has been characterized as a partnership, senior executives at Procter & Gamble have also noted that the initial impetus came from Walton. The partnership required Wal-Mart to switch from its internal proprietary standard to a more widely adopted electronic data interchange (EDI) standard, as well as to bar codes that were already in use by other retailers, particularly Kmart. Although Kmart was the first major retailer to experiment with EDI, Wal-Mart led the way in structuring supply relationships and its overall competitive strategy around information exchange. The program soon expanded to other vendors, including apparel suppliers, who entered their own "trading partnerships" with Wal-Mart. Thus, what began as a system focused on efficient distribution eventually evolved into the modern system of lean retailing.

National Chains: J. C. Penney

J. C. Penney built an internal data communications network well in advance of its use with suppliers.[33] Point-of-sale terminals first appeared at its stores in the mid-1970s, allowing the company to capture information on store-level sales. Penney was also one of the first retailers to adopt scanner technologies. Although early forays into electronic data management relied on mainframe computers, between 1988 and 1991 the company installed 45,000 cash registers equipped with microprocessors and storage capabilities.

These store-level investments were accompanied by major capital investments in central computer processing capacities, continuing development of store- and corporate-level software systems, and improvements in distribution operations. In the late 1980s, Penney drew on these systems to allow corporate buyers in its Plano, Texas, headquarters to display potential products to geographically dispersed individual store merchandisers who, with store managers, had considerable autonomy within the company. This information infrastructure proved most beneficial when it gave Penney's major vendors access to sales data via direct broadcast satellite. There was initial resistance, however. Despite the company's offer to provide suppliers with EDI downloads, many declined because of their inability to process the data. It was only when Penney provided aggregated reports via fax to account executives that a thousand vendors agreed. By 1993, Penney was using EDI for processing 97 percent of purchase orders and 85 percent of invoices with 3,400 of its 4,000 suppliers. Nonetheless, many small suppliers did not have electronic links with the company.[34]

It is no accident that such innovative information and distribution relationships with key suppliers emerged through Wal-Mart, Kmart, and a national chain like J. C. Penney rather than among department or specialty stores. The larger size of these mass merchants facilitated adoption of rapid-replenishment practices as a result of economies of scale in inbound and outbound transportation, information technology, and distribution center operations. Indeed, the adoption of these distribution innovations parallels the emergence of department stores and mail-order houses a century earlier.

Both mass merchants and national chains cover a more narrow range of products—primarily basic apparel items—than department stores. Basic products are prime candidates for lean retailing because such a product style remains in a retailer and apparel company's product line over much of the selling season and often over several years. That makes it easier to use information acquired during the selling season for replenishment during the same season or for forecasting future demand. Basic items also represent a major percentage of all apparel goods sold. In our 1992 HCTAR sample, 45 percent of all shipments by business units, weighted by sales volume, could be classified as basic. Therefore, given their scale and product mix, it is not surprising that Wal-Mart, Kmart, and J. C. Penney were among the early pioneers of lean retailing.

Department Stores: Dillard's and Federated

Although providing consumers with low prices for a limited range of goods underpins the strategy of mass merchants and national chains, department stores (going back to Wanamaker) rely on offering consumers a diverse and exciting collection of goods. The focus of department stores tends to be on the middle and higher portion of the fashion triangle; consequently, lean retailing came later to this segment of the industry.

Dillard's was a pioneer in the use of information technology for tracking and responding to sales. Dillard's became one of the first department stores in the late 1980s to build a centralized inventory-tracking system to provide its headquarters in Little Rock, Arkansas, with real-time information on sales, by both store and item.[35] This entailed buying and then adapting early scanning technologies for use at sales counters and for point-of-sale data collection. Dillard's also purchased computing capacity for individual stores and its headquarters office, along with the necessary equipment to connect stores to the head office via electronic data transmission.

With these systems in place, it began to develop distribution centers capable of being efficient intermediaries between its suppliers and stores. Finally, like the mass merchants and national chains, Dillard's started insisting that its suppliers invest in corresponding technologies to allow electronic reordering and to meet its increasingly stringent service requirements. But unlike a mass merchant that typically manages over 125,000 separate items in a large store, the Dillard's system uses this information to manage over *one million* SKUs in one of its flagship stores.[36]

Federated originated as a decentralized "federation" of well-known stores like Rich's and Bloomingdale's, with wide variation in both its merchandising and back-room activities. Like Dillard's, its stores carry a vast array of products: a typical department store may have 800,000 items; its flagship Macy's in midtown Manhattan offers more than two million separate SKUs. During the 1980s, however, the amount of inventory held by Federated ballooned while it faced bankruptcy.

Under CEO Alan Questrom, the company addressed these problems by attempting to increase its inventory turns (the number of times a year that goods turned over in its stores) and reduce its exposure to losses from excess inventories. This entailed instituting aggressive markdown policies in the short term to remove large inventories that had built up in many divisions and stores. At the same time, the company began to redesign its logistics system—the method it used to move goods from suppliers, through warehouses, and to delivery at stores.

The size of Federated's logistics challenge can be captured by the following figures. In 1997, the company moved over 700 million units from its suppliers to its stores, requiring an average of 500 truck deliveries per day, which amounted to thirty million miles for deliveries per year.[37] Like Dillard's, J. C. Penney, and others, Federated spent millions of dollars on installing scanners, adopting bar codes and EDI to communicate internally and with suppliers. Given the size of its logistics challenge, Federated also chose to redesign its methods of moving goods from suppliers to stores. With the establishment of an independent operating unit, Federated Logistics, this retailer reduced the amount of time required to process merchandise in distribution centers by 60 percent, to an average of two days.

Meanwhile, the company sought to maintain the strengths of its divisions—Macy's and Bloomingdale's, in particular—in merchandising. It created, among other innovations, a "team buying" system that centralizes certain buying functions to benefit from potential economies of scale while taking full advantage of divisional expertise regarding different customer groups within Federated's stores. Yet a tension exists between its desire to provide customers with a changing variety of apparel fashions and the need to increase its capacity to replenish a higher percentage of products, thereby taking advantage of its expertise in logistics.[38] Increasingly, a department store must be successful at both pursuits. We discuss the trade-off arising from providing new products with little information on consumer demand (fashion products) and replenishing items on the basis of sales (historically limited to more basic products) in detail in Chapter 6.

Although Wal-Mart's rapid climb has created the most sound and fury, a variety of retailers adopted and adapted different pieces of lean retailing in the early 1990s. Note that the push toward rapid replenishment, reduction of lead times, and what has often been called "quick response" came predominately from retailers rather than from their apparel suppliers.[39]

The next chapter analyzes the building blocks of lean retailing, drawing on the retailers described above as well as others. Chapter 5 discusses how the retail revolution has led to a tremendous shift in bargaining power within the channel—away from manufacturers and suppliers and toward lean retailers.

4

The Building Blocks of Lean Retailing

> We're probably in a better position to determine specifically what the customer wants to buy than is the manufacturer.
> —*David Glass, Chief Executive, Wal-Mart, 1992*

Let's reconsider the keys to effective retailing: providing customers with a variety of desirable products, procuring those products at a low enough cost to make a profit, marketing them well, and charging prices that reflect customers' willingness to pay. Lean retailers still adhere to these principles—offering a variety of products, good marketing, and merchandising—just as a traditional player like Wanamaker did. But, as the opening quote indicates,[1] today's retail powerhouses have added a new twist: They also focus on continuously adjusting the supply of products offered to consumers at each retail outlet to match actual levels of market demand, thereby reducing their exposure to the risks of selling perishable goods. Lean retailers now incorporate into their total cost functions for sourcing both direct product costs (as reflected in the wholesale prices charged by suppliers plus transportation costs) and the indirect costs associated with demand uncertainty—including stock-out costs, costs of markdowns and write-offs, and inventory carrying costs.[2]

The goal of adjusting the supply of products at each retail outlet to market demand is not new. Successful buyers for traditional retailers sought to achieve this objective for a given product line by making the right guesses about future demand. Yet to do this consistently across a diverse range of products requires something more than prescient buyers. It takes timely information on the state of sales and an ability to transmit that information efficiently to a network of suppliers.

Given the quantity of SKUs carried by retailers and the enormous number of daily transactions, manually capturing and using this information on a timely basis is not practicable. Lean retailing requires several building blocks to be viable. First, it is based on the promulgation of industry standards for identifying products. Second, there must be affordable methods of information acquisition, storage, and transmission. Third, integrating computer technologies and automation for materials handling in distribution centers is crucial. Finally, this strategy requires the development of other standard practices among retailers and their suppliers, particularly regarding the preparation of packages and products for shipment and delivery to stores. After a more detailed description of the basic elements of lean retailing, this chapter examines each of these building blocks.

The Elements of Lean Retailing

Figure 4.1 depicts the relationships underlying lean retailing. In contrast with the infrequent, large bulk shipments between apparel manufacturers and retailers under the traditional model, lean retailers require frequent shipments made on the basis of ongoing replenishment orders placed by the retailer. These orders are determined by real-time sales information collected at the retailer's registers via bar code scanning. SKU-level sales data are then aggregated centrally and used to generate orders to suppliers, usually on a weekly basis.

However, collecting and generating orders electronically is only part of the story. Lean retailing also requires a system for efficiently handling incoming shipments from suppliers, checking them against

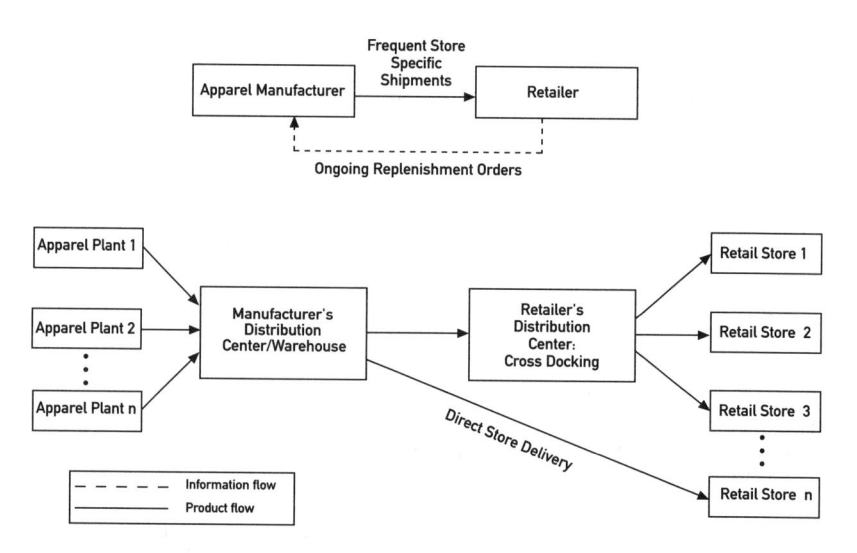

Figure 4.1. Lean Retailing-Apparel Supplier Relations

retail orders for content, processing receipts from and payments to suppliers, and rapidly routing those orders to the proper store. These elements rely on centralized distribution centers that serve logistical management functions. Unlike a simple warehouse—or retail store back room—that functions as a holding station for inventory ordered well in advance of sale, a distribution center quickly routes incoming supplier shipments to stores.

The lean retailer collects information from its stores on sales of particular products at the style, size, and color level, compiling that information at the end of the week—usually on Sunday night after weekend sales are known. It then transmits an electronic order to the appropriate supplier on the same night. On Monday or Tuesday, the supplier ships the products ordered in containers that can be electronically scanned at the retailer's distribution center. The shipment, unloaded at this center, moves through an automated sequence of scanning, weighing, and routing. At another bay of the distribution center, a truck is loaded, destined for the store requiring replenishment. By Wednesday or Thursday, shipping clerks at the store unload the truck and stock their shelves. Apparel items move without being touched by human hands from the time they are loaded into a container by a supplier to unloading at a specific retail store.

Just as Wanamaker fashioned a distinctive retailing system by drawing on a set of recently invented technologies and business practices, lean retailing's underpinnings arise from a set of technologies, standards, and practices that date from the 1980s. Lean retailing—and the apparel-textile channels that support it—rests on four foundations: bar codes; a set of enabling computer technologies; the modern distribution center; and the promulgation of standards across firms. In this chapter, we review each of the building blocks that have transformed the ways retailers compete with one another.

Building Block 1: Bar Codes and the Uniform Product Code

A system that continually replenishes products on the basis of actual sales relies on the acquisition of accurate information. Providing customers with a choice among thousands of SKUs is an essential component of retailing that vastly increases the amount of information that must be processed. The technologies behind the bar code, as well as the underlying standards it relies on, are fundamental to lean retailing.

These developments in the 1970s, including the emergence of the private nonprofit Uniform Code Council (UCC) to allocate the first five digits of bar codes to individual companies, were first established among grocery manufacturers and food chain stores. From this food sector beginning, bar codes have spread throughout the world; indeed, they are one of the major innovations of the last quarter of the twentieth century. Yet as Figure 4.2 illustrates, it was not until the mid-1980s that use of bar codes spread, to an appreciable extent, to the retail apparel sector.

A brief sketch of the origins of bar codes in the food sector will help to explain its contributions and adoption a decade later by general merchandise retailers in their relations with apparel, textile, and other suppliers.[3] Moreover, the UCC and its predecessors, which initiated the program, continue to administer bar codes throughout all sectors.[4]

Because labor costs in supermarkets were so high in the early 1970s, automated checkout had been a vision for some time, and the commercialization of the laser and other technologies enhanced these prospects. Chain store executives also envisioned much larger stores that could handle a wider range of products than the traditional 6,000

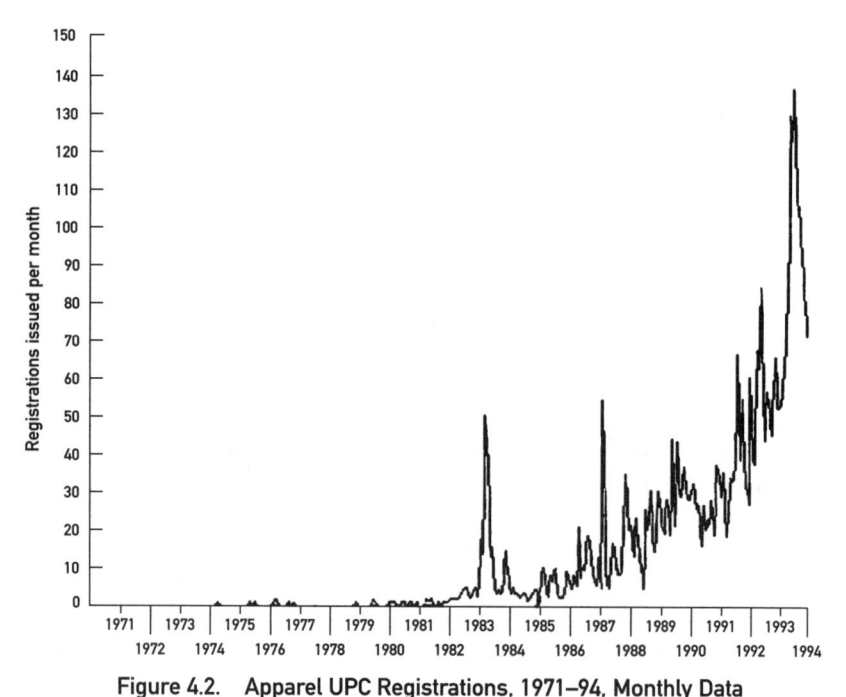

Figure 4.2. Apparel UPC Registrations, 1971–94, Monthly Data

Source: Based on analysis of Uniform Code Council, UCC Registration database, 1971–94

or so SKUs for grocery, meat, and produce items. Their "one-stop" shopping goal required a much more productive front end of the store to handle at least 25,000 SKUs.

Meanwhile, grocery manufacturers, the suppliers to food stores, were developing numerical and alphabetical systems for attachment to shipping cartons to facilitate ordering and warehouse operations. A number of factors pushed them and others to come up with common standards. For one thing, individual manufacturers tended to create distinctive and inconsistent programs; they wanted to avoid inconsistencies with the National Drug Code and a growing array of company identification codes. Manufacturers also needed more accurate and timely information on sales for better production planning and controlling the coupons they issued to stimulate retail sales. Last but not least, both retailers and food manufacturers were required by the federal government to adapt to wage and price controls in the early 1970s, enhancing their interests in productivity.[5]

In August 1970, six major associations in the grocery manufacturing and food chain sectors formed the Grocery Industry Ad Hoc Committee on Universal Product Coding. It was composed of twenty-two members—CEOs or senior officials from five grocery manufacturers and five distributors or food stores—and chaired by R. Burt Gookin, CEO of H. J. Heinz Company.[6] The Ad Hoc Committee's work was significantly enhanced by the extraordinary technical ferment of the previous decade; progress in basic sciences and research efforts launched during World War II and the Cold War were starting to bear commercial fruit. Developments in laser technology and holography played a role, and advances in integrated electronic circuits reduced the costs of real-time, interactive computing. The automated checkout counter would have been prohibitively expensive, perhaps technically impossible, just a decade earlier.[7]

The committee first recommended a Uniform Product Code composed of a ten-digit, nondescriptive, all-numeric mixed code; the leading five digits were to identify the manufacturer, the trailing five digits the merchandise item.[8] The committee then went on to recommend the choice of a standard symbol, the familiar vertical lines of the bar code. It suggested that a continuing organization—currently the UCC—be established to issue a distinctive code to manufacturers for a one-time fee that would vary with the gross sales of the enterprise. Most important, the committee played a distinctive role in visiting leading companies in grocery manufacturing and retail food chains to urge adoption and acceptance of this program, building critical mass for standardization.

Possible labor cost reductions and increased productivity helped persuade companies. Members of the committee and others estimated that automated checkout would operate two-thirds faster than conventional hand checkout, substantially increasing labor productivity and reducing customer lines at the checkout counter. Store trials with checkout scanning systems yielded a reduction in mis-rings and failures to include items, which also increased productivity. Checker training would be simpler than with conventional keyboards, an important factor considering the part-time and labor turnover usual in the industry; and end-of-day summaries could be compiled much faster with computers. Thus, hard savings exceeded the allocated capital costs of these installations and the costs to grocery manufacturers. Estimated direct savings at the time did *not* include further economies likely to be derived from better transactions information for space allocations, scheduling of workers, and inventory control.[9]

The manufacturers, agreeing to place bar codes on the merchandise that identify both manufacturer and product, were expected to profit from far better information on sales, reducing the extent of out-of-stock situations and the elimination of conflicting proprietary product identification systems. In addition, manufacturers' coupons for price reductions could be automatically matched at the register.

In 1974, the first item marked with a UPC bar code—a double-pack of Wrigley's chewing gum—was scanned in a supermarket in Troy, Ohio.[10] By 1975, bar codes and automated checkouts began to spread throughout the retail food-grocery manufacturing sectors. Food chain stores grew in size, taking on drugstore products, deli departments, and bakeries, and the number of SKUs climbed to 40,000 and more.[11] In April 1976, less than two years after the first bar code experiment, 75 percent of the items in a typical supermarket carried a bar code based on the UPC code.[12] Ironically, however, retail food chains did not become seriously concerned with inventory management issues until the late 1980s, when they had much to learn from the general merchandise and apparel channels.[13]

Widespread introduction of bar codes in apparel waited until the 1983–1987 period (see Figure 4.2, page 58), when Kmart, followed by Wal-Mart, seized the new technology and began requiring apparel suppliers to use bar codes for product identification. Registrations with the Uniform Code Council reveal the impact of these two retailers' forays into bar codes: in 1983, the year Kmart began its UCC requirements for soft good sales, UCC registrations among apparel manufacturers jumped to 400 registrations from seventy in the previous year. And in 1987, when Wal-Mart instituted similar requirements, UCC registrations among apparel manufacturers jumped by 300 over that of the previous year.[14]

But unlike the food chains, the driving force behind bar codes in apparel retailing was not the front end of the store but precise product identification and inventory management. Mass merchants have 150,000 SKUs and department stores may have over a million, indicating the variety of styles, colors, fabrics, sizes, and products that constitute apparel sales. Bar codes permit organizations to handle effectively the kind of vast product differentiation that would have been prohibitively expensive in an earlier era. They also facilitate instantaneous information at the point of sale, with significant effects on inventory management and logistics.

The promulgation of bar codes as the industry standard for apparel product labeling was further bolstered in 1986 when a group of supplier, manufacturer, and retailing executives established the Voluntary Interindustry Communications Standards (VICS) committee. The VICS objective was, and remains, to encourage the use of standards and protocols to improve customer service. Its first major effort was to ensure that the Uniform Code Council's UPC-A and associated bar code became the standard for point-of-sales scanning devices.[15] From 1987 to 1992, this largely came to pass as a growing number of retailers began requiring their suppliers to provide products using this labeling scheme. In our sample, 69 percent of business units using bar codes reported adopting the UPC-A by 1992.

To be sure, large capital investments are required to move from a paper-based sales system to one drawing on bar codes. When a major U.S. department store, for example, decided to adapt a system of bar codes in the late 1980s, it needed to modify 40,000 registers, at a cost of $200 to $300 per register. Additional major investments were required in software and hardware for operating the system at the store and enterprise level, as well as the costs associated with training workers to use those systems.

But the savings far outstrip the initial costs, which is why virtually all major retailers have adopted bar codes and scanning. The growth in UCC registrations by apparel companies vividly illustrates the trend. In 1981, less than half a percent of all bar code registrations were issued to apparel manufacturers. By 1994, 7.3 percent of UCC registrations were for apparel companies.[16] Even more telling are the changes at specific retailers. In 1996, Federated Department Stores, with $15 billion in annual sales, had more than 95 percent of its goods labeled with bar codes.

Building Block 2: EDI and Data Processing

The technology and standardization underlying the bar code provided a platform for fruitful investments in complementary technologies. The most important related technology is electronic data interchange (EDI). EDI facilitates rapid transmission of large amounts of information with far greater accuracy than possible via paper transactions.[17] Like bar codes, EDI involves both technological developments and standardization of methods for data transfer. At this point, standards have been developed for business-to-business communications, including purchase orders, shipping invoices, and funds transfer. And by eliminating the clerical and mailing activity associated with paper-based information, EDI reduces costs, time delays, and errors.[18]

Technologically, EDI requires hardware and software systems capable of capturing and moving information efficiently in an electronic format. By the 1980s, the development of software, coupled with the falling costs of computing, made EDI an increasingly attractive addition to the basic foundation of lean retailing. Kmart, Wal-Mart, and Dillard's were early users of EDI, partially because they developed their own internal standards and systems. Other retailers, like Federated Department Stores and Sears, adopted EDI systems considerably later than bar codes (in the case of Sears, some five years after registers capable of using bar codes had been fully installed).

One reason for this is that exchanging information electronically also requires a common software platform. Without such a communications interface, information sent by a retailer might be unreadable or require extensive translation by a supplier. From the retail perspective, the reverse flow of information is even more problematic, given that many retailers use thousands of different suppliers. As with bar codes in the 1970s, an array of potential information standards existed in the 1980s, including proprietary and publicly available communication platforms (such as GEIS and IBM). The VICS committee, following its success in helping to promulgate the UCC bar code standard, once again worked to establish a standard, EDI 856, as the platform most commonly in use.[19] In the 1992 HCTAR survey, 78 percent of the business units using EDI worked with the IBM platform. Having EDI capabilities has become a prerequisite for dealing with a growing percentage of retailers, an issue we will return to in the next chapter.

Developments in both hardware and software further augment the lean retailer's ability to use the vast amount of information collected at store registers. Software packages (and a niche of software companies and consultants) for more complex data processing are available commercially or can be tailored for a particular company on a proprietary basis. These packages assist retailers in using point-of-sales information for inventory management and vendor management, as well as for new activities such as category management and "micromerchandising" in which a retailer can tailor product selection to specific regions or stores.[20] Like EDI, more sophisticated database management methods are slowly spreading from the early lean retailers to those that have adopted the strategy more recently.

Building Block 3: The Modern Distribution Center

A distribution center is the antithesis of a warehouse. Warehouses serve as the physical expression of the need to store large inventories of goods, the main artifact of traditional retailing. Distribution centers, in contrast, form the nexus between retailers and their suppliers. They serve to process incoming goods efficiently, ensure that incoming deliveries match purchase orders, and route orders for shipment to the correct store. Rather than being a place for storage, a distribution center consists of bays for inbound and outgoing trucks, an automated, fast-moving conveyor network connecting them, and a sophisticated information system to control movement from receiving to shipping docks as well as process the transactions relating to those shipments.[21]

The comparative physical size of a warehouse and a modern distribution center provide one indication of the fundamental differences between the two. A warehouse built to support the flagship retail stores of a major retailer in Manhattan, circa 1980, required about 650,000 square feet of floor space and was equipped with about fifty bays (or "doors") for loading and unloading trucks. But the ideal distribution center constructed for the same set of stores currently would be no more than 300,000 square feet, with 150 bays for servicing trucks.[22]

The size and composition of the workforce are also quite different. Traditional warehouses require hundreds of people, usually working on a single shift. In addition to loading and unloading trucks, a large number of jobs were devoted to receiving and inspecting incoming packages and stocking storage bins in the warehouse. A second group of workers was involved in "picking and packing," that is, assembling outgoing orders for stores by going to storage areas and bins and picking the required items and packing them for outbound shipment. Additional workers moved goods within the warehouse to adjust to space limitations arising from unexpected delays in shipping out orders, unexpected early arrival of goods, or holding unsold inventory. Capital per worker reflected the relatively low level of technology in place in the warehouse (primarily equipment, such as forklifts, to load, lift, and unload pallets and boxes).

Not surprisingly, the capital investment in a new distribution center is substantial. The capital investment entailed in building a traditional warehouse operation to service a large regional area is approximately $8 to $10 million (in 1997 dollars). A new distribution center for servicing an area of similar size required expenditures of between $60 and $70 million in 1997.[23] Even the cost of retrofitting an existing warehouse to operate as a distribution center can range between $10 and $25 million. But just as the initial costs of implementing bar codes and other information technologies are quickly superceded by hard savings, a distribution center usually has a relatively short payback period.

A state-of-the-art distribution center to service a large regional area requires between 400 to 500 employees and operates in two shifts. It includes workers for the traditional jobs of loading and unloading trucks, as well as a group of highly skilled employees who are responsible for information processing and maintenance of sophisticated equipment like scanners and automated conveyer systems. Capital intensity is much higher than in warehouses for reasons described below, typically more than $10,000 per worker.[24]

Managing the Flow of Goods

The demands placed on distribution centers are substantial. Take the case of a distribution center for a major department store retailer. A single flagship store requires up to eight trucks a night during a typical week—and anywhere from ten to thirty trucks a night at peak season—to keep it stocked. A smaller store, in the normal course of operations, still needs a shipment at least every other day. A single, state-of-the-art cross-docking facility for such a retailer can service a geographic region as large as southern California. Such a distribution center handles up to 70,000 containers and pallets each day of various size, weights, and fragility, loading and unloading between fifty and seventy-five trucks at any one time.

The distribution needs for a mass merchant are just as significant. A typical Wal-Mart distribution center may serve about 150 stores located within a radius of 200 miles, with each store receiving approximately five deliveries each week. Wal-Mart's fleet of trucks delivered more than 688,000 trailer loads of merchandise from its distribution centers to its stores in 1995.[25]

A description of the flow of goods from vendors to the retail sales floor provides a picture of the central role played by the distribution center in lean retailing. Incoming shipments from apparel suppliers may come as full truckload deliveries direct from vendors; from consolidators that have merged the shipments from multiple vendors; and from vendors as less than truckload deliveries.[26] Also, while retailers historically maintained their own fleet of trucks for delivery, they have increasingly contracted this work out, both in terms of deliveries from vendors and even in handling shipments from distribution centers to their individual stores.[27] This reflects, in part, a desire to take advantage of the cost economies of shippers, which still must operate within the tight performance guidelines laid out by the retailer.[28]

Within a distribution center, there are two main flows for goods. The most advanced set of practices are applied to incoming shipments that can be "cross-docked." In this case, goods are unloaded at one bay of the distribution center and moved to another bay by conveyer for shipment in the same day. The other category of incoming goods require some sort of manual processing, such as "picking," in which packages are opened and items selected for repackaging and delivery. This is more labor intensive, and products remain in the distribution center for longer periods of time. Of the incoming containers per day processed by a major distribution center of a lean department store, 60 to 70 percent are cross-docked, while 30 to 40 percent need to be manually processed.

The cross-docking procedure begins when trucks are unloaded (manually, with some lifting equipment for heavier items or pallets); packages are positioned so that the bar code on the shipping container marker (SCM) can be scanned.[29] This initial handling step is important, because goods come in three forms: cartons, hanging boxes, and pallets. The bar code on the SCM, containing information on the products and the number of items in the package, is immediately scanned. The package then moves onto a scale and its weight is checked against the weight indicated on the label. If a discrepancy exists, the package is routed to an audit area for examination. At the same time, the information on the SCM is matched against data in the distribution center's database on purchase orders. Once again, discrepancies between the label and the original purchase order issued by the retailer will send the shipment through a separate auditing process.[30]

Shipments that pass weight and purchase order verification move on to the main conveyer line, which has multiple sublines, or "spurs," that correspond either to docks where packages are being consolidated directly for shipment to stores or to areas in the center devoted to opening certain types of goods for price marking, reconsolidation, or other manual processes.[31] However, the aim of the distribution center is to minimize the percentage of goods that flow anywhere but directly to a dock for shipments to a store. Those packages that have been prepared by manufacturers with price tags, bar codes, hangers, and other features necessary to make them "floor-ready" move rapidly to a loading dock, specified on the computer file associated with the SCM, destined for a specific store delivery.

The various spurs of the main conveyer system end up at truck loading bays—often located on the opposite side of the distribution center—where storebound trucks can be docked. Trucks are loaded for delivery to specific stores. The computer completes its file associated with the particular shipment by indicating that the package has been loaded for shipping. Financial payments to the vendor are then initiated, along with a shipping manifest for the truck. The trucks are then sent out for deliveries to stores, where they will be unloaded and products stocked directly on the sales floor.[32]

Technological Requirements for a Distribution Center

Four technologies have made the modern distribution center possible: (1) bar codes and associated software systems; (2) high-speed conveyers with advanced routing and switching controls; (3) increased reliability and accuracy of laser scanning of incoming containers; and (4) increased computing capacities. Once again, bar codes are essential. Rapid processing in a distribution center requires methods of identifying unique incoming shipments. This is provided by means of product identifiers on the shipping container marker. Distribution centers draw on bar codes to provide unique identifiers for packages, pallets, and other shipping containers.

Modern distribution also involves sophisticated materials-handling technologies. Conveyers in a typical distribution center can process about ninety cartons a minute, while a state-of-the-art conveyer can move 120 cartons a minute.[33] Sensors and switches, controlled by microprocessors, provide the control to route packages on conveyer lines on an individual basis through the multiple branches that make up the handling system. These conveyer technologies have reached the point where the limiting factor on physical conveyance is the time it takes to load a truck.[34]

In addition, improvements in scanner technology, particularly in the depth of field of laser diode scanners, provide the means for the scanners along the conveyer to identify and route packages once they are unloaded from trucks. The range of size, shape, condition (e.g., dirt or rips on the box or bar code), and orientation of packages requires a robust means of scanning. Accompanying improvement in these technologies has been the rapid fall in their price, and thus improved payback for retailers integrating them in distribution centers. The falling price of related information technologies, such as handheld scanners, makes the system even more viable.

The data-processing needs in a distribution center are enormous: A typical center must handle hundreds of thousands of transactions associated with incoming and outgoing shipments on a daily basis. Accordingly, the reduction in costs of computer memory, storage, and processing capability has been critical in providing affordable capacities for processing and operating these systems. For example, increased RAM and high-speed CPUs enable computer systems to process incoming bar code data, matching them with purchase order data.[35]

To make any of these technologies effective, a distribution center requires a set of standardized practices between the retailer and its vendors. Two areas of standardization are crucial for the distribution center. First, a bar code on a standard shipping container marker identifies the contents of a package and links them to purchase orders, increasing the potential efficiency of the distribution center. The benefit of SCM adoption grows if retailers and suppliers also use related communication standards regarding the financial aspects of the transaction that can be processed electronically.[36] Second, standards regarding physical aspects of shipping—size, shape, and weight of shipments, as well as the placement of SCMs or other scannable markings—have become increasingly common. Too much variation in the physical characteristics of incoming shipments can lower the percentage of goods that can move through a distribution center on a fully automated basis.

From Distribution Center to the Sales Floor

The modern distribution center and the shipment of floor-ready merchandise also transform the operation of the retailer at the store level. Because incoming and outgoing orders are electronically scanned, processed, and routed to individual stores, inventory control resides at the retailer's distribution center(s) rather than at the individual store. As a result, individual retail stores no longer take inventory of incoming orders as they are unloaded from delivery trucks.[37] Instead, when trucks—fitted with an "electronic seal" to avoid pilferage—arrive from the retailer's center, they are immediately unloaded and products sent to the sales floor, ready to sell. This reduces the number of workers required at each store's shipping dock and lowers the cost of losses arising from clerical mistakes and theft.

Under the traditional retailing model, the elapsed time between the arrival of a delivery truck at an individual store and the stocking of products from that truck on the sales floor was one to five days, with a significant proportion of the truck's merchandise remaining in storerooms for longer periods of time. A crew of workers from the store's back room would undertake inventory control—counting individual items in each carton and comparing the count to the truck's manifest—unloading, bringing items up to the sales floor for stocking, or storing them in the basement for display in the future. Given the time required for this type of physical stockchecking, inventory control at the shipping dock was not typically done by individual SKU. For example, workers would simply check to see if the total number of shirts received at the store of a certain style matched the truck's manifest, without verifying that the assortment of sizes, colors, and designs conformed to the manifest or original order.

Under a lean retailing operation at a leading department store, however, a forty-eight-foot truck arrives at 4 A.M. and is unloaded by two workers by 5 A.M. Then a team composed of sales associates and managers works with staff from the shipping dock to prepare and bring the merchandise to the sales floor by 6 A.M., holding only damaged items for storage. By working as a coordinated team, and unencumbered with the need for manual inventory control, they are able to ensure that goods are ready for sale to shoppers when the retailer opens at 9:30 A.M. Drawing on such a system, a department store receiving 19,000 apparel items in a week, typical for a large store, requires less than sixty person hours to transfer those items from loading dock to the sales floor.

Building Block 4: Standards Across Firms

This brings us to the final building block. Under traditional retailing, the line between activities undertaken by the retailer and those by apparel suppliers was clear: Apparel manufactures made the products; retailers received, prepared (unpacked items, put on price tags and hangers), and displayed the products. However, lean retailing blurs those distinctions. This can be seen in part in the standardization of practices regarding product identification, EDI, and shipping labels already described. It should be clear by now that getting companies to adhere to common standards throughout the retail-apparel-textile channel is a major part of the story; even with compelling competitive reasons and an organization like the UCC advocating integration, standardization across industries is not easy. But the growing influence of lean retailing has forced the use of standards in many respects, as in the new degree to which products must be "floor-ready" on delivery.

A logical extension of the lean retailer's desire to reduce the amount of time between when product orders are placed and filled is to make incoming shipments ready for the sales floor—that is, prepared for display the moment they arrive at the retail store from the distribution center.[38] That means the product must have a price tag carrying the *retail* price to the consumer. To make this work, retailers must provide apparel suppliers with both retail price labels, tags, and/or stickers, and the price for each product shipped; they need a means for accurately sending timely pricing information to the manufacturer. This transfer of information would be almost impossible under the traditional retail system—and of little value, given the large time lags in that system and the time-sensitive nature of retail pricing. However, the availability of an EDI platform that draws on UPC bar code information now allows suppliers to provide this service.[39]

In addition to pricing, a number of other things can be done by suppliers prior to shipping products to the retail distribution center. They can place apparel items on hangers, which are used immediately by the retailer, and otherwise prepare clothing items for display on the sales floor. This reduces the time required for unpacking, folding or refolding, and/or hanging the garment. As in the other areas described above, the VICS committee has issued extensive guidelines regarding standardized practices for hanging garments, based in part on a January 1993 study commissioned by the group, which indicated cycle-time and direct-cost savings from standardizing practices across the industry and shifting these tasks back to suppliers.[40] In 1998, a group of the largest retailers agreed to craft industry standards for the next generation of point-of-sale technology as well.[41]

Not only do retailers establish standards, they impose penalties for failure to comply with those standards. For example, Federated levies penalties based on vendor "noncompliance" with a variety of UPC ticketing standards. Failure to mark merchandise with bar codes results in a penalty of $25 plus ten cents per unit not ticketed. Similar charges are applied to cases of poor-quality UPC tickets, affixing tickets improperly or using a ticket that does not conform to industry standards. Failure to provide UPC electronically (via EDI) results in a fine of $1 per UPC key entered, while locating shipping container markers improperly on a package results in fines of $5 per carton.[42] Federated is hardly alone in enforcing its practices so aggressively; a large percentage of lean retailers have systems in place to ensure compliance.[43]

Yet the need for retailers to specify such detailed and rigorous standards underscores how important the four building blocks have become. In the next chapter, we assess how these practices have affected the performance and growth of retail adopters. We then address the implications of lean retailers on their suppliers in the apparel and textile channels, drawing on HCTAR's survey and other data. Lean retailing has not only conferred competitive advantage to its adopters; it has profoundly changed the competitive dynamics in the entire supply chain.

5

The Impact of Lean Retailing

> You're constantly faced with a decision: Can I afford to deal with these guys? You can't afford not to.
> —*Ronald Best, President, Totes Inc., 1992*

So said one of Wal-Mart's apparel suppliers in the early 1990s.[1] If anything, even more suppliers at the close of the decade have found they must deal with lean retailers. An increasing number of manufacturers have adopted technologies that support the information exchange and distribution practices discussed in the previous chapters. Consider KGR, a New England supplier of women's fashion clothing to major department stores. One executive noted in 1996,

> Three years ago, KGR had a problem. One of our largest accounts announced that we had only four months to implement EDI invoices with U.P.C.-level detail. Non-compliance meant losing business.... Implementing U.P.C.s seemed impossible, because over 90 percent of the company's products are custom-made to order and have a life cycle of a single shipment. Many retailers now require EDI capability as a prerequisite for doing business, but three years ago [1993] it was a novelty in the fashion apparel industry. Fortunately, KGR's president, Chet Sidell, and CFO, David Guido, agreed that EDI and UPC numbers would some day be the rule, not the exception.[2]

Most retail players have also felt pressure to change in order to compete. The better-known lean retailers—including Wal-Mart, Lands' End, Dillard's, Federated Department Stores, The Limited, J. C. Penney, Sears Roebuck and Co.—have forced the majority of other major retailers to incorporate these principles within their enterprises. Although business commentary in the late 1980s focused on the need to develop specialty products and segment consumers, by 1993 the Standard & Poor's retailing report began with this statement:

Merchandising is fundamental to retailing. Though perhaps less obvious, logistics is just as essential an ingredient for success. If you can't get the merchandise on the shelves, you can't sell it. And if you don't have the right merchandise on the shelves, you'll lose that sale to a competitor that does. What goes on behind the scenes is of great importance: efficient warehousing, transportation, and delivery systems are among the elements of successful merchandising.[3]

This chapter describes the performance and growth of lean retailing across all major retail segments. It then examines the implications of this growth for the apparel industry. Lean retailers transform the basis of competition for all suppliers by radically reducing the amount of time manufacturers have to respond to orders. That means suppliers must be able to provide frequent deliveries, in smaller quantities, of more diverse products. Moreover, they must do so with a far greater level of accuracy in fulfilling orders and meeting delivery standards than in the past. In short, the retail revolution alters the basic rules of both domestic and global competition for the apparel and textile industries, a theme we will revisit throughout.

The Relative Performance of Lean Retailers

Let's start this analysis by comparing the performance of lean retailers with that of their competitors between 1985 and 1994, the years in which lean retailing practices emerged. The figures and tables in this section are based on our calculations of data from Standard & Poor's Compustat Services.[4] For these comparisons, we chose Dillard's and Wal-Mart to represent "Lean" in Table 5.1, combining data for both in our analysis. Figure 5.1 (page 73) adds J. C. Penney, The Gap, and The Limited on the lean retailing side. We do not mean to suggest that their rivals (or "Average" in the first table) are not lean retailers, only that the designated lean retailers led the way during the crucial period between 1985 and 1994.

If successful, lean retailers should be able to sell their products more efficiently and be exposed to less inventory risk than their rivals. One method of looking at the impact of lean retailing is to compare the relative costs of selling goods.[5] Table 5.1 compares the basic cost structures of lean retailers with those of their less lean competitors for two retailing segments: department stores and mass merchants.[6] The table presents the cost of goods sold (COGS); selling, general, and adminis-

Table 5.1. Comparative Performance of Retailers: 1985–1994
Comparative Costs of Selling Goods

Cost of Activity as a Percent of Sales Revenue

	1985		1988		1991		1994	
	Lean	Avg.	Lean	Avg.	Lean	Avg.	Lean	Avg.
Mass Merchants								
Cost of goods sold	74%	72%	77%	72%	78%	73%	78%	74%
SGA[a] costs	18	21	16	21	15	21	16	21
Operating income	8	7	7	7	7	6	6	5
Department Stores								
Cost of goods sold	63	68	63	67	63	66	64	64
SGA costs	25	22	24	23	24	25	23	26
Operating income	12	10	12	10	13	9	13	11

Source: Authors' calculations based on Standard & Poor's Compustat data. See Note 4 and Appendix C for details of calculations and definitions of variables.

[a] SGA: selling, general, and administrative costs.

trative expense (SGA); and operating income before depreciation and taxes as a percentage of sales in 1985, 1988, 1991, and 1994.

For both department stores and mass merchants, the table reveals that the lean retailers reduced SGA expenses over the time period relative to their competitors. At this point, it makes sense to examine the individual numbers for our two lean retailers. In fact, Dillard's had higher SGA expenses in 1985 than its competitors (25 percent of sales revenue compared with 22 percent for other department stores). But, by 1994, its SGA expenses had decreased to 23 percent, while the average for other department stores rose to 26 percent. The growing difference in these expenses for lean and other mass merchants is even more striking. By 1994, Wal-Mart's SGA expenses were 16 percent of sales revenue compared with 21 percent for its competitors.[7]

It is interesting to note that these two lean retailers did not use improved SGA performance entirely to augment their bottom line. In other words, operating income before depreciation and taxes for both Wal-Mart and Dillard's did not rise by the full decrease in SGA expenses. Although both companies outperformed their competitors in regard to operating income throughout this period, reductions in administrative expenses seem to have been used to maintain lower prices and presumably expand sales.

74   *A Stitch in Time*

Improved competitive performance, however, is most significantly portrayed in the growth rates of lean retailers relative to their retail segment. Figure 5.1 compares the growth rates (measured in constant 1993 dollars) of lean retailers against growth for the retail category that they were a part of from 1983 to 1993. In that period, Wal-Mart had a compound annual growth rate (CAGR) of 25.8 percent compared with an average CAGR of 9.9 percent among mass merchant retailers. Similarly, Dillard's, an early advocate of lean retailing among department stores, had a CAGR of 15.4 percent compared with an overall annual *decline* of –1.6 percent for the department store category as a whole. The Gap and The Limited outpaced the growth in revenue among specialty stores, as did J. C. Penney for national chains.[8]

As a result of these pronounced differences in growth rates, the percentage of all sales accounted for by lean retailers within their segment has grown significantly in recent years. After slipping in market share in the early and mid-1980s, J. C. Penney's sales as a percentage of total sales for the national chain group increased from 22 percent in 1988 to 26 percent by 1994. Dillard's sales increased steadily from the onset of its lean retailing practices, from 5 percent in 1984 to 12 percent of all department store sales by 1994. Most dramatic of all, Wal-

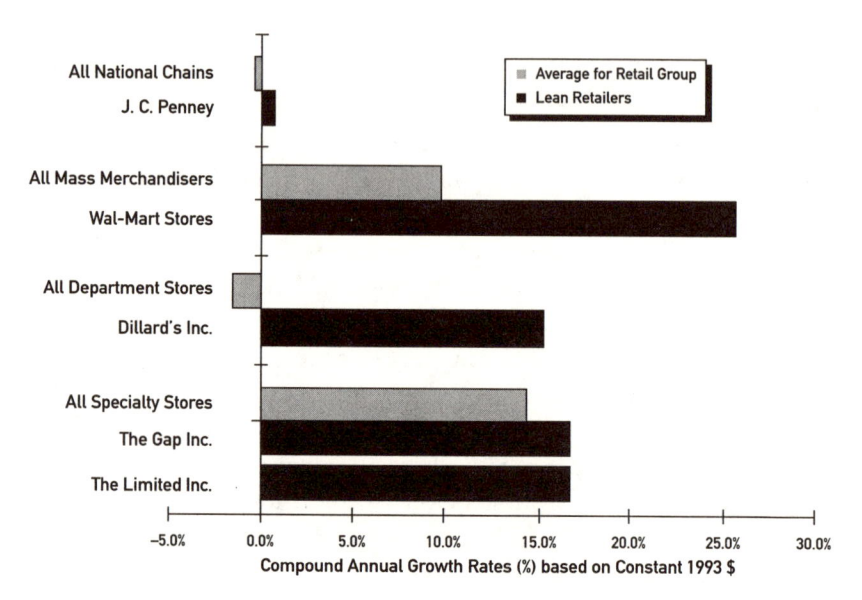

Figure 5.1.   Lean Retailer vs. Retail Groups:
Comparative Growth Rates of Retailers: 1983–93

Source: Standard & Poor's Compustat Database, selected years.

Mart increased its market share among mass merchants, rising from about 17 percent of total sales in 1984 to 54 percent of sales by 1994.

Concentration in the Retail Sector

The enormous impact new retailing methods can have on the way consumer goods are distributed in an economy is not a new phenomenon. As we described in Chapter 2, the rise of lean retailing in recent years parallels the first retail revolution a century ago. In 1937, leading retail analysts, McNair, Gragg, and Teele commented on the outcome of that earlier transformation:

> One of the notable changes in retail distribution during the last twenty-five years has been the growth of large-scale operations. The so-called "big" retailers comprise principally department stores, chains, mail-order houses, and supermarkets....[B]arring some mechanical developments which would greatly increase the "sales output" per person employed in large retail enterprises, it does not seem likely that the advantages accruing from some integration of the marketing functions will give big retail business in the future a great enough margin of superiority over small retail business to make probable the ultimate disappearance of the latter.[9]

The integration of the four building blocks of lean retailing, is the modern equivalent of the "mechanical developments" mentioned by McNair, Gragg, and Teele. These modern "mechanical developments" have led to the disappearance not only of small, family-owned department stores but also of regional department stores and even venerable national retailers like Montgomery Wards and F. W. Woolworth.[10] These retailers have been unable to survive in a retail environment characterized by over-capacity, ever-growing exposure to risk from product proliferation, and continuing pressure to lower prices. The diffusion of lean retailing practices has led to increasing concentration in much of the retail industry.

Table 5.2 shows the increase in retail concentration between 1977 and 1992 as lean retailing practices emerged and diffused across retail sectors. It presents the percentage of sales in 1977 and 1992 in two groupings: for the fifty largest firms and for the four largest firms in various retail categories.[11] Concentration in almost every retail segment rose during this period. In particular, the table shows an increase for general merchandise retail stores (SIC 53), with the share of sales accounted for by the top fifty firms going up by 14.5 percentage points—from 77.3 percent to

Table 5.2. Concentration in the Retail Sector, 1977 and 1992

SIC Code	Industry	Portion of Sales (Percent) Accounted for by the 50 Largest Firms			Portion of Sales (Percent) Accounted for by the 4 Largest Firms		
		1977	1992	Change	1977	1992	Change
52	Building materials and garden supplies	16.6	35.1	18.5	5.4	16.0	10.6
521	Lumber and other building materials	23.0	45.7	22.7	8.3	23.2	14.9
53	General merchandise stores	77.3	91.8	14.5	37.7	47.3	9.6
531	Department stores	86.5	98.2	11.7	44.0	53.1	9.1
533	Variety stores	78.1	85.8	7.7	49.1	54.8	5.7
54	Food stores	40.7	47.6	6.9	16.3	15.4	−.9
541	Grocery stores	43.5	49.9	6.4	17.4	16.1	−1.3
56	Apparel and accessory stores	27.8	52.4	24.6	9.1	17.9	8.8
561	Men's and boys' clothing stores	24.2	48.6	24.4	8.5	20.0	11.5
563	Women's accessory	28.4	63.8	35.4	12.7	37.7	25.0
565	Family clothing stores	45.9	76.6	30.7	23.1	35.3	12.2
566	Shoe stores	48.6	68.2	19.6	22.8	38.6	15.8

Source: U.S. Department of Commerce, Bureau of the Census, Census of Retail Industries.

91.8 percent. Sales of the top fifty firms in apparel and accessory stores (SIC 56) also rose significantly, by 24.6 percentage points, from 27.8 percent to 52.4 percent.

These changes in retail industry concentration are consistent with retail analysts' forecasts of continuing concentration in retail markets through the end of the decade.[12] More important, the link between lean retailing principles, performance, and market power is changing the relationships and expectations of retail suppliers in consumer product sectors generally.

How Lean Retailing Affects the Apparel Industry

Companies that have adopted lean retailing principles now dominate most retail segments.[13] Therefore, lean retailing performance standards provide the benchmark for competition in the retail-apparel-textile channel. Specifically, lean retailers operating with the systems described in detail in the previous chapter require frequent replenishment of a growing percentage of their products and demand that shipments meet standards concerning delivery times, order completeness, and accuracy. Lean retailers also want suppliers to adopt standards regarding bar codes, EDI, and shipment marking. Finally, as our research documents, they are relying on a smaller number of companies to serve as their suppliers, given the greater complexity and investment necessary for retail-supplier relations.

Replenishment Requirements, 1988 Versus 1992

With the advent of lean retailing, replenishing products within a selling season is the most fundamental challenge for apparel manufacturers. Instead of specifying that manufacturers respond to a single, fixed order placed far in advance of required delivery time, lean retailers may now require that a replenishment order be filled in as little as three days. We discuss some specific ways to approach the problem of replenishment from the manufacturer's perspective in Chapter 7. Here we will simply document that it has, indeed, become a challenge for suppliers.

Data from the HCTAR survey of apparel business units provide a comprehensive and striking measure of the tremendous shift in replenishment demand engendered by lean retailing. Table 5.3 (page 78) compares the degree of replenishment pressure faced by business units in the sample for different retail segments in 1988 and 1992. Specifically, it reports the percentage of total dollar volume shipped on a daily, weekly, bimonthly, and monthly replenishment basis, along with the percentage of volume shipped on a nonreplenishment basis in three retail segments as well as for all of them.[14]

For all retail categories, the percentage of total dollar volumes shipped on a daily or weekly basis quadrupled—from 8.7 percent in 1988 to 33.9 percent in 1992. At the same time, the percentage of nonreplenished goods plummeted, from 61.7 percent in 1988 down to 22.5 percent in 1992. Because the composition of retail sales segments served by the business units in our sample changed little between the two time periods, these enormous changes reflected shifts in what retailers required within each of the three categories.[15]

The degree of replenishment activity varies across retail segments. For example, apparel business units shipped 34 percent of their dollar volume to mass merchant retailers on a daily or weekly basis, compared to 25 percent for department stores. These differences reflect the evolution of lean retailing described in Chapter 3: It was adopted first by mass merchants, then national chains, and then department stores. Even though department stores are relative newcomers to lean retail-

Table 5.3. Replenishment Rates by Retail Channels, 1988 and 1992

Average Percent of Sales Replenished at Different Frequencies	1988	1992	Change
	Mass Merchants		
Daily	1.49	8.38	6.89
Weekly	5.40	34.06	28.66
Biweekly	3.56	11.07	7.51
Monthly	17.31	23.82	6.51
Never	68.96	22.90	−46.06
Total[b]	100%	100%	
% of all sales	26%	27%	
	National Chains		
Daily	0.72	8.90	8.18
Weekly	7.46	33.61	26.15
Biweekly	5.70	8.81	3.11
Monthly	26.19	23.59	−2.60
Never	56.04	25.10	−30.94
Total[b]	100%	100%	
% of all sales	18%	14%	
	Department Stores		
Daily	0.00	0.05	0.05
Weekly	1.92	26.70	24.78
Biweekly	3.41	11.95	8.54
Monthly	31.74	38.83	7.09
Never	60.51	22.22	−38.29
Total[b]	100%	100%	
% of all sales	28%	32%	
	All Channels[a]		
Daily	1.56	3.74	2.18
Weekly	7.17	30.14	22.99
Biweekly	3.56	11.07	7.51
Monthly	26.03	30.71	4.68
Never	61.69	22.52	−39.17
Total[b]	100%	100%	

Source: Harvard Center for Textile and Apparel Research survey (see Appendix B).

[a] Represents the sales-weighted average of all retail channels, not only those cited above.

[b] Totals do not sum to 100% in all cases due to a small percentage of shipments that could not be classified by business units under these categories.

ing, the percentage of sales volume shipped to them on a nonreplenishment basis still fell dramatically—from 61 percent in 1988 down to 22 percent over the study period. Regardless of their late conversion to lean retailing techniques, department stores were receiving over three-quarters of their shipments on a replenishment basis by 1992.

Federated Department Stores provides a more recent example. Federated—especially, its Macy's and Bloomingdale's divisions—is known for its wide collection of medium- to high-end fashions. As a traditional retailer, it historically depended on single-order, long lead-time deliveries for much of its collection. But since the early 1990s, this has drastically changed: In 1991, less than 20 percent of its merchandise was bought on a replenishment basis (with more than 80 percent purchased as one-shot purchases), but that number climbed to 30 percent by 1996. A review of Federated operations in 1997 indicates the time for replenishment is now just four days from placing a computer order to having the merchandise on the sales floor.[16]

The Growing Adoption of Information Technology

Beyond replenishment speed, lean retailing implies other performance requirements that are at odds with traditional retailing/supplier relationships. Table 5.4 (page 80) summarizes the differences arising from the retail revolution.

The recent experience of Federated once again indicates dramatic changes in supplier requirements. In 1992, Federated introduced the Federated Accelerated Sales and Stock Turn (FASST) Plan that set out an ambitious technology strategy intended to "realize significant sales increases, cost reductions, stock turn increases and mutual profitablity" for Federated and its vendors. In pursuance of this goal, Federated currently establishes the following requirements in its literature for vendors:

1. Mark 100 percent of your merchandise with quality UPC tickets.
2. Provide "floor-ready" merchandise with our retail price on your UPC ticket when appropriate.
3. Provide us with an accurate electronic UPC catalog via. . .a direct EDI transmission.
4. Send us an accurate ship notice at the carton level and mark all cartons with corresponding UCC-128 shipping container labels.
5. Follow our Federated Corporate Transportation Routing Instructions for shipping merchandise.
6. Follow our Federated Merchandise Accounting Services requirements for submitting EDI invoices and related correspondence.
7. Provide an industry standard hanger for hanging merchandise.[17]

As noted in Chapter 4, Federated—like many major retailers—has a monitoring and penalty system to ensure compliance with these stringent standards.

Table 5.4. Comparative Supplier Performance Requirements
Traditional versus Lean Retailer

Retailer Requirement	Traditional Retailer	Lean Retailer
Product replenishment	No replenishment within season	In-season replenishment: 1 week from order to receipt of product by retailer
Order reliability	Total no. shipped consistent with order; accept discrepancies	Accurate at the SKU level; reject discrepancies
Penalties for non-compliance with retail standards	None	Monetary penalties for late or incomplete shipments; charges for retail preparation of certain merchandise for display
Adherence to transaction-related standards (e.g., product identification)	None	UPC; EDI; SCM; floor-ready merchandise; etc.
Provision of floor-ready merchandise	Limited	Growing requirements re: retail pricing; display
Lead time for new products	One- to two-year lead time expected	Significantly less than 1 year lead time required

Source: Harvard Center for Textile and Apparel Research.

In general, implementing the practices listed in Table 5.4 is costly. Take the various activities that must be done by a supplier to prepare shipments for handling in a retail distribution center. A 1993 analysis undertaken by a major apparel manufacturer, Haggar Apparel Co., calculated the costs of adopting these practices. For example, a typical hanger that met VICS standards cost $.325 a unit; attaching price tags ranged from $.05 to $.10 a unit. These costs rapidly mounted when a supplier ships large volumes of merchandise. For Haggar, the fully loaded cost for providing shipping container markers with relevant UCC-128 information accessible via EDI was $5 a carton. Providing automatic shipping notices entailed similar costs.[18]

Nevertheless, the rise of lean retailing between 1988 and 1992 led to big changes in the use of a variety of information practices by apparel manufacturers. Based on the HCTAR survey, Figure 5.2 shows the growing adoption of these information technology and retail service practices.[19]

Our survey indicated, that in 1992, only 60 percent of apparel products were marked with the manufacturer's UPC bar code. Today, the results are more dramatic; very few products carry no manufacturer's bar code. Only a food store chain such as Trader Joe's, which makes a point of doing business the "old-fashioned way" (and perhaps cuts its costs in the short term), carries products without bar codes.

EDI usage also exploded between 1988 and 1992. Its use for transmitting purchase orders exhibited a sixfold increase, rising from 4.5 percent of volume in 1988 to 32 percent in 1992. And while we do not

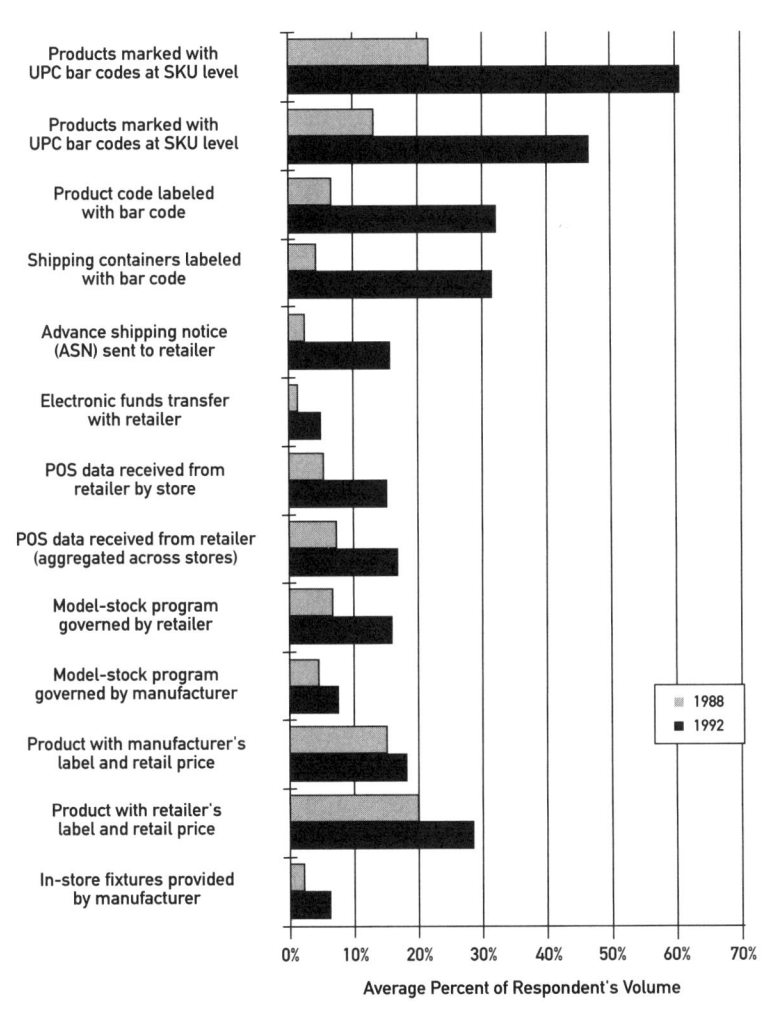

Figure 5.2. Information and Retail Services, 1988 and 1992

Source: Harvard Center for Textile and Apparel Research.

have survey data to prove the point, we are quite certain that the vast majority of all purchase orders today are transmitted by EDI.

In 1992, retailers more frequently provided their apparel suppliers with point-of-sales (POS) information than in 1988, either on an individual store basis (increasing from 6 percent to 15 percent of volume) or aggregated across stores in the retail chain. But despite the extensive information links established between retailers and apparel suppliers by 1992, analysis of our survey data reveals that 44 percent of orders were still not accompanied by POS data or sales forecasts. Production planning by suppliers in a world of rapid replenishment makes the receipt of such point-of-sales information critically important.

Figure 5.2 indicates that adoption of information technologies allowing apparel shipments to move through a lean retailer's distribution center increased dramatically between 1988 and 1992. Shipping containers marked with bar codes rose from 7 percent of volume to 33 percent. Manufacturers provided more and more electronic advanced shipping notification (ASN) to retailers as well, going from a mere 3 percent of volume in 1988 to 17 percent in 1992. And, as with the prevalence of bar codes on products themselves, these practices have become increasingly commonplace during the last five years. Today it would be nearly impossible for a supplier to have a replenishment product accepted at a lean retailer's distribution center without a shipping container bar code. Automated cross-docking cannot function without the internal identifications provided by container bar codes.

In addition, the decisive role played by lean retailers in driving apparel firms to adopt the new information technology can be seen by comparing the information practices of firms facing a high volume of replenishment orders with those that face a relatively low volume. In Figure 5.3, the business units in our survey have been split into one of two categories based on the degree of replenishment pressure they experienced from their retail customers. Apparel suppliers that shipped more than 15 percent of their volume to retailers on a daily or weekly basis in 1992 were classified as operating under high levels of lean retailing pressure—the "Frequent" category. All others were considered "Infrequent" replenishers.

Figure 5.3 shows that those apparel suppliers facing more frequent replenishment requirements also relied more extensively on information links with their retailers. For example, "Frequent" business units marked products with bar codes for more than 70 percent of volume shipped versus about 50 percent for the low-pressure group. Even more

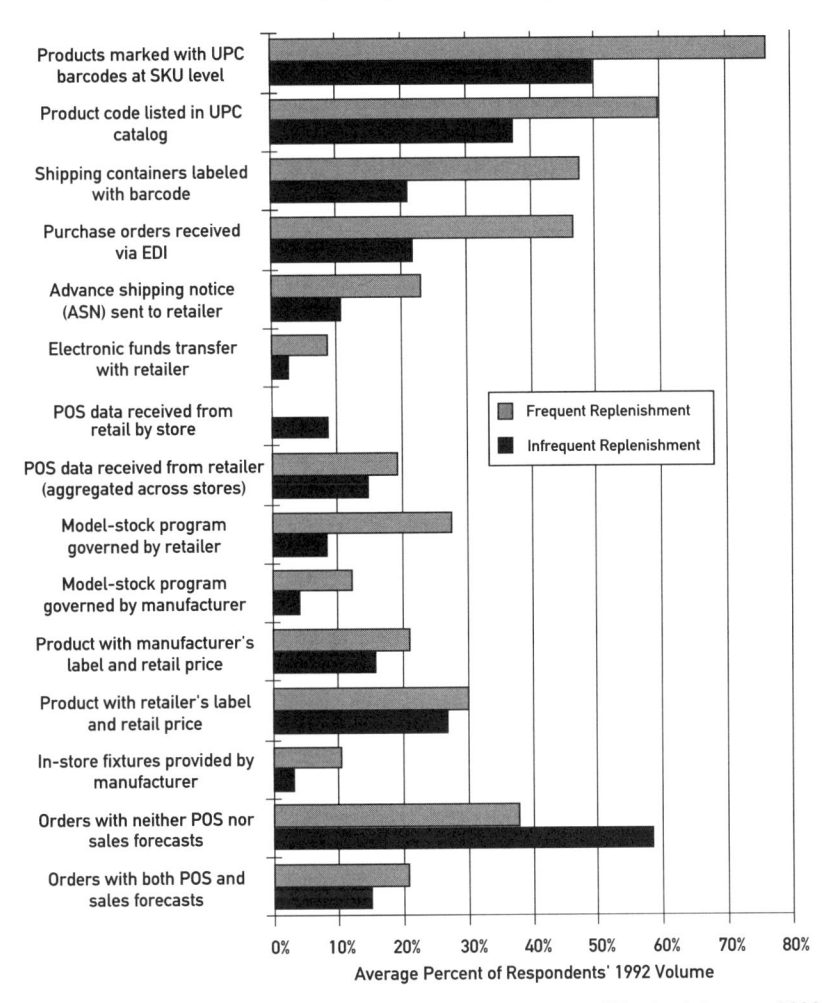

Figure 5.3. Information and Retail Services by Frequency of Replenishment, 1992

Source: Harvard Center for Textile and Apparel Research.

striking, suppliers facing high pressure provided EDI purchase orders for 45 percent of orders compared with only about 20 percent for the "Infrequent" replenishers. The other practices show similar differences between the two.[20]

As we have already noted, the diffusion of lean retailing has become far more pervasive now than it was in 1992. The results illustrated in Figures 5.2 and 5.3 suggest why the adoption of bar codes, EDI, ASN, shipping-container markers, and other information practices have become common among apparel manufacturers. Adoption of these practices, however, does not ensure that manufacturers will make full use of the vast amounts of information now available to them concerning retail and consumer demand. We will delve into the opportunities and pitfalls of information use by manufacturers in Chapter 7.

What It Takes to Supply a Lean Retailer

Apparel suppliers now face a new set of demands, many of which depart from historical practice. The current picture becomes even more complicated when one includes the multiple channels that textile manufacturers operate in, an issue we examine in detail in Chapters 11 and 12. But in the next five chapters, we focus primarily on changes in the retail-apparel relationship. In general, apparel manufacturers must at least have the following capabilities to meet retail requirements. They should be able to

- Label, track, and respond to product orders in real time on the basis of style, color, fabric, and size;
- Exchange (send and receive) information concerning the current status of a retailer's products on an electronic basis;
- Provide goods to a retailer's distribution center that can be efficiently moved to stores—that is, containers marked with bar codes concerning contents; shipment of products ready for display in retail stores.

These are now the basics for manufacturers. Adoption of these practices is, so to speak, an entry cost of working with lean retailers and not based on joint investment by "channel partners."[21] Diffusion of these practices across the apparel industry, which is generally characterized by small-scale enterprises, reflects the market power exerted by lean retailers. Although some manufacturers—like VF Corporation and Haggar—have embraced the opportunity to work with retailers and take advantage of potential joint benefits arising from timely information about demand, the increasing pressure exerted by retailers has engendered a fair degree of hostility by some suppliers.[22] Whatever the nature of relationships, information integration across the channel changes the rules of the standard retail-supplier game, and our research makes clear that new practices and relationships in the retail-apparel-textile channel are still evolving. Bar codes are now the *lingua franca* of these businesses, but the industrial transformation is far from over, particularly in the realm of inventory management.

The manufacturing capabilities required to respond in an information-integrated manner challenge the way in which apparel firms are structured internally and, in turn, interactions with their own suppliers—especially textile firms. Specifically, apparel suppliers are under pressure to fulfill retailers' orders rapidly, efficiently, and flexibly. It also requires manufacturers either to hold more finished goods inventory or to innovate production processes to meet retailer requirements and reduce their exposure to risk. In the next two chapters, we focus on the problem of inventory control—first from the retailer's perspective, then from the manufacturer's. On both sides, companies are making profound changes in their inventory policies in response to lean retailing.

6

Inventory Management for the Retailer: Demand Forecasting and Stocking Decisions

> You can only sell what is on your wagon.
> —*William T. Dillard, Founder, Dillard's Inc.*

William Dillard's simple maxim[1] succinctly captures the central—and perennial—inventory challenge facing retail managers. To make a sale, a retailer must have "on its wagon" the product the customer wants. Absence of an item often translates into a lost sale and reduced revenues and profits. The magnitude of such lost sales for retailers can be significant. For example, in 1994, roughly 25 percent of customers who entered a Macy's store left without making a purchase because the product they were seeking was not available.[2] On the other hand, the retail "wagon" should not be too full, since stocking retail shelves with unpopular items also results in excess costs—the cost of capital tied up in unwanted goods, the opportunity cost of the space that could be used for products that customers would buy if present, and, ultimately, lost margin when retailers must resort to price markdowns or product disposal to clear languishing items from their shelves.

The main goal of retail inventory strategy is to maximize profitability by managing the inherent tension between stocking too much and stocking too little. Retail buyers of old grappled with this problem as they do today. But as product variety has increased and product life cycles have shortened, this tension has become increasingly acute, prompting inventory management practices to evolve in recent years to meet rapidly changing market demands. Although a seemingly mundane, tactical aspect of business, a firm's inventory strategy reflects its approach to managing risk. Indeed, the inventory strategies chosen by firms in a supply channel—and the congruence of those policies across channel partners—have enormous implications for the channel's speed, flexibility, and profitability.

Conceptually, retail inventory management is straightforward enough: Forecast demand for a product; order the product in the appropriate quantity; stock it in the right retail locations; keep track of its sales and the resulting inventory levels; and replenish its store inventories if possible (either from the manufacturer if it offers replenishment services for that product or from the retailer's central warehouse if the retailer had purchased a large quantity of the product in advance of the selling season). In practice, however, retail inventory management is fraught with challenges, such as long and uncertain order-fulfillment lead times, and errors in product identification and record keeping. Consider, for instance, how many store clerks still scan items incorrectly at the register. A customer may purchase three similar polo shirts in different colors or sizes, but because the price is the same for all, the clerk may simply scan one of them three times—losing important information about consumer color and/or size preferences. Even without such obvious errors, forecasting demand at the SKU level has become difficult, as an ever wider array of products cycle through stores. Many lean retailing practices are rooted in retailers' attempts to deal with growing demand uncertainty. In this environment, ordering large quantities of products far in advance of the selling season is simply too costly. Retailers now prefer to place relatively small orders before the season and then observe consumer response to the product offering before ordering more. As we described in Chapter 4, many have transformed their warehouses into modern distribution centers to facilitate the receipt and distribution of these smaller orders.

The forecasting and inventory models presented in this chapter are not new; they have been recommended for years by statisticians and operations researchers.[3] However, until the 1990s, retailers had neither the data collection and computing capabilities required to execute these models effectively nor the tremendous impetus to implement them that lean retailing has precipitated. Because the effects of lean retailing are sweeping across many industries, it is imperative that everyone involved understand how inventory policies have been affected. This chapter covers the key steps in retail inventory management: forecasting demand, choosing appropriate stocking strategies, and determining order quantities and frequencies. Although few retailers have embraced the complete set of forecasting and inventory models described in this chapter, lean retailers are moving in that direction.

The Retail Forecasting Challenge

We first turn to the problem of forecasting sales in retail stores. Imagine trying to predict how many women will walk into a particular downtown Boston store next week prepared to pay $48 (full price) for a size-8 pair of Levi blue jeans, with "long" pant length, "loose" fit, stonewashed finish, and a pleated waist—in other words, one particular SKU out of thousands. How will that compare to the number who would buy the same product but with a "short" pant length? How does a retail buyer even begin to approach the problem of making forecasts at such a minute level of detail?

The buyer might start by trying to get historical data on the weekly sales of those Levi jeans in the store. But wait—should that be on the sales of those jeans throughout the Greater Boston area? Should the buyer base her prediction on sales of only this particular size and style or would it be more accurate to look at the sales of all jeans in this style and then multiply by the percent of all jean styles sold that were size-8 long? Maybe she should restrict herself to this year's data to ensure that it is as current as possible. On the other hand, one would hate to lose the information that might be contained in past years' selling patterns.

The complexity of the problem, even for basic blue jeans, is staggering. Now consider the same exercise for a new dress style not previously available at retail—perhaps a style that gained attention when worn by a controversial film star at the most recent Academy Awards ceremony. How many of these dresses will sell this season? Specifically, how many will sell in a dark-peach tone in size 14?

If the challenge of making such predictions for this season's sales is not sufficiently daunting, try predicting how many of each item will sell during a given period next year. The impossibility of making accurate predictions of demand long in advance of the selling season—especially at the SKU level—is clear. But because products are manufactured and ordered by SKU, some attempt must be made to forecast demand at that level. Most retailers have to make demand forecasts for products in two different categories: existing products for which historical sales data are available and new products with no selling history. The following section discusses the first category and provides general background on the elements of a demand forecast. It is followed by a short discussion of new product forecasting.

Forecasting Demand for Products with a Selling History

Creating a forecast for a product that the retailer has sold in the past starts with collecting and analyzing historical selling data. Those data provide insight into historical trends and suggest how the product's sales are related to other factors like weather, holidays, special advertising campaigns, general economic indicators, or simply the passage of time. Air conditioners sell in greater quantities during summer months, for example, neckties just before Father's Day, and consumer electronics when the economy is booming. Once these relationships are understood, predictions of future sales can be made, although a high level of uncertainty is always involved. Before discussing how one might analyze the trends in historical data, it is important to recognize three often overlooked aspects of demand forecasting.

Three Caveats About Forecasting

First of all, a product's selling history is only representative of future sales if the product is sold in a stable environment. For the blue jeans discussed above, the selling environment will remain stable as long as competitors do not introduce competing products that draw from Levi's demand; fashion preferences do not change; a new, more desirable type of denim is not introduced that customers prefer; and the economy does not dip into a recession. However, even for a basic product like blue jeans, it is unlikely that all these assumptions will hold. Given the volatile nature of demand in many industries, an assumption of stability is suspect, meaning that forecasts based on historical sales data may be less accurate than the historical data suggest. Consequently, lean retailers prefer to forecast demand, set target inventory levels, and place orders on a weekly basis, because the selling environment is much more likely to be stable into the next week than months into the future.

Second, most firms gather *sales* data, not *demand* data. Customers rarely inform the sales clerk in a typical retail store if a desired product is out of stock; they either buy a different product or leave the store without making a purchase. Direct-mail firms, such as catalog companies and those that sell via television or the Internet, are important exceptions. Because the customer must write, call, or e-mail these retailers with a specific purchase request, these firms are able to capture actual consumer demand rather than sales numbers alone. Such retailers can also gather data about customer demographics, past purchases, and responses to potential substitute items, all of which add up to a gold mine of information about consumer preferences.[4]

In fact, the value of such data may induce traditional store retailers to offer incentives for customers to share their demand preferences, even when the product is not available in stock. In the mid-1990s, Nordstrom ran newspaper ads promising, for certain products, that if the size or color of an item the customer wished to purchase was not in stock at the store, Nordstrom would locate the desired item and mail it to the customer at no additional cost—both the item and its delivery were free. (Not surprisingly, Nordstrom limited this offer to a small number of basic styles and sizes and to one item per customer.) The only thing a customer had to do was tell a sales clerk what he or she wanted.

This approach has benefits on three fronts: the retailer avoids a lost sale and its associated margin; a potentially dissatisfied customer is delighted by the store's additional service and free product; and last, but certainly not least, for a very small fee—the wholesale cost of the product and shipping fees—Nordstrom gains critical information about consumer demand. Without such programs, retailers may find it difficult to judge how demand is faring after a product stocks out at the retail site and therefore may have trouble making sensible reordering decisions.

The third caveat to bear in mind is that a "point forecast" (a single number) alone has relatively low value. If a buyer forecasts that customer demand for size-8 Levi jeans next week in one of its stores will be ten pairs, what does that mean? Will exactly ten pairs sell? Is ten the most likely number to sell—or will at least ten pairs sell? A forecast consisting only of a single number provides no indication of the degree of uncertainty.

Indeed, the purpose of the forecasting process is to provide a basis for deciding how many units of a given product should be shipped to a store to minimize the costs—that is, risks—of over- and undersupply. But risk exists precisely because retailers are uncertain about what demand will be for their products. Therefore, to provide a useful basis for making decisions that minimize risk, a forecast should include an explicit assessment of the relative likelihood of different demand levels occurring. Our buyer might capture this information by saying that there is a 90 percent probability that weekly demand for size-8 jeans in the store will fall between two and seventeen units, with an "expected value" of ten units. She might add that there is a 50 percent probability that demand will fall between six and thirteen units. Figure 6.1 shows a demand distribution having these properties. (Note that there is a 95 percent chance that demand will be less than seventeen units next week—thus, if our buyer decides to stock seventeen units at the beginning of the week, the store should be able to offer a 95 percent order fulfillment rate on this SKU.) It is only with such probabilistic forecasts, which explicitly characterize uncertainty, that retailers can make inventory stocking decisions that minimize risk.

Four Components of Historical Demand Data

With these caveats in mind, let's assume our store buyer has representative historical demand data for blue jeans for the last few years. She will first analyze the historical data by separating the causes of past changes in demand into the following categories: (1) trend, (2) seasonality, (3) cyclicality, and (4) random fluctuation.[5]

The *trend* in demand data describes a medium- to long-term growth or decline. Such trends occur in all industries and can be steadily increasing, steadily decreasing, or varying over time. *Seasonality* describes within-year trends that are associated with the season of the year and that occur year after year. For example, Figure 6.2 shows weekly demand for men's dress shirts at a particular retailer: There are seasonal peaks in demand at Father's Day and Christmas, when many shirts are bought as gifts. *Cyclicality* in demand describes longer-term, gradual rises and declines that are typically associated with aggregate business activity. For example, demand for new automobiles tends to

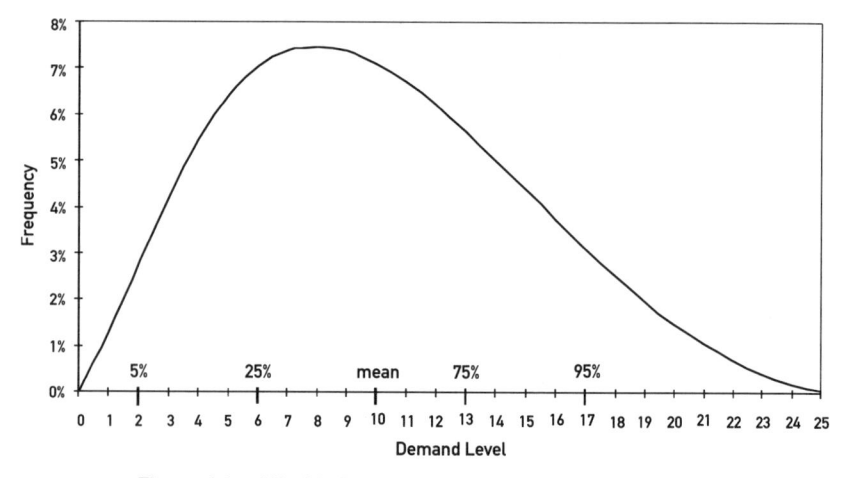

Figure 6.1. Weekly Demand Distribution for Size–8 Jeans

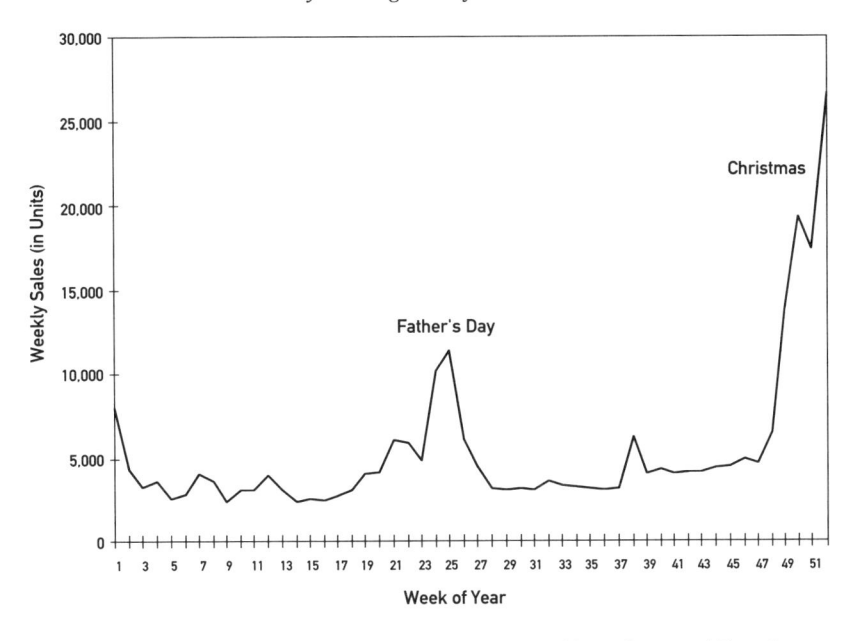

Figure 6.2. Weekly Sales of Men's Dress Shirts Show Seasonal Trends

increase during times of economic prosperity and decrease during recessionary periods.

The final component of a demand distribution, *random fluctuation*, is perhaps the most critical; it is also the most difficult to assess and incorporate into inventory planning. Essentially, random fluctuation in demand cannot be explained by trends, seasonality, cyclicality, or other factors like advertising and new product introduction. Examine Figure 6.2. In addition to the seasonal trend associated with major holidays, random fluctuation in shirt sales occurred from week to week. For our purposes, note that high demand fluctuation decreases one's ability to forecast demand accurately.

Building a Demand Forecast

After completing an analysis of how different factors relate to past demand fluctuations, our buyer can draw inferences about what future demand for women's blue jeans might be in her store next week.[6] In this case we assume a stable environment: specifically, that past relationships among variables are representative of future relationships among those variables. Although this may not be a realistic assumption for many situations, it makes it easier to understand the fundamentals of demand forecasting here.

Let's assume that the store's demand for the size-8 Levi's jeans last week can be described by the distribution in Figure 6.1. Let's also assume that the average demand each week has been growing at a rate of about 1 percent, so that the average demand for the next week should be 10*(1.01) = 10.1 units, for the following week about 10*(1.01)² = 10.2 units, and so on. Then the expected (average) demand is the solid black trend line shown in Figure 6.3.

The buyer could incorporate demand uncertainty into the forecast by indicating different possible values of demand, and the likelihood of that actual demand will fall within those values. For example, in Figure 6.3, the lines directly above and below the solid trend line indicate a range of demand for which the likelihood of demand falling within that range is 50 percent. The lines further from the trend line indicate the range with a likelihood of 90 percent. Thus, for week 1, there is a 90 percent probability that demand will be between two units and seventeen units, exactly as depicted in Figure 6.1. Predicting what customers will do when they walk into the store will always be challenging, but the buyer can be confident that if she stocks seventeen units at the beginning of the next week, she has a 95 percent probability of meeting all consumer demand on this product.

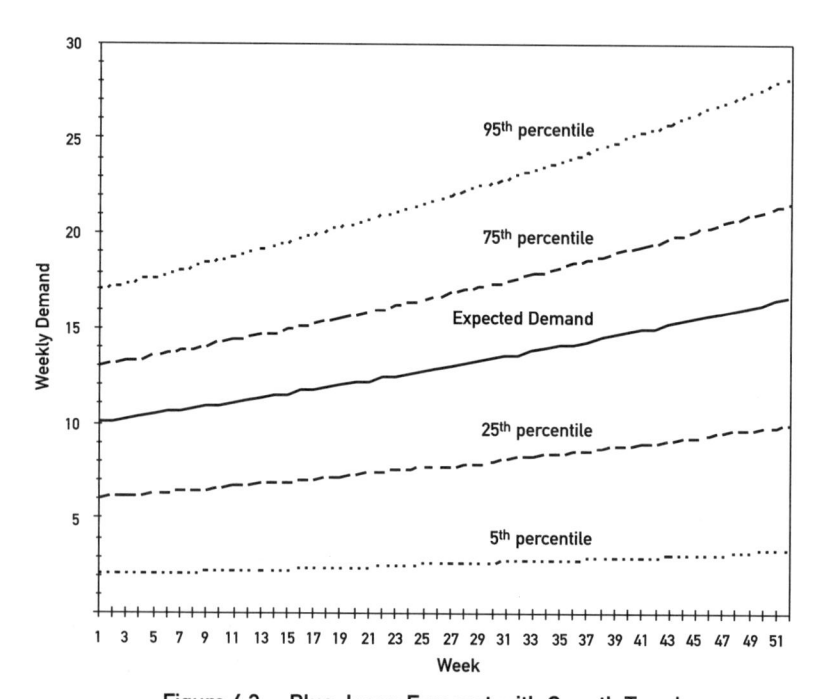

Figure 6.3. Blue Jeans Forecast with Growth Trend

Forecasting Demand for New Products

Of course, when a product has just been launched and no historical data exist on which to base a forecast, retailers confront additional challenges. In this case, most companies resort to informal forecasting methods. A common approach is to forecast "by analogy," using data for similar products that have been on the market previously. One might assume, for example, that sales for this year's new fashion will be similar to those for last year's new fashion. This is clearly a subjective call; but once made, it gives retailers a basis for predicting demand patterns for a new product.

Obviously, forecasting demand for new products accurately requires a broad understanding of consumer preferences and market trends. Fisher, Hammond, Obermeyer, and Raman have introduced a method that proved successful in predicting demand for new fashion skiwear as part of an "Accurate Response" forecasting and planning approach.[7] This approach combined individual forecasts by members of the company's Buying Committee, creating a probabilistic forecast whose uncertainty was determined by the level of agreement among forecasts made by individual managers. Statistical analysis showed that those garments for which the Buying Committee had the greatest disagreement were indeed those with the greatest demand uncertainty. The skiwear firm has credited the Accurate Response approach with increasing its profits by nearly two-thirds.[8]

The Impact of Product Variety on Forecast Uncertainty

The forecasting challenges retailers confront have been amplified in recent years by product proliferation in almost every category. As a result, demand forecast uncertainty has grown substantially, thereby increasing the level of inventory that must be held to meet customer service requirements. High demand uncertainty, previously associated only with fashion products, is now pervasive, characterizing even those items once regarded as basics—such as power tools, industrial seals, men's dress shirts, and blue jeans.

A good rule of thumb for understanding how product proliferation affects demand uncertainty is that the demand uncertainty for a product category increases as the square root of the number of products in the category (assuming that the total demand for the product category remains unchanged and that the individual items in the category have demand distributions that are statistically independent and identically distributed). A common standardized measure of demand uncertainty, the *coefficient of variation* (C_v)—defined as the standard deviation of the demand distribution divided by the mean of the demand distribution—for a specific product is proportional to the square root of the number of products offered.[9] For example, increasing the number of products offered in a category by a factor of four (say from fifty items to 200) without increasing total demand in the category would increase the coefficient of variation for each individual product by a factor of two. And, as we'll see in the next section, doubling the demand uncertainty roughly doubles the amount of finished goods required to provide the same level of product availability in the store.

Therefore, product variety is costly due to the increased demand uncertainty associated with each unit. Retailers thus must either limit product variety or change their way of doing business so as to minimize the impact of high variety. Lean retailing is the major such change that retailers are adopting to reduce significantly the costs associated with product variety.

Setting Inventory Levels in the Store

After completing the process of developing a demand forecast for each SKU, a retailer must determine how much of each item to stock on the shelves of its stores. Retailers have an incentive to stock high levels of inventory: They want both to provide sufficient display stock to attract customers—empty shelves are not inviting—and to have products available for those who wish to purchase them. Yet carrying inventory is expensive: Retailers pay capital costs for having their money tied up in inventory, for the physical floor space necessary to store goods, and for handling, managing, and monitoring the inventory.[10] Most important, they pay a "risk premium" for carrying products that might become obsolete, either because they are damaged or fall out of fashion.

A retailer's decision about what to stock will depend on a variety of considerations, including the demand forecast for the product, the level of product availability it wishes to provide to customers, the frequency with which it will place replenishment orders, and the lead time to acquire replenishment units. We'll describe later in this chapter how these factors affect retail inventory policy. A number of other straightforward costs are associated with any inventory stocking policy, such as the cost of ordering and transporting product; the cost of determining inventory levels; and the impact on purchase price of any quantity price discounts.

In order to evaluate the performance of different inventory options, it is important to emphasize the less straightforward costs involved. Take the two primary types of inventory "errors" a firm can make: stocking too much of an item the customer does not want and stocking too little of something the customer does want. Although the categories for the costs of mismatched supply and demand are simple in concept, in reality they are difficult to measure accurately. Evaluating forced markdown costs is hard, for example, because one must separate markdowns made for promotional reasons from those made to liquidate stock that cannot be sold at full price. The difficulty of measuring these costs is further exacerbated by the fact that a given product may be attractive to different consumers at different prices, so determining the appropriate "full price" for a product is not an easy task.

Stock-out costs are also complex. To determine the magnitude of a stock-out cost for a unit, one must understand consumer behavior. Will the customer buy a substitute item if a particular item is out of stock or return to the same store at a later date to purchase the item when it is again in stock? In these cases, stock-out costs are minimal. But the customer may leave the store because a desired item was not in stock, thereby not purchasing anything else; that means the stock-out cost would equal the margin on all the products the customer would have otherwise purchased. In the most extreme case, a stock-out might cause a customer to switch retailers, costing the lifetime value of that customer and others who might defect due to negative word-of-mouth.

In addition, it is useful to divide the items retailers order into two groups: those for which additional units can be obtained from the supplier during the selling season for that product and those that cannot—that is, replenishable products versus nonreplenishables. This distinction matters, because inventory management differs for products in the two categories. All else being equal, a retailer would prefer to have replenishment opportunities for every product. Lean retailers' rapid replenishment arrangements radically reduce the risk of undersupply—the retailer can essentially "correct" for those items that it ordered too little of prior to the start of the season—and of oversupply, since the retailer orders smaller initial quantities. In contrast, orders for nonreplenishable products must be placed in full prior to observing consumer demand for the product. The retailer "rolls the dice" and makes its entire order commitment based on preliminary demand forecasts, considerably increasing the risk of over- or undersupply.

Inventory Models for Nonreplenishable Products

When a retailer has no ability to replenish a product, the inventory decision is reduced to a single question: How many units of the item should a buyer order to maximize that product's profitability? Retailer managers are relying less and less on their "gut" and past experience; lean retailers are increasingly using more sophisticated statistical models, even in the risky realm of nonreplenishables, to help guide stocking decisions. In this section we review briefly the well-known "news-vendor" problem to illustrate the basic trade-offs retailers must make when determining inventory stocking levels.[11]

To determine the optimal quantity for a SKU, the retailer finds the number of units to order so that the expected marginal cost of stocking an additional unit and not being able to sell it equals the expected marginal cost of not stocking that unit when it would have sold if available. Mathematically, this relationship translates as follows.

Find the optimal inventory stocking quantity, Q^*, that satisfies the relationship:

[Probability the unit cannot be sold](C_o) =
 [Probability the unit could have been sold](C_u),

that is [Prob$(D<Q^*)](C_o)$ = [Prob$(D \geq Q^*)](C_u)$.

where Q^* = the optimal order quantity
 D = demand for the product
 C_o = cost of oversupply
 C_u = cost of under-supply

At the simplest level, the optimal stocking policy for nonreplenishable goods is to stock the quantity (Q^*) that satisfies [Prob$(D<Q^*)$] = $(C_u)/(C_u+C_o)$. For example, suppose a retailer can purchase a dress for $200 that it sells for $440. Suppose also that if the retailer stocks too many of these dresses, it can only sell the leftovers for $120 each. In this case, the cost of oversupply comes to $80 = $200 − $120 because the retailer loses that much on every leftover dress. Conversely, the retailer loses $240 = $440 − $200 whenever it stocks out of a dress that a customer would have purchased at full price. According to the model, the retailer should purchase the quantity Q^* that will yield [Prob$(D<Q^*)$] = 240/(240+80) = 240/320 = .75—that is, a 75 percent probability that demand for the dress will be less than the quantity purchased.

Inventory Management for the Retailer

With this analysis completed, the retailer must next forecast demand for the dress at the SKU level. A sample demand forecast for the dress appears in Figure 6.4. The buyer should order 250 units, since there is a 75 percent probability that demand will be less than this. Note that this buyer would be ordering more than she expects to sell (the mean value of the distribution, 180 units). This makes sense, because the margins on these dresses are high relative to the cost of buying additional dresses and having to dispose of them below cost.

Inventory Model for Replenishable Products

Although determining an inventory policy for nonreplenishable products continues to be an issue for retailers, inventory decisions that involve replenishables have undergone the most change with the advent of lean retailing. Indeed, many products sold in retail outlets, particularly basic and fashion-basic items, can now be replenished after the start of the selling season. The jagged heavy line in Figure 6.5 (page 100) depicts a typical inventory pattern for a replenishable product like our blue jeans in size 8. Note that the inventory level drops gradually as consumers purchase the item. Once a week, this retailer places a replenishment order with its supplier and receives a shipment. On July 17 and 24, the replenishment order arrives in time to restock the inventory before selling out; however, during the week of July 24, high demand led to rapid depletion of stock, so the retailer stocks out of the product prior to the end of the week.

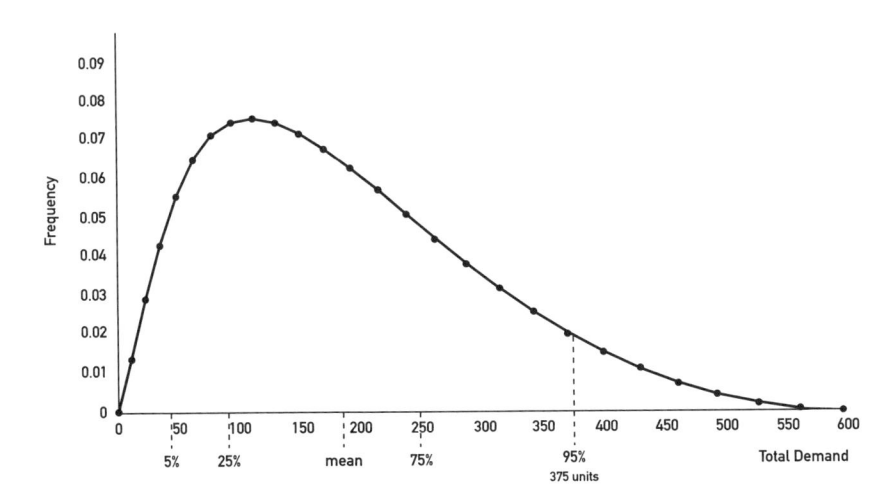

Figure 6.4. Demand for Nonreplenishable Fashion Dress

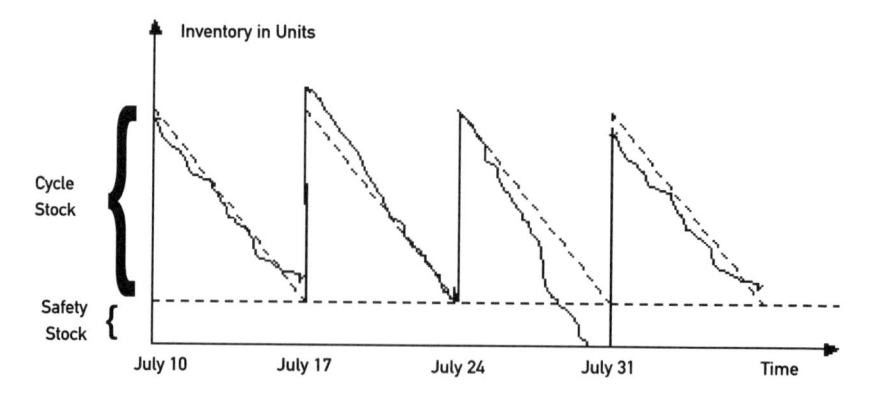

Figure 6.5. Typical Retail Inventory Pattern

To understand this product's inventory requirements, it helps to divide the inventory into two separate components: cycle stock, which is held to cover expected demand for the product; and safety stock, which is held to cover higher than expected demand. Figure 6.5 breaks out these two components of stock. The straight dashed lines show the inventory pattern that would result if there were no variation in demand—that is, if exactly the same number of units were bought each day. Specifically, the dashed lines indicate the inventory pattern that would result if demand each day were equal to the average, or expected, demand. In the figure, cycle stock is the amount of stock necessary to meet average demand. Below the cycle stock sits the safety stock, a buffer that is held for those weeks (such as the one following July 24) in which demand exceeds the average. If there were no uncertainty in demand, this retailer would need no safety stock. But the higher the demand uncertainty, the more safety stock is required to ensure a low probability of stocking out.

As Figure 6.6 shows, the safety stock needed to achieve a given customer service level is proportional to the standard deviation of the demand forecast.[12] Simply put, the less certain retailers are of the demand for their product, the more safety stock they must hold to meet consumer needs. In the figure, we assume that the order-fulfillment rate equals 97 percent and the order-fulfillment lead time is three weeks. The parameter choices for the figures, although based on data from actual apparel firms, are for illustrative purposes only. By reducing order-fulfillment lead times, lean retailers are able to reduce the level of safety stock required to deal effectively with a given level of demand variation.

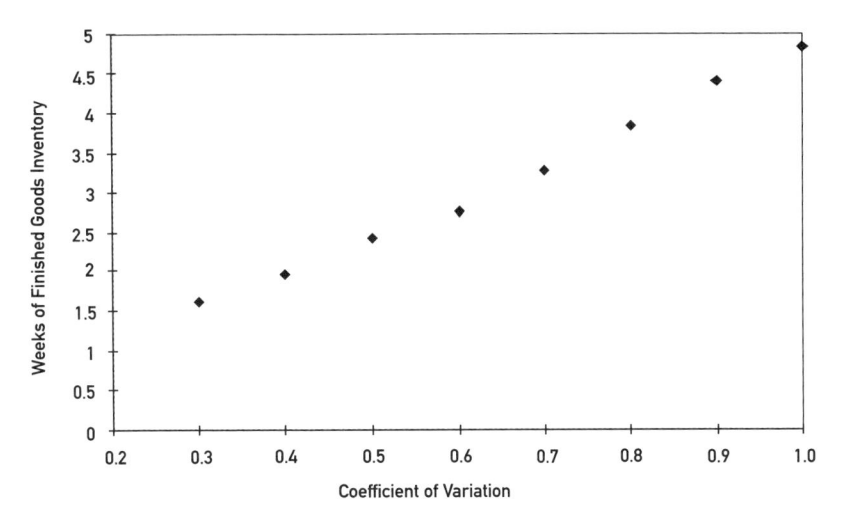

Figure 6.6. Finished Goods Inventory as a Function of Demand Variation

Because safety stock is directly dependent on demand uncertainty, increasing product variety increases retail safety-stock requirements. For example, when the coefficient of variation increases from 0.5 to 1.0—which would happen if the number of products offered increased by a factor of four—the amount of finished goods required to provide the desired service level doubles. Formally, one determines safety-stock levels by weighing the costs of having too much inventory (overstocking) with the costs of having too little (understocking), in much the same way as we did for nonreplenishables.

From the retailer's point of view, the only way to mitigate the effects of increased demand uncertainty is to have frequent replenishment opportunities, in which replenishment orders can be filled by manufacturers with very short lead times. Chapter 7 examines what this entails from the manufacturer's perspective. At this point, however, we will introduce the standard inventory model that many retailers use for rapid replenishment items, considering the implications of demand uncertainty raised above.

(R, s, S) Models: Traditional Inventory Policy for Replenishables

A standard inventory policy for a retailer proceeds as follows: At the end of every week, check the inventory of your product. If the inventory has fallen below a stated amount, s, termed the reorder point, place an order for more units. The amount ordered should be sufficient so that the number of units on hand plus those that are on order equal some "maximum" stocking quantity, S.[13] For a particular item, our store buyer may reorder when the inventory level falls below s equals 4 units, in a quantity that brings the current inventory up to S equals 8 units. With this policy in place, if at the end of a day she notes that inventory has dropped to 3 units, she would order 5 more, as shown in Figure 6.7. The parameter R in this model refers to the length of the time period between inventory status checks; in this case, the buyer checks inventory weekly, so R is 7 days.

Note that there is a short delivery lead time from the time the order is placed: one day during the first two cycles shown in the figure, two days for the third cycle. Because units typically are sold during the delivery lead time, the actual inventory in stock rarely reaches eight units. Instead, at the time of ordering, inventory in stock plus that on order equals eight units. But if order lead times are long, the buyer must order up to a larger number S to meet demand during the replenishment lead time. Once again, if lead times are uncertain, retailers must hold additional safety stock to meet demand in the event of an unusually long lead time. It can be shown that high variability in lead time means higher costs for retailers than somewhat longer, but more reliable lead times; that is, it may be better to have a longer reliable lead time than an unpredictable one with a shorter average duration.[14]

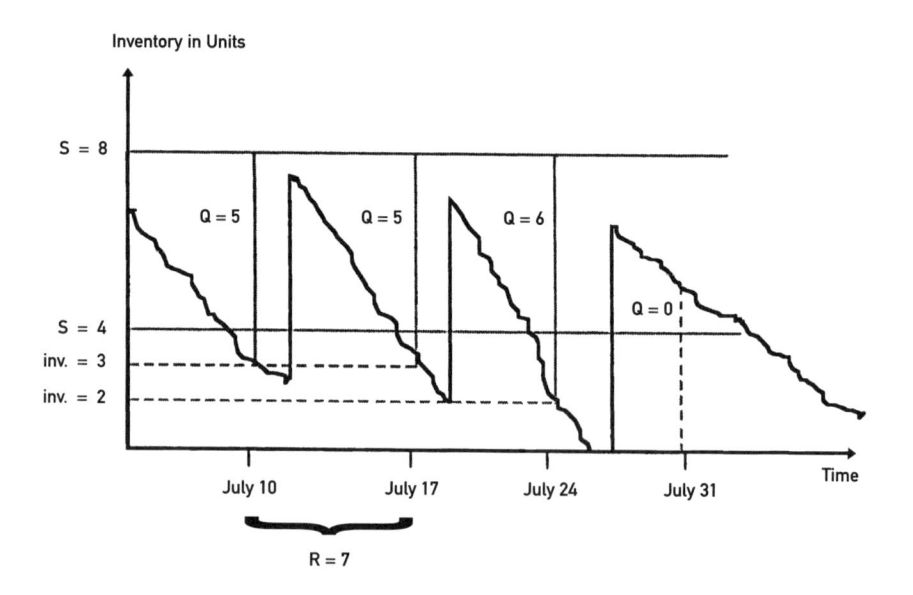

Figure 6.7. Sample (R, s, S) Policy

The lean retailing policies described previously attempt to reduce both average lead times and lead-time variability through the imposition, for example, of penalties for late deliveries.

We noted earlier that a retailer's decision about how much to stock depends on the demand forecast for the product, the level of product availability it wishes to provide to customers, the frequency with which it will place replenishment orders, and the lead time to acquire replenishment units. Let's see how these factors would combine to create a stocking policy for our size-8 blue jeans. We continue to assume that this SKU has the weekly demand distribution shown in Figure 6.1 (page 92). Assume that the retailer wishes to provide a 95 percent order-fulfillment rate for this SKU, that the retailer checks inventory once per week, and that the manufacturer's lead time to deliver replenishment units is overnight. (This last assumption is unrealistic in many situations[15]; we choose it only to simplify the exposition. It is not difficult to extend this analysis to the case in which the replenishment lead time is longer.) Finally, we assume that like most retailers, our retailer replenishes each week exactly the number of units that sold the previous week. (Formally, this translates into an (R, s, S) policy with $s = S − 1$: that is, if the current stock is $S − 1$ or less, the retailer orders $S − s$.)

Given the desired 95 percent service level, the retailer should set a target stock level of seventeen units. Thus, the retail replenishment system would check the stock of these jeans every Sunday night; if the current stock is thirteen pairs of size-8 jeans (meaning that four pair sold the previous week), then it would automatically order four more pairs, bringing the amount of this SKU up to its target level of seventeen units. This order would be combined with other replenishment orders for Levi jeans destined for the same store, thereby reducing shipping costs.[16]

Periodic Versus Continuous Review

The policy described above involves what is known as periodic review. After a fixed period of time (e.g., every week), the retailer checks the inventory level. If the level of inventory is less than the specified reorder point s, the retailer "orders up to" the specified level S. This is still the most common practice today.

An alternative approach offers continuous review—or an (s, S) model—in which the retailer continuously checks the inventory level. The moment the level hits s, the retailer orders up to a specified quantity S. Unlike a periodic-review policy, in which retailers may order when the inventory level is less than s, with a continuous-review policy, they always order when the inventory equals s. Thus, under a continuous-review policy, retailers always order the same quantity ($Q = S - s$) but after a variable amount of time since the last order was placed. Conversely, under periodic review, they order after a fixed length of time, but the quantity differs because it depends on the amount that is in stock when inventory was checked each period. Use of continuous review allows retailers to achieve a higher service level with a lower amount of inventory. By monitoring the inventory continuously, they ensure that it never falls below s before placing an order.

The choice of which model to use depends on a number of factors. Prior to the use of bar codes, implementation of a continuous-review policy at retail was nearly impossible because it was extraordinarily difficult to keep track of actual inventory levels on a continuous basis.[17] Today bar codes and retail information systems allow access to stocking levels on a continuous basis, but most retailers choose to use periodic review systems to restrict ordering activities to set times of the week; that way, they can save on transportation and other costs by ordering multiple products from the same vendor at the same time.

Finally, a complete economic analysis of the appropriate parameters for an (s, S) or (R, s, S) policy must include consideration of some of the "softer" costs and benefits of inventory. A retail buyer may choose to stock more of a product than indicated by an economic analysis because she believes that more stock is necessary to attract the customer and sustain the desired level of sales. In recent years, many retailers have been hampered in their efforts to reduce in-store stocking levels by the size and shape of the fixtures in which their products are displayed. If the fixture was designed to hold ten shirts of a particular color and size, for instance, it is both wasteful of space and visually unappealing to put only three shirts out—even if an economic analysis recommends the lower quantity. In fact, many stores have introduced new fixtures with smaller slots for each SKU (or flexible slot sizes) that can hold a more economically desirable quantity of stock without sacrificing pleasing appearance.

Vendor-Managed Inventory

One of the most significant changes in retail inventory management in recent years has been the introduction of vendor-managed inventory (VMI) programs, also known as Continuous Replenishment Programs (CRP) or Continuous Product Replenishment (CPR). These programs involve having either the retailer, the manufacturer, or the retailer and manufacturer together determine desired inventory stocking levels for the manufacturer's product in the retail store. After these "model stock" levels are set, data about product sales and current retail inventory levels are transmitted electronically to the manufacturer. The manufacturer then decides how much to ship—and, in many cases, when to ship—to the retailer in such a way that its own costs of manufacturing and shipping are minimized while still meeting retail inventory policy requirements. Typically, these programs result in the frequent delivery of small quantities of items to the retailer—it would not be uncommon for a blue jeans manufacturer to ship a carton of one dozen blue jeans of mixed styles and sizes to a particular store.

The benefits of such policies are significant. In the grocery industry, the implementation of VMI programs has been shown to increase retail inventory turns from 50 percent to 100 percent over those achieved prior to implementation, even if the retailer and manufacturer had previously used electronic data interchange for communication of retail orders.[18] The advantage of using VMI programs stems from the retailer and manufacturer working together to determine a flow of shipments that optimizes the economics of the two parties as a system. Otherwise, the two parties make independent decisions that myopically optimize their own profits, without complete consideration of the impact these decisions may have on other players in the channel.[19]

A few caveats are in order, however. According to HCTAR's survey, the incidence of retail model stock programs increased significantly over the 1988–1992 period, from 7 percent to 16 percent of total volume shipped by the business units in our sample (see Figure 5.1, page 73). But there was a much smaller increase in the prevalence of model stock programs governed by apparel suppliers, reflecting the dominance of retailers in instigating new channel relationships as well as the reluctance of most retailers to allow suppliers to control merchandise on the shelf. As in all cases where partnerships might benefit the various parties involved, real-world considerations—who has the most power, who is responsible for instigating change, who will make the initial investments—often slow integration.

Managing Inventory in a Lean Retailing Environment

The new world of rapid replenishment implies additional capabilities for both the retailer and manufacturer. The retailer must be able to gather and synthesize point-of-sales data quickly to determine what has sold and then update its demand forecast for the product accordingly. The manufacturer must deliver the ordered product quickly to the retailer. As we describe in Chapter 7, manufacturers have essentially two choices in supplying replenishables. They can hold finished products in inventory, thereby reducing their processing requirements during the replenishment lead time to picking, packing, and shipping the order. However, this approach increases the risk to the manufacturer: It has to commit to holding finished goods of a product for which it has little or no consumer demand information.[20]

The alternative is to adopt quick-response manufacturing strategies that allow items to be produced to order. But given the increasingly short lead times dictated by retailers (often just a couple of days), most manufacturers cannot produce in this way.[21] Therefore, it is not surprising that most replenishment products are basics or fashion-basics with relatively stable demand: Manufacturers are unwilling to hold speculative stock to meet replenishment requests from retailers for fashion products because the risk of holding those fashion goods in finished goods inventory is too high.

Ironically, replenishment capabilities would be of most value to the retailer for fashion products, but because of their short product lives and the unpredictability of demand, fashion products are typically not offered on a replenishment basis. From the apparel supplier's perspective, that's a good thing—at least for the time being. As the next chapter will make clear, the demands of lean retailing have already created plenty of inventory challenges for manufacturers.

7

Inventory Management for the Manufacturer: Production Planning and Optimal Sourcing Decisions

Retailers' calls to apparel manufacturers about late delivery are the basis for many a tall tale at retail conventions. In the past, the standard reply to a query about what had happened to an order was "It's on the loading dock." Information systems at apparel factories were primitive. If all the SKUs for an order were not in the warehouse, substitutions of the same style in a different size would be offered to the retailer. Or retailers might not even notice if an unplanned substitution had been made because their information systems were equally as primitive. If there were insufficient SKUs of the requested style, the order would be shorted or a phone call made to the retail buyer to negotiate a solution to the problem. If no SKUs of the order were in the finished goods warehouse, then the search of the factory floor—where there might be tens of thousands of partially completed items to look through—would begin.

Then along came lean retailing and the need for rapid replenishment—manufacturers are now expected to replenish products in less than a week. At first, only a few retailers required this, and apparel manufacturers tried to meet these needs with minimal changes in their internal practices. Often, this was done at the expense of a manufacturer's non-lean retail customers. For example, the CEO of a men's dress-shirt supplier reported to us in 1992 that its finished goods warehouse was divided into two areas. A locked section contained finished goods reserved for orders from Dillard's, Inc., this manufacturer's biggest customer and its only one with stringent rapid-replenishment requirements. The rest of the warehouse held inventory for all other retailers. If the locked section had insufficient inventory for a Dillard's order, product from the rest of the warehouse could be picked and sent to Dillard's, but no retailers could receive products from the locked section reserved for Dillard's, no matter how severe their needs. This arrangement worked well from Dillard's perspective; it found this firm to be one of its best rapid-replenishment suppliers, with high order-fulfillment rates and on-time deliveries—the main criteria for success. For the manufacturer, it meant a larger finished goods inventory and worse service for its other customers.

As long as only one or two retailers required rapid replenishment, manufacturers could get away with this type of solution. But it didn't take long before most retailers wanted orders for basic apparel items replenished this way and they became very demanding. As an increasing number of suppliers are dancing to the demands of rapid replenishment, they are finding it a complex tune. Manufacturers suddenly have much more to do than just make clothing—they are being asked to do work previously done by the retailer, such as picking and packing the order for each store from the retailer's warehouse. Each store's order has to be put in a separate carton, labeled with its own bar code, and accompanied by an advance shipping notice. Moreover, retailers want an order to arrive at their distribution center at an exact time. If the truck is late, the driver often has to wait until the end of the day to unload, if allowed to do so at all. Deliveries made a day late are sometimes refused and sent back.

Such retail requirements have certainly put substantial pressure on apparel manufacturers to change their own practices. Chapter 5 described some of the basic changes many manufacturers are making to stay in the game with lean retailers. But even if lean retailing has led to suppliers' wide-scale adoption of bar codes and EDI-related capabilities, divergent production strategies among suppliers have emerged. Conceivably, two business units could each meet the same lean retailing requirements yet have very different internal practices and performance. One could raise finished goods inventories substantially (like the dress-shirt manufacturer described above); the other could make crucial operational changes to reduce manufacturing lead times. However, in light of the growth of rapid replenishment, our research predicts that the performance of these two units will vary over time, with the supplier that has implemented flexible planning and short-cycle production processes coming out ahead. By investing in these practices, apparel suppliers have the potential to satisfy lean retailing performance standards *without* bearing the costs of greatly expanded inventory in their own operations. From our standpoint, holding high inventories to meet rapid replenishment demands is strictly a short-term strategy for manufacturers.

The increasing emphasis on rapid replenishment raises a related question: can offshore manufacturers meet retailers' requirements for such short delivery lead times and so many services? More specifically, what are the characteristics of products for which inexpensive, long lead-time production is preferable to more costly production with extremely short lead times? The models and analyses presented in this chapter help shed light on this critical question.

We begin this chapter with an overview of the impact of demand variability on a manufacturer's own inventory and production planning processes. Next, we describe how apparel manufacturers can use statistical analysis and simulation to gain insight into inventory planning and production scheduling for products they offer in their rapid replenishment collections. The first of two case studies illustrates how demand uncertainty affects a firm's target inventory levels. The second case study demonstrates how short-cycle production translates into inventory reduction for a manufacturer, thereby radically reducing the increased exposure to inventory risk a manufacturer would otherwise face to meet lean retailers' demands. The chapter concludes by emphasizing the relationships among demand volatility, manufacturing lead times, and inventory levels, addressing a critical decision apparel manufacturing firms face today: Given two different apparel sources, with different variable production costs and lead times, how does a firm decide which products to make in each of the two plants?

The Key Role of Demand Variability

> The most important thing we are doing is "consumerization," to be the best in the business in delivering products customized for what the consumer wants. All of our initiatives are to drive consumer value. And as we reduce costs, we reinvest those savings in improving our consumer responsiveness.[1]
>
> —*Mackey McDonald, President and CEO, VF Corporation, 1998*

Because being responsive to consumer tastes is central to lean retailing, dealing with variability in demand has become crucial to suppliers competing in a lean retailing world. Even for basic products, demand varies from day to day and week to week. Thus, if a retailer follows the simplest strategy of ordering at the beginning of each week exactly those items that sold during the previous week, manufacturers must be prepared to ship an unknown number of items each week. Very few manufacturers can produce items in production quantities in the limited lead time retailers allow for replenishment and consequently they must fill such orders from finished goods inventory. And, as one would expect, the higher the variation in week-to-week demand, the more inventory a manufacturer must hold to meet a retailer's high service expectations.

Because weekly demand variability is a key determinant of the finished inventory a manufacturer must hold, each firm should conduct an assessment of the demand variability of each item in the product line.[2] Retailers require orders to be filled at the SKU level, so such demand variability analyses should be conducted at the SKU level as well.

We conducted such an analysis of weekly demand for a U.S. manufacturer of men's coats, suits, and blazers. Figure 7.1 depicts the weekly demand for one SKU—a single-breasted coat in one of the firm's most popular sizes (46-regular)—during the first twenty-four weeks of the year. Each week's demand has been divided by the average demand over the twenty-four weeks; therefore, the average weekly demand is simply equal to 1.0 on this normalized scale. (The important features of

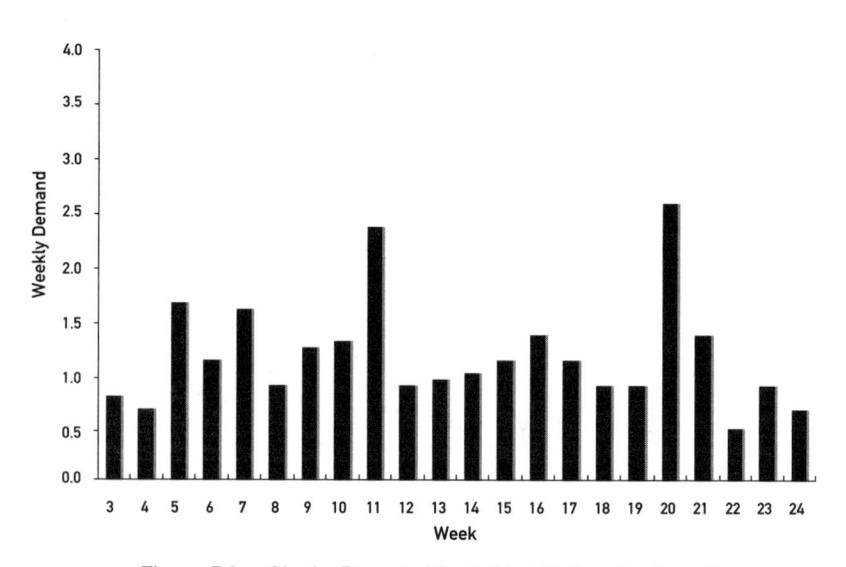

Figure 7.1. Single-Breasted Coat, Size 46 Regular Length
Average Weekly Demand = 1.0, Coefficient of variation = 0.55
Source: Harvard Center for Textile and Apparel Research.

demand for scheduling coat production are contained in demand data presented in this normalized fashion. Normalizing the data also allows us to keep this manufacturer's actual demand volume confidential without obscuring the central information contained in the data.)

Plotting the data in this way allows us to focus on the deviation of the weekly demand from the average weekly demand. Figure 7.2 depicts the weekly demand for a different SKU—the same single-breasted coat—but this time in a less popular size (43-regular). Again, the normalized data highlights the weekly deviation from the average demand. In this case, there is greater week-to-week variation than for the more popular size.

The amount of variation in weekly demand exhibited in Figure 7.2 is quite remarkable, especially if we consider that the manufacturer's demand is based on the total sales of this SKU in over a thousand retail outlets each week. It is important to note also that this product was not promoted at retail with discounted prices at any time during this period, so the variation is not due to consumers preferring to purchase a product when it was "on sale." In addition, the demand peak for the 43-regular occurs in week 10, which was only an average demand week for the 46-regular.

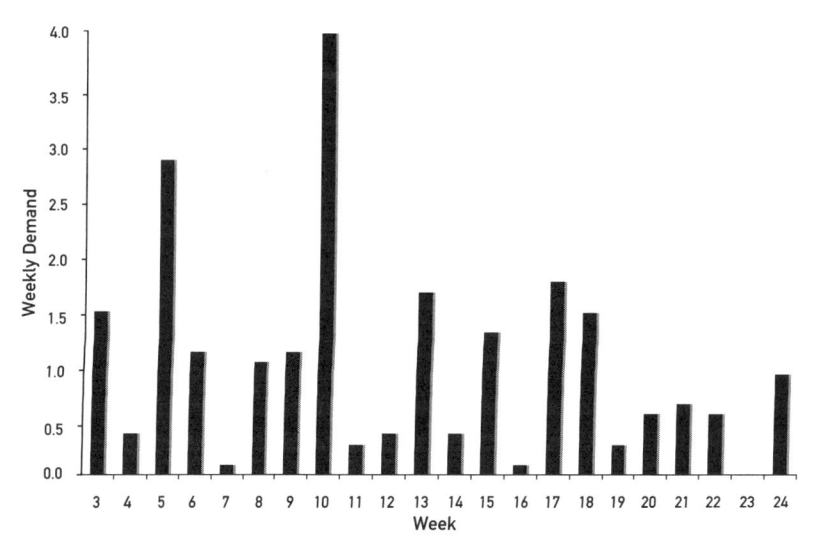

Figure 7.2. Single-Breasted Coat, Size 43 Regular Length
Average Weekly Demand = 1.0, Coefficient of variation = 1.0
Source: Harvard Center for Textile and Apparel Research.

It is useful to outline the ordering and manufacturing processes on a weekly basis to see how this manufacturer's inventory policies might differ for the two different sizes. Suppose that, as described in Chapter 6, the retailer consolidates POS data for the previous week's sales each Sunday night and places a replenishment order with our manufacturer. On Monday, the manufacturer (1) processes the order; (2) picks and packs the desired items from finished goods inventory and ships them to the retailer; and (3) places a factory order to manufacture those items that it shipped that day. Assume that the manufacturing lead time—the amount of time required to go from a production order to a product ready for shipping to retail—is less than one week. Then, by the following Monday, the items ordered the previous week would be completed at the factory and available in the manufacturer's finished goods inventory. At this point, the manufacturer's inventory is restored to the "target" level it had the previous week and is ready to fill the next week's retail replenishment order.

For the popular 46-regular coat, weekly demand never exceeds twice the coat's average demand. Thus, as long as the lead time for producing more coats in size 46-regular is less than a week, the manufacturer could hold two weeks' worth of inventory and be able to fill—immediately—retail orders that replenish the previous week's demand. That is, it could set a target stock level of two weeks of finished goods inventory and be able to provide a very high customer service level (defined here as order-fulfillment rate) to retailers.

However, for the low volume 43-regular, the maximum weekly demand is about four times the average. To provide the same service level to retailers for both sizes, our manufacturer must hold twice as many weeks of demand of finished goods for the 43-regular than for the 46-regular. Note that we are comparing the inventory levels in terms of weeks of average demand, which measures the ratio of the units of finished goods to average weekly sales. In fact, the actual number of units of finished goods inventory would be higher for the popular 46-regular than for the low volume 43-regular. The point to keep in mind here is that, compared to a product's average demand, more popular products required relatively less finished goods inventory than less popular ones. Bear in mind that the actual sales of our manufacturer's coats showed no seasonal variation. If a product has seasonal sales trends, then the manufacturer's inventory must rise to meet customer demand during peak seasonal demand. Furthermore, if the manufacturing lead time exceeds one week, the manufacturer faces more demand risk and therefore must hold even more inventory.

As explained in previous chapters, variation in weekly demand can be characterized by a standardized measure, the coefficient of variation, or C_v. Formally defined as the standard deviation of demand divided by average demand, the coefficient of variation can be considered a measure of variation that is normalized; it allows us to compare the variation of demand for different products, even if the average demand of the two products is quite different. The value of the coefficient can vary from zero (if demand is exactly the same every week) to numbers much greater than one for wildly fluctuating weekly demand. In our analyses of demand patterns for different apparel products, we have found that the most predictable items have C_vs in the 0.4 to 0.6 range. But in most situations in which a firm provides a wide range of goods to customers, some of its products will have low or moderate demand variation, while others' demand will vary a great deal. As illustrated in the previous examples, high volume products often have lower coefficients of variation than low volume products. (In Figure 7.1, the high volume 46-regular has a low C_v of 0.55. In Figure 7.2, the lower volume 43-regular has a C_v equal to 1.0, which means the weekly demand departs much more from the average.) This is a result of the familiar "demand pooling" argument, which shows that the total variation for the sum of many customers' demand is less than the sum of the variation in individual customers' demand.[3]

The same argument can be used to explain why growing product variety has increased demand variation at the SKU level: As variety grows, demand is distributed among an increasing number of SKUs, thereby reducing the pooling effects of demand aggregation. Take the single-breasted coat of our manufacturer, which is sold through more than a thousand retail outlets. The total yearly sales of all SKUs of this kind of coat are in the tens of thousands. Yet sales of some of the less popular sizes, such as the 43-regular, are only a few hundred a year. When considered on a weekly basis, this translates into average weekly demand across all retail outlets of less than ten units. Therefore, even a small swing in demand from week to week translates into high relative variation—that is, into a high coefficient of variation.

Figure 7.3 (page 114) plots the coefficient of variation for men's single-breasted coats. The graph shows that the SKUs with the lowest total yearly sales have the highest C_v values (the largest variation in week-to-week demand). The coat manufacturer will have to hold relatively more finished goods inventory of the low volume SKUs than of the high volume SKUs.

Taking demand variability into account becomes even more important given recent trends toward product proliferation. Over time, suppliers must manufacturer more and more goods that have the joint characteristics of low volume and high variability. As a result, product proliferation represents a shift in the curve relating sales volume and variability (see Figure 7.4).

High demand variation similarly occurs during the beginning and end of a product life cycle. This variation is due in part to the lower demand volumes during those periods relative to the middle of a product's life, but such fluctuations also occur because of the inherent uncertainty during the ramp up or ramp down of a product's life.

Demand variation plays a central role in determining a manufac-

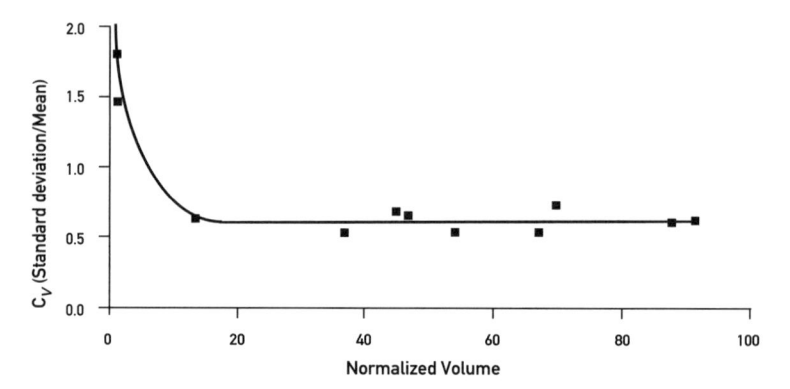

Figure 7.3. Coefficient of Variation versus Sales Volume for Various SKUs
Single-breasted coat, 1 style, multiple SKUs
Source: Harvard Center for Textile and Apparel Research.

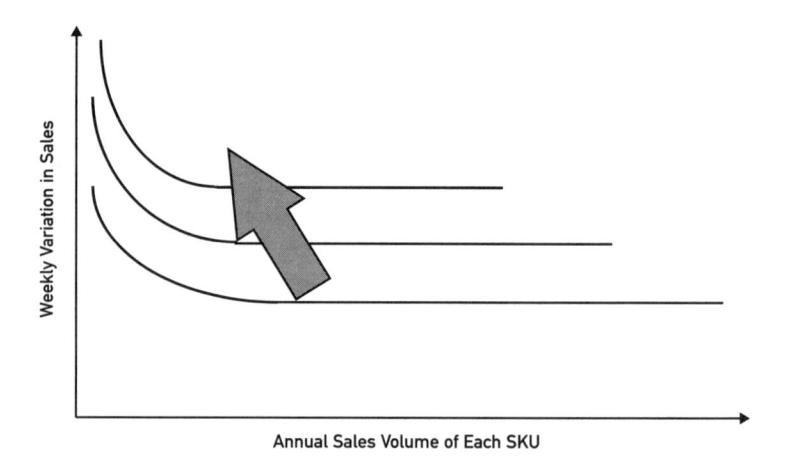

Figure 7.4. Product Proliferation Increases Weekly Variations in Sales

turer's finished goods inventory levels. In the following case studies, we describe how demand variation can be used to determine a firm's production and inventory planning processes. These cases offer a rational approach to inventory management for manufacturers, one that is premised on receiving accurate POS information from retailers and maintaining good working relationships with all channel players—for example, retail orders are not placed at the last minute and textile suppliers come through when they say they will. Reality is messier of course: retailers and suppliers often "surprise" manufacturers, and the POS data are rarely perfect or may not even be available. Yet these nagging problems do not negate the need for a new approach to inventory management; they merely indicate how complicated supplier relationships have become.

Case 1: Inventory Control at a Men's Coat Manufacturer

Our first case study examines the inventory management practices at the men's coat manufacturer previously described. This manufacturer's standard approach to rapid replenishment requests was simply to carry large inventories. The firm treated all SKUs alike; it held the same number of weeks of demand for each SKU. Specifically, our manufacturer checked inventory of every item each week. If the inventory of any item was ten weeks of demand or less, the firm would place a production order for that item so that the current inventory plus the planned production was equal to fourteen weeks of demand. (This manufacturer essentially followed an (R, s, S) policy as described in Chapter 6, with R = time period between orders = seven days, S = target inventory level = fourteen weeks, and s = reorder point = ten weeks.)[4]

Note that this response is not unusual. Many manufacturers do not explicitly track and use information like weekly demand variation for different SKUs. Currently, no manufacturer we know of has implemented all the changes described here and in the following chapters. In that respect, this men's clothing supplier is representative of the industry.

In our initial assessment, we found that this manufacturer was in stock for most SKUs most of the time—a pretty good result. However, we also noticed that the firm was out of stock for some items, especially those with the most variable demand. Managers first thought that was true just for its largest sizes, but further analysis revealed that the company had the same problem with some small sizes as well as with some less popular styles. The firm was stocking out of the low demand items, which, as described above, suffered from relatively high demand variation. This is illustrated in Table 7.1, which shows the average order-fulfillment rate for products with different levels of demand variability, assuming the same level of average demand is held for each SKU.

The data suggest that when a manufacturer chooses the same inventory policy for all products, its order-fulfillment rate for highly variable products is usually worse than for low variation products. Such a policy rarely maximizes profits; the manufacturer stocks out, thereby losing the margin on the sale, and the retailer, which typically desires a consistent (or at least predictable) order-fill rate across items in a product group, is unhappy. Simply increasing inventory for all SKUs would be a poor allocation of investment, further increasing the order-fill rate for those SKUs for which service levels are already high. Thus, for most manufacturers, tracking weekly variation for different SKUs is essential and will help to guide a firm in setting appropriate inventory targets for each SKU. To do this, firms need a planning tool that translates demand variation into inventory targets by weighing, for each SKU, the opportunity for more sales against higher inventory carrying costs.

Once demand variation for each SKU was determined for our men's coat manufacturer, its managers faced the question of how to manage the inventory of the items in its rapid replenishment collection while maintaining a smooth flow of products through the sewing room. Using traditional sewing operations, it typically takes eight weeks to produce a coat, from the time an order is issued for cutting to the moment the finished goods are hanging in a manufacturer's distribution center. Two weeks are spent in the cutting room, where the cloth is spread, cut, inspected, and has backing material fused to appropriate

Table 7.1. Order-Fulfillment Rate as a Function of Demand Variability

Coefficient of Variation	Order-Fulfilment Rate
0.50	98.2%
0.65	95.8
0.75	95.4
0.90	93.7

Source: Diehl, Gregory, Frederick H. Abernathy, and Janice H. Hammond, "Customer Demand and Scheduling for Clothing Manufacturers," HCTAR Working Paper Series, November 1996.

parts of the outer ("shell") fabric. Four weeks are spent in assembly processes. The last two weeks involve final inspection, repairs if necessary, shipping to the distribution center, and hanging the finished coats so they can be picked to fill individual orders for a given store.

A men's suit coat or a blazer requires more than a hundred assembly operations (compare this with only forty operations for a men's shirt); it is one of the most complicated and expensive apparel items to make. Although the number of operations partly determines how long it takes to get a garment through production, other factors come into play, including the firm's policy about how many finished coats should be allowed to build up in work-in-process and finished goods inventory. Given this manufacturer's policy of ordering production only when inventory levels dropped below ten weeks, with the production quantity set to restore the inventory to fourteen weeks, the minimum production quantity for each item was four weeks of demand. Thus, at least four weeks of demand—a large quantity for most products—of the same style and size could move through the sewing plant at one time, minimizing setup costs for thread changes and the like.

The diagram in Figure 7.5 depicts the production process, including all product and information flows relevant to the inventory decision. In general, to maximize operating profit, a manufacturer must know the factory's overall cycle time, work-in-process carrying costs, finished or hanging goods carrying costs, unit production costs, and unit selling price, as well as the C_v for each SKU of a given style. The manufacturer in this example effectively had limitless capacity to produce the single-breasted coat, since only approximately 30 percent of the plant's total capacity was devoted to producing a variety of rapid

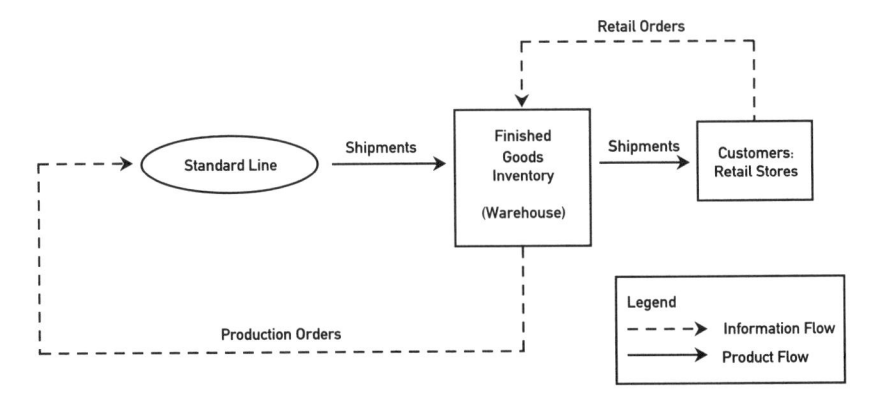

Figure 7.5. Product and Information Flow in a Single Factory Production System

replenishment items. This capacity could be invoked when necessary by putting aside the lower priority products made in the factory.

Our approach to the problem was to use operations research techniques and computer simulations of demand to explore the appropriate inventory levels, taking into account the statistical nature of the weekly demand for each of the SKUs for a style. In our approach, we assumed that an unfilled order was a lost sale with a lost profit. Table 7.2 reports the recommendations derived from the method.[5] Setting a target inventory level for each SKU that maximizes profit is the first step; we did this using a computer simulation. As expected, the target inventory levels depend on a product's demand variation. The larger the variation is, the higher the inventory level should be for an item to satisfy demand, as shown in the fourth and fifth columns of Table 7.2. The second and third columns of the table indicate our manufacturer's standard approach to inventory and are included to allow comparison with the optimal policy.

The optimal policy is one for which marginal increases or decreases in chosen inventory levels will not confer additional profits. For example, when demand for an item was quite variable, with the highest C_v of 0.90, the optimal policy called for placing a production orders when inventory dropped to twelve weeks of demand, rather than the lower standard level of ten. Put in a different way, increasing the amount of inventory from the company's uniform level to the optimal level raised the manufacturer's order-fulfillment rate to more than 97 percent for all SKUs, which raised profits more than it cost the manufacturer in terms of added inventory carrying cost. As a result, overall profits increased because of the change in inventory policy.

Following this strategy, it is true that a manufacturer will carry

Table 7.2. Comparison of Optimal Policy with Manufacturer's Policy

Coefficient of Variation	Manufacturer's Standard Policy (Min. Inventory, Max. Inventory)	Actual Order-fulfillment Rate Using Standard Policy	Optimal Inventory Policy (Min. Inventory, Max. Inventory)	Estimated Order-fulfillment Rate Using Optimal Policy
0.50	10 weeks, 14 weeks	98.2%	11 weeks, 15 weeks	99.5%
0.65	10 weeks, 14 weeks	95.8%	11 weeks, 15 weeks	97.6%
0.75	10 weeks, 14 weeks	95.4%	11 weeks, 15 weeks	97.6%
0.90	10 weeks, 14 weeks	93.7%	12 weeks, 16 weeks	98.0%

Source: Diehl, Gregory, Frederick H. Abernathy, and Janice H. Hammond, "Customer Demand and Scheduling for Clothing Manufacturers," HCTAR Working Paper Series, November 1996.

more inventory for certain items. Yet the percentage of time (97.6 to 99.5 percent in our simulation) that the firm is in stock for these SKUs translates into more sales and fewer stock-outs, which increases gross margin and, ultimately, operating profit. Because margin is primarily determined by the difference between the selling price and manufacturing and materials costs, if the margin for a unit is high, it pays to be almost always in stock. The resulting profit accrues, even after the higher finished goods carrying cost associated with larger inventory has been considered.

This view of production and inventory planning also provides a manufacturer with a more sophisticated tool for balancing alternative plant operating choices to maximize profits. For example, consider whether a manufacturer should cut fabric and assemble garments in smaller lots. In order to make this decision for a SKU with a given level of demand variation, this firm's managers should weigh the increased unit costs arising from manufacturing smaller lots against the benefits this might create in shortening production lead times, which would reduce the amount of inventory the firm must hold for that product. Similarly, the impact of alternative methods for reducing plant cycle time depends not only on the direct costs of changes, but also on the reductions in inventory levels allowed by shorter lead times.

Fundamental to any resulting scenario is the idea of coupling inventory carrying costs to other manufacturing costs in order to make optimal production planning decisions. This allows manufacturers to balance the potentially higher operating costs associated with decreasing lot sizes (the minimum number of units in a production run) with the opportunities to reduce inventory carrying costs and increasing sales. The failure of most suppliers in the apparel industry to make inventory carrying costs an explicit part of their decision-making process remains a significant impediment to enhanced profitability. On the flip side, the performance results presented in Chapter 14 indicate that moving toward this more sophisticated method of handling production decisions can yield significant competitive advantages.

Case 2: Multiple Plants and Production Planning

Of course, a firm that relies on multiple production plants has a more complex problem than the example just presented. Not only must it set inventory levels and schedule production for each product, but it must choose which products to assemble in each plant. In many cases, the choice is between a more expensive plant—probably located close to the market—that provides shorter lead times and a more distant supplier that takes longer to make items but does so at a lower unit cost. Under the traditional retailing system, suppliers filled an order by carrying out assembly in the least costly plant, as long as its quality was adequate for the market for which the product was destined. In a lean retailing world, however, factors other than the direct costs of assembly and transportation need to be considered.

Caught between lean retailers' need for immediate replenishment and the high risk of carrying inventory for products with uncertain demand, a manufacturer today must go beyond traditional direct costs and also include manufacturing lead times and inventory carrying costs in its sourcing equation. Most production managers instinctively believe that having at least some manufacturing capability close to the market adds value to the company, but expressing that value in dollars and cents, and making specific allocations of products to plants, are difficult.

Manufacturers—whether of suits, CDs, office products, or pasta—generally classify products in terms of product lines. Planning, therefore, is done for fall fashion lines, jazz ensemble CDs, yellow legal pads, or fettuccine pasta products. Even if this method of categorization is important from a marketing perspective, it often glosses over what is, in fact, common to many products that seem different and different about products that seem the same. Once again, demand variability is key. For our men's suit manufacturer, the men's size 43-regular coat may have less in common with the size 46-regular coat in the same size and color than with a fashionable boy's blazer.

To set an optimal policy for a multi-plant or multi-source setting, the first step is to determine the coefficient of variation for each SKU and then to arrange the SKUs into groups that have similar variations in weekly demand (i.e., the same C_v). Figuring out how to assign products to plants rests on two findings explored in this chapter. First, the previous case study suggests that SKUs with large demand variance (high C_vs) will require larger amounts of inventory than low variance SKUs to provide a high order-fulfillment rate to the retailer. Second, we argued earlier that reducing manufacturing lead times can lower the amount of inventory needed. The combination of these factors suggests that high variance SKUs are the best candidates for a plant with short lead times—the higher direct costs of production are balanced by the reduction in inventory carrying costs resulting from the shorter manufacturing lead times.

The Two-Plant Model

Our second case study is based on a prominent apparel manufacturer that acted as one of our research sites. Here we will show how a decision tool can be used to make the transition from general intuition to specific decisions about (1) which products to make in each plant and (2) how to schedule the time and quantity of production for each product.[6] This analysis can help manufacturers allocate production among existing facilities. It also illustrates what plant characteristics a close-to-market production facility must have to be competitive with low-cost, offshore suppliers. For this analysis, we assume that that the two facilities already exist—that is, we do not evaluate the option of building a new plant or modifying an existing plant (i.e., we are seeking a solution to a short-run optimization problem.)

A simple depiction of the production situation is presented in Figure 7.6. Block diagrams represent this manufacturer's plants and distribution center as well as the retail stores involved. There are two production lines or plants; in the "quick-line" plant, it costs more to produce an item of apparel but it does so more quickly than in the

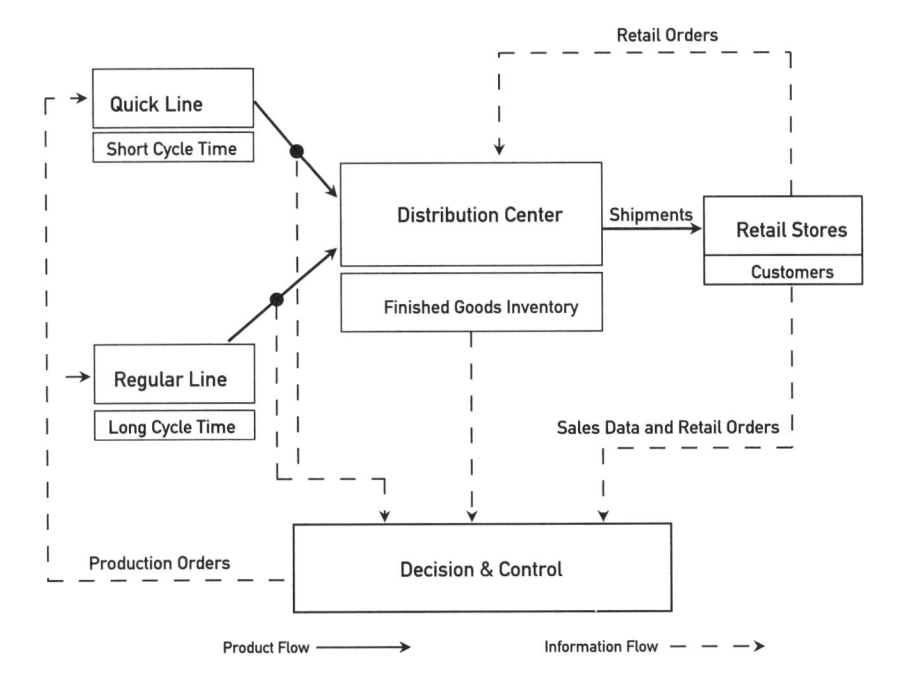

Figure 7.6. Production and Information Flow in a Multiple Factory Production System

"regular-line" plant. The flow of goods is shown in solid lines, and information flows are represented by broken lines. Both plants are capable of making the same set of products. We assume that once a week, orders from all retail stores selling the product are received, picked, packed, and shipped to the retailers from the manufacturer's distribution center. On receipt of the weekly orders, production managers total the quantity of each SKU ordered and determine production needs to restore each SKU's distribution-center inventory to its target level. The total production quantity for each SKU is allocated between the two plants. The cost to produce a unit and deliver it to the distribution center is known for each plant, as well as the time it takes.[7]

For confidentiality reasons, the actual costs and weekly sales volumes for our manufacturer are disguised; however, the cost numbers and sales volumes that appear in this case are reasonable numbers for, say, an upscale dress-shirt manufacturer. Let's assume that we have a single style of dress shirt and that the shirt can be made in one of two plants. In the plant with the "regular" production line, the average direct cost of producing one shirt is $13.15: $7.15 in materials costs (including all buttons, thread, and lining material) plus $6.00 in labor and transportation costs (including direct labor at the plant level; transportation costs for fabric and other supplies shipped to the sewing plant; the cost of transporting finished goods to the manufacturer's distribution center, any customs fees or insurance associated with transportation, and any other costs associated with producing an acceptable unit of finished goods). The other plant (the "quick-line" plant) has production costs that are 10 percent higher than for the regular line, but the manufacturing lead time from the time a production order is placed until a shirt is available in finished goods inventory is two weeks, compared to eleven weeks for the plant with the "regular line."

The question a manager faces in this situation can be stated as follows: For which dress shirts is it more profitable to pay $13.75 per shirt ($7.15 materials plus $6.60 production costs) but have a two-week production lead time, rather than $13.15 with an eleven-week lead time?

If this case involved traditional production strategies in the apparel industry, there would be no problem to study. Managers would just decide to make all these dress shirts in the regular plant because its unit production cost is lower. But in the world of lean retailing, the decision becomes more complicated. Now the unit wholesale selling price, assumed to be $22.00 a shirt, is relevant to the decision because managers must weigh the cost of carrying shirts in inventory with the foregone revenue if they stock out of shirts in the distribution center.

In addition, these managers need to know weekly demand variation as well as average weekly demand for each SKU. In this case, we assume that total weekly demand for all of our SKUs averages 10,000 shirts a week. We classify the SKUs into three categories: those with high demand (averaging 5,700 units a week) and low demand variation (C_v=0.6), those with medium demand (averaging 3,000 units a week) and medium demand variation (C_v=0.7), and those with low demand (averaging 1,300 units a week) and high demand variation (C_v= 1.3). These particular volumes and C_vs were chosen based on the values shown in Figure 7.3 (page 114).

Finally, to allocate production appropriately, managers need to know the inventory carrying cost for carrying work-in-process and finished goods inventory. The inventory carrying cost should reflect not only the cost of capital tied up in inventory, but also the risk of holding that inventory. One indicator of risk is the cost of markdowns manufacturers must make to clear inventory that retailers are not willing to purchase at full wholesale price—if at all.[8] For example, the HCTAR survey found that an average apparel business unit discounted its products to retailers by 24 percent in 1992.

Determining Optimal Allocations

Next, the manufacturer must determine what percentage of its total capacity should be allocated to the quick line (we call this percentage the quick-line capacity ratio), with the remainder allocated to the regular line. Once this decision is made, specific SKUs must be allocated between the two plants on a weekly basis. As in the first case study, we assume that the retailer places an order every Sunday night and that the order must be filled during that week.

We have developed a software package that solves this problem by using computer simulations of the weekly demand and production that determine the consequences of different quick-line capacity ratios and production scheduling policies for the manufacturer's inventory and service levels (order-fulfillment rate) to the retailer. For a given quick-line capacity ratio, the computer program searches for a target inventory level for each SKU and finds the values of the target inventory for each group of SKUs that maximizes profit. The number of computer searches necessary is very large, but with a fast desktop computer and by using special search reduction techniques,[9] the computations can be carried out in just hours.

The results of a search for the maximum profit in this two-plant case appear in Figure 7.7 (page 124), which shows how the quick-line ratio

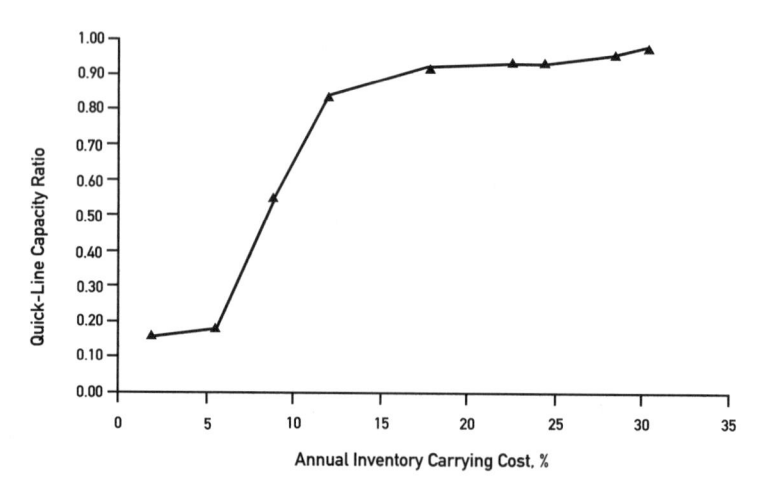

Figure 7.7. Optimal Quick-Line Capacity Increases as Inventory Carrying Costs Increase*

*Assumes quick-line and regular-line lead times of two and eleven weeks respectively

increases as the inventory carrying costs increase.[10] As we would expect, if the cost of carrying inventory is very low, the quick line is not used; that is, the quick-line capacity ratio equals zero. As inventory costs rise, the percent of units allocated to the quick line increases; eventually, when the annual inventory carrying cost approaches 30 percent, the ratio equals one—that is, all the production is allocated to the short-cycle plant. With higher values of inventory carrying costs, it is more profitable to shift more production to the quick-line plant to allow reduction in work-in-process and finished goods inventory.[11]

The major point here is that inventory carrying cost is a critical variable in making such plant capacity decisions. A 24-percent annual inventory carrying cost amounts to approximately 2 percent a month. For the long-cycle plant, work-in-process and finished goods inventory will cover about sixteen weeks on average before the unit is sold. At 2 percent a month, this results in an inventory carrying charge of just 8 percent of the cost to assemble (plus materials). This 8 percent charge against materials and production should be compared with the 24 percent of wholesale selling cost our survey reported as the average markdown needed to clear inventories.[12]

Figure 7.8 shows the full relationship between inventory carrying costs, lead times, and the quick-line production ratio. Again, our earlier intuition is confirmed. The decreasing lead time of the quick-line plant makes it competitive at a lower inventory carrying cost. The

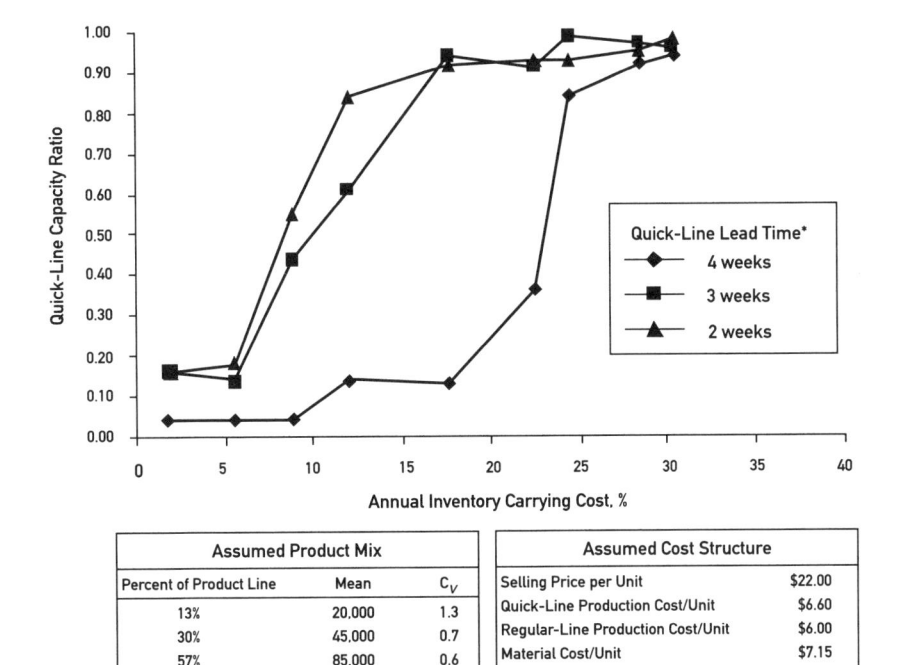

Figure 7.8. Optimal Quick-Line Capacity Depends on Lead Times and Inventory Carrying Costs

Assumed Product Mix		
Percent of Product Line	Mean	C_v
13%	20,000	1.3
30%	45,000	0.7
57%	85,000	0.6

Assumed Cost Structure	
Selling Price per Unit	$22.00
Quick-Line Production Cost/Unit	$6.60
Regular-Line Production Cost/Unit	$6.00
Material Cost/Unit	$7.15

*In all three cases, we assume the regular line lead time is 11 weeks

short-cycle plant becomes more competitive for two reasons: (1) there is less work-in-process; and (2) the finished goods inventory level necessary to satisfy retail demand for each SKU is less because the short-cycle plant can respond to actual demand more quickly.

In this figure, the cycle time of the slower plant has been set at eleven weeks; the short-cycle line can make our products with three different times—namely, two, three, or four weeks. In this case, the cycle time for the long-cycle plant represents the number of weeks typical for offshore production. Note that some outsourcing of production for fashion items is done in Pacific Rim countries and flown directly to distribution centers in the United States. For example, executives at The Limited have often claimed that its firm can produce an item offshore in a thousand hours—or just six weeks—using air-freight delivery to its center in Columbus, Ohio. But most firms that use foreign plants take longer, which is why we have chosen eleven weeks as the cycle time of the slower production line. Figure 7.8 shows the curves for the various lead times listed in the legend on the right-hand side.

Both components of total inventory (work-in-process and finished goods) decrease as the most profitable production shifts to the short-cycle plant. Less finished goods inventory is required because finished goods can be rapidly replenished after a peak selling week.

Therefore, the amount of finished goods in the manufacturer's distribution center needed to satisfy weekly demand for all SKUs depends on the cycle times of the plants supplying finished product, and what fraction of production is made in each plant. In the single-breasted coat example of the previous section, there was only one plant involved, which made the most profitable target inventory level a single number for each SKU.[13] Increased profit came from missing fewer sales by being in stock a higher percentage of the time. In the second case, the finished goods in the distribution center are generally a blend of the output of two plants and the target inventory level varies with the quick-line capacity ratio. *Most important, when a manufacturer considers two sourcing options, the one that offers the lowest direct cost is not always the most profitable.*

The Manufacturer's Dilemma in a Lean World

This chapter shows that suppliers must take additional dimensions into consideration when they make decisions about sourcing. To maximize profits, a firm must consider the complete set of benefits and costs of production decisions. The disadvantage of lower cost, slow production today is that it is necessary to risk large inventories to provide reasonable levels of service to retailers. The omission of such costs from sourcing decisions—as well as the failure to consider the benefits a supplier gains by being in stock on certain items—will reduce a manufacturer's profitability as well as its ultimate ability to compete.

This dilemma in a lean retailing world is summarized in Figure 7.9. Exactly how a manager divides production between plants with different production costs and cycle times depends on the details of the situation, such as those presented in the cases above. However, at least one general rule emerges from the cases we have studied: The cycle time of a fast production facility can be no more than a week or two. Needless to say, a local, more expensive production line with long cycle times cannot compete with slower, low-cost producers, even when allowances are made for late deliveries, markdowns, and the like.[14] But as Figure 7.9 suggests, a manufacturer can pay somewhat more to make certain units—those with high weekly variation in sales—in quick production

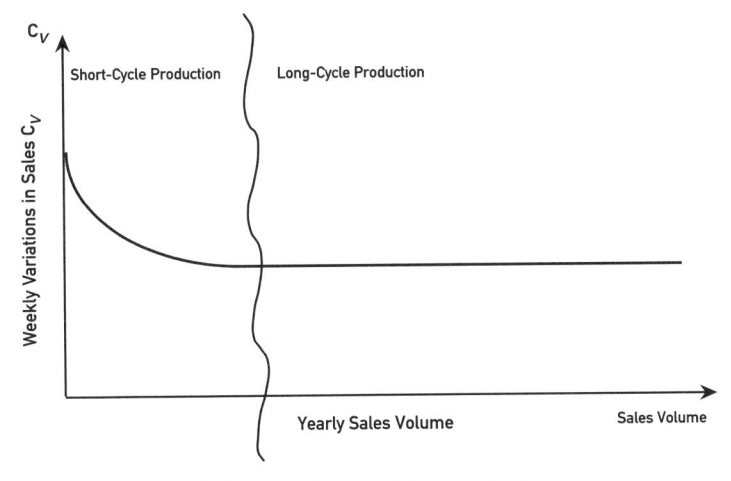

Figure 7.9. Optimal Allocation of Short- and Long-Cycle Manufacturing Capacity

[Chart: C_V (Weekly Variations in Sales C_V) vs. Sales Volume, showing a curve that decreases steeply then levels off. The area to the left of Yearly Sales Volume is labeled "Short-Cycle Production" and the area to the right is labeled "Long-Cycle Production."]

Maximum profit occurs with appropriate fraction of short-cycle and long-cycle manufacturing

lines and still reap a better return than it would by making all of the product in a less expensive, slower plant.

Balancing these production alternatives clearly has implications for foreign competition and the current transformation of the U.S. apparel industry. It also requires changes in internal processes, including manufacturing innovations and the sophisticated computer tools necessary to do this kind of production planning. Although many U.S. apparelmakers are only beginning to incorporate these changes into their operations, lean retailing practices will continue to push suppliers in this direction.

The next two chapters examine apparel operations, starting with a look at the use of information technologies and automation equipment in the preassembly stages of garment-making (Chapter 8) and then the sewing room (Chapter 9). Chapter 10 considers how new human resource practices that allow for short-cycle production, in concert with the use of information technology, can positively affect the performance of suppliers.

8

Apparel Operations: Getting Ready to Sew

The late Joseph Gerber, founder of Gerber Garment Technology Company in Tolland, Connecticut, invented automated fabric cutting and introduced it to the market in 1969. This innovative company went on to create a new industry in automatic-cutting equipment. By the late 1970s, Gerber Garment Technology was supplying the automotive and apparel industries with its GERBERcutter, allowing firms to cut cloth and nonwoven material more effectively. The Gerber system first made it possible for a computer to guide the cutting knife anywhere on the cutting table. Gerber's automatic-cutting equipment, as well as that of several other international competitors, has continued to improve; cloth from a single ply to layers up to six inches thick can now be cut quickly and accurately.

Gerber is also a major worldwide supplier of information systems for the sewing products industries. Its Product Data Management software provides users with all the information about an apparel product, including design, patterns, markers, sewing instructions, and assembly costs. This single software package can be made available through an in-house local area network or the World Wide Web. Computer data systems like this have enormous potential for the apparel industry. Private-label apparel for U.S. department and specialty stores, for instance, is generally designed in this country and produced by domestic contractors or overseas. Regardless of geographic location, it is always difficult for a contractor to know if it has the latest information on sewing patterns and other construction details. But via a network that allows contractors access, manufacturers' headquarters can make sure that the information available is the most recent and complete. In addition, video instructions, which do not rely on spoken language, can demonstrate to foreign contractors what is acceptable and what is not.

In previous chapters, we have described the impact of crucial information technologies, such as the use of bar code scanning and electronic data interchange, on the retail-apparel-textile channel. The ability to transmit order information in unambiguous electronic forms between retailers and apparel manufacturers, along with the possibility of sharing point-of-sales information, allow these manufacturers to understand in real time what is happening in the marketplace. It is then up to the manufacturer to use this information in product design and production planning. Indeed, for many apparel firms, speed in the market now means using modern computer tools that make the process of creating a piece of clothing—from conceptual design to fabric cutting to sewing—smooth and efficient. From the first use of computer-assisted pattern layout in the 1970s, computers and specialized information technologies have spread widely in the industry. Such systems have the potential to develop patterns and color fabrics; adapt apparel patterns for custom-made suits, shirts, pants, and other garments; and evaluate production sourcing alternatives to maximize profit while allowing for demand uncertainty.

Yet not every aspect of apparel production depends on new technologies; in fact, automated sewing processes and the use of robots on the apparel shop floor have not turned out to be profitable or effective.[1] People do a better job than computers of adjusting fabric alignment through sewing machines and compensating for prior sewing and cutting errors. As a result, the marginal costs for human sewing operators are lower than those of the complex robotic systems needed to guide sewing of limp fabric in most operations.

In discussing apparel manufacturing, it is important to make a distinction between preassembly of garments—design, marker-making, spreading, cutting, and bundling operations that are the focus of this chapter—and garment assembly, the subject of the next chapter. Most of the innovations in production and information technology are taking place in preassembly processes, which can be more readily automated. Although changes in how managers orchestrate production flow through the sewing room are starting to make a difference, shifts in the practices of shop-floor workers have more to do with new human resource policies than equipment.

As most observers of the apparel industry know, contracting out the assembly of garments has become common for American manufacturers, although the use of contracting differs between the men's and women's industry. Men's clothing has generally been made in long production runs with only small variations among styles in a given year and relatively little change from year to year. This has allowed men's clothing manufacturers to capture the benefits of their own highly efficient sewing rooms through long production runs. Women's clothing is characterized by great diversity in styles and short production runs. Small contractors' sewing shops are the norm for most women's apparel. The use of contractors has grown at the international level in the 1970s and 1980s.

We will examine some of the complex issues related to international sourcing in Chapter 13. But we want to stress here that today's apparel supplier usually does not produce all of its own garments, from start to finish. Apparel manufacturing can involve many contractors and subcontractors, creating a complex web of supplier relationships. Jobbers—suppliers that may contract out every aspect of clothing production except for design—represent one extreme. Companies like Liz Claiborne and MAST Industries are essentially current versions, although their operations are much larger than those of jobbers in the past.

Many U.S.-based apparel firms, not to mention the apparel union, have long recognized that producing higher quality garments may be the best means for competing against low-cost foreign labor. One way to increase quality is to control fabric purchasing, marker-making, spreading, cutting, and parts preparation in a central facility. The manufacturer can then transport the cut parts for assembly to sewing rooms, which may be either local or out of the country. In fact, HCTAR's survey indicates that the average cutting room services 4.5 sewing rooms. Quality assembly of garments from pieces of material cut according to a particular pattern involves operations that can be carried out almost anywhere in the world. Whether a unit of apparel is assembled in China or the United States, the overall process is quite similar. The differences from country to country remain in the details—principally in the layout of the pattern on the cloth and in cutting the patterns.

For instance the high-end design of a women's jacket, made from $300-a-yard cashmere plaid fabric, can still be of very poor quality if the plaids do not match on the lapels, the inseams of the sleeves, or along the seam joining the back panels. Pattern layout may not seem important at first, until one sees a plaid mismatch when this jacket is buttoned. A very small amount of plaid mismatch in cutting can be overcome by a skilled sewing operator, but the essential step in achieving a quality product is to make the pattern parts correctly. This chapter describes the various steps involved before a garment is sewn, focusing on the technical innovations that are having the greatest impact.[2] Before looking at preassembly operations in apparel-making, however, we will examine the very beginning of the process—garment design and the creation of a pattern.

The First Step: Apparel Design and Patterns

When most people think of apparel design, they see fashion designers and models on runways. Yet the vast majority of design in the apparel industry has little to do with the way clothing is created in the high-fashion world. Often apparel design and pattern-making are done by department stores, private-label offices, and small manufacturers in addition to major firms. The name designers generally create fashion directions and the next tier of designers fill out the new directions into many levels and for many items of apparel.[3] Department stores also have designers at headquarters who prepare designs and patterns for their private-label collection.

Although many apparel manufacturers do have in-house designers, most of the work of garment design comes in adjusting previous patterns or small elements of existing garments—say, the trim or the fabric—and is more a matter of technical creation than a flight of fancy. Consider the expansion of basic and fashion-basic garments in the U.S. market. For T-shirts, sweatpants, and different types of jeans, the design elements that change annually may only amount to a change of color, fit of the jeans, or the addition of a pocket to sweatpants.

Traditionally, a new apparel design was created by asking the designer/artist to make a watercolor sketch. If the fabric was to have a pattern, there might also be a close-up colored sketch of it. Many designs would be grouped together into a storyboard, which was then presented to managers for final decisions. Next the designs that passed this stage went through a technical design step in which details were added and patterns made. After this step, fabric might be cut and a sample made to see how it would look on a mannequin. If the new garment was a blouse, for example, the designer might wish to see how it looked with skirts planned for the collection. If the designer was not satisfied with the drape of the garment, the fit, or the pattern, he or she might go back to square one. Several iterations of these initial design steps could add weeks or months to the process before production began.

Although some haute couture or high-end apparel designers may still work in this manner, each year more garments are designed using computer technology. In our survey, 40 percent of the business units reported using Computer-Aided-Design (CAD) systems to prepare new products in 1992. Employing CAD was particularly common among the largest business units in our sample. The use of modern design tools and information technology can collapse the design time so that managerial decision-making becomes the longest step in the process—and even the time for that step can be shortened with information technology. The new way allows the designer to work creatively with a computer pen or brush to outline the sketch, which appears on a computer screen. The computer can "watercolor" the sketch and produce the storyboard for presentation. Once past the first steps, these systems let designers drape fabric patterns on sketches or photographs of people on the computer screen. For example, sketches or photos can be draped with material of different colors and patterns. The size of the pattern can be changed and the visual images compared to get a sense of their appeal. And a colored ink-jet printing of the pattern can be made on basic plain fabric to help identify and demonstrate the desired colors in future discussions with textile mills.

Design changes can be implemented in minutes. For example, if the apparel item is a skirt, the proposed material on the computer image can be changed with a few key strokes. Prints can be scanned into the computer and used as the pattern for the visual image. Entire collections can be created in a day with the selected materials draped on a sketched figure or actual photograph of a model. The colors of the blouse can be changed with a few computer steps. The color and texture of the rest of the garments in the photograph can be changed with equal ease. Computerized design systems collapse the time needed to explore new design ideas into hours of work, rather than the traditional work time of days or weeks. The resulting visual images can be shared with other decision-makers in the company wherever they might be, without the need to wait until everyone is in town for a meeting. Computer images can be viewed on the local area network or even put on the Internet in a secure form.

Other development applications allow designers to begin with an actual garment and make appropriate changes to achieve the desired design or construction modifications. In this case, designers pin the garment to a special design table. A computer pen is used to outline a panel of the garment with a sequence of contact points. The computer, on command, then connects the image of the points on its screen with a series of line segments that form the silhouette of the pattern piece. Another computer command adds the seam allowance and, after the desired modifications have been made, a piece of the new design is created. When all the individual pieces of the garment have been modified and entered into the computer system, the final garment pattern is ready to be cut and sewn into a sample garment. Numerically controlled fabric cutters are now available that can rapidly and accurately cut patterns from a single ply of cloth, removing the usual obstacle to sample garment-making. The cutting equipment is driven by the output of a pattern-grading and marker-making program.

Note that this entire design sequence can take as little as part of a day, yielding a sample garment hung on a mannequin. Again, the time it takes managers to reach a decision is what determines the length of this process. However, it may take months to produce a sample garment in a desired fabric simply because that fabric takes months to make.

Design information systems, such as the Gerber Garment Technology software discussed above, can also greatly affect how and when design changes are made. Gerber's Web version of such a system (WebPDM) allows worldwide access to designated users with information stored on a single host server about relevant apparel products. Naturally, contractors for sewing assembly will not be allowed access to estimates of production costs and information about other suppliers; however, once a change is made in a garment's design, then everyone involved will have access to and can work from the identical information base. The system can store design, costing, measurements, and detailed construction information, all in multiple languages.

Preassembly: Marker-Making

An order to an apparel factory—whether from a retailer, jobber, or a manufacturer contracting out different stages of the work—specifies the total number of units to be made of a particular design, with a given fabric, and with a certain number of units in each size. Because a retailer normally will have already seen a sample garment before placing an order, the manufacturer therefore will have the pattern pieces for all sizes in-house, with coordinate outlines of the pieces on its computers. The manufacturer might also have the patterns cut out from stiff fiberboard so that the individual pieces can be traced by hand onto a large sheet of paper. But several preassembly processes have to be performed before the cloth can be cut. The order must be broken down into groups of units to be worked on together. Then all the pieces of the patterns must be laid out for the various units so that they can be cut at the same time. The silhouette for each individual pattern piece is generally traced or imprinted on a sheet of paper, which is called a "marker." Finally, the cloth must be spread in as many layers of thickness as necessary to achieve the number of units requested or as many as can be properly cut at one time.

Each piece of the pattern in a marker has a seam allowance added to the basic outline. This allowance serves two purposes: First, the sewn seam must be made far enough in from the edge of the cloth so that it will not pull free of the cloth; second, the seam allowance provides a region into which small alignment notches can be cut. The notches are the basic instruction to sewing operators regarding where the fabric pieces to be joined should match up or be aligned. In a sense, these notches visually encode the basic sewing instructions into each pattern piece of the garment. This means that skilled sewing operators do not need to be able to read a language to follow instructions. They can follow the general outline of assembly from supervisors' or video demonstrations.

Before the pattern layout is made, there is the assortment problem of determining which apparel sizes should be included in a given marker. Because each roll of cloth has a particular width, grouping different sizes together will result in varying percentages of cloth utilization for each width. For example, if one is laying out a marker of men's pants, there are four large panels for each pair, along with fourteen other small pieces like waistbands and trim.[4] Yet the four panels of a pair of forty-inch waist pants will not fit in the typical sixty-inch-wide bolt of cloth. To achieve the 90 percent cloth utilization typical of this kind of production, one needs to combine six pairs of pants into one marker. An efficient marker will have larger sizes of pants balanced with smaller sizes.

A typical marker for men's pants is shown in Figure 8.1 (page 137). At first glance, it might appear that almost all of the cloth is used in the marker; in fact, only 90 percent has been covered in the layout of 108 individual pieces. Given the basic shapes of the pants pieces, it is unlikely that a substantial increase in marker efficiency can be achieved. At best, experience with different combinations of waist sizes and leg lengths for a given design allows a scheduler to aggregate the units to be made into groups of large and small sizes, which means marker-makers can achieve efficiencies near 90 percent for casual pants. Higher cloth utilization is possible with jeans, but lower levels are normal for blouses, jackets, and intimate apparel (see Figure 8.2).

Making a marker is a complicated task, even with modern computer assistance. Because fabric is generally the most expensive part of finished garments, the skill of the marker-maker is critical for achieving high cloth utilization and lower fabric costs. Marker-making is easier with fewer pieces, but with fewer pieces, overall cloth utilization is generally lower. A typical production pants marker is about 265 inches long and 59.75 inches wide. This marker, over 22 feet long, contains all of the 108 individual pieces of the shell fabric that make up six different pairs of pants. An operator with six months or more of experience with pants markers can take up to ninety minutes to achieve an efficiency of 89 to 90 percent. Manipulation of the arrangement of these pieces, whether on a computer screen or not, is a time-consuming task. It resembles putting a jigsaw puzzle together, except that the cloth pieces do not fit together exactly. The separate pieces can be moved around on a computer screen by the normal drag and drop procedure, but even this involves a complex mixture of trial and error and relies heavily on a marker-maker's experience. A trial marker might leave the right-hand end very uneven, for example, resulting in low utilization when the cloth is cut straight across the bolt in the standard "guillotine" cut. Such a marker would not be acceptable for production. A marker-maker would have to reconstruct the layout to give it the appearance of those in Figures 8.1 and 8.2.

Computer layout systems also improve the quality of the finished apparel by preventing marker-makers from tilting the pieces by more than a predetermined amount, typically three or four degrees. These restrictions ensure that the weave of the cloth is aligned along the length of the garment. After all, stripes should be vertical—a quality feature of the final product determined when the marker is made, not later in the process. Such quality is difficult to achieve with hand layout and manual tracing of the silhouette onto the marker cloth. When the layout is done by hand through tracing on a sheet of paper, there is always a temptation for the operator to tilt a particular piece a bit more, squeezing it into the marker or "shrinking" the silhouette of

Width: 59.75 in.; Length 268.69 in.; Pieces 108; Efficiency 89.66%

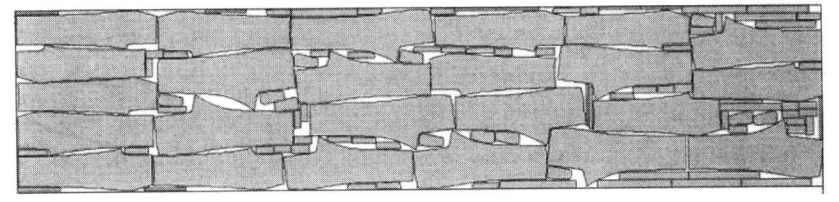

Figure 8.1. Typical Pants Marker
Source: Harvard Center for Textile and Apparel Research.

Width: 52.00 in.; Length 249.12 in.; Pieces 508; Efficiency 81.43%

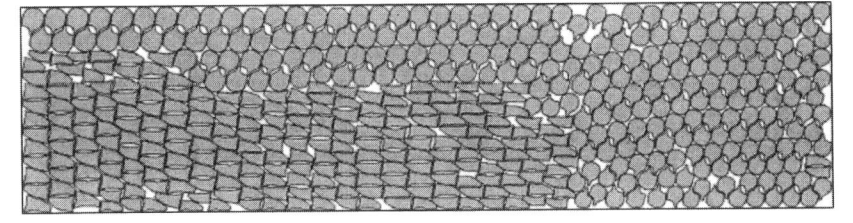

Figure 8.2. Typical Intimate Apparel Marker
Source: Harvard Center for Textile and Apparel Research.

some of the pieces to get them all on the marker. Subcontractors who might do cutting as well as sewing are provided with enough fabric to make the order. Any fabric left after the order is completed is kept by the subcontractor, providing an incentive to "squeeze" the pattern pieces more than a designer might want.

When the computer screen layout is finished, it is automatically printed full-size on paper by large computer-driven printers. The paper marker identifies each piece in the layout so that the cloth pieces for individual apparel items can be put together after the fabric is cut. Computer-assisted marker-making can offer large savings with basic garments, like men's pants or women's intimate apparel, which may be manufactured repeatedly over several years. The same assortment of sizes might be needed many times in a month, and the finished layout can be called up from computer memory and used over and over again, provided the width of the fabric remains the same. There are, however, small variations of fabric width from bolt to bolt, and from one supplier to another. If the cloth runs wide or narrow, an efficient manufacturer would remake the marker to take advantage of the full width. Variation of just a quarter inch in a sixty-inch width can yield a 0.42 percent change in cloth utilization.

Part of HCTAR's research effort has resulted in new automatic marker-making software based on computational geometry techniques. The software allows a manufacturer to take existing production markers and automatically "compact" the arrangement of pieces by translation or a combination of translation and allowable amounts of rotation.[5] It automatically adjusts for changes in fabric width by moving the pieces to the left and up or down to fill the available width most efficiently. The more pieces in a marker, the more effort required to make an efficient marker of a given width. Therefore, if the cloth of a given bolt of fabric is half an inch wider than the marker, there is a tendency to cut the marker as is. Yet some users of this software have been able to decrease the amount of cloth lost in this way by as much as 2 percent.

The pants marker shown in Figure 8.1 was produced by this automatic layout software and yielded cloth utilization of 89.66 percent. The equivalent production marker made by the manufacturer's highly skilled operator, using a computer but without HCTAR's software, achieved a utilization of 89.54 percent, or just a little less than the fully automatic software system. Sometimes a human operator can beat the automatic system by a small amount, but the following example is typical. The production marker for the intimate apparel item in Figure 8.2 was initially laid out by a trained operator with 79.96 percent utilization; the HCTAR software compacted the marker and achieved cloth utilization of 81.54 percent, an improvement of 1.47 percent. One-third of the wholesale price of apparel is typically fabric cost. A 1 percent savings in fabric over the entire production goes directly to the bottom line. Such savings can add up to many millions of dollars for large manufacturers.

Based on our survey results, about two-thirds of the business units in 1992 generated markers by trained operators with computer assistance; when the survey response is weighted by dollars of yearly sales, however, 99.5 percent of the business units' production came from computer-generated markers. In contrast, apparel operations in developing nations generally do not use computerized layout systems. Markers are made by hand, tracing pattern pieces onto sheets of paper from thick, pre-cut cardboard pattern elements. The primary alignment tool is the meter stick for measuring distances from the edge. It is not hard to imagine a tendency to allow a slight twist in individual pieces to achieve a closer fit between neighboring pieces.

There are also stories of subcontractors, in this country as well as overseas, crumpling a marker up so that when it is laid out again it will be just a little smaller in width and length—a trick to save a fraction of a percent from each piece. The savings can add up for the contractor, since the apparel manufacturer that supplied the cloth might not notice. As far as final quality is concerned, however, such arrangements create the wrong incentive—another reason why it may make more sense for U.S.-based manufacturers to control all aspects of preassembly, including marker-making and cutting.

Preassembly: Spreading

Every meter of fabric destined for apparel production is normally inspected by the textile manufacturer. As a part of this inspection and repair, a detailed map is made that locates any remaining defects; the minimum width of the bolt is measured along with the overall length of the unstretched material. After final inspection, the cloth is wound "without tension" on a roll for shipment. But it is actually impossible to wind the fabric onto a roll without leaving some stresses in the cloth. Variations in storage temperature and humidity also cause changes. Indeed, all the residual stresses in the cloth cause problems when it is spread on the manufacturer's "lay" table prior to cutting.

Spreading cloth out on a table in a way that leaves it flat but unstretched, without tension in the cloth, is more difficult than one would think. To get the cloth flat, without mechanical help, two workers could hold the cloth by both ends and stretch it out flat, then release just one end. But the friction between the table and the cloth will leave this layer ("ply") of cloth stretched; just how much will depend on the amount of friction between the two. Putting another ply on top the same way creates an additional problem. The friction between the second ply and the first can create a wrinkle in the first ply. When plies of cloth are piled high—a foot or more is not unusual—there are often wrinkles in the plies after they are cut. This is especially true for knit goods, which are easily stretched and adhere well to neighboring plies in a stack of cloth.

The number of plies of cloth spread at one time depends on the fabric, which, in turn, determines how many are cut at one time. Thirty plies of denim might be cut together, whereas a hundred to three hundred plies of men's dress-shirt fabric might be cut at one time. In contrast, a men's dress suit might be cut from a single ply, or from five or six plies of the same or different material.

Spreading the cloth many plies thick without stressing the cloth is, again, one of the quality steps of getting ready to sew. If the cloth has tension before it is cut, then it will contract after it is cut into separate pattern pieces. Because it is easy to stretch many fabrics by up to an inch in a yard, one can imagine the amount of distortion possible in the final garment. But technical innovations have aided the operators. Stresses in the cloth on the lay table can be minimized with the help of mechanical spreading machines, and such devices come in all sizes and costs. The most elaborate allow an operator to ride the machine, which holds the rolls of cloth, so that it can feed the cloth onto the table at a speed that just matches the speed of the machine as it moves along rails fixed to the table. On-board computers compare the location of cloth defects with pattern pieces in the marker. If the type of defect and its location are deemed unacceptable, then the bolt of cloth is cut and a new ply started with enough overlap to ensure that all pattern pieces are whole and without defects. In our sample, business units used some type of automatic spreading for about 39 percent of the volume of goods they shipped.

Simpler spreading machines have no on-board computer, but they do unroll the bolt of cloth "unstressed" and properly aligned with the edge of the ply below. However spreading is done, it is important for the plies to lie directly on top of each other. Misalignment of the edges can ruin many pattern pieces and the final garments for which they were intended. Once a ply is laid down, it is almost impossible to shift it because of the friction between the plies. With simple spreading machines, the operator must look for fabric defect indicators placed in the selvage by the textile manufacturer.

After the cloth is spread, it is ready for the appropriate marker to be fit on top and fixed to the lay of fabric. Sometimes staples are driven through the paper into the underlying cloth. If the lay is made by hand, then the cloth is generally cut directly by hand-guided electric knives that slice through the cloth on the table. If computer-controlled cutting is used, the lay of cloth is pulled onto the cutting table by an underlying paper sheet. In either case, the pattern pieces can now be cut.

Preassembly: The Cutting Room

Since the early twentieth century, the cost to a manufacturer of a cutter's mistake has been much greater than one committed by a sewing machine operator. Wrong stitching can be pulled out and a seam redone in the sewing room, but a big mistake by a cutter can involve the loss of many yards of cloth—and cloth costs range from one or two dollars a yard for inexpensive fabrics to three hundred dollars for some cashmeres. Even relatively small errors in cutting can degrade the final quality of garments. If the fabric is defect free, the marker efficient, the lay flat and unstressed, then everything else is up to the cutter.[6]

Some magazine advertisements for upscale men's dress suits tout hand-cutting by experienced tailors. Occasionally the ads include a drawing of a man with a large pair of scissors. But cloth is rarely cut this way, even when only one ply is cut at a time. An eight- or twelve-inch pair of scissors is an unwieldy instrument, difficult to guide within the 1/32th of an inch of the pattern outline. It is even harder to accurately cut the notches used by sewing operators to align cut parts.

Most often, an electrically driven vertical reciprocating knife is used to cut the fabric. The vertical knife oscillates less than three-quarters of an inch but can cut cloth plies a foot or more in thickness. The knife and motor are supported above the base plate by a frame. The frame also gives the cutter a place to grip the machine for hand-guided cutting. The base plate is a smooth cap with a slit to contain the moving end of the knife. The knives have built-in sharpeners that run a stone up and down the blade every few minutes. In such a "hand-cutting" operation, the operator guides the knife along the outlines on the paper marker fixed to the fabric lay. One hand holds the marker on the lay, the other guides the electric knife. When a pattern piece is cut from the lay, the cutter then makes the notch cuts indicated on the marker. These slits should be about one-eighth of an inch cut into the three-eighth-inch sewing margin around the pattern. The chances are high of making the slit too deep or forgetting it entirely. Computer-controlled cutting machines, on the other hand, do not forget.

Joseph Gerber solved the major problem in cutting—how to hold the cloth while the knife cuts through the material—by putting the entire lay on a vacuum table. The fabric lay with the marker on top is covered with a thin sheet of clear plastic. When the vacuum pump comes on, five pounds of force per square foot push down on the fabric. The thin plastic sheet effectively cuts off the flow of room air through the fabric. The vacuum holds the cloth firmly and compresses the thickness of the lay, typically by half.

Gerber's automatic-cutting equipment holds the knife on a frame that spans the cutting table and moves back and forth along the table. The location of the knife anywhere on the table can be precisely controlled by a computer, allowing it to cut its way along the silhouette of the patterns. Finally, Gerber's equipment enabled the knife to slice through all the cloth without hitting the top of the vacuum table, supporting the lay of cloth on a brush between the fabric and the inlets to the vacuum table. The stiff bristles of the brush were made of plastic with flat tops, similar in appearance to a flat-headed nail. The flat tops supported the fabric. The plastic bristles were stiff enough to support the fabric layer under the force of vacuum while remaining sufficiently flexible to deflect out of the path of the knife.

The most up-to-date versions of automatic-cutting equipment, including the GERBERcutter, are even more effective. Cloth is cut by having the knife oscillate up and down while it moves along the silhouette of the apparel pieces in the marker. The knife support tilts to keep the blade erect when going along curves. Software can prevent lines from being cut twice; it can control the touchy job of cutting the apex of wedge-shaped pieces by approaching the point from both sides of the wedge rather than attempting to cut around the tip. The vacuum tables have also become "smart." One level of vacuum is maintained over the general lay area; a higher level is arranged under the region being cut to keep the cloth fixed.

Yet despite the obvious advantages of computer-controlled cutting, only a minority of the business units in our survey (21 percent) were using this kind of equipment in 1992. Most continued to use manually guided electric knives to do their cutting, including some of the largest business units in the sample. Manufacturers have told us that hand-cutting with skilled cutters is as accurate as computer-cutting. Small factory operations, without sufficient volume to support two shifts of cutting, claim that they cannot justify the capital cost of computer systems.[7]

Those that do have computer equipment say that the consistency of cutting was their primary reason for purchasing computer-driven cutting systems. The computer cutter does not tire during the day nor forget to cut the notches, and the operator of computer-cutting equipment does not need the skills of a manual operator. As with many new technologies that have developed since the 1970s, adoption of innovative equipment is still occurring in fits and starts and depends on a given firm's size and mix of products. In the case of computer-controlled cutting, however, there appear to be long-term advantages for manufacturers, especially those that produce large runs of basic or fashion-basic products. Apparel producers providing garments with multiple dimensions—for example, men's shirts that are sized according to collar, sleeve length, and often torso length—require much more consistent cutting than suppliers whose apparel is sold only in small, medium, and large sizes.

Knit material, which is easily stretched, poses other challenges for cutting. Tubular knits are often cut in a die-cutting press. With most tube T-shirts, for instance, the die-cutter serves the twin functions of pulling the knit material into the machine and centering it under the die before cutting. The machine then presses the die down on the fabric, cuts through the fabric, and unloads the machine. The centering operation is important because the diameter of a knit tube varies slightly along its length, and it is necessary to reference cutting from the midline of the tube. Some die-cutting operations allow for a number of knit tubes to be centered, placed on one another, and then cut.

Like computer-controlled cutting equipment, large-capacity knit die-cutting presses are expensive machines; they can cost up to $400,000 and are generally found only in factories of the largest producers. The die is a razor-sharp steel outline of the desired item to be cut. Like a cookie cutter, it is pressed down on the fabric and, if all is aligned, a replica of the die is cut from the tube. To change the size of the item to be cut, the die must be removed and a new one installed. The machines are massive in size because they must be rigid to achieve cutting along the entire silhouette. Die-cutters are much safer when fully automated, but building computerized loading and unloading features into the machine adds cost. Therefore, such machines are used only where long production runs of a given size of T-shirt or sweatpants will allow a payback of their capital costs through round-the-clock or multi-shift operations.

One other technical innovation deserves mention here, partly because it illustrates why the most sophisticated equipment is not always appropriate for factory operations. Laser-cutting of fabric remains a little used technique in the United States and abroad. The HCTAR survey indicated 0.6 percent usage among responding business units in 1992 and, if the survey results are weighted by the dollar value of production, then the use drops to only 0.0002 percent. We have seen such equipment working in a production setting in a knit goods manufacturer's facilities; however, we believe that its immediate potential use is limited for several reasons. Laser-cutting equipment must be totally enclosed to be safe for human operators. A high-energy light beam vaporizes a very narrow path around the silhouette of the patterns to be cut. The enclosure contains the vapors and conducts them to an exhaust outlet as well as prevents human access to the cutting region. A laser beam can seriously harm humans, and people may not notice the small-diameter beams of light in an industrial environment.

Twenty or more years ago, when lasers were first used to cut cloth, a mixture of polyester and wool as well as 100-percent polyester cloth was common. Attempts were then made to cut several plies of cloth at the same time. The light beam did cut through the plies, but it melted the polyester fibers at the sides of the burn and fused the edges of the cloth together. No matter what is done, the beam affects the edge of the cut. With the lower-intensity laser beams of the past, the bead of fused material at the edge of the cut formed a rough edge and was unpleasant to touch. Some over-edge sewing operations common with knit goods actually trim the edges of cloth just in front of the needle; in these cases any fused material from the laser cutting could be trimmed away. But, if nothing else, the temperature effects on fabric, combined with the cost of installation, appear to limit the use of this technology to those applications in which the connection between plies before sewing could be an advantage.

The great advantage of laser-cutting is speed. Modern laser-cutters, developed both in this country and Japan, leave the laser fixed in position and move the light beam around simply by computer-controlled tilting of the mirrors that guide the beam along the desired path. With high-powered lasers, the beam can be moved quickly and still cut through the cloth. There may come a day when the demand for single-ply cutting and the economics of continuous laser-cutting will allow this technology to be more cost effective. Until then, it will not be widely used in the garment trade.

Bundling the Parts

When cutting is completed, the pieces are removed in stacks and arranged in bundles for sewing. For many, if not most, applications, each ply in a bundle is marked with a sticker to indicate the actual garment to which the piece belongs. This can be an important step in men's dress-suit assembly. Each suit is ideally made from pattern pieces cut from the same ply of cloth and the same region of material. This is done to avoid cloth matching problems, especially if the shade of the cloth varies along the roll. The point is to make sure that even very slight shade variations will not be apparent in the final assembly. It is also necessary to identify the individual pieces in order to assemble the correct pieces for a garment of a given size. As we have already noted, garments of various sizes are often grouped together on each ply of cloth.[8]

Some stacks of parts are further broken down into smaller bundles of parts so that sewing operators can use the same thread for everything in a bundle. Suits and pants require thread colors that match or blend with the shell fabric, and it is important to reduce the number of thread changes the sewing operator has to make. A work ticket is attached to each bundle of cloth, indicating the garment style, size, and all other necessary parameters. The main tag generally has subtags or tickets that the sewing machine operator collects to indicate that a sewing operation has been completed.[9]

This final preassembly step and those that precede it affect the assembly operations that follow. As we will see in Chapter 9, work processes in the sewing room have been designed to minimize the direct labor content in a garment. To ensure that sewing workers remain busy and operate at high productivity, apparel manufacturers traditionally carry large ready-to-sew cut goods in front of their sewing lines. In 1988, business units carried a median of twenty-four hours (three days worth) of such goods. However, our sample also reveals that some manufacturers began to adjust to the new demands of lean retailing: By 1992, the median dropped to ten hours, reflecting their desire to reduce the amount of work-in-process at this beginning stage of apparel assembly.

Mass Customization

The percentage of the population wearing factory-made apparel has grown steadily since the nineteenth century. Some still rely on custom-made clothing, especially those who have to go this route because of their size and shape or those with the money to afford custom tailoring. Although many might like to have customized clothing, few consider it a realistic option. It is only recently that "mass customization" may make sense for both consumers and apparel-makers.[10]

Mass customization involves a number of preassembly innovations. When somebody orders custom-made clothing, his or her measurements are taken by a fitter in a store and, three to six weeks later, the garment appears. In this case, how was the suit, shirt, pants, or pair of jeans made? Were all the preassembly steps followed or did an individual tailor cut the cloth and make the entire garment? The answers depend on the garment as well as on just how "custom-made" it really was. Regardless of how customization was done in the past, consumers paid more for the end product. Mass customization, however, has the potential to make "tailor fit" at least somewhat less expensive, as new systems combine features of the efficient factory system with attention to at least a few critical customer measurements.

There are two different approaches under way. The first modifies an existing apparel design in a few dimensions to improve its fit for an individual customer. Levi Strauss, which is currently offering custom-fit jeans for women in some stores, provides the best example of this kind of mass customization. Many women have a difficult time finding a pair of jeans that fits to their satisfaction. Buying jeans is based on both style and fit; for many people this means trying on several different brands and finally making compromises. Jeans-makers have tried to satisfy the majority by making many different styles and sizes, but for some customers there still are not enough choices.[11] Fit for a given style involves at least four different measurements. Obviously, waist and hip measurements are important, but where the waist should be also matters and, once that is determined, there is inseam length.[12]

A customer for Levi's custom jeans is asked to try on the style that comes closest to the fit she wants. The store sales associate then takes the four key measurements: waist, hips, where the waist should be, and inseam. These measurements, along with the style of jeans and the type of fabric, are sent to a sewing plant where they are cut, sewn, and then mailed to the customer. Levi's uses proprietary software to make these modifications, but other software systems are commercially available for modifying standard patterns and producing a marker to guide fabric cutting.[13]

The actual making of custom jeans or any other item of custom apparel is slightly more complicated than making an equivalent item under standard production conditions. The pattern pieces for each individual pair of jeans must first be modified. Then a unique marker must be created that combines different orders using the same fabric. Under these conditions, a marker will not be as efficient as the standard production markers shown in Figures 8.1 and 8.2 (page 137) because the amount of cloth that can be saved for a single ply does not justify the time required to reach high levels of cloth utilization. Indeed, fabric-cutting costs are higher for custom clothing than for mass-produced items simply because just one item of apparel is cut at a time.

Mass customization of this sort also means that a single garment must pass through the sewing room at a time. Apparel assembly is described in the next chapter, but for now it is enough to say that all the pieces for a custom garment must be kept together during assembly. If the sewing room is making garments one at a time, it is probably not using the progressive bundle system. Instead, items will be assembled by teams of a few workers, who will do all the assembly operations. Such a short-cycle production system adds to the cost of customized apparel.

You cannot make a completely customized item of apparel with just four measurements. The Levi's process merely adjusts the pattern pieces of a basic style of jeans with these measurements. If a customer wants more areas or features customized, many more measurements are necessary. Achieving consistent measurements presents a major problem because two trained fitters will generally come up with important differences in the body measurements of the same person. No matter how the measurements are taken, most people being measured in this way have a difficult time standing up straight and holding in their stomachs.

The second approach to mass customization attempts to overcome some of these problems by optically scanning the customer with light beams in a private area of the store. In this case, the person needs to be dressed in appropriately tight (form fitting, but not form modifying) athletic shorts and a top. The computer-processed results of such a scan are shown in Figure 8.3 (page 148), with a sample of the extracted body dimensions in inches printed on the right side of the figure. For reference, some of the measurements are highlighted and presented as darkened lines on the processed image.

The optical system that produced this image was developed by [TC]^2 and is now ready for commercial demonstration.[14] This system will probably cost $100,000, and a demonstration in a shopping mall is currently under way. When in place, customers will be scanned at a central location in a mall. They would then take their body measurements to any of several participating retailers, who pass the information on to their apparel suppliers and have the clothing custom-made.

Computer-generated body measurements are just the first, if most important, step in achieving success in fit for customized apparel. The

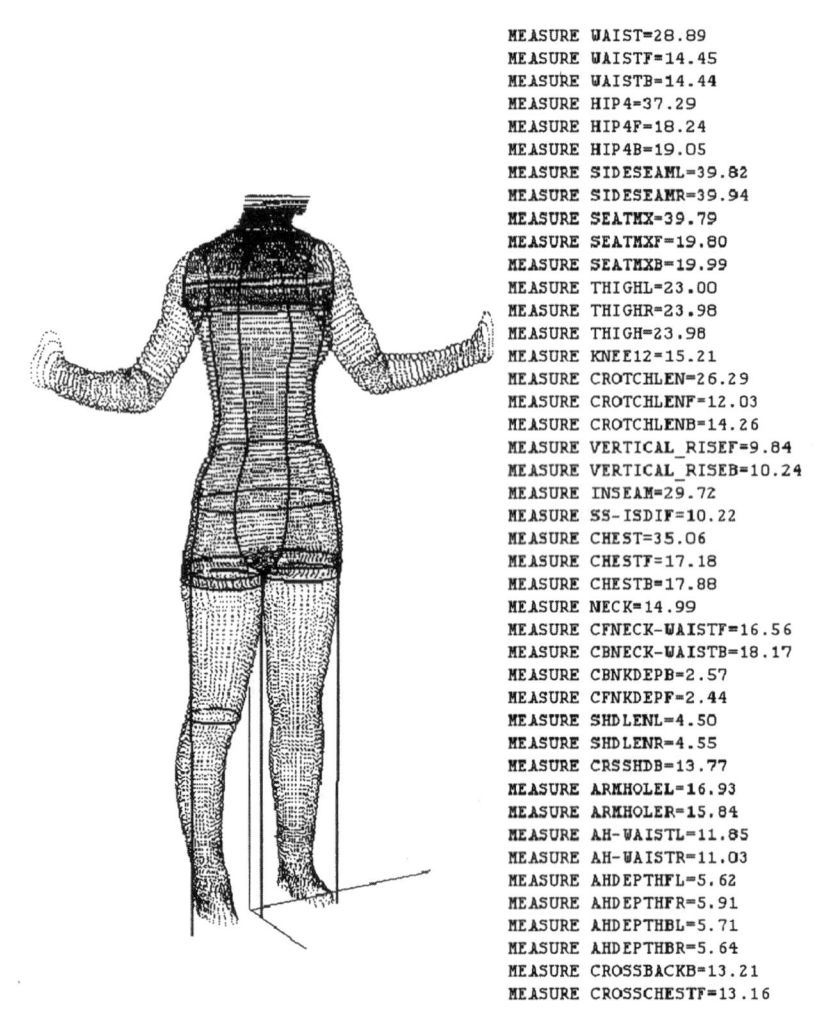

```
MEASURE WAIST=28.89
MEASURE WAISTF=14.45
MEASURE WAISTB=14.44
MEASURE HIP4=37.29
MEASURE HIP4F=18.24
MEASURE HIP4B=19.05
MEASURE SIDESEAML=39.82
MEASURE SIDESEAMR=39.94
MEASURE SEATMX=39.79
MEASURE SEATMXF=19.80
MEASURE SEATMXB=19.99
MEASURE THIGHL=23.00
MEASURE THIGHR=23.98
MEASURE THIGH=23.98
MEASURE KNEE12=15.21
MEASURE CROTCHLEN=26.29
MEASURE CROTCHLENF=12.03
MEASURE CROTCHLENB=14.26
MEASURE VERTICAL_RISEF=9.84
MEASURE VERTICAL_RISEB=10.24
MEASURE INSEAM=29.72
MEASURE SS-ISDIF=10.22
MEASURE CHEST=35.06
MEASURE CHESTF=17.18
MEASURE CHESTB=17.88
MEASURE NECK=14.99
MEASURE CFNECK-WAISTF=16.56
MEASURE CBNECK-WAISTB=18.17
MEASURE CBNKDEPB=2.57
MEASURE CFNKDEPF=2.44
MEASURE SHDLENL=4.50
MEASURE SHDLENR=4.55
MEASURE CRSSHDB=13.77
MEASURE ARMHOLEL=16.93
MEASURE ARMHOLER=15.84
MEASURE AH-WAISTL=11.85
MEASURE AH-WAISTR=11.03
MEASURE AHDEPTHFL=5.62
MEASURE AHDEPTHFR=5.91
MEASURE AHDEPTHBL=5.71
MEASURE AHDEPTHBR=5.64
MEASURE CROSSBACKB=13.21
MEASURE CROSSCHESTF=13.16
```

Figure 8.3. Mass Customization: 3-Dimensional Optical Scan with Derived Measurement

Source: Textile/Clothing Technology Corporation

measurements must still be transmitted to a CAD system that will automatically alter the pattern to conform to specific body measurements. From that point, the pattern must be laid out, cut, and sewn by a group of sewing specialists.

The technology now exists to do mass customization, whether that involves a pair of jeans based on four measurements or a garment custom-made from a whole body scan. Five U.S. firms, including [TC]², offer 3-D scanners, and there are at least two firms with systems that can adjust basic patterns to conform to individual body measurements. Custom clothing may therefore be financially available to a wider audience in the future, opening a new market in which domestic apparel manufacturers can compete. The general public interest in the possibilities of mass customization is evidenced by a recent article in *The New York Times* describing the techniques and reporting that representatives of several apparel firms expressed interest in exploring the public willingness to pay for better fitting clothing.[15]

From Preassembly to Assembly

Mass customization represents an innovative combination of new technologies in information, design, marker-making, and cutting. For the short term, its impact will be on a relatively small niche market. However, lean retailing and product proliferation place much more general pressure on suppliers to decrease time and cost per SKU associated with the design and preassembly steps we have described.

In many American apparel plants, central spreading and cutting rooms abut the area of fabric inventory. Finished goods distribution is often a part of the same complex. Centralization of this kind makes financial sense because trucks that take out cut parts to a firm's sewing rooms or contractors can return with finished goods for inventory. Having spreading, computer-cutting, fusing, and inspection in the same areas also allows teams of cross-trained workers to prepare the order for sewing, finishing, final inspection, and packaging. This is one place in apparel manufacturing where teamwork has been quite successful. In many cases, it has shortened the cycle time from order to ready for sewing by half. In addition, computer-cutting or die-cutting makes the team less dependent on the skill of a manual cutter and allows all team members to operate automated-cutting equipment.

These centralized spreading and cutting facilities generally operate at least two shifts per day and, in some large companies, around the clock. The equipment is capital intensive, especially if computerized or die-cutting machinery is used; therefore, plant managers try to keep these lines producing as much as possible. We have visited a large knit goods manufacturer that combined final fabric finishing operations in the same building with cutting and initial automated sewing, all of which operated around the clock. Although automation of sewing operations is generally not cost effective, these innovations have made some inroads in particular segments. T-shirts, which are consumed in the United States every year by the billions, are a good example. A commercially available machine can automatically make the sleeves of T-shirts. This machine picks up cut material from a carousel at one end and delivers finished sleeves at the other. One operator can tend to the needs of two such machines. Yet because the investment per worker is several hundred thousand dollars, it only makes sense if the equipment is used nearly continuously.

Sewing factories, in contrast, are not capital intensive and are rarely operated for more than one shift. Because of this, most expensive automation equipment is concentrated in preassembly, drawing on multi-shift operations. Marker-making, fusing processes, sleeve-making for T-shirts, die-cutting, and computer-driven knife-cutting fall into this automated "getting ready to sew" category. As always in a world of lean retailing and rapid replenishment, the need for faster production is what drives these capital-intensive technical innovations. Because some U.S. manufacturers have found that centralizing preassembly operations also improves the quality of products, this may provide another edge for American apparel-makers in the future.

Our survey indicates that the average length of time it takes to get a garment ready for sewing, from issuing the order for a given marker to having the pieces cut and otherwise prepared, is 4.9 working days. The cut parts are then sent to sewing areas or other factories. If the sewing room is in the same building as the cutting room, then cut goods are sent over many times a day. If the sewing factory is far away, then a shipment once a week is typical. Reducing the time from placement of the order to cut goods in the sewing room requires decreasing both the time it takes to complete preassembly and the wait for delivery to the sewing room. Indeed, logistical considerations enter assembly well before garments are finally sewn together. Time really is money in today's apparel industry, a theme we will expand on in the next two chapters.

9

Apparel Operations: Assembly and the Sewing Room

Forty years ago, home economics courses in high schools across the country taught cooking, nutrition, and sewing to most schoolgirls. The sewing machine, in its polished wooden cabinet, was an expensive and valued wedding gift. Now the sewing machine, like the typewriter, is fast disappearing. The typewriter is being replaced by the computer, and the home sewing machine has become a small, inexpensive portable unit stored in the closet and used for minor repairs and alterations—if it is used at all. There are many reasons for this shift away from home sewing, including the growing number of women in the labor force. But perhaps the main reason is that production of factory-sewn clothing has become increasingly cost effective. It has taken away a time-consuming and often wearying task from the round of daily chores, providing consumers with a wide array of products and styles at reasonable prices. The popularity of casual-wear items like T-shirts and jeans—quintessentially factory-sewn garments—has also shifted sewing from home to the factory.

The annual number of units of outerwear created in the United States has remained remarkably constant over the last several decades, varying from 12.5 units per capita in 1967 to 13.4 units in 1995,[1] while the number of production workers has continued to drop, from 1,098,200 in 1960 to 664,400 in 1997.[2] This employment decrease is associated with the impact of casual wear, an increase in worker productivity, and the significant import penetration in garments with high labor content. Casual clothing is not only less expensive to purchase and maintain but also requires less labor to assemble.

Whether the apparel item is casual or formal, the stitching in the garment must accomplish one or more of the following objectives.

The primary reason to sew, of course, is to join individual pattern pieces. The second objective is to leave no raw edge of fabric to unravel. This feature is sometimes combined with the joining operation, as in the "felled seaming" on the inseam of jeans or the sleeve seam in men's dress shirts. The felled seam was first used in work clothing because of its strength and has since migrated to other apparel items because of its visible stitch pattern. Decorative stitching is the third objective of sewing. In the felled seams of shirts and jeans, for example, the visible stitches might be of a color designed to decorate the garment.[3] No matter which stitch pattern is being used or which seaming operation carried out, the sewing machine operator must guide one or more pieces of cloth together through the machine. That is the basis of modern sewing operations in manufacturing facilities.

As we have noted throughout, the actual sewing of a garment may take place far away from its design: the translation of that design into a pattern, and the making of a marker of that pattern, which is arranged on layers of fabric for cutting. Consequently, the assembly of that garment often involves sewing together pieces from prearranged bundles sent by the manufacturer. In the contemporary world of contractors, subcontractors, and complicated sourcing decisions, assembly is usually the step in the manufacturing process that is farmed out to lower-cost firms.

Yet just because many U.S. manufacturers rely on foreign contractors for a good portion of garment assembly, it does not mean sewing in a factory requires little or no skill. Only a very few sewing operations involve a machine that is fully automated, in which the operator's job comes down to stacking parts at one end of the sewing system and re-threading the machines if a thread breaks. Today's factory sewing machine is generally dedicated to a single operation and most likely will be fitted with specialized fixtures in the area of the stitch plate—to help guide the seaming a fixed distance from the fabric edge, for example, or fold the edge of the cloth under, or with other attachments that feed elastic tape and so on into the seaming operation as needed. More complicated sewing operations require the operator to guide differential stitching, with more fabric in each top stitch than in the bottom one. Regardless of which individual sewing operations are required, the operator must be trained and given practice time to achieve a quality product, at least at the standard production rates.

The time required for a new worker to achieve production standards, while maintaining quality, can range from days for the simplest operation to nearly a year for joining the sleeve to the body of a suit coat. A few sewing operations are so demanding that some operators are never able to achieve the minimum acceptable production rate for them. With different skill levels required for different operations, it is not surprising that piece rates vary with the difficulty of the operation. In this chapter, we will describe what actually goes on in today's sewing room—the machines used, what operators do, the flow of operations—and how sourcing decisions for replenishable products may affect assembly operations in the future.[4]

Sewing Machines and Garment Assembly

There are two major types of sewing machines used in garment assembly: the lockstitch and the chain-stitch machine. Each type feeds in separate threads above and below the fabric, and these two threads must be connected in some fashion to form a stitch. Both have one top thread for each needle above the seam and one or more different threads on the bottom below the surface of the sewing table. The primary difference between these sewing machines is in the way the two threads interact.

The Lockstitch Machine

Almost all home machines are lockstitch machines. The top thread comes from a spool or cone of thread above the machine and goes through many thread guides, a thread tensioner, a take-up arm, and, finally, the needle. The bottom thread is wound on a bobbin, a small spool, that is below the needle and the sewing surface. To make a stitch, the needle with the top thread is plunged through the plies of fabric, and a loop of the top thread is formed below the surface of the stitch plate (often called a "throat plate").[5] The loop of top thread is passed over the bobbin and around its thread. The take-up arm then pulls up the top thread to set a stitch. The top and bottom threads are locked together by passing the loop of the top thread around the bobbin.

One part of the art of sewing comes in adjusting the thread tension.[6] With a lockstitch machine, when the needle withdraws from the cloth and the take-up arm pulls the top thread tight, the stitch begins to be "locked" or set in place. If the tension on the top and bottom thread is too high, the seam puckers and the seam length becomes less than that of the cloth. If the tension is too low, the seam will be so loose one can see through it when holding up the joined pattern pieces. Indeed, a well-formed lockstitch is smooth and appears the same when viewed from either the top or bottom ply. Note that even if a sewing machine is properly adjusted for sewing a particular weight and color of fabric, it will generally need to be adjusted again if the fabric color changes because the mechanical properties of a given type of fabric can depend on the dye color used. The lighter the fabric weight, the more sensitive seam quality is to machine adjustments and thread tensions as well as to the ability of sewing operators to make necessary adjustments.

In a factory setting, lockstitch machines are used for the decorative stitching that is necessary whenever the undersurface of a garment piece will be seen during normal wear, such as in the collar and cuffs of a dress shirt. The primary disadvantage of this kind of machine is that the bobbin must be small enough so that it can pass through the top thread loop, but it then quickly empties of thread. When this happens, sewing must be stopped and a newly loaded bobbin inserted to replace the empty one. Since the bobbin is reached by sliding back the stitch plate, if a bobbin runs out in the middle of an operation, it might be necessary to rip the seam out from the beginning and start over. Therefore, sewing operators generally keep track of the number of items sewn on a bobbin and stop before the thread runs out. If it were not for the limited thread capacity of the bobbin and the need for the operator to wind thread onto the bobbin, the lockstitch would be more widely used in factory assembly operations.

While men's dress shirts are normally sewn with white thread, regardless of the fabric color, most apparel items use a thread color to match or contrast in a decorative way with the cloth. This means that after sewing a bundle of items of one color, an operator must not only change the needle thread but also put in a new bobbin for each new color of fabric. If an operator has a choice of thread color for the next lot to be sewn, she will always choose the color of the last bundle. Changing the type of fabric, even if the thread color is the same, generally demands adjustment of the thread tensions and other parts of the machine. Long production runs of the same basic item of apparel, with the same fabric, allow sewing operators to make major machine settings once a day, with only a few additional adjustments required throughout the shift.

The Chain-Stitch Machine

This machine overcomes the bobbin thread limitation and can operate at higher speeds, but it does have disadvantages. In this case, there is no bobbin. Below the sewing surface, the lower thread is manipulated by a mechanical arm called a looper. The looper inserts a loop of the bottom thread into a loop of the top thread that is created when the needle pierces through the fabric plies and begins to withdraw from the cloth. The top thread is then pulled up by the take-up arm. The top thread cannot be pulled through the cloth because it is held below the fabric by the inserted loop of the bottom thread. The bottom thread is formed into a continuous sequence of very small loops by the looper arm. Although the top and bottom threads are not interlocked, as in the lockstitch machine, the stitch is fixed in place and the seam has a bit more flexibility.

Because the bottom thread does not have to be encircled by the top thread, the bottom thread can come from a large cone stored above the machine. A new cone of looper thread contains miles of thread and generally does not have to be replaced more frequently than a few times during a shift. The operator can glance up at the cones of both top and bottom threads and replace them before they run out in the middle of a seam. The disadvantage of this kind of machine is that it makes seams that are not as secure as the lockstitch; in addition, the appearance of the seam from the top and bottom of the fabric is different. If a stitch is skipped—the looper thread is not inserted or may not get caught in the loop of the top thread—then the resulting thread loop could pull the seam out if it were to catch on something. Factory inspectors look for such flaws, but they are hard to find because they end up on the inside of a garment.

Nevertheless, the advantages of the chain-stitch machine far outweigh its disadvantages. A chain-stitch seam is strong and can be produced more quickly than a lockstitch seam. Most of the long seams in factory-sewn apparel are made with a chain-stitch machine or with variations of it. The felled seam commonly used for the inseam of jeans comes from a two-needle chain-stitch machine. Such stitching generally outlasts the fabric of jeans, as one can see from looking at the holey knees of jeans worn by many teenagers.

Other Sewing Machines

A wide variety of specialized sewing machines are also used in factories. There are machines with multiple needles and loopers that attach elastic waistbands to boxer shorts, for example. Knit fleece goods are commonly joined by a seaming operation called over-edging in the factory (and overlocking sewing in home use). The over-edge or overlocking machine automatically aligns the fabric by trimming off the edges of the plies to be joined just before the stitch is made. At least one thread wraps around the edge of the fabric during the stitching process. There are one-, two-, three-, four-, and five-thread overlocking or over-edging machines, each one designed to meet a given requirement of seam, strength, flexibility, and security. Over-edge machines can run at more than 8,000 stitches a minute. At eight or ten stitches an inch, it is possible to seam thirteen to sixteen or more inches a second. In the factory, however, a sewing machine's maximum speed is generally not what limits production; it is the time it takes to set up the work on the machine and guide the fabric to the needle as the seam is being made.

What the Sewing Operator Does

In a typical apparel factory, a sewing operator is actually sewing only one-quarter of the time. The operator must first select the work to be done, put aside the tickets that indicate she performed the sewing appropriate for those bundles and should be paid at the specified rate for the job, open the appropriate bundles, and position the pieces to be joined on the sewing table in preparation for sewing.[7]

If the sewing machine is correctly threaded, the operator then lifts the presser foot—a device that comes down on either side of the needle to hold the cloth—and, if the needle is in the up position, inserts the fabric. Otherwise, the operator turns the machine wheel to get the needle in the up position, lowers the presser foot, sews the beginning of the seam, backstitches to lock the seam, grabs the two plies of cloth near where the seam will end, and guides the cloth through the sewing machine. Usually, she will backstitch at the seam end, then cut the thread. Some machines have an automatic thread-trimmer to do this step; if not, then the threads must be cut and the finished work put in an appropriate pile to be tied together when all the pieces of the bundle have been finished.[8]

Machine-tending, material placement, and off-loading operations are all considered part of a sewing operator's job. Although none of these operations actually involves sewing, they do take time to complete and are taken into account when determining the piece rate and normal workload for an operation. If a new sewing table or a new sewing machine with programmable features is added at a particular workstation—that is, any device that reduces the time it takes to complete various tasks—then the allowable time and wage rate for that operation must be changed.

These issues aside, there is one other major task a sewing operator performs. She must make the pieces of the pattern fit together at the end of the sewing process. This is certainly not possible if there has been a big mistake in cutting, but it is never easy, even without serious cutting errors. If two plies of flat cloth of identical length are placed on top of each other and sewn together, then the ends of the two pieces will not line up without the intervention of a sewing operator. The two ends of a thirty-inch leg seam on a pair of jeans, for instance, might be a quarter of an inch out of alignment unless the operator takes control. During sewing, the feed-dog on the machine—a part that comes up through two slots in the stitch plate and engages the bottom ply of cloth—will pull the bottom ply under the presser foot and against the pull of the thread. The top ply of cloth is carried along by the bottom ply; hence, one ply is stretched more than the other.

This simple fact of sewing makes it very difficult to automate the process. In reality, the two seam lines to be joined are rarely exactly the same length. Cutting introduces differences from the top to the bottom of the layers of fabric. No matter how good spreaders and cutters are, preassembly operations are never perfect. The sewing operator must overcome all these prior minor variations, as well as the differences introduced by the sewing process, and make the joining seam come out even at the end. She accomplishes this magic by stretching the two plies differently. First, the plies are stretched to get the pattern notches in the two to align; then the ends are pulled together, causing them to align. The operator uses the elasticity of the cloth to overcome minor errors in cutting and prior sewing. Indeed, most trained sewing operators see this defect correction simply as part of their job.

The Sewing Room

The vast majority of workers in the apparel industry are involved in assembly. This is illustrated in Table 9.1 (page 158) for the men's and boys' shirt industry. In 1990, 73 percent of all workers in this industry were classified as working in the sewing department; 91 percent were sewing machine operators. Given the predominant share of workers in assembly, organization of work in the sewing room has been the central focus of management attention.

The sewing rooms of most apparel factories are similar in overall appearance. Apparel parts, trim pieces, buttons, zippers, and thread arrive at one end of the room and are separated for each operation, or subassembly. As the last chapter noted, large apparel firms usually operate a central cutting room that provides cut parts to an average of five sewing plants.[9] About two-thirds of the production volume of our

Table 9.1. Occupational Breakdown, Men's and Boys' Shirts, 1990

Department Occupation	Number of Workers	Occupation as Percent of Department	Occupation as Percent of All Workers
Cutting Room			
Assemblers	687	31.5%	1.9%
Cutters	662	30.4	1.8
Markers	172	7.9	.4
Spreaders	501	23.0	1.4
Total[a]	2,175	100.0	5.9
Sewing Department			
Collar pointers/trim	333	1.2	.9
Inspectors	427	1.6	1.2
Loaders	1,402	5.1	3.8
Sewing-machine operators	24,953	91.4	67.1
Underpresser	188	.7	.5
Total	27,303	100.0	73.5
Finishing Department			
Baggers and boxers	911	17.4	2.5
Folders, garment	1,350	25.7	3.6
Garment repairers	448	8.5	1.2
Inspectors, final (& thread trimmers)	1,590	30.3	4.3
Pressers, finish	735	14.0	2.0
Total[a]	5,245	100.0	14.1
Miscellaneous Occupations			
Janitors	450	18.3	1.2
Sewing Machine repairers	601	24.4	1.6
Shipping and stock	409	16.6	1.1
Work distributors	1,003	40.7	2.7
Total, Misc.	2,463	100.0	6.6
Total, All	37,186	—	100.0

Source: U.S. Department of Labor, Bureau of Labor Statistics, *Industry Wage Survey: Men's and Boys' Shirts, September 1990*, Bulletin 2405, September 1990. Washington, D.C.: U.S. Department of Labor, April 1992, pp. 14–15.

[a] Several additional small occupational groups are included in this total but not listed individually, due to the small number of workers in these categories

surveyed business units did their marker-making, spreading, and cutting in a single location. Most would deliver cut goods to sewing plants many times a week; however, when cutting is done hundreds of miles from the sewing plants, weekly deliveries are the norm. Trucks take fresh parts to the plants and return with finished goods for the distribution center.

Sewing rooms are generally arranged in rows of workers, each seated at a machine doing one operation on a bundle of parts. Traditionally, the progressive bundle system assumed that maximum worker productivity could be achieved by breaking down the steps of assembly into a series of discrete operations. Each sewing operator would be trained in the correct approach to one specific task. Through repetition of the task and coaching by experts, the operator would become very productive. Although new work practices are evolving in the apparel industry, many workers still specialize in one operation or at most two. In fact, long product runs in men's and unisex product lines, such as jeans, have made U.S. sewing operators extremely efficient.

Workers in most plants are paid on a piece-rate basis—that is, they are paid a fixed amount for each seam sewn correctly. If a part must be reworked, it is done on the operator's own time. This incentive system means that each operator needs to have work-in-process waiting; if there is a machine breakdown or no work waiting, then the operator will be paid at some average earnings rate during the waiting period. But to avoid this, there is always work waiting; for example, in a men's dress-shirt factory there can be a day's worth at each sewing station. On the sewing room floor, there are generally piles of items ready to be sewn or moved to the next assembly step. The time it takes for a given item of apparel to pass through a plant is determined by the average hours of work-in-process before each operation and the total number of operations along the critical path.

Work Flow in a Plant

The flow of operations through a typical men's dress-shirt sewing factory is shown in Figure 9.1 (page 160). The subassemblies for the collars, backs, fronts, cuffs, and sleeves might be on one side of a center aisle down the factory floor and the major assembly steps on the other side. The factory manager needs to keep track of the flow of items through the plant to assure that the subassemblies, such as the sleeves, are ready to join the shirt. A given shirt must have a specified collar size and a given sleeve length. Clearly, the fabric, color, and style must also

FLOW CHART CURRENT TECHNOLOGY
MEN'S DRESS SHIRT, SINGLE NEEDLE CONSTRUCTION

CUTTING

COLLAR | BACK | FRONTS | CUFFS | SLEEVES

- BUILD UP LINING
- FUSE STAY
- RUN TOP
- TURN AND PRESS
- TOP STITCH
- FUSE HANG. LABEL
- CREASE BANDS
- INSERT TOP
- TRIM THREADS
- HEAT SET
- BUTTONHOLE BAND END
- BUTTONHOLE SEW BAND END

BACK: FUSE LABEL — TACK SIZE LABEL — YOKING

FRONTS: UNDER FR. HEM — BUTTON SEW — CENTER PLAIT — BUTTON HOLE — HEMPOCKET — TURN AND TOP STITCH — ATTACH POCKET — BUTTON HOLE — BUTTON SEW

CUFFS: HEM CUFFS — RUN CUFFS

SLEEVES: RUN ON BINDING — BOX TACK PLACKET

ASSEMBLY:
- JOIN SHOULDERS
- ATTACH COLLAR
- RUN ON SLEEVES
- ST. DOWN SLEEVES
- FOLDER FELL
- ATTACH CUFFS
- HEM BOTTOM

TYPICAL SHIRT:
ALL OPERATIONS: 40
TOTAL SAM: 12.00
CRITICAL PATH OPERATION: 20
CRITICAL PATH SAM: 9.00

PACKAGING: LABEL/BOX — BODY PRESS — BUTTON AND FOLD — EXAMINE AFT. FOLD — BAG AND BOX → TO DISTRIBUTION CENTER

CRITICAL PATH

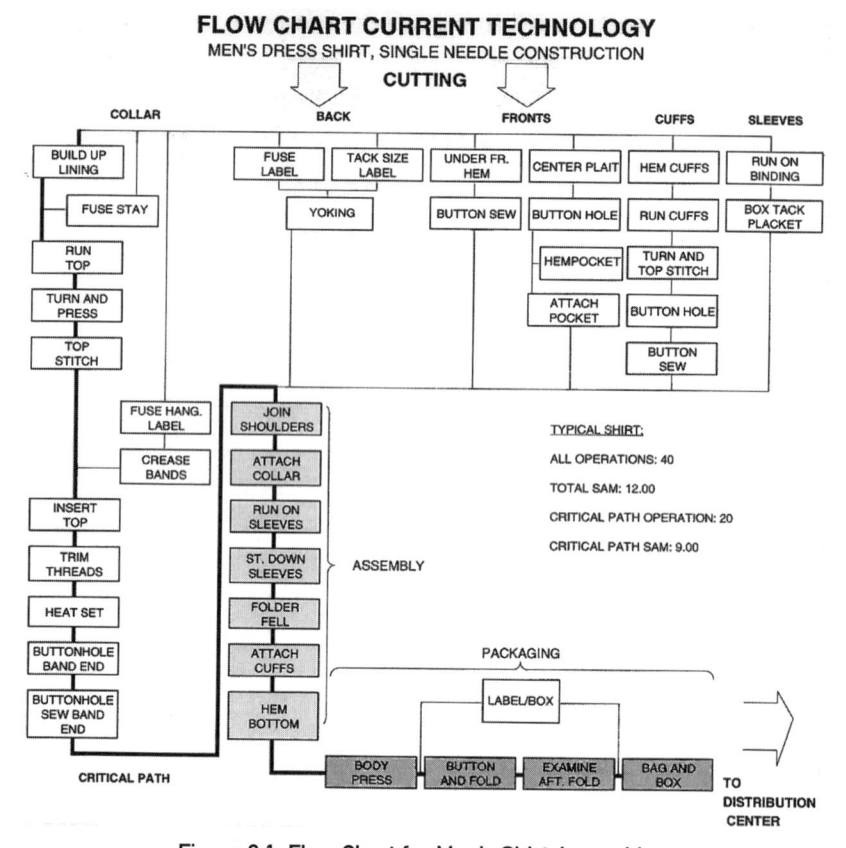

Figure 9.1 Flow Chart for Men's Shirt Assembly

Source: Adapted from Schramyr, Ernst, "Jets-in-time: 13 Operation Can Go," *Bobbin Magazine,* May 1987. Reprinted with permission from *Bobbin® Magazine,* May, 1987. Copyright © Miller Freeman Inc.–Bobbin Publishing Group. All rights reserved.

match. If the cut bundles are sent to the factory once a week, this manager might then put that week's bundles into carts identified by a flag flying the color for that week. Note that the work in a shirt plant is generally grouped into production lots of 1,500 shirts if the progressive bundle system is used. Shirts are normally counted by the dozen, so a production lot comes to 125 dozen.

Each day, the manager looks over the factory floor to see if any carts with a particular flag color are falling behind the others of that group. Delays in product flow can result from machine problems, worker absence, or if priority is given to special orders. In some plants, the carts may contain up to a day's worth of work. Although this may appear to be a crude way of keeping track of the work flow, it is simple and generally effective. Still, work almost never progresses in perfect lockstep through a factory. Finding the correct parts for a shirt can often involve a hunt through the plant. For example, a worker might accidentally leave a bundle of unfinished work in the cart when it goes back to be loaded again. Because a worker may have a day's work in the carts in front of her, it is easy to see how individual bundles of parts can be misplaced—which, in turn, will hold up the assembly of some SKUs. Partially finished shirts and shirt subassemblies will then be in a number of places in the factory.

This shirt factory employs 250 workers. If the shirt in question is rated to require twelve minutes to assemble, such as the one in the figure, a forty-hour work week will produce 4,167 dozen shirts when the factory is operating at standard efficiency. (Of course, many plants may fall below the standard and take longer than twelve minutes to make that shirt.)[10] A typical time for a shirt to go through the plant is four weeks, which means the plant will have 16,667 dozen shirts as work-in-process (WIP). The forty operations indicated in the figure may require only twelve minutes if the operators are working at 100 percent efficiency, but any given shirt still takes twenty working days to pass through the plant. To shorten the time significantly, the work-in-process in front of each of the twenty operations listed as part of the critical path would have to be reduced from a day to just several hours. Not all the forty different operations are sequential; the parts assembly goes on in parallel, but the final assembly involves a series of eleven operations that require all the subassemblies to be completed and ready to be mated with the correct parts.

Needless to say, reduction of throughput time is not a simple task. Some of the forty operations require very little time; others are much longer. Hemming the top of a shirt pocket is a short operation, for example, but it takes longer to attach the pocket and longer still if stripes must be matched. If there is one operator for the short operation, then there will have to be several operators for the longer one just to keep the production line in balance. If any one of the several operators speeds up or slows down, the line becomes unbalanced. If the imbalance lasts for more than an hour or so, the factory manager would have to take corrective action. A utility operator skilled in several operations might be brought over from another area to move work past the slow sewing station. Clearly, it is easier for the manager to keep all operators supplied with work, especially since in most cases the work-in-process for each operator is large. The large buffers are designed so that natural daily variations in work rhythm do not cause a major disruption. In fact, a production line is probably never in perfect balance. If it were, when even one worker in the plant changed her pace, the line would drift out of balance.

As work progresses through a typical sewing plant, it is also common for a special order to disrupt the flow. Even if the special order does not require a thread change, as with most dress shirts, someone will have to move the order to the front of the queue at each sewing station and combine the parts for final assembly.

We have visited a top-of-the-line men's suit plant in Sweden where a special order would go through the plant in four working days, rather than the normal six weeks, just by allowing the work to go to the head of the work buffer at each sewing station. In this suit plant, work was moved from one station to the next by a Unit Production System (UPS). A UPS is a mechanical overhead transport system that moves a unit of clothing from one work station to the next. The mechanical device generally carries all parts of the finished garment. After a sewing operator finishes one step, the carrier is sent on its way to the next. There is a finite mechanical buffer area before each operator; when the buffer fills, the next unit is automatically sent to another operator who does the same operation.

With a UPS delivery system, factory throughput time can be dramatically reduced. But the cost required to install such a system is steep, running to $4,000 or more per workstation. The high cost and lack of production-floor flexibility after the mechanical conveyers are installed have limited the number of factories adopting these systems. In 1992, only 3.5 percent of the output of our surveyed business units was assembled using UPS. A competing approach to reducing plant throughput time involves team-based sewing or modular production, which we will discuss at length in the next chapter. In that case, groups of sewing operators are trained in more than one assembly operation. Workers move from one sewing station to another, guiding the work-in-process through the plant.

The assembly of most items of apparel follows the work flow sketched here. Subassemblies are manufactured in small lines and join the critical path at the appropriate point. But while a T-shirt, for example, might include sleeves made in the cutting room, its collar might be inserted, the sleeves attached, and the garment finished in a sewing room far removed from the cutting room. A suit manufacturer might cut the cloth for the suit in one plant, ship the coat parts to another, and ship the pants parts to yet another plant in another state. Eventually, regardless of where particular operations are carried out, the finished garments return to a central distribution center to be shipped to customers. In the case of the suit manufacturer with plants in different locations, each individual suit is made from shell fabric cut from the same roll and generally the same ply of cloth on the lay table. Matching the coats, pants, and vests is carried out in a special section of the distribution center. The items are then stored in a way that makes them easy to pick for an order about to be shipped.

The Costs of Assembly

The investment per worker in a sewing room is quite modest. A simple new commercial sewing machine may cost $2,000 to $3,000, but a rebuilt machine can run as low as five hundred dollars and still provide a good dozen years of production. The average annual capital investment in sewing machines and attachments per operator in our survey was $720 (in 1992 dollars). Some of the machines in an American men's dress-shirt plant like the one previously described will cost $20,000 or more, but such automated sewing systems are rare. As we have already noted, the general requirement for return on investment forces expensive capital equipment to be operated under more than single-shift conditions, unless it is essential to produce a given item. The automated sewing systems that create the closely spaced regular stitch patterns used as decorative top stitching on men's dress shirts, collars, cuffs, and pockets are examples of expensive machines operated for a single shift.

Because assembly operations are driven more by labor costs than capital-intensive equipment, a typical American sewing factory operates just a single shift a day, with an average of about thirty-seven hours of work per week.[11] On the men's side of the industry, factories of up to several hundred workers are common, but smaller loft shops are typical for women's apparel. Factories are located where the workforce lives. And the infrastructure needed to support a sewing room is relatively modest. Power in the form of electricity, water—especially if items like jeans are to be washed—and a phone are about all that is required. In some developing countries, workers are brought to the factories, which are generally located at the outer reaches of the local industrial infrastructure. These workers often live in dormitories on the factory compound for a period of a year before returning to their villages or moving into the city. Similar worker dormitory arrangements were part of the men's suit industry in Japan as recently as fifteen years ago.

Apparel Assembly and the Demands of Rapid Replenishment

The traditional system of apparel assembly was designed to minimize the direct labor costs of assembly, not production throughput time. The progressive bundle system, with up to a day's WIP waiting for each sewing operator was an efficient way of operating when the costs of carrying mountains of WIP did not enter into production costs. Generally, under this system of apparel assembly all production was made to fill an actual order. The risk of inventory was carried by the retailer who placed the order, so apparel operators carried large WIP (in 1988 for our sample an average of 3.65 weeks worth).

But under rapid replenishment arrangements, the inventory risk is now assumed by the apparel manufacturer; consequently assembly time is now very important. As shown in the cases studied in Chapter 7, production-cycle time and inventory carrying costs are two crucial parameters in making rapid replenishment sourcing decisions. When the assembly cycle time is reduced, both the WIP and finished goods inventory levels necessary to meet a given rapid replenishment demand go down.

The possibility of mass customization for some apparel items presents another market opportunity that demands short-cycle production. If a retail customer pays a premium for a custom pair of jeans, dress shirt, or suit, that customer will expect the item to be delivered to her home within days, not weeks or months. We are a nation of last-minute shoppers, and mass customization will have to compete against overnight delivery of apparel items with less than perfect fit from a specialty catalog company. Speed of delivery has increasingly become part of the competitive equation.

There are a number of ways to organize apparel assembly to minimize cycle time. One way is to use a UPS assembly process. Another involves reorganizing the workers themselves through a team of sewing operators responsible for the entire critical path of assembly. In this case, sewing operators achieve production-line balance by moving from one workstation to another advancing the work smoothly through the line. As in life, there are few if any absolutes in methods of apparel assembly. Each method of organizing production has advantages and problems associated with it. Chapter 10 takes up these issues in detail.

10

Human Resources in Apparel

Throughout the early 1990s, a major American shirtmaker faced steady erosion of its markets and profits. Like many other apparel manufacturers in the 1970s and 1980s, the company had sought to improve its competitive performance by reducing the direct labor content of its shirts. Specifically, it had perfected its system of apparel assembly to minimize the labor content in each step of the assembly process, but that left little room for further productivity improvements when the company faced a new crisis. For one thing, the small size of this shirt manufacturer compared with its textile suppliers meant it did not have the necessary clout to reduce the costs of materials; for another, the growing power of its retail customers, combined with the presence of offshore competitors, provided almost no leeway in terms of the prices it charged for products. To reduce the time it took to produce a specific item, the company turned to team-based assembly, but this also proved costly and time consuming. The shirtmaker confronted the very real possibility of bankruptcy.

In fact, this manufacturer was not alone. Over the past decade, many apparel-makers have tried to address competitive problems by focusing on the aspect of production over which they exercise the greatest control: the people who work for them. As we emphasized in Chapter 2, this focus served apparel manufacturers well in the first half of the century, leading to the creation of an extremely efficient assembly process, particularly in the men's sector—the progressive bundle system (PBS). Yet the advent of lean retailing has not only changed the nature of competition in the apparel industry but also reshaped human resource practices in the 1990s.

In order to explore the impact of lean retailing and the information-integrated channel, the first section of this chapter revisits traditional human resource practices in the sewing room. Later sections describe team-based assembly systems, or modular production, and assess their patterns of adoption in the 1980s and 1990s. We compare the impact of traditional and team-based systems on apparel manufacturer performance, relating this performance to the larger changes arising in retail-apparel-textile channels, then conclude with a description of Levi Strauss's innovative partnership with UNITE!, the major apparel union. Although the situation of our shirtmaker sounds dire, new work practices can affect a company's profitability—as long as they are linked to other technological innovations such as bar codes and information-sharing.

Increasing Productivity in the Traditional Sewing Room

Traditional manufacturers survived in the price-driven markets surrounding the apparel industry by keeping unit costs as low as possible. For an apparel-maker, the majority of input costs are still composed of materials and labor. In 1995, for example, 50 percent of the value of shipments for men's shirts was composed of cost of materials, while 25 percent arose from compensation costs.[1] Although some apparel manufacturers place orders large enough to exert pressure on suppliers to lower fabric costs, much of the industry does not have that influence. But even small sewing shops have some control over what they pay workers. Finding methods to reduce labor costs has driven much of human resource policy in apparel, including cooperating with union leaders in both the men's and women's industry to promote methods of "scientific management," industrial engineering, and labor-cost standardization.

In the traditional sewing room, productivity enhancements are achieved by improving the performance of the bundle system, which can be done in a number of ways. Productivity can be increased by reducing the amount of time required per operation. Such improvements historically came from time-motion studies, undertaken in the unionized segments of the industry by the garment-worker unions' efficiency and engineering experts. Improvements also arise from shortcuts introduced by individual workers. In addition, the skill level of operators can be increased via informal and/or formal training or by bringing new workers "up to speed" more rapidly through new training methods in an industry with high turnover.[2] The rate structure can also change to increase the incentives for attaining or exceeding the production rate associated with the standard allocated minute (SAM) standard. Moreover, frequent style changes, particularly in the women's branch, provide regular opportunities to review and set piece rates.

Since its beginnings in the 1930s, refinement of PBS led to an increasing pace of work. Consequently, labor productivity has grown steadily in terms of direct labor content per assembled apparel product. Given average hourly earnings in 1995, the dollar value of direct labor content in a typical shirt was about $2.16, for pants $2.88, and for a T-shirt $.19. Even the most complex garment among men's collections—suits—involved only about $14.18 of direct labor content.[3] Productivity in specific apparel segments measured as constant-dollar value of output per employee hour rose steadily over the past quarter-century. In men's and boys' suits and coats, for example, output per employee hour increased 60.7 percent in the period 1973 to 1995, or 2.8 percent a year.[4]

One major consequence of PBS is its dependence on buffers between assembly operations to minimize downtime for workers. The point is to keep everyone in the sewing room occupied—always a challenge for apparel-makers because of uneven assembly time requirements for different operations. Standard practice is a one-day buffer between operations. The target buffers between different steps vary within an assembly line in order to achieve overall line balance. As we made clear in the last chapter, a large amount of in-process inventory can be created for an individual garment. Take a pair of pants, which involves roughly forty operations. Under PBS, this pair of pants may require *forty days* or more to move from cut pieces to final product. The need to create large buffers to minimize direct labor content leads to dramatic differences between the total time directly required to sew a garment—the total SAMs—and the plant throughput time for a given garment. As Table 10.1 (page 168) indicates, while SAMs are measured in minutes, throughput times for the same items are measured in days or, in some cases, months.

Given the increasing demands of lean retailing and rapid-replenishment arrangements, the fact that it can take one pair of pants over a month to get through a plant is anything but ideal. Yet the bundle system presents impediments to large-scale modifications of the sewing room. Although changing capital investments could theoretically enhance labor productivity, this option is limited by the need to bal-

Table 10.1. SAMs Versus Throughput Times for Selected Apparel Products

Apparel Product	SAM per Unit[a] (Minutes)	Throughput Time[b] (Days)
Tailored suit	105	30–40
Tailored shirt	18	20–25
Separate trousers	24	15–25
Knit pants	3	5–10
T-shirt	1.5	5–8

Source: Harvard Center for Textile and Apparel Research survey (see Appendix B).
[a] Based on estimates of average industry SAMs, collected by HCTAR.
[b] Throughput defined as elapsed time between receipt of cut textiles by sewing room to shipment to manufacturer's distribution center. Estimates collected by HCTAR.

ance the assembly line as a whole. Introducing changes at any step of the process will unbalance the system as it stands, slowing the introduction of technological innovations. Such changes may also involve shifting ownership of the production process itself, particularly at the sewing stage, by breaking up assembly into the work of multiple subcontractors.[5]

Team-Based Assembly and Its Initial Challenges

Throughout the 1980s, a number of alternative assembly systems were heralded by the trade press, the American Apparel Manufacturers Association, major fiber and textile producers, and the labor union UNITE!. The most prominent among those alternative systems is team-based, modular production.

Modular production is based on a fundamentally different notion from bundle assembly. Instead of breaking sewing and assembly into a long series of small steps, modular production entails grouping tasks, such as the entire assembly of a collar, and assigning that task to members of a "module," or a team of workers. Such a team, ranging from five to thirty operators, works together to produce part, or in some cases all, of a garment. In our HCTAR sample, 81 percent of the business units that had implemented modular assembly in 1992 indicated that at least some modules are used in assembling an entire product. Although most operators in the team still spend the majority of their time on a single assembly task, they are cross-trained and move to other tasks if work builds up at another step in the process. Compensation is primarily determined by the module's output, and these teams are partially self-directed. In most cases, operators decide on task assignments, pace, and output targets based in part on the incentives provided by the group compensation system.[6]

Modular production has been heralded by some advocates as the answer to a number of persistent problems facing the industry. Because more interesting work may attract a more stable and dedicated workforce, a number of commentators have argued that modular assembly may be a cure for labor shortage problems in urban areas. In a similar vein, other advocates have cited its positive impact on absenteeism and motivation.[7] Yet another group of proponents, including textile and fiber suppliers, claim that modular manufacturing is key to the long-run survival of U.S. apparel firms. By using multi-skilled team production, the argument goes, modular systems can dramatically decrease the time required for a garment to move from fabric to a packaged product for shipment. Such a manufacturer can be far more responsive to changing customer demands than those locked into a bundle system with long throughput times. This may further enhance an inherent advantage U.S.-based firms have—their proximity to American retailers.

Focusing production at the group level means that modular assembly lines rely on far smaller buffers between sewing steps than under PBS. Because sewing operators are compensated at the group level, production activities are geared toward completing the entire sequence of steps delegated to the team, which creates a disincentive for accumulating work-in-process. Indeed, if mass customization ever becomes a competitive option, the assembly process would change even more; a mass customizer might be willing to incur higher labor costs to decrease throughput times.

Regardless of what the future holds, modular systems entail considerable modification of the human resource practices associated with PBS. The differences in human resource practices for the two methods of assembly can be compared in Tables 10.2 and 10.3 (pages 170, 171). By breaking down assembly into discrete operations undertaken by individual operators, PBS relies solely on piece-rate compensation and draws on line supervisors and, where present, union stewards to deal with problems and disputes on the line. The use of group assembly shifts the incentive structure away from individual performance to the team. As a result, only one-third of assembly workers on modular lines are paid by piece rates, with the majority of operators receiving some type of group incentive. Training requirements also differ because modular operators need to be able to perform multiple assembly tasks.

Table 10.2. Impact of Production Organization on Human Resource Practices

HR Practice	Bundle System	Modular Systems
Job design	Single skill; 1 operator, 1 job	Multi-skill; job rotation
Compensation	Individual piece rates and incentives; individual rate based on task	Group rates and incentives; individual rate based on skill acquisition
Mobility/internal labor market	Flat internal labor market	Mobility based on skill acquisition
Training	On the job; refinement of skills	Formal and on the job; substantive and process
Supervision	Shop floor supervision	Group-based supervision—fewer supervisors required
Union role	Grievance system—"administer the rate"	Involvement in teams/ informal dispute resolution
Safety and health	Repetitive motion problems	Inexperience-related accident risks

Source: Dunlop, John T., and David Weil, "Diffusion of Human Resource Innovations: Historic and Current Lessons from the Apparel Industry," working paper, Harvard Center for Textile and Apparel Research, 1994.

Table 10.3 suggests, however, that modular production relies on training for a more limited number of jobs—a median of two jobs compared with one for PBS—than popular industry accounts indicate.

Clearly, the diffusion of innovative practices like group incentives, team-based supervision, and multi-skilling is fundamentally linked to the diffusion of underlying production systems. In this sense, new human resource practices can be more usefully described as a set of complementary practices associated with a certain manufacturing system, rather than as a separate and independent variable. The complementary relationship between assembly methods and human resource practices also illustrates why firms are often reluctant to innovate in the sewing room. Introducing modular production requires far more than rearranging plant layout; it means changing the incentive system and training requirements for production workers along a number of dimensions.

Despite the accolades for modular systems, the 1980s saw little

Table 10.3. Human Resource Practices in PBS and Modular Assembly

	Percent of Business Units Drawing on Human Resource Practice		
	Overall[a]	PBS	Modular
Compensation practices			
Individual piece rates	91.4	98.1	30.0
Straight hourly rate—target output	2.0	0.0	20.0
Straight hourly rate—skill or quality	3.5	0.0	20.0
Group incentive—target output	8.2	0.0	80.0
Group incentive—skill or quality	7.8	0.0	80.0
Split incentive (individual and group)	23.3	20.4	50.0
Penalty for rework	34.3	31.5	60.0
Other compensation system	1.7	1.9	0.0
Training Practices			
Workers are trained for one job only	54.1	58.9	10.0
Workers are trained for two jobs	31.7	28.6	60.0
Workers are trained for three jobs	6.8	5.4	20.0
Workers are trained for four jobs	7.4	7.1	10.0
Percentage of volume shipped by business unit using assembly system	88.9[b]	80.0	8.9

Source: Harvard Center for Textile and Apparel Research survey (see Appendix B).

[a] Results are the incidence of practices weighted by the overall percentage of dollar volume shipped by business unit using each assembly system. Overall incidence includes Unit Production System.

[b] Remaining volume shipped using UPS (2.2 percent) and other systems related to PBS.

change in the dominance of the progressive bundle system. A series of industry surveys conducted in 1985, 1988, and 1992 shows that the majority of apparel manufacturers continued to use PBS for most assembly. Although the use of modular lines increased from 7 percent of our survey respondents in 1988 to 15 percent by 1992, bundle systems remained in use in over 82 percent of all firms surveyed by the American Apparel Manufacturers Association in 1992.[8] In addition, even modular assembly does not eliminate bundles altogether. For the HCTAR sample, an average buffer of sixty apparel items between production steps accumulated on modular lines. Only 30 percent of the business units using modular systems indicated that workers directly hand off garments to other team members, which would imply a "zero" buffer.[9]

This low level of diffusion for team-based production should not be surprising. Because the modular system requires a fundamental shift from individual- to group-based assembly, almost every associated human resource practice has to change as well. If only part of an assembly process is done on the basis of modular principles, balancing the line for nonmodular steps must be done from scratch. And if firms have to rebalance entire assembly operations, they must change the basis of compensation, spend more on training and retraining, change supervision methods or supervisors, invest in additional machinery, and lose productivity at least during a transition period. In addition, high performing sewing operators often dislike team-based assembly because it leads to a reduction of their hourly earnings. In many of the plants using modular systems, special arrangements for high piece-rate workers were arranged to adjust for potential earnings loss, or those workers opted to remain on traditional PBS lines.

For most manufacturers in the late 1980s, the potential benefits of modular adoption paled in comparison with the costs of introduction, even if those costs were relatively modest. The majority of retailers continued to demand goods on the old principle of low price. Although some studies indicate that modular lines result in higher job satisfaction, lower absenteeism, and improved quality, those benefits do not radically reduce cost.[10] The positive impact of modular production on throughput time similarly did not seem to benefit manufacturers directly because at the time most retailers were uninterested in such reductions and unwilling to pay for them. Without substantial changes in retailing practices, introducing dramatic innovations on the production floor or in human resource practices made little financial sense. Therefore, the vast majority of domestic producers chose to focus on further streamlining the bundle system or reducing labor costs by sourcing assembly offshore, although they continued to do fabric cutting in centralized, U.S.-based operations.[11]

Lean Retailing and the Benefits of Modular Assembly

By the mid-1990s, of course, the emergence of lean retailing changed the environment for human resource practices.[12] Since lean retailers adjust the supply of products at their sales outlets to match consumer demand on the basis of daily point-of-sales information, apparel suppliers can compete through replenishment speed, flexibility, and services as well as price.

These industry changes have direct implications for the adoption of modular assembly systems. The reduction of throughput time compared with PBS may mean that an apparel supplier that implements team-based assembly has an enhanced ability to deal with retailer demand for rapid replenishment. Lean retailing may justify the effort and cost required for implementation of modular assembly, at least on short cycle lines, since it gives a competitive edge to systems that minimize throughput time. Under these economic conditions, it is even possible that team-based assembly will have an impact comparable with that of PBS in earlier decades, when the latter system minimized direct labor content for products.

Given the new competitive terms in a lean world, let's look at HCTAR's survey results in more detail. In our sample, sixteen business units used modular systems at some point during the past decade.[13] These business units can be divided into two groups: "experimenters"—those that tried but abandoned modular systems at some point before 1992—and "adopters"—those that implemented modules after 1988 and continued to use them, at least up to 1992.

Experimenters tried team-based assembly for, on average, eight months. The most commonly cited reason that modules were abandoned after this trial period concerns the costs of modular systems in terms of lost labor productivity and the consequent inability of modules to provide a sufficient payback to justify their continuation.[14] Because the majority of experimenters implemented modular systems before or around 1988, their responses suggest that these business units did so primarily because managers were interested in cutting down on direct internal costs.

Adopters, in contrast, introduced modules in more recent years for very different reasons.[15] Table 10.4 (page 174) presents business-unit respondents' rankings of the reasons why they adopted modular assembly systems.[16] These responses by managers indicate that retailer pressure played a greater role in the decisions of this group than the justifications for modules commonly cited in the 1980s.

Ability to meet retailer standards for product delivery was cited as the most important reason for adoption. This was followed by reduction in work-in-process inventories, faster throughput times, and improved quality. Attributes related to the impact of modular production on human resource factors—worker satisfaction, turnover, safety, and health—come next. Repetitive motion injuries arising from PBS have been a major problem for business units in many apparel sectors. Reducing these costs by increasing each operator's task variety can therefore be a motivation for introducing modular assembly. Managers

Table 10.4. Reasons for Modular Adoption

Reasons for Modular Adoption[a]	Ranking[b] Mean (S.D.)
Improves ability to meet retailer standards on product delivery	2.8 (0.4)
Reduces work-in-process inventories	2.6 (0.7)
Improves first pass product quality	2.5 (0.7)
Reduces throughput time for product assembly	2.5 (0.7)
Improves worker safety and health	2.3 (0.8)
Decreases turnover and absenteeism	2.2 (0.7)
Improves job satisfaction of workforce	2.2 (0.8)
Reduces number of material handlers and support workers	2.0 (0.7)
Reduces number of supervisors	1.7 (0.8)
Helps attract new workers	1.1 (0.9)
Reduces direct labor content required for garment assembly	0.9 (1.3)
Number of business unit observations	10

Source: Harvard Center for Textile and Apparel Research survey (see Appendix B).

[a] Based on business-unit managers' responses for those business units that adopted modular systems between 1988 and 1992.

[b] Based on a scale of 1–3 where 0 = "not important"; 1 = "somewhat important"; 2 = "important" and 3 = "extremely important."

considered the following reasons the least important: the potential impact on reducing the number of support workers and supervisors; increasing space availability; and improving the attractiveness of assembly jobs.

Table 10.5 (page 176) provides further evidence of the compelling role retail change has played in adoption of modular assembly since 1990. The table presents characteristics of both experimenters and adopters, along with those business units that did not implement modules throughout the entire period. Among other differences, modular adopters were under greater pressure from lean retailers than nonadopters. On average, adopters of team-based production provided 53 percent of their products to national chains and mass merchants—the retailers that are "leanest"—compared with 44 percent of nonadopters and only 30 percent of those business units that had experimented and then abandoned modular assembly prior to 1992. When the other differences between adopters and nonadopters were held constant using statistical methods, replenishment pressure remained a significant reason for why firms implemented modular assembly practices.[17]

The Performance Effects of Modular Assembly in a Lean Environment

Even so, team-based production is currently used by only a few apparel firms. The ten adopters in Table 10.5 drew on modular lines for an average of 36 percent of total volume assembled, ranging from a low of 10 percent to a maximum of 70 percent. As a result, by 1992, only 8.9 percent of the volume shipped by business units in the HCTAR sample as a whole had been assembled by modular systems, compared with 80 percent assembled by PBS.

There are several possible explanations. First, low levels of diffusion may reflect the fact that modular systems do not have the expected impact on throughput time and replenishment speed. Second, modular systems may yield benefits, but high switching costs still inhibit their adoption. Third, the benefits from modular assembly may pay off only when a firm has invested in other innovations associated with lean retailing. Without these investments, the competitive advantage of team-based assembly may be small or unattainable. In the following sections, we will analyze the relationship between modular assembly and other practices related to retail replenishment.

Modular Adoption and Information Investment

Because a growing number of retailers require rapid replenishment of at least some products, most apparel suppliers are investing in information systems that can receive and transmit detailed sales and order information. Bar codes and EDI provide the two basic information links with an apparel supplier's retail partners. As noted in Chapter 5, overall investment in these basic information-transfer technologies increased dramatically in the 1990s.

Table 10.5 Characteristics of Modular Adopters and Nonadopters

Business Unit Characteristics	Overall	Nonadopters	Modular Users	
			Experimenters Pre-1992[b]	Adopters, 1992[c]
Number of business units[a]	42	26	8	10
Replenishment pressure[d] 1988	41.5 (39.2)	44.5 (39.8)	24.9 (31.9)	39.2 (40.0)
Replenishment pressure[d] 1992	44.6 (36.2)	44.0 (37.6)	30.4 (32.4)	53.2 (32.0)
Percent of volume in basic product lines, 1988	54.3 (30.3)	56.2 (32.8)	57.5 (25.2)	44.6 (23.2)
Work-in-process inventories held in sewing operations (weeks), 1988	3.6 (2.3)	3.3 (1.6)	5.0 (3.6)	3.1 (2.3)
Size (1988 $million sales volume)	151.9 (267.4)	82.0 (89.8)	144.4 (161.2)	356.2 (469.8)
Average length of modular trial (years)[e]	—	—	.7 (1.0)	1.8 (0.6)

Source: Harvard Center for Textile and Apparel Research survey (see Appendix B).

[a] Two business units adopted, abandoned, and readopted modular systems and therefore are classified in both experimenters and adopters categories.

[b] Business units that adopted and then abandoned modular systems before 1992.

[c] Business units that adopted modular systems after 1988 and continued to have them in operation in 1992.

[d] Percent of volume shipped to national chains/mass merchants.

[e] Length for experimenters indicates the average reported time for those who abandoned modular assembly; length for adopters measures the average length of time between adoption and 1992.

Modular adoption must therefore be understood as part of a set of sequential decisions necessary to adapt to changing retail requirements. Meaningful changes to the modular assembly of apparel make little sense if one has not made investments in information technology regarding product demand. Similarly, if one is unable to ship products efficiently to retail distribution centers, there will be little to gain from the throughput-time reductions that result from modular assembly.[18]

Observations of sophisticated apparel manufacturers support this notion of sequential manufacturing investments. In the late 1980s, Levi Strauss and Haggar—two of the largest manufacturers of jeans and men's trousers—invested heavily in developing methods to identify uniquely products and exchange information electronically well in advance of any changes in design, cutting and sewing rooms, or relations with textile manufacturers. Compare this with two of HCTAR's early experimenters, business units in the men's separate-trouser and dress-shirts segments that had abandoned their modular lines by 1992. In those cases, neither manufacturer had developed electronic data interchange with their retail customers.

Indeed, in 1992, *every* business unit in our sample that had implemented modular assembly had also made the basic information technology investments necessary to deal with lean retailers; only 75 percent of the nonadopters had done so. Yet, before 1992, no such connection existed between the presence of basic information technology investments and modular production. Only two of the eight experimenters that adopted and abandoned modular systems before 1992 also had electronic information links with retailers in 1988. This corresponds to the overall incidence of information investments in 1988, which comprised just 26 percent of business units at that time—once again suggesting that manufacturers were motivated to adopt modular production prior to 1988 for other reasons.

Measuring Performance Effects

For our sample of apparel business units, we assessed the effect of modular assembly through three performance outcomes. First, plant *throughput* is the time it takes for a single garment to go from cut goods to packaged product. As discussed previously (Table 10.1), throughput-time reductions are a direct result of the reduction of buffers between assembly steps. Second, *lead time* measures the total time required in the apparel production process, from the time fabrics are ordered to when finished products are ready for shipment. Unlike throughput times, which are limited to assembly, lead times provide a more comprehensive measure of a business unit's ability to compete in a market increasingly dominated by lean retailing practices. Third, if lead times capture a unit's external performance, *operating profits* reflect its internal performance.[19]

Throughput Times

In HCTAR's sample, the average reported throughput time for sewing operations on modular lines was 1.7 days compared with 9.2 days for PBS lines. Our observations of particular plants show even more dramatic results. For example, the throughput time required to complete a pair of pants fell from twenty days to just four on a line that had adopted modular principles.[20] Note that such throughput reductions can be achieved without changes in other manufacturing practices.

Lead Times

Business units in the HCTAR sample with modular systems had significantly lower lead times for their products. If we hold constant other factors that might also be associated with both lead times and the adoption of modular systems—such as size of the business unit and mix of basic versus nonbasic products—a 1 percent increase in the volume of production assembled via modular systems leads to only a 0.6 day decrease in lead time, or less than a 1 percent decrease in average lead times. However, for the typical adopter, which drew on modules for 36 percent of assembly, these results imply lead-time reductions of between twenty-three and twenty-five days.

Unlike throughput reductions, shorter lead times are closely tied to the adoption of innovative information practices. Without information integration, neither retailers nor apparel suppliers have much to gain from lead-time reductions. As such, the changes in performance cited above must be interpreted in conjunction with a basic platform of bar codes, EDI, and related practices that link retailers and apparel manufacturers.

Operating Profits

Regardless of the assembly process, apparel firms' investment in information links with suppliers is associated with higher operating profits. Business units in our sample that used bar codes and EDI in 1992 earned average operating profits as a percent of sales that were 6.5 percent higher than those of units lacking these basic information links. But, more to the point, operating profits rose further when firms also used modular production. Our study indicates that even a 1 percent increase in modular production can raise operating profits as a percentage of revenues by 0.1 percent. For a typical adopter, this estimate implies increased profits of 3.5 percent, or about one-third more in average operating profits. The impact of modular assembly is about half that of bar code and EDI adoption but is still statistically significant.

Although team-based assembly appeared to have little effect on lead times, it mattered more to operating profits, probably because of the increased responsiveness to retailers without holding excessive inventories.

Modular assembly has an effect on business performance when it is associated with investments in other practices, particularly those that are necessary for information sharing. At this point in apparel industry development, having these basic information links dramatically changes the external and internal performance of business units. The impact of other manufacturing innovations in the cutting or sewing room, or in distribution operations, is small in comparison. Although this dynamic may change as more and more apparel firms adopt baseline practices, understanding the sequence of investments necessary for responding to market changes is central to interpreting the potential of human resource innovations like team-based assembly.

Case in Point: The Levi Strauss/UNITE! Partnership Agreement

Consider human resource developments at Levi Strauss in the mid-1990s. The "Partnership Agreement" reached in 1994 between Levi Strauss and UNITE! represents a landmark in labor relations for the apparel industry and beyond. It would be inaccurate, however, to assess the agreement without an understanding of how it fits into the larger strategic decisions made by Levi Strauss executives.[21]

The Partnership Agreement emerged in the context of other major changes at Levi Strauss. In 1984, newly appointed CEO Robert Haas took the company private through a $1.7-billion leveraged buyout.[22] One immediate impact of the buyout was a round of plant closings and acrimonious relations with ACTWU—the union representing workers in the men's apparel industry before the formation of UNITE!—in the plants under agreement, which accounted for 50 percent of Levi Strauss's facilities. At the same time, in order to reposition itself competitively, the company undertook a major study of its customers. This became the centerpiece of a new strategy to create a "customer service supply chain." Levi's wanted to improve its ability to replenish products rapidly, use information efficiently, distribute products effectively, manufacture them flexibly, and build better relationships with key suppliers like denim producers.

Back in the 1970s, the company had developed some of the most efficient and productive assembly plants in the jeans industry by perfecting its PBS operations. But the new initiative to improve manufacturing flexibility challenged this traditional organization of production. The company also faced growing costs from repetitive-motion injuries among sewing workers, another more unfortunate result of its highly efficient PBS.[23] Despite the desire to change, senior managers were frustrated by their inability to persuade plants to adopt more flexible systems. Although some of this opposition arose from those assembly plants represented by ACTWU, it was also due to the recalcitrance of plant-level managers and supervisors.

Indeed, early discussions about creating more cooperative labor relations between the company and the union received little support from top executives and faced strong opposition from plant managers, particularly nonunion ones. After almost four years, the discussions had generated few results. But this stalemate ended in 1991 when Levi CEO Haas agreed to meet with ACTWU President Jack Sheinkman. These intensive discussions over a five-month period led to the outlines of a partnership agreement, one aimed at involving Levi union and nonunion workforce in many of the changes required by its emerging customer-focused strategy. The outlines of the agreement were taken to the Levi and ACTWU boards for separate discussions. After each board had separately drafted proposals, a Strategic Steering Committee, composed of members from both organizations, was created to draft the text of what became the Partnership Agreement. It includes six innovative features:

1. The Strategic Steering Committee deals with all issues except financial (borrowing, stock issuance), executive-compensation, and capital-investment decisions.
2. The agreement directly involves UNITE! in work redesign and human resource decisions in all plants, regardless of union status, in exchange for a pledge by Levi to remain neutral during union elections.[24] By 1997, this led to three nonunion plants voting in the union by wide margins.
3. The partnership calls for implementing modular production in all facilities. Both parties view PBS as antithetical both to short-term goals and their desire to make plants flexible and responsive through employee involvement.
4. The partnership has now been supplemented by two other types of agreement: plant-level partnership agreements that are locally negotiated and a detailed document drafted by the Strategic Steering Committee on guidelines for implementing work redesign.
5. The overall agreement stresses that each plant should devise its own system of work redesign and associated human resource practices. These should follow the principles laid out in the company- and plant-level agreements, as well as the guidelines on work redesign.

6. The local partnership agreements allow each team within a plant to develop a formal charter concerning how it will achieve production goals within a stated range of costs. This includes creating models for work design, compensation, training, and job rotation.

Note that Levi Strauss was one of the first companies to invest in information links with retailers. In fact, the company helped to create one of the early systems for information exchange before an industry standard had been established. Levi also invested heavily in its logistical operations, consolidating a large number of traditional warehouses into four distribution centers that rapidly process shipments from plants to retail customers. Management's understanding of the critical effect of information and speed on competitive performance has therefore motivated much of Levi Strauss's strategy, including its program to provide customers with personally customized jeans (see Chapter 8).

Levi's strategy, in short, is premised on providing customers with the right product, when they want it, without holding vast amounts of inventory in the process. The Partnership Agreement is a necessary extension of this effort, one that has helped its union and nonunion production facilities become more capable of responding rapidly and flexibly to retailer and, ultimately, consumer demand.

Once again, however, we want to point out that partnerships among the various players in the channel remain hard to sustain and represent only one piece in the larger puzzle. Economic conditions for these three industries continue to fluctuate, and the transformation we describe throughout is still in process. Even the Levi Strauss partnership has not been without its problems, including the decision by the company to close eleven production plants, which resulted in a loss of 6,395 jobs in November 1997.[25] In addition, the company has had difficulties in implementing teams in many of its plants and encountered resistance among many workers who favor PBS methods of assembly and related rewards.[26] Team-based assembly and related human resource practices are not a panacea, but are only one type of innovation for reducing cycle time along with other organizational changes.

Other Human Resource Issues

Modular production systems, along with the accompanying compensation, training, worker involvement, and supervisory practices, account for less than 10 percent of all assembly. This system makes the most sense in apparel workplaces that have close relationships with retailers and sophisticated inventory management. Where this suite of information investments and relationships exists, it can improve performance along a number of dimensions. But to call modular production either the driving force behind plant-floor changes or the savior of the industry is to misunderstand fundamentally the dynamics of the channel and the benefits of those systems. The modest impact of team-based assembly indicates that the attention this innovation has received in the trade press is misplaced when compared with other human resource changes that are underway. Two other issues merit particular attention.

The New Strategic Workers

The advent of lean retailing creates a new category of strategic workers who become of special interest to unions seeking to develop collective bargaining relationships in the sector: workers in retail distribution centers. Historically, the cutters in the apparel industry were strategic in the sense that in the absence of a cutter the sewing plant would be unable to operate. Labor organization of cutters often led to plantwide collective bargaining.[27]

With the emergence of the information-integrated channel, the workforce in the distribution center has become strategic to the whole channel operation.[28] With lean inventories in retail stores and in supplier plants, the prompt, efficient, and uninterrupted operation of the distribution center is decisive to the whole channel. It should not be surprising that unions have clearly realized this strategic role.

For example, in 1997, UNITE! organized distribution centers of Marshall's acquired by TJX Companies in Georgia and Virginia, each with 600 to 700 employees. In 1998, the union organized an additional center in Massachusetts that employs 900 workers.[29] Distribution workers now represent some 25,000 of UNITE!'s 300,000 members. It remains unclear how this bargaining power will be used in the future elsewhere in the channel. The widespread effects of the strike by the International Brotherhood of Teamsters at United Parcel Service during 1997 illustrates how important workers involved in logistics are to a wide variety of sectors where lean retailing and related methods of distribution have become important. One of the first business groups to encourage the Clinton Administration to intervene in that strike was the National Retail Federation.

The Recurring Problem of the Sweatshop

For more than a century, the sweatshop has been of concern to public policy investigations and legislation in this country, often focused on the role of shifting generations of immigrants and the apparel industry, particularly in women's clothing. The Industrial Commission, 1898–1901, appointed by President McKinley, composed of ten members of the Congress and nine private citizens, defined the sweatshop in its reports:

> The term "sweating" or "sweating system" originally denoted a system of sub-contract, wherein the work is let out to contractors to be done in small shops or homes. "In practice," says the report of the Illinois Bureau of Labor Statistics, "sweating consists of the farming out by competing manufacturers to competing contractors of the material for garments, which in turn is distributed among competing men and women to be made up."[30]

The report documents extensive abuses: long hours of work, often seven days a week, small pay, and unsanitary shops.[31] Foreshadowing contemporary argument, the Commission noted,

> Witnesses who discuss the effects of immigration on industry take two opposing standpoints. On the one side, it is held that they add to the productive energy of the country, and that immigrants of low intelligence are desirable to do the rough work. On the other side, it is claimed that the rapid influx of low standard population, especially those of southern and eastern Europe, depresses wages and lessens the amount of employment available for American labor.[32]

Another era in the century-old public policy concern with the sweatshop is reflected in the Fair Labor Standards Act (FLSA) of 1938.[33] This act created federal minimum wage, hour, and working condition standards, including those relating to child labor. Enforcement of FLSA standards provided a means for defining minimum conditions applicable to all apparel workers and created a federal agent for controlling sweatshop conditions. At the same time, collective bargaining agreements between the International Ladies Garment Workers' Union (ILGWU) and apparel manufacturers set out minimum working conditions not only for those companies, but for any contractor doing work for them.[34] The success of these government and collective bargaining efforts led *Life Magazine* in 1938 to run a lead story on the ILGWU in which it reported, "Still numerous in 1933, the sweatshop is virtually gone today."[35] Optimism about resolving or eliminating sweatshops, as well as concern over their reemergence, have been recurring themes this century.

The mid-1990s have seen a revival in public policy interest in sweatshops in the apparel industry, along with renewed immigration (particularly from China, other Asian countries, and Latin America) and the decline of the extent of collective bargaining and the unions in that sector. Although one reason government labor standards continue to be flouted is the ever-present pressure to reduce the labor-cost component of garments, the growing importance of replenishment also explains the recent reemergence. Sweatshop operations offer the dual "advantage" of low labor costs and proximity to the American market. Suppliers relying on contractors that violate wage and hour laws can achieve timely replenishment without holding large inventory risk and still pay low wages.[36]

The activities of Secretaries of Labor Robert Reich and Alexis Herman have sought to raise public awareness of sweatshops in this country and abroad, as have the work of a variety of union, consumer, and student groups.[37] Yet rooting out sweatshops becomes even more complicated in the presence of lean retailing. We will discuss this significant public-policy problem, arising as it does from integrated channel production, and a possible means to redress in Chapter 15. The next two chapters will focus on the textile industry, where plant automation and technological innovation involve a quite different set of human resource issue.

11

Textile Operations: Spinning, Weaving, and Finishing Cloth

If Samuel Slater, the "father of American manufactures," kicked off the textile industry in the United States through an act of industrial espionage, Francis Cabot Lowell also used his wits to bring the power loom to the new country. As we discussed in Chapter 2, Slater avoided British prohibitions on the export of technology and built the first U.S. water-powered carding and spinning mill in 1790. But as successful carding and spinning mills spread in New England, the absence of mechanical weaving became more limiting. Hand weavers could not fully absorb the growing spinning capacity, which set the stage for Lowell's innovations. As historian Robert Dalzell writes, "The crowning glory of Britain's textile technology—the ingenious power loom, which wove the yarn into finished cloth and which had earned the inventor, Edmund Cartwright, a £10,000 bonus from Parliament—remained beyond the reach of American manufacturers."[1]

Until Lowell made his mark, that is. A well-off Boston merchant, he and his family spent several years in Britain, including the Manchester textile region and Edinburgh, and returned to Boston on the eve of the War of 1812. Through close observation of the power looms he saw in England, Lowell, like Slater, memorized enough details to reproduce this key technology in his own country. He established the Boston Manufacturing Company in 1813 as a joint-stock enterprise, rather than a traditional business proprietorship or partnership, and the next year the company completed its first factory on the Charles River in Waltham, Massachusetts. This single factory combined the entire process of mechanized textile production—from handling the raw material, ginned and baled, through spinning and weaving to produce finished cloth.

Lowell did more than pioneer a new form of business organization;

he also established an innovative system of employment. In Britain, he had been disturbed by the plight of English factory workers living in urban slums. For the Waltham plant, therefore, Lowell and his associates hired young farm women at a higher rate of pay than that usually given to the urban poor, housed them in special homes with matrons, and provided churches. The young unmarried women were encouraged to save and to return to their farm areas in several years with a tidy sum. Lowell believed that this arrangement would avoid the creation of industrial slums that could lead to social unrest.[2] His factory system was much praised in comparison with the unwholesome conditions found in British plants. Its use spread to the Massachusetts towns of Lawrence and Lowell, which became major New England textile centers in the nineteenth century.[3]

It appears that Yankee ingenuity, at least in textiles, consisted of much more than mechanical inventiveness. As economic historian David Landes comments, "So a few machines came from England, but only a few, and Americans were soon adapting them to the needs and tastes of the home market. (They were also inventing new devices and exporting them to Britain—the best sign of technological independence.)"[4] In fact, since its beginnings in the Industrial Revolution, the mechanized textile industry has spread not only south of New England to the Piedmont states but around the world by a variety of processes, including those that resist national regulation. As Chapter 12 will indicate, textiles have led the industrialization process in many recently developing countries.

The textile industry forms a crucial link in the supply channel dynamics we discuss throughout this book. In many respects, it is the beginning of the channel. Clothing cannot be made without knit or woven cloth, and apparel manufacturing would not exist without textiles. Because textiles are so indispensable to a discussion of garment-making, firms in this sector often have more clout than those in the apparel industry; they also play a different role. The textile industry, whether considered globally or domestically, is generally larger in scale and less affected by labor costs. Unlike apparel operations, which have only been automated in certain steps, modern textile operations rely on factory automation. In a contemporary textile plant, one sees very few people. Instead, floor space is occupied almost entirely by sophisticated machines—such as shuttleless or air-jet looms, the descendants of Lowell's power loom. Although labor costs still affect the overall cost of textile production, expensive equipment plays a strategic role.

That does not mean the U.S. textile industry will continue as it is or that it has been untouched by lean retailing practices and the increasing call for rapid replenishment. Many American textile firms now operate in multiple channels; they supply not only apparel-makers but also work directly with retailers. Lean retailing practices have also opened new opportunities for both apparel and textile manufacturers, especially those that can produce faster, smaller runs for short-cycle production. Traditionally, textile plants created items through long runs and lead times to keep their capital-intensive equipment operating almost continually. Yet the current transformation of the channel may push textile firms to create products in smaller runs for their retail and industrial customers much more quickly. The next chapter will explore multiple textile channels and the implications for growth in the industry.

More to the present point, new kinds of partnerships between apparel manufacturers and textile producers, which involve information-sharing of demand data in a timely manner, are necessary if rapid replenishment of retailers' orders is ever to achieve optimum efficiency. Textile producers need to anticipate fabric demand, with a high level of certainty, in order to supply apparel-makers appropriately on a periodic basis. Although the industry has had little motivation to do so in the past, lean retailing has created new financial incentives for textile firms to supply their products to apparel-makers faster and more flexibly. Given the capital intensity of textile operations, however, just how these new partnerships are to be brought about remains an open question.

In this chapter, we examine the technological and production processes that turn raw materials into finished fabric. Our description is not meant to be definitive, since this book emphasizes the apparel industry and many textiles are produced for nonclothing items that fall outside its boundaries. But to appreciate the performance of the modern textile sector, one must understand the interdependent machine processes and the changes that have contributed to enhanced productivity.

From Lowell to the Modern Textile Mill

Since the emergence of spinning, weaving, and finishing textile plants, technological changes have mainly come from improvements in the machinery and combination of processes rather than from revolutionary innovation. As the labor historian Herbert Lahne notes,

The development of ring spinning and its perfection for high-speed production in the 1870s, the invention and adoption of the automatic loom which began in the middle nineties, and the introduction of the tying-in machine[5] shortly after the beginning of the present century set the pattern of change which dominated the industry until after the First World War.[6]

Increasing automation has been the norm in textiles. Since the mechanization of spinning and weaving, most jobs in textile mills have involved machine-tending, with wages distributed in a narrow band.

Production Processes and the Stretch Out

The introduction of faster machinery with more automatic controls led mill owners to increase the number of machines tended by each worker. As workers put it, managers were engaged in the "stretch out;" to managers the issues were appropriate "work assignments." Whatever the term used, these issues and associated questions of compensation for the work became a source of conflict and strikes in mills with unions and the basis for sporadic walkouts in plants without union organization. These included the Fall River strike of 1904[7] and outbursts in the South between 1929 and 1930 that arose from, as Lahne writes, "the objections of the workers to increases in the work load which they considered excessive."[8] In 1932 and 1933, bills were introduced into the South Carolina legislature, although they were not enacted, to limit the number of looms that could be assigned to a weaver.

Under the National Recovery Administration, 1933 to 1935, a Cotton Textile Work Assignment Board was established to work out a permanent plan for regulating work assignments in textiles. When the Supreme Court invalidated the underlying statute providing for the industry codes, this board disappeared. But the workload associated with the wage rate of textile mill operators remained a persistent problem in the industry. In this respect the human resource issues of textiles have been quite different from those in apparel where setting piece rates for each particular garment was the operating question.

A careful review of workload or "stretch out" issues during the 1930s and 1940s showed that much depended on the way work operations were organized and managed in a mill. Weavers, for example, could be relieved of loading bobbins, cleaning the looms, and removing the finished cloth, leaving them to watch the operation of the looms and tying up broken ends of warped yarn. Higher quality materials and yarn, as well as better maintenance and relief from some routine duties, would permit a weaver to tend two or three times as many looms as previously.[9]

In the past generation, another round of intense technological change in textile production has created new processes, that do more than merely speed up or make older machines automatic. The quality of product has become more significant and the issues of workload and stretch out have receded in significance. These technological developments have, however, affected occupational distributions in textile mills.

New Technologies and Job Classifications

In the 1970s, several innovative technologies emerged, such as open-end spinning and shuttleless or air-jet looms. A shuttleless loom "not only produced fabric three times faster than its wooden fly shuttle predecessor, but it also could produce seven or eight times more fabric because it was able to weave wider widths. Open-end spinning boosted the rate of production of yarn four times over the older ring-spinning technique and reduced the number of steps involved in manufacturing some kinds of yarn from 15 to 3.6."[10] Further technologic improvements have led to looms that can bring yard across the warp at a rate above 1,000 movements per minute. This has resulted in enormous growth in loom productivity: In 1975, a typical loom could produce 8.3 square yards of fabric per loom hour; by 1997, loom productivity increased to 34.7 square yards per loom hour. Put in a different way, a shuttle machine required 13 minutes to weave the material necessary for a man's shirt while today's air jet loom takes only 3 minutes. There are machines under development that will require less than one minute.[11] There have also been significant innovations in reactive dyes, continuous operations, and finishing. These innovations have further raised the capital intensity of textile operations and increased the scale of enterprises and productivity.

Even before these developments, textile operations largely came down to machine-tending except for the loomfixer—who repairs looms—and some weaving job classifications.[12] Automation has eliminated some operations altogether, such as the picker tender who opened bales of fiber. In recent years, at least two changes in job classifications, which involve relatively few workers in a plant, have led to their higher relative wages: (1) shuttleless loom weavers, and (2) electronic technicians in maintenance departments that handle new equipment and receive higher pay than traditional maintenance electricians.

One indication of the rate of innovation in these technologies is reflected in industry wage surveys conducted by the Bureau of Labor Statistics in textile plants.[13] In the June 1985 study, 40.3 percent of all loomfixers were reported to be working on shuttleless looms; by the August 1990 survey this share had risen to 63.3 percent. Similarly, in 1985, 50.1 percent of all weavers were working on shuttleless looms and by 1990 the figure had jumped to 78.6 percent. In 1985, 12.3 percent of all weavers operated air-jet looms, which increased to 23.2 percent by 1990. It is significant that an August 1971 survey did not even report on shuttleless loomfixers or weavers, including air-jet weavers. In contrast, the 1990 survey listed an electronic technician job classification for the first time, one that included 13 percent of all maintenance electricians.

Size of Establishments and Wages

The larger scale of textile operations, with more workers in each plant, has enhanced productivity in these larger and more modern establishments. Some facilities now employ more than a thousand employees and handle much more of the textile industry's overall production than those plants with fewer than fifty employees.

Table 11.1 represents the relative employment size of establishments in textiles and apparel reported by the Census of Manufacturers in 1994. The median size class for establishments in textile was 250 to 499 employees as compared to 100 to 249 employees in apparel.

In addition, the intense capital expenditures and increased labor productivity in textiles since 1960 have enhanced the relative wages of textile production workers when compared with other industries—despite the concentration of domestic textile production in low-wage Piedmont states, the high proportion of women workers,[14] and the absence of appreciable collective bargaining. Table 11.2 (page 192) reflects the changes in the average hourly earnings of production workers in a number of sectors. Textile average hourly earnings were actually below those in apparel until the 1950–60 period; thereafter, textiles moved well ahead of apparel—almost 22 percent more by 1997. And the hourly earnings of textile workers went from 71 percent of the manufacturing average in 1960 to 76 percent by 1997.

Textile Machinery

At one time, the United States produced most of the machinery developed and used in its domestic textile industry. By 1985, William Cline

Table 11.1. Textile and Apparel Establishments and Employment by Employment-Size Class, 1994

Size Class	Textile[a] Establish.	Textile[a] Employees	Apparel[b] Establish.	Apparel[b] Employees
1–4 employees	1,702	2,657	9,153	13,286
5–9	694	4,621	3,632	24,485
10–19	729	10,219	3,432	47,525
20–49	993	32,035	3,753	117,808
50–99	701	50,001	1,973	138,854
100–249	783	126,660	1,534	235,554
250–499	492	172,808	51	174,956
500–999	198	129,599	179	119,946
1,000 or more	57	89,199	35	50,754
Total establishments	6,349	—	23,742	—
Total employees	—	617,799	—	923,168

Source: U.S. Department of Commerce, Bureau of the Census, *County Business Patterns, 1994, United States*, Washington, D.C.: Government Printing Office, 1996, pp. 12, 14.
[a] Textile mill products (SIC 22).
[b] Apparel and other textile products (SIC 23).

reported that the United States "Now imports approximately half of its textile machinery."[15] Because less of the sophisticated equipment that goes into textile operations is made in America and designed with U.S. companies in mind, various commentators have been concerned that domestic textile mills will lag behind in innovations and access to new technology when compared with mills in the countries that produce the latest machinery.

The critical issue for future trade policy is whether new innovations and machinery can continue the U.S. industry's high rate of productivity and quality. Our discussions with American textile company executives indicate that foreign machinery manufacturers thus far have established good working relations in this country with their companies, generating ongoing improvements and responding to domestic problems.

The United States is not solely a textile machinery importer. In 1995, the U.S. imported $1.7 billion in textile machinery drawn largely from Germany, Japan, Italy, and Switzerland. Yet it also exported $600 million in machinery to a wide range of countries, especially Canada and Mexico. American exports were composed of a wide

Table 11.2. Average Hourly Earnings in Textiles and Apparel Compared with Other Industries, 1960, 1997

	1960	1997
Manufacturing	$2.26	$13.17
Durable goods	2.42	13.74
Nondurable goods	2.05	12.34
Textile mill products	1.61	10.02
Apparel	1.59	8.25

Source: U.S. Department of Labor, Bureau of Labor Statistics, Employment and Earnings, various years.

variety of machines and equipment and their parts. The imports were quite diverse as well, with spinning machines, parts of weaving machinery, and embroidery machines heading the list.[16]

The industry that has developed to transform cotton, wool, other natural fibers, and synthetics into fabrics for apparel, home furnishings, and industrial use involves a sequence of highly capital intensive manufacturing operations that provide competitive products primarily to the domestic market. The processes can be grouped into three major activities: yarn spinning, weaving and knitting, and finishing. We will detail all of these in the sections that follows. Some firms are fully integrated from fiber to retail products, while others specialize. The elapsed manufacturing time from fiber to finished fabric is long—generally several months—primarily because the capital-intensive equipment used in each of the three steps forces managers to plan production schedules in advance to assure round-the-clock production.

Spinning Yarn from Natural or Synthetic Fibers

A wide variety of fibers are found in textiles—mohair, alpaca, silk, jute, flax—but the most extensively used are cotton, wool, rayon, and other synthetic fibers. The type used, of course, depends on style, serviceability, and price. Representing less than 10 percent of the market in 1940, synthetics had captured nearly 68 percent of total textile fiber consumption by end use by 1996, but synthetics constituted only 45 percent of fiber used in apparel, compared to 53 percent for cotton and 2 percent for wool.[17] Synthetics may be used in various combinations with natural fibers; unlike in earlier years, it is now hard to draw a line between the cotton textile industry and other branches.

The spinning of staple yarns is the first and perhaps most capital-intensive step per worker in the sequence of operations necessary for producing textiles. We have visited a relatively new spinning plant with capital investments of several hundreds of thousands of dollars for every worker in the factory, secretaries and security guards included, only to be told by managers that even more expensive spinning mills are being built.[18] In such factories, most operations, other than repair, have been automated. For example, floors are continuously swept and vacuumed by battery-powered robotic machines that move throughout the plant; spinning rooms have vacuum systems continuously moving on overhead rails with hoses hanging down that pass over the spinning equipment. These vacuum systems gather up the lint on the machines to prevent it from being spun into the yarn and creating imperfections, as well as to keep the atmosphere clean for breathing, drastically reducing respiratory diseases among workers.

Consider the fabric used for a men's dress shirt. Making quality yarn is not easy, and the task becomes harder still when one takes into account the length of uniform yarn required for, say, a pinpoint oxford shirt. Lands' End advertises that such a shirt is made from 80s two-ply cotton yarn. The "s" indicates how fine the yarn is, with 80s being quite delicate compared with the 40s typical of oxford shirts, or the rougher 20s yarn of T-shirts and the 6s of jeans.[19] A pound of cleaned cotton ready to be spun will be converted into 38.2 miles of 80s yarn. More to the quality point, the yarn must have nearly constant fiber density over its entire length to prevent the fiber from breaking in weaving or causing a flaw in the woven or knit fabric.

Two such 80s yarns are then wound together to make the two-ply yarn that later will be woven into shirting fabric. The diameter of an 80s yarn is comparable to the thickness of a sheet of paper in this book. A finished dress shirt requires between 11 and 12 miles of 80s two-ply yarn that weighs less than a pound. Because an 80s yarn is finer than those used in most items of apparel, it cannot successfully be made from short-length (staple) fibers. Cotton fibers less than an inch in length may be used in the thicker yarns found in denim, for example. Longer fibers go into making yarn that will be woven into bed sheets, and still longer fibers are used for fine cotton apparel.

Preparation for Spinning: Cleaning, Blending, Carding

Bales of cotton or wool are graded according to individual fiber fineness and length as well as other characteristics. The process of yarn spinning starts with bales of raw fibers that must be opened, blended together, and cleaned. Cleaning and opening wool is much more involved than the process for cotton, since natural grease, dirt, dried sweat, and the like must be removed from wool fibers before processing can begin. Most items of apparel are made from cotton and synthetic fibers, and for brevity this description will focus primarily on the processing of these two types. The detailed processes in the conversion of fibers into textiles vary from plant to plant and depend to a large extent on the desired properties of the final fabric. What follows is meant to be a general discussion without the subtleties that distinguish a high-quality operation from others.

Preparation for spinning begins by blending cotton from a dozen or more bales. A machine will remove a few inches of cotton from each bale in turn as it circles around from bale to bale. This is just the first of many steps to achieve uniformity of the fibers along the length of the yarn. The cotton is cleaned and opened to expose the individual fibers and separate them from grains of sand and dirt. The final stage in cleaning and opening is to rake the fibers through an array of closely spaced pins in a process called "carding." This resembles the way pet owners take a wire brush to the matted fur of a dog or cat, separating the individual hairs of the animal. Naturally, the automated cotton carding process is more extensive and controlled, and includes the addition of blowing air to carry away debris.

The net result of opening, fiber blending, and cleaning is a continuous puffy strand of fibers, with the feel and appearance of household surgical cotton, which is lightly coiled and wound into collection barrels. This output of carding, called "sliver," is combined in a drawing operation with sliver from a number of other machines. Combining and drawing accomplish two things: They blend the output of several carding machines and align the fibers along the length of the output sliver. The drawing operation leaves the output sliver with about the weight per unit length of each of the individual input streams. Cotton and synthetic slivers are often combined in the drawing operation.

Drawing may be done several times to improve quality and, if the desired yarn is to be of high-quality, it is generally combed after the last drawing operation. Combing removes the shortest fibers and any "neps" (very small masses of tangled fibers) that have passed through earlier cleaning and opening operations. The output sliver strand is now ready for spinning into yarn. Any defects in fiber uniformity and alignment at this stage will appear in the finished yarn and diminish its quality.

The Three Types of Spinning

Three major techniques are used to spin yarn. The oldest is *ring spinning*, which produces the smoothest yarn with the same amount of twist or rotation of each of the fibers across the strand. The yarn is twisted by passing through a ring guide that rotates around the spinning spindle onto which the finished yarn is wound. An 80s yarn, for instance, would have about forty twists per inch if it were intended for weaving and somewhat less if it were used in knitting.

One disadvantage of ring spinning is that the size of the output spindle must be small because of the kinematics of the spinning ring and rotating spindle, and the yarn must be rewound onto a much larger separate package for shipment to weaving mills. Yarn from each spinning unit can be produced up to only forty meters a minute.[20] The production rate depends on the diameter of the yarn being produced. If one could produce 80s yarn at forty meters a minute, it would take 25.6 hours to convert one pound of cotton sliver into a pound of yarn from a single spinning unit.[21] In contrast, it takes just 6.4 hours to convert a pound of cotton into 20s yarn. Clearly, the finer the yarn, the longer it will take to spin a pound of cotton; therefore, the consequent cost per pound is higher. When the finest yarn is woven into fabric—such as for that men's pinpoint oxford dress shirt—there will be more yarn crossings in each inch of cloth and the weaving costs will also be higher.

While ring spinning produces smooth twisted yarn, its production rate is much lower than that of either of the two newer techniques: rotor or open-end spinning and air-jet spinning. *Open-end spinning* relies on a rapidly rotating rotor to twist the yarn, and *air-jet spinning* uses an air jet to swirl or twist the fibers in the spinning chamber. These machines can produce yarn up to six times as fast, although the output yarn is not as smooth and the fibers are not uniformly twisted as with ring spinning. The output yarn from both open-end and air-jet spinning can be wound directly into large cylindrical packages, avoiding the separate step of rewinding the small bobbins of ring-spun yarn. Yet even with these two important advantages, the newer techniques have not completely replaced ring spinning, because their yarn quality is not as good and the range of yarn sizes and fiber blends they produce is not as large.

Because the output of a single unit of spinning can be as little as several pounds a day, it is necessary to have many thousands of units in a typical mill, each supplied with clean sliver ready for processing. The units are grouped in frames with a single drive motor. The frames are almost entirely automated; for example, they automatically load and unload yarn, and detect and connect yarn breaks as they occur. A typical spinning mill runs continuously; any particular unit might be down only a few hundred of its 8,760 hours in a year.

The installed cost of new units of spinning equipment reflects the importance of the U.S. market to equipment suppliers and indicates the amount of capital invested in this portion of the textile industry. Ring-spinning equipment with tandem winders, which has the capacity to produce thirty-five pounds of 37s single-ply yarn an hour, costs $700,000 installed.[22] The equipment to produce the same yarn at the same rate using air-jet spinning would cost $400,000 installed. From these two numbers, we estimate that it would likely cost between four and eight billion dollars today to handle the current U.S. yarn capacity with new equipment.[23] From 1991 through 1995, the U.S. average value of annual imported spinning equipment was 210 million dollars.[24] Assuming that installed equipment costs twice the import value, it would take from 9.5 to 19 years to achieve replacement of the installed capacity. A new yarn plant involves a great deal more than just spinning equipment, so the replacement cost of capital investments in yarn production mills is even higher. Clearly, investment in this stage of the textile industry is substantial and not easily replicated in a developing nation trying to enter into the industry.

Because yarn is produced on standard equipment available to all, producers must compete through product quality and customer service. Keep in mind that the final quality of any apparel or houseware fabric will never be higher than the quality of the yarn used. The quality of the raw cotton matters most, followed by the execution of the steps leading up to spinning. As we have already noted, while there are some firms whose primary product is yarn, most large textile manufacturers are vertically integrated, usually with yarn spinning and weaving operations in the same plant complex. This allows control of the delivery of yarn to the weaving or knitting room, as well as quality control.

Weaving and Knitting

Weaving fabric in a factory setting follows the same general steps and procedures used in home weaving. The difference is in the quality control of the yarn and the complexity of the equipment that inserts the fill yarn (the yarn that crosses the width of the loom).

Preparation for Weaving: Slashing and Threading

Yarns must be conditioned before they can be woven or knit into fabric. Warp yarns run the length of the fabric, and the fill yarns are those that pass through the warp from one side of the loom to the other. Yarn intended for the warp of a fabric must have special chemical surface treatments to minimize the yarn damage during weaving. Each segment of a warp yarn will undergo several thousand cycles of stresses associated with the individual manipulations that accompany its alternating lifting and depressing; this allows the fill yarns to pass between the warp yarns, creating the weave pattern. Because a fill yarn passes through the warp just once, the yarn coating added at the end of spinning is often adequate for weaving. In contrast, the coating and treatment of warp yarns, called slashing, is extensive.

The coatings, or "sizing," added to protect, strengthen, and reduce the hairiness of warp yarns must be removed later in the fabric finishing process. Sizing may be starch, polyvinyl alcohol, or many other chemicals, depending on the chemistry of the synthetic and cotton fibers involved. Before the yarn is sized, it may be dyed if the fabric, such as shirting, is designed to have stripes of different colors. The dyeing and sizing of yarn involve a complex process of fiber chemistry and process control. Therefore, slashing is a critical step in preparation for weaving. The knowledge, experience, care, and skill of slashing operators make significant contributions to the quality of woven fabric.[25]

Slashing follows the process of forming the warp yarns into a parallel sheet of individual yarns that are wound onto a beam. This beam provides the supply of warp to the loom. If the final fabric will contain multicolored stripes, the arrangement of the individual yarns during the warping process is another critical operation. The varying reactions of sizing with different yarns add more complexity to the chemical processes during slashing. The tension on the yarns, which can stretch when wet, is just one of the parameters to be controlled as the yarns pass through the sequence of treatment baths and drying operations of the slashing process.

Before weaving can begin, the warp yarns must be threaded into the loom through the harnesses, the devices that raise and lower the yarns to form the passage across the warp for the fill yarn. This connection process is called drawing-in. Fabric woven for apparel is about sixty inches wide; household sheeting can be more that twice that, if the fabric is intended for king-size sheets. The number of yarn ends to be threaded through all of the control devices and tensioned can exceed 10,000, depending on the fineness of the yarn and the width of the loom. Advertisements for household bed sheets often mention 200-count, 250-count, or 300-count sheets. A 200-count, for instance, means a total of 200 individual yarns in one square inch of fabric. The number in each direction is nearly equal, though it need not be exactly the same. What matters most to the customer is the feel of the fabric. A sheet with 300 yarns in one square inch feels softer and smoother than a 200-count sheet.

The impact of technological change on sheeting quality is illustrated by comparing modern cotton sheeting to that produced on Lowell's Waltham power looms. The original product was thirty-seven inches wide with forty-four picks, or insertions of yarn, per inch and used 14s yarn.[26] Modern sheet fabric is much wider and comes in a variety of widths. The yarn is a much finer 37s and usually contains 100 to 150 picks per inch. Although some people may still live in homes built in 1813, it is hard to imagine anyone using this original low-cost, low-quality fabric for sheets, even if it were finished in the modern way.

High-Speed Looms and Knitting Machines

The production rates of new looms have kept pace with the improvements in spinning provided by new technology. Modern looms for apparel and houseware fabrics use one of three different methods to insert the fill yarn across the width of the loom. In some cases, a projectile carries the fill yarn between the lifted and lowered yarns. This is a modern version of the original power shuttle looms, which used a mechanical impulse to launch a wooden shuttle, carrying the fill yarn in a bobbin, across the warp. After crossing, the fill yarn is pushed tight against the finished fabric and the order of the raised and lower warp yarns is reversed, creating a new region through which the next fill yarn or pick will pass. As all of this is going on, the warp beam lets out one unit of length and the finished fabric takes up the same length. Needless to say, all these motions must be undertaken quickly and with precision. In fact, projectile looms can have machine speeds of 425 picks per minute on a two-panel-wide loom that inserts 1,416 yards of fill yarn per minute.[27] This is nearly a mile of yarn in a minute.

In another method of fill insertion, a metal rapier carries the yarn halfway across the loom, where it then passes the yarn off to another rapier from the other side, which then pulls the fill yarn the rest of the way across. The last and most recently developed insertion technique involves a series of air jets that pull the fill yarn across the warp at very high speeds, from 110 to 180 miles an hour.[28] The process happens so fast that one cannot see the crossing. Today's looms are capable of up to nearly 1,000 picks per minute, over four times faster than the speed of old shuttle looms. Open-end and air-jet spinning, coupled with improved looms, are two major reasons for the productivity increases in the textile industry over the past several decades. Installing these new looms, however, comes with substantial capital costs, ranging from $55,000 for a narrow air-jet loom to $110,000 for a projectile or air-jet loom 330 centimeters wide.[29]

Knitted goods, which have become increasingly popular, are made on a different kind of machine than woven cloth. Knitting can either be done in a flat sheet or in the more common circular tube. Machine knitting is difficult to describe in detail without a series of illustrations; however, almost everyone is familiar enough with knit products to know that a broken yarn will lead to a run in the continuous intersection of loops. Runs in women's pantyhose are the most common example. Therefore, the quality of yarn is perhaps even more important to knits than it is to woven fabrics. Yarn for knits is spun with fewer turns of the fibers per inch to allow for greater flexibility. Slashing is omitted because yarns do not have to be processed to endure the mechanical manipulations of knitting. Tubes of knit fabrics are the major building block of T-shirts and most sweatshirts and sweatpants; stockings and pantyhose are also a product of tube knitting machines, while sweaters are often made from flat knits.

Fabric Finishing

Whether fabrics are woven or knitted, they are not yet ready for the consumer or apparel markets when they come off the machines. They first must undergo a series of individual operations that are collectively called "finishing": heat setting, singeing, scouring, bleaching, dyeing, printing, and surface finishing. Not every fabric passes through each of these steps, but many do. A majority of the operations involve chemical treatments, heating, and washing between steps, and therefore most generate a wastewater stream that must be treated before discharge. Boilers for heat generation, waste-treatment facilities, and sophisticated process controls can be shared among most finishing operations; therefore, textile establishments often run large central facilities that operate twenty-four hours a day and serve many smaller weaving plants.

Some finishing plants contain a million or more square feet of process space, which means they are likely to represent the biggest single capital investment for an integrated textile manufacturer. In addition, finishing is perhaps the most important operational step for product differentiation in the market. Fabric for dresses, for example, can have unique proprietary prints and surface finish; T-shirts can be screen-printed to create different products; no-iron or easy-care cotton twill pants are a product of finishing; and color alone allows many product variations. In fact, the list of possibilities for creating different fabric SKUs is nearly limitless.

Although the modern operations of spinning, weaving, and knitting use common equipment found on the world market, printing and surface modifications can produce items that are copyrighted or difficult for others to duplicate in the short run. Therefore, finishing plants that use proprietary techniques can create unique products. Malden Mills' Polartec® comes immediately to mind. This is a 100-percent polyester knit fabric finished in a special way to create a popular fleece product used primarily in winter outerwear. Massachusetts-based Malden Mills has now created Synchilla®, a fuzzy smooth fabric also designed for outerwear. This company's fleece comes in 100 styles, 5,000 colors, and 1,000 patterns.[30] Of course, Polartec was the result of a $100-million investment in research and development. In this case, one manufacturer created a new product that consumers liked and other producers are scrambling to catch up. Designer bed sheets and drapes are another example of unique products, created in finishing through proprietary printed patterns.

Dye Preparation: Singeing, Desizing, Bleaching

It is impossible, in these pages, to mention all finishing operations. Instead, we will describe a few of the main steps taken in finishing woven cotton and blends. Generally, a roll of greige, or unfinished, fabric arrives at the finishing plant and is first fed through singeing equipment, which removes the protruding fiber hairs by exposing the fabric briefly to a gas flame. From there, the fabric goes into a bath to remove sizing from the fabric. Scouring and bleaching steps follow. Again, the chemistry of these steps must be matched to the particular fabric fibers. While high temperatures might be ideal for cotton processing, hot alkaline can degrade polyesters. Washing follows each of these steps, creating an additional waste stream to be treated.

Dyeing the Cloth

After these preparatory operations, the fabric is ready for dyeing, another stage in which fiber chemistry plays a critical role. Uniformity and colorfastness of the dyed fabric are characteristics that determine which dyes will be used for a given fabric construction. Consumers expect modern fabrics to be colorfast in dry cleaning and washing and not to fade unduly when exposed to the sun. With the end use and cost in mind, a dye is selected. Modern reactive dyes form strong chemical bonds with fibers, while older coloring processes relied on pigments that do not chemically bond to the fibers. The result is excellent colorfastness of reactive dyes during washing but at a higher cost.

Many seasonal knit products are created with unique colors, which may give the manufacturer a comparative advantage for at least one selling season, if the color becomes a hit in the market. Some apparel fabrics have yarn-dyed warps, which must first go through dyeing and then return to slashing before weaving. Such dyed yarns, however, normally constitute a special order, except for a few common colors. Once dyed-yarn orders for a season are set, textile firms cannot make more during that season because of the time it takes for dyeing, weaving, and finishing. In this way, textile suppliers can offer apparel manufacturers a unique fabric for that year.

Large-volume multicolor fabric printing requires multimillion-dollar printing ranges. Printing machines with twenty colors are available, although it is common to use half the print rolls for one order while the second set of rolls is cleaned for the next. Registration of the individual colors is critical for a quality product, and full microprocessor-speed control is necessary to account for fabric stretch. Most of the print dyes are heat-set and naturally must be colorfast if the fabric will be used for bedding. Given the sophistication and precision of this equipment, the capital intensity of this stage of textile operations is quite high.

Surface Finishing

The last stage in finishing is often the mechanical step of surface modification. The fabric can be "calendered" by passing it between a series of contacting rolls. The rolls press on the cloth, flattening and polishing it. Heat may be added or not, depending on the desired surface finish.

There are techniques to raise the surface rather than to polish it. Malden Mills' polyester fleece, for example, is created by brushing the knit surface with thousands of small hooked needles that open loops in the knit.[31]

Recently, cotton twill pants are being offered with a brushed or raised finish. Such finishes give the fabric a softer feel and add another style, increasing the SKUs a casual pants manufacturer can offer. Chemical finishes also have become popular. Both wash-and-wear and soil resistance fabric properties are the result of surface treatment.

Competitive Challenges

The story of textile production presented here, while somewhat truncated, is designed to highlight the following points: (1) it still takes many weeks or months to produce finished cloth from fibers; and (2) to match changes occurring in the rest of the channel, textile firms must focus on quality, service to customers, and uniqueness of products, which can often be achieved through the finishing process. The technical realities of the textile industry mean that—like it or not—a number of time-consuming steps are required to convert fibers into useful textiles. The capital intensity of spinning, weaving, and finishing often requires producers to schedule continuous operations. Because setup times are long and costly, companies prefer to run long fabric lengths for weaving and finishing.

This type of manufacturing was well suited to the traditional markets served by textile producers, especially the apparel market. As Chapter 12 details, textile operations have achieved tremendous productivity growth over the past four decades through their incorporation of new technologies and practices in all phases of production. Yet the demands of lean retailing, increasing product proliferation, and the growth of other markets for textiles outside the apparel industry have put new pressures on these manufacturers. In the next chapter, we explore the overall performance of the U.S. industry as well as the new competitive dynamics involved in multiple textile channels.

12

The Economic Viability of Textiles: A Tale of Multiple Channels

From the outset, we have emphasized that separate enterprises in the retail-apparel-textile channel, which traditionally maintained arm's-length relationships with one another, are now becoming increasingly integrated through information and inventory links. For that reason, channel operations must to be reported and analyzed as a whole. Still, there are a variety of separate connections between textile enterprises, retailers, and ultimate consumers and purchasers. The upshot is that a large and growing segment of the textile industry appears to be far less dependent on the apparel industry than it was in the classic retail-apparel-textile channel.

Textiles are best understood as part of three major channels: the traditional textile-apparel-retail flow, the textile-retail direct connection, and the textile-industrial purchaser pattern. The textile sector has developed specialized production at some stages for all three types of end markets. Traditional spinning and weaving provide cloth for apparel manufacture; knitted T-shirts and fabricated household furnishings go directly from textile plants to retail stores; and industrial products, such as automotive trimmings, fishnets, and tire cord, flow from textile plants to other industries and their customers.

In fact, the definition of "textile industry" requires clarification in any discussion of U.S. textiles. The Census of Manufacturers classifies "establishments" as a whole according to the "type of activity in which they are engaged."[1] Although an establishment may manufacture a range of products, it is only given one code, or standard industrial classification (SIC). For example, SIC 22 encompasses all textile mill products,[2] and it is subdivided into nine three-digit and at least twenty-four four-digit industries.[3] The numbering sequence within

SIC 22 follows the flow of product through the production process—from cotton, wool, or synthetic fibers to woven or knit products and finishing operations. But some establishments in SIC 22 have almost nothing to do with the textile-apparel channel, such as carpets and rugs (SIC 2273) and cordage and twine (SIC 2298).[4]

This clarification matters because it indicates that the U.S. textile industry now operates in multiple channels—part of the reason for its continued growth. Historically, most textile products went into apparel-making; but by the late 1990s, only about one-third of the American industry's output goes into making clothes. A closer look at the scope of the U.S. textile sector also avoids a simplistic use of data in the aggregate form of SIC 22 textiles and SIC 23 apparel when more focused data are required.[5] For our purposes, it is essential to examine data presented in three- and four-digit codes or on an individual enterprise or even establishment basis. That way, we have a much clearer picture of which segments of the textile industry are expanding and contracting.

This chapter shows how vital the U.S. textile industry has become on a global scale. It does so by looking at the performance of the industry as whole, then considering the multiple channels in textiles. The conventional wisdom, often repeated, holds that this American sector is in its sunset stage, soon to be eliminated by import penetration, and is one the country would be well advised to abandon. But such a stance has failed to predict the outcome for U.S. textiles, in part because the industry has shifted over the years toward high-value items like bed sheets, carpets, and industrial products. These have become far less standardized commodities than greige, or unfinished, goods. Indeed, the current textile industry is a far cry from the classic greige goods producers that faced competitive commodity markets.[6] In an earlier day, cotton greige goods brokers were concentrated in the Worth Street district of New York City, analogous to a bourse in primary products. Today textile firms may create their own finished products for sale, buying materials from other suppliers around the world. This shift in focus not only accounts for the current health of American textiles; it also points to what is required to keep the industry vibrant in the future.

The Global Industry

The contemporary textile industry, which provides fabric to apparel producers as well as an array of products to retail and industrial customers, truly spans the globe. The past fifty years have witnessed widespread emergence of new nation states like Pakistan and Indonesia, and in almost all of them industrialization in the textile sector, and related apparel enterprises, has played an historic role in establishing a foundation for economic growth. Developing countries with an abundance of cheap labor but little capital have produced textile and apparel products for domestic and export markets.[7] The different stages of economic development among countries are reflected in the changing distribution of the world's textile industry, production, and employment.[8]

The world production of synthetic fiber grew from 4.8 million tons in 1970 to 16.2 million tons in 1993.[9] The percentage distribution of this production among types of economies in 1970 and 1993 is shown in Table 12.1.

As synthetic and artificial fiber use expanded, a number of developing countries increased their basic textile production, mainly for clothing and industrial purposes, with the assistance of investment by multinational companies in fiber facilities. Typically, firms in these developing countries started out with less capital-intensive fabric and clothing technology, then invested the export earnings from this relatively inexpensive form of production into setting up more advanced textile facilities. According to a 1996 report of the International Labour Office, "Most countries in South-East Asia succeeded in this way to make their mark on the international textile scene."[10]

Employment among the major textile-producing countries over the past several decades shows a similar global redistribution. Because labor productivity varies substantially among these countries, employment figures are an inadequate proxy for actual output. Nonetheless, Table 12.2 (page 206) indicates how location of textile employment has shifted with expansion of the industry in China, Indonesia, Bangladesh, and other developing countries and its contraction in Germany, France, Italy, the United Kingdom, Japan, and the United States.

Table 12.1. Production of Synthetic Fibers in Different Economies (Percent of all Production)

	1970	1993
Industrialized countries	85.3%	43.6%
Eastern Europe and China	8.0	16.3
Developing countries	6.7	40.1

Sources: International Labour Office, *Globalization of the Footwear, Textile and Clothing Industries*, Geneva, Switzerland, International Labour Office, 1996, p. 5.

Table 12.2. Employment in Textiles (ISIC 321 in Thousands)[a]

Country	1970	1980	1990	1992	1992/1970 (Percent change)
China	—	3,119	5,060	5,060	
India	1,356	1,695	1,403	1,398	103.0
United States	1,113	986	829	795	71.4
Japan	1,144	757	634	597	52.2
Bangladesh	131	273	512	—	—
Indonesia	143	230	467	490	371.0
Korea	204	393	349	336	165.0
Germany, F.R.	498	317	229	210	42.1
France	411	303	210	184	44.7
United Kingdom	621	349	224	198	31.9
Italy	419	291	224	234	55.8

Source: International Labor Office, *Globalization of the Footwear, Textile and Clothing Industries*, pp. 34–35.

[a] ISIC refers to International Standard Industrial Classification Standard of all Economic Activity, 1968, Revision 2 used in the International Labour Office (ILO) study. The Soviet Union and Eastern European countries have been excluded from the above summary.

The U.S. decline has been substantially less than that of Western Europe and Japan, and differing productivity levels offer some clue as to why the American industry is still thriving. In 1993, the textile industry in the People's Republic of China used an estimated 16.7 billion pounds of fiber compared with only 12.5 billion pounds in the United States. If productivity levels in China had been equal to those in the United States, the Chinese industry would have needed about one-fifth the number of workers that were actually employed. In the same vein, a draft report on the U.S. textile industry states, "If all the world's textile industry were as productive [as the U.S.], the world output could have been provided by 4.48 million textile workers [instead of 15 million]."[11]

U.S. Performance and Productivity

In this global setting, the U.S. textile industry continues to perform well. In 1997, textile yarn and fabric imports were $11.9 billion compared with exports of $9.0 billion; in contrast, clothing exports were $8.4 billion compared with imports of $48.4 billion.[12]

In fact, the productivity rate in textiles has been much higher than the average of manufacturing in the United States. For instance, multifactor productivity in textile mill products from 1949 to 1996 increased faster than for manufacturing—a 2.2 percent compound average annual growth rate in textiles compared with just 1.2 percent for manufacturing. Multifactor productivity indices compare output to five categories of input: capital, labor, energy, nonenergy material, and business services.[13] Compare the 2.2 percent annual growth rate in multifactor productivity for textiles during the 1949–96 period with a few other sectors: It was 1.1 percent for chemicals and allied products and 0.7 percent for transportation equipment (including motor vehicles and trucks); electrical and electronic equipment with an annual average growth rate of 3.2 percent, has increased the fastest in the years since 1979.

If we refer to the more familiar measure of productivity—output per employee hour—we see textile sector growth rates in excess of the private sector or manufacturing as a whole. For cotton and synthetic broadwoven fabrics (SIC 221 and 222), output per hour for all employees increased between 1973 and 1995 by 145.8 percent, with an average annual increase of 6.6 percent a year. The increase for hosiery (SIC 2251 and 2252) was 101.1 percent, with an average annual increase of 4.6 percent; and in nonwool yarn spinning mills (SIC 2281), output per employee went up 138.3 percent for the same years, with an average annual increase of 6.3 percent.[14] For the business sector of the economy as a whole, however, output per employee increased only 28.2 percent, with an average annual increase of 1.3 percent; for all manufacturing, productivity measured in this way went up a decent 72.7 percent during the same period, with an average annual increase of 3.3 percent a year, but this rate was still lower than the segments of textiles for which the data are presented. Not all branches of textile mill products increased labor productivity at the same rate in these years, but the segments cited are substantial in their proportion of total industry volume.[15]

The U.S. Bureau of Labor Statistics' outlook for output and employment of textiles to the year 2006 projects a continuation of the patterns shown in Figure 12.1 (page 208), which depicts the course of aggregate textile production and employment since 1950.[16] Note that while textile production has increased almost threefold during this period, the number of workers has been reduced by more than half. The course of U.S. textile production and employment since 1950, as well as the steady growth in productivity, reflects a number of significant developments

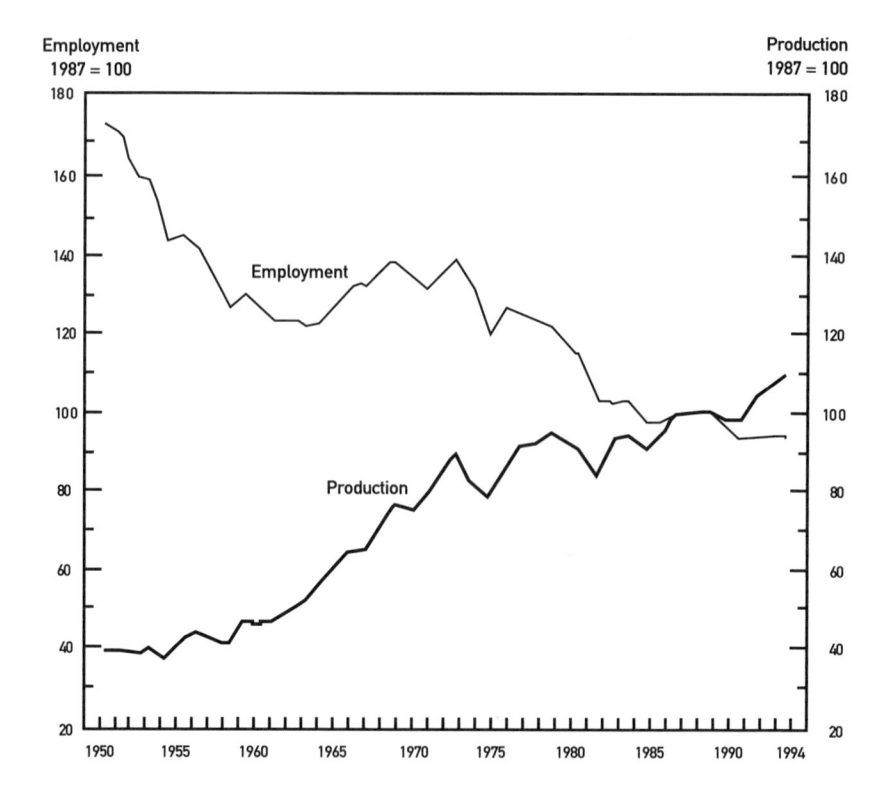

Figure 12.1. Employment and Production in Textiles, 1950–94.
Source: Monthly Labor Review, August 1995, p. 65.

described in the last chapter: technological changes and automation in textile manufacturing processes; shifts to large-scale establishments; restructuring and consolidation of enterprises in spinning, weaving, knitting, and specialized finishing operations; substantial capital expenditures in these activities; and a shift to textile products with expanding markets.[17] The vibrancy of the textile industry can best be understood, however, by examining three separate but related channels: the traditional retail-apparel-textile channel; the textile-retail channel that produces home furnishings and other products; and the channels that connect textile producers to industrial users.

The Impact of Different Textile Channels

It would be ideal to measure the performance of the textile industry over recent years according to the end uses of textiles, at least for the three major channels through which textile products flow to consumers. But the data for spinning, weaving, knitting, dyeing, and finishing operations among and within establishments according to destination of products is not available. Therefore, this section will examine other ways of estimating the growth of different channels. The most striking point overall is that, together, textile-retail and textile-industrial outflows now represent the largest part of textile output in the United States. These markets have grown, despite the fact that the classic textile-apparel channel has been favored by the preferential duties for sewn apparel imports made of U.S. textiles.[18]

To begin with, Table 12.3 shows major changes in the composition of the domestic industry. This lists aggregate employment figures for each of the main segments of the industry for 1960 and 1997.

The expanding areas of the industry have been knitting mills—now the largest segment—textile finishing, carpets and rugs, and yarn and thread mills. The miscellaneous fabricated textile products category, classified as a part of apparel (SIC 239) and included here for comparative purposes, has also grown in employment, while broadwoven fabric mills cotton and wool have declined significantly. The data on relative employment levels reflect the fact that the textile-retail and textile-industrial channels have grown significantly. On this basis, apparel markets would appear to provide little more than a quar-

Table 12.3. Employees in Thousands in Major Textile Sectors, SIC 22[a]

		Employment (Thousands)		Segment as Percent of All Textile Employment	
		1960	1997	1960	1997
22	All employees	924.3	607.7		
221	Broadwoven fabric mills, cotton	254.0	71.2	27.5	11.7
222	Broadwoven fabric mills, synthetics	84.4	64.9	9.1	10.7
223	Broadwoven fabric mills, wool	55.6	14.4	6.0	2.4
224	Narrow fabric mills	27.6	20.9	3.0	3.4
225	Knitting mills	219.2	171.8	23.7	28.3
226	Textile finishing, except wool	77.0	64.9	8.4	10.7
227	Carpets and rugs	37.6	61.6	4.1	10.1
228	Yarn and thread mills	102.5	87.2	11.1	14.4
229	Miscellaneous textile goods	66.4	50.8	7.2	8.4

Source: U.S. Bureau of Labor Statistics, Employment and Earnings, Establishment data.
[a] SIC 239, Miscellaneous fabricated textile products had 139.9 employees in 1960 and 216.3 employees in 1997.

ter of aggregate textile employment. Meanwhile, industrial markets are catching up, providing almost a quarter of aggregate textile employment. And direct retail from textiles, including fabricated textile products, accounts for almost half. The substantial size of the textile-retail channel is related to the growth of knit goods and household products like sheets, towels, and carpets.

Another way to estimate the relative size of different channels is to follow the flow of fibers. A study by the U.S. Office of Technology Assessment placed "apparel's share of fiber consumption at approximately 37 percent between 1979 and 1985, whereas the share of home furnishings grew from 31 to 38 percent. Industrial textile products still consume over 20 percent of fiber production."[19] It also appears that, from 1980 to 1996, a larger share of the fiber used in apparel was cotton (increasing from 35 to 53 percent), while a declining share of synthetic fiber was used in apparel (from 62 to 45 percent).[20]

We can also estimate the relative size of the classic textile-apparel channel by measuring the value of shipments to apparel production from the textile industry. For instance, approximately one-third of total textile shipments currently appears to flow to apparel manufacture from woven fabrics.[21] With these estimates of the scale of the three channels in mind, let us turn to their current operations in more detail.

The Retail-Apparel-Textile Channel

The traditional retail system permitted the accumulation of large amounts of inventory at both the finished goods and work-in-process stages of production. With retail orders placed months in advance of expected time of receipt, apparel manufacturers could gear up production to smooth output and gain maximum efficiencies. This method of doing business rippled backward in the channel to the relationship between apparel manufacturers and their textile suppliers.

Orders for textile products were placed with even longer lead times than those placed by retailers, and apparel manufacturers were committed to purchases of significant production runs. On the men's side of the industry, the relatively low fashion content of products meant that the number of different fabric types being ordered was limited. On the women's side, intermediate parties played a role in providing more diverse products in shorter runs.[22] Overall, however, the considerable length of lead times and the acceptance of large minimum orders for fabrics fitted well with the economies of scale arising in textile manufacturing operations.

With the advent of lean retailing, apparel manufacturers are under pressure to change these traditional relationships. In particular, apparel-makers would like to order fabric with lead times measured in weeks, rather than months, and order lot sizes often less than a thousand yards. The growing tension between these two channel players produces intense discussion whenever garment-makers and textile executives meet to address quick response in the apparel industry. Retailers, in turn, would like to place their orders for fashion merchandise close to the season and with a minimum order size. Reorders of only the fashion SKUs that are selling would be ideal. But replenishing fashion apparel within a few weeks is impossible for apparel-makers, unless the piece goods are available. If it were possible to create fabric in a few weeks, in small lot sizes, and at reasonable prices, then rapid replenishment of fashion apparel would be a major new business opportunity for U.S. apparel firms.

Our survey of the apparel industry asked manufacturers to report their minimum order quantities for basic and fashion textiles. The results for 1988 and 1992 are shown in Figure 12.2 (page 212). Almost no progress in decreasing the minimum order size was made between the two designated time periods. The reason for lack of movement has a great deal to do with the high costs in textile production. Although a number of major textile manufacturers have been exploring new methods to reduce setup costs in weaving, progress has been slow. Newer methods of finishing, including the widespread use of computer-controlled finishing operations, also promise to reduce minimum order sizes. But change was modest at best during the years in which lean retailing emerged.

The same lack of change can be seen in comparing lead times for basic and fashion textiles between 1988 and 1992. Once again, inherently long lead times arise from the complex sequential processes required to produce textile products. Although lead time reductions are possible, they cannot be as easily or as inexpensively achieved as lowering throughput time in apparel assembly processes. Figure 12.3 (page 213) presents the average minimum lead times for basic and fashion fabrics from the time an order is placed by the apparel business unit to receipt of those products. The survey revealed relatively little change between the two time periods, despite the dramatic increase in lean retailing practices. In fact, our analysis of the survey data found that minimum lead times offered by textile suppliers were about the same in 1992, whether the business unit faced a low or high level of demand for rapid replenishment by its retailers. Shorter fabric lead

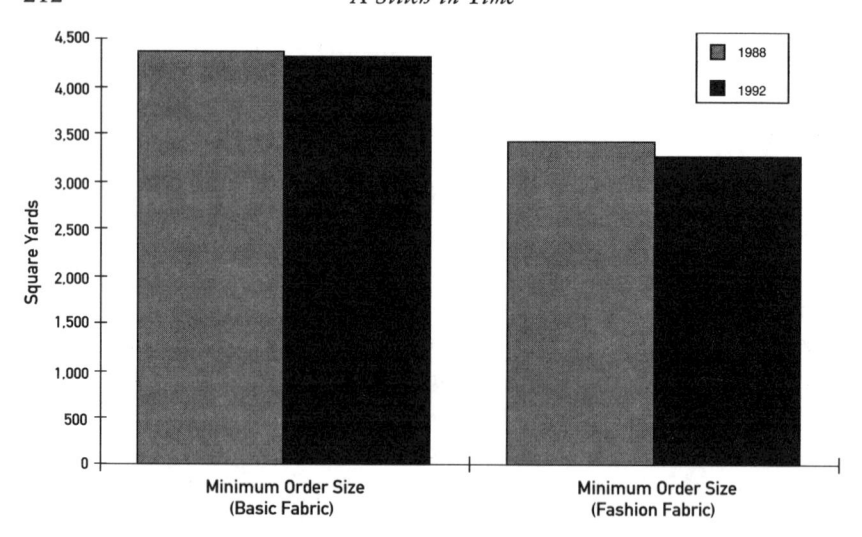

Figure 12.2. Average Minimum Order Quantities of Textile Manufacturers, 1988 and 1992

Source: Harvard Center for Textile and Apparel Research.

times offer potential competitive advantages for apparel firms—and presumably their textile suppliers—but in 1992 business units had to wait, on average, more than two months to receive fashion fabrics.[23]

Clearly, work needs to be done to decrease order size and lead times. The information systems that allow retailers to follow retail sales are in place, but the channel requires quicker response between textile suppliers and apparel manufacturers, if replenishment of fashion items within a selling season is ever to become a reality. Although we do not have survey data to report on changes after 1992, we know of a number of instances in which fashion fabrics have been made available in shorter order times. Then again, not all fashion apparel requires fashion fabrics. A fashion apparel item may just need a change in silhouette and trim from a basic item. Or it might take a special color, using only a basic greige fabric that is readily available and can be piece-dyed.

Malden Mills represents a well-known case of a textile manufacturer that has successfully capitalized on its ability to produce a wide variety of high quality textile products with market responsiveness. The success of its Polartec line has a great deal to do with the company's attention to retail requirements (such as those specified by Lands' End and L. L. Bean) and what its apparel customers (Patagonia, North Face) need. Malden Mills' manufacturing operations have focused on both productivity and providing varied products.[24] The success of a number

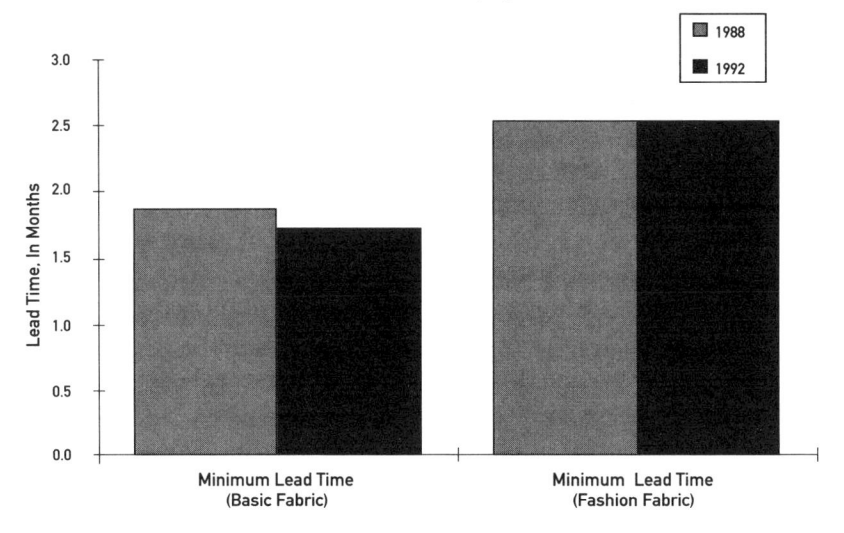

Figure 12.3. Average Minimum Lead Time of Textile Manufacturers, 1988 and 1992

Source: Harvard Center for Textile and Apparel Research.

of other smaller mills in New England, which make small runs of high-quality products for apparel and industrial users, offers similar examples of the potential in this area.[25]

However change in the relationships in the retail-apparel-textile channel can be brought about, it is sure to involve long partnership discussions and the development of trust. That is the only way to ensure that firms in different parts of the channel will share order information and accurate forecasts of retail sales. Smaller, quicker orders might be made in special offshore textile factories with lower operating costs, as long as these factories are located in a region with good enough logistics to ship fabric quickly for finishing in this country. There are many ways to shorten the supply chain, which would then enable U.S.-based apparel firms to sell into the fashion replenishment market. But, from our perspective, textile and apparel firms have yet to make these connections. In part, that is because of the inherent capital intensity of textile operations. It also requires new agents in the channel, as we discuss at the end of this chapter.

Direct Channels for Retail and Industrial Products

Non-apparel channels have characteristics quite different from the classic retail-apparel-textile channel described in earlier chapters. In that channel, textiles flow to apparel enterprises that manufacture a variety of women's, children's, and men's wear, as well as to large producers of jeans, casual wear, and various uniforms. Now we want to focus on the textile-retail direct channel made up by the textile enterprises that produce and market household items like bedding, bath accessories, and carpets or sell major products like tire cord automotive trimming to industrial purchasers.

Such textile firms, particularly the largest, are integrated from the primary textile operations of spinning and weaving, which produce greige goods, to the dyeing, printing surface finishing, and fabrication of these products. They make direct shipments to mass merchandisers and major department stores or to industrial companies. These enterprises tend to produce the great majority of the greige goods they require internally, but they purchase yarn or fabric from smaller companies to meet short-term fluctuations in demands and volumes that do not warrant building or purchasing new primary plants.

Note that large-scale multi-plant textile enterprises have established in recent years the same sort of information-integrated channels with retailers that many apparel-makers have. Instead of an intermediary link between textile firms and retailers, as in the classic channel, many textile enterprises and retailers/industrial purchasers now deal directly with one another. One such textile company reports that, between 1988 and 1997, it increased its electronic data interchange (EDI) partners from 26 to 400; the types of EDI documents from 3 to 25, and the aggregate of EDI documents processed from 60 thousand to 15 million.[26] An information-integrated channel appears to have been established in this instance, providing evidence of the links between suppliers, production operations, distribution centers, retailers, and, in turn, customers.[27]

As we have already reported, HCTAR's research shows a reduction in inventories for apparel manufacturers facing rapid replenishment pressure from retailers, as well as shorter times to market, at least for basic and fashion-basic items. These features are also emerging in the textile-retail channel. Take product proliferation. One textile company now has more than 20,000 SKUs in its bed-products line, as well as more than 10,000 bath products. New technologies and innovations in dyeing, finishing, and color printing have contributed to these developments. More important, the emphasis on an information-integrated channel, with related changes in production and distribution of bed and bath products, has substantially reduced cycle time in this company. In fact, cycle times have been reduced by about half over a decade, from five or seven weeks to little more than two weeks.

As with textile companies in general, firms that work directly with retailers and industrial purchasers have made very large capital investments in new equipment. But they also continue to invest in information systems and product development. One company we know of expends about $30 million a year on product development and the same amount in operations on information systems. Over the last several decades, this textile company has shifted from producing cotton and synthetic fabrics for apparel to creating bedding, towels, rugs and carpets, and various industrial products. These items, with ever growing variation in SKUs by size, color, fabric, and design, require machinery and equipment to process textile products with larger dimensions than conventional weaving and fabrication. This heavy capital investment also involves continuous and multi-shift operations.

Another major U.S. textile company has largely withdrawn from the production of greige goods and cloth for apparel markets, except when it purchases product from outsiders for further processing. With approximately the same number of total employees as a quarter of a century ago, this firm has expanded the value of its shipments by about five times. The continuing shift toward higher value product lines and markets is a major feature of this segment of the textile industry. The design and diversification of products in a given line require continuing adaptations in the production and distribution processes of the enterprise.

In addition, not all suppliers of purchased materials to these textile companies are domestic producers. Such textile firms may, on occasion, purchase product from overseas contractors to meet short-term demands for items they regularly produce. Most suppliers of yarn and greige goods fabric are smaller domestic companies close to the main manufacturing facilities, yet one major company sourced some basic commodity-type supplies from Indonesia, Thailand, and China.

The retail-textile channel in household products, like the retail-apparel-textile channel in jeans and some knitwear, involves integrated information flows, inventory management, and at least a limited form of partnership rather than classic market relationships. This channel encourages long-term interests and business relations, and the price and terms of transactions cannot readily be imposed by any party in the purchase or sale process. Because of the size and clout of textile enterprises in this channel, retailers have far different relationships with them—more of a partnership—than they do with most apparel manufacturers and their contractors, save for a few large-scale suppliers in a few product lines. Yet even major textile producers note the increasing pressure they face in their direct relationships with retailers. The latter want suppliers to provide products within tight time limits, use bar codes and EDI, and ship in a manner in which products can be rapidly cross-docked in retail distribution centers.

As for industrial textiles, their market share, according to Sabit Adanur, "has increased tremendously within the last thirty years."[28] Although industrial textiles are highly diverse, the largest market segments in 1995 were geosynthetics, automotive, and safety and protective items, which constituted three-quarters of the market as measured in square yards. Among rapidly emerging new markets are airbags and geosynthetics, or so-called "smart" materials, which change characteristics according to outside conditions. The textile-industrial channel often involves the same lean retailing features: information integration, inventory replenishment, business partnerships, product proliferation, distribution centers, and production processes geared toward retail markets.

We want to stress, however, that these different textile channels do not correspond exactly with the retail-apparel channel. For one thing, the capital equipment in textile plants means that planning shorter production runs may require different human resource changes than those discussed in earlier chapters for apparel manufacturers. For another, inventory control and sourcing decisions in textile firms may be based on different considerations than those of the apparel plant cases detailed in Chapter 7. For example, the additional cost of running a short-cycle line in apparel arises from differences in labor productivity between assembly workers on PBS and modular lines, as well as differences in wage rates that depend on the location of the lines. In textiles, the differences between operations that offer shorter turnaround times or smaller minimum order sizes may arise from more fundamental technological changes in the way that fabric is woven, knitted, or finished. Therefore, the effects of lean retailing requirements on textile producers—whether from apparel manufacturers, retailers, or industrial users that have moved to just-in-time order methods—involve technological complexities much greater than those found in apparel and beyond the scope of this volume.

Channel Integration: Still a Challenge

Despite the development of information sharing and partnerships between major textile companies and retailers—or across textile companies, apparel companies, and retailers in some product lines like denim jeans and knit goods—there is little evidence of an increase in vertical integration in these sectors. As we have already noted, Levi Strauss and a few other apparel-makers also have retail outlets; there are several instances of textile enterprises engaging in retailing beyond the usual company store. But some of the most significant boundaries have yet to be crossed and may never be—textile firms entering apparel manufacturing or retailing, apparel enterprises also producing textiles, retail enterprises moving into either apparel or textile manufacturing. In fact, the presence of abundant accurate information on demand and the falling costs of conducting transactions across the boundaries between sectors may lower the benefits arising from formal integration of enterprises. We take up this issue in the concluding chapter.

Decades ago, lower Sixth Avenue in New York City formed a large and vigorous community of garment-makers. We have been told that apparel suppliers could walk down the street and find buttons or fabric to satisfy their needs. This community has now shrunk in size for many economic and social reasons. Yet given the rigors of lean retailing, it is clear that independent apparel manufacturers and contractors cannot exist for long operating along traditional lines in metropolitan areas like New York City, Los Angeles, and San Francisco or scattered throughout the country in small rural communities. Some method of linking apparel firms to fabric suppliers—a modern equivalent of lower Sixth Avenue—will be an essential aspect of the U.S. softgoods industry in the future.

In the 1980s, some analysts assumed that as low-wage countries began to compete with the United States in textile production, the domestic industry might have to follow the successful example of the Italian Prato textile region near Florence. In their account of this region, Michael Piore and Charles Sabel note that employment in Prato remained nearly constant at 45,000 workers from 1966 to 1976, while employment in the textile industries of West Germany and France declined by 25 percent.[29] They suggest that Prato's success was due to the reorganization of production from large integrated mills to that of individual units with just a few looms, each creating new fashion woolen fabrics.[30] These small firms formed flexible production networks coordinated by an *impannatore*.

The *impannatore* in Northern Italy plays a key role: They coordinate information between textile producers and apparel manufacturers. The network of producers can only compete by virtue of such coordination among the region's separate, relatively small enterprises and final consumers. Finding agents to serve an equivalent function also has the potential to address the problem of linking U.S. textile firms and apparel manufacturers. One possible candidate for playing the role of information coordinator is the Internet.

A project called DAMA (Demand Activated Manufacturing Architecture) has recently been undertaken jointly by [TC]^2 and some of its industry members along with the U.S. Department of Energy's national research laboratories. The DAMA project seeks to link the U.S. apparel and textile industry through a computer-based information system. Part of the project has been to sponsor a Web page where textile suppliers and apparel manufacturers identify their availability and provide information on what service or products they offer. This National Sourcing Data Base (NSDB) has the potential for creating a virtual community of apparel and textile providers in various channels of the softgoods industry.

Although still in the development stages, NSDB can provide an apparel supplier looking for different fabrics with a range of information concerning textile sourcing. Factory views of several of the textile operations discussed in Chapter 11 are shown at this site to give apparel manufacturers a sense of the textile company's capabilities. In addition, the NSDB offers links that provide images of textile products—for example, color printing operations. Although it is difficult to describe multicolor printing in words, the site can show a print pattern after it passed through each color stage of a print range. This information could be invaluable for a company making sourcing decisions. NSDB also has information concerning the size of minimum orders and current availability of listed companies.

The next step toward providing part of the *impannatore's* role is for NSDB—and other agents offering similar functions—to maintain active and comprehensive links on the Internet. Being able to find detailed and up-to-date information on textile suppliers, including their capacity to provide specific products in specific delivery periods, will be critical for the competitive future of segments of the apparel industry. For example, the capability of apparel-makers to replenish products with a high fashion content rests in part on access to smaller runs of textile products with relatively short lead times.[31] Although specific segments of the textile industry must make their own operational changes to offer such products economically, establishing information links is a critical step in this direction.

Direct textile channels to retailers and industrial users will also continue to be affected by the capacity of textile firms to use information regarding demand from their customers in effective ways. There is less of a need for new intermediaries in these channels than in the retail-apparel-textile channel, but the dangers of not adjusting production strategies to deal with more frequent orders of smaller quantities of more diverse products remain.

When one considers the three channels that compose the textile industry as a whole, it is clear that competition from offshore producers has ended up affecting this industry quite differently than it has apparel-makers. It has undergone waves of concentration, while apparel firms have remained small with just a few exceptions. Regardless, the domestic textile industry has not been subject to import penetration in the same way. The major factor influencing its success has been improved product management and technology, which has led to productivity increases more rapid than the average of American manufacturing. The next chapter picks up the global trade story in more depth, emphasizing new sourcing possibilities for both the U.S. textile and apparel industries.

13

The Global Marketplace

Although much of this book has focused on the U.S. apparel and textile industries, it is impossible to provide a complete picture of the current transformation they are undergoing without discussing global trade patterns. Indeed, the volume of *all* goods and services traded in *all* industries across borders has grown enormously in recent years, accounting for about 45 percent of world gross domestic product in 1990 compared with only 25 percent in 1970.[1] As for the growth of trade in the American economy, in 1960 all international trade—exports plus imports—was equivalent to only 9 percent of gross domestic product. That figure has jumped to a healthy 25 percent, even though trade remains a much smaller component of the U.S. economy than in most countries.[2]

Technological and related changes have significantly enhanced all trade, making the world easier to navigate. Goods, capital, people, and ideas travel faster and more cheaply today than ever before. According to a 1995 World Bank report, "By 1960 maritime transport costs were less than a third of their 1920 level, and costs have continued to fall. Communications costs are falling even more dramatically—the costs of an international phone call fell six-fold between 1940 and 1970 and tenfold between 1970 and 1990."[3]

Globally, the textile and apparel industries have certainly been affected by better communications and faster transport. But a number of other factors particular to these industries have also determined trade patterns, and are still determining them, as speed to market, increasing product proliferation, and lean retailing practices continue to mold supply channels both within U.S. borders and without. This chapter begins with a look at how textile- and apparel-making have helped industrialize developing economies, then focuses on the shifting flow of American imports and exports in both industries.

It is important to reiterate here that the U.S. textile and apparel stories are not the same, and that the fates of these two industries are not inextricably linked. For instance, in 1997, the United States imported $48.4 billion of apparel,[4] up from $24.5 billion in 1989, $6.5 billion in 1980, and just $283 million in 1961.[5] At the same time, apparel exports have been relatively small, $8.4 billion. And although 1997 apparel imports at foreign port values accounted for about one-third of domestic consumption, the mid-1990s level of apparel imports constituted approximately one-half the value of apparel consumed in the United States when measured by retail prices.[6]

Meanwhile, import penetration has been much less dramatic for textiles. In 1997, the United States imported approximately $11.9 billion of textiles, up from $6 billion in 1989, $2 billion in 1980, and $590 million in 1961.[7] Yet textile exports in recent years have almost kept pace with imports; at the end of the 1970s, textile exports were actually larger in value than textile imports, and in 1997 textile exports were $9.0 billion.[8] The mid-1990s level of textile imports accounted for only about 12 percent of domestic textile consumption when measured at retail prices.

The link between these two industries may be growing more tenuous. Because the American textile industry supplies most of the cloth and other materials used by domestic apparel-makers, the rapid growth of apparel imports has adversely affected the 35 percent of the textile market derived from U.S. apparel manufacturers. The only exceptions are Mexican and Caribbean imports of apparel made from U.S. textiles, which we will address in the following trade sections. For good reason, American textile firms have entered other markets, including the direct retail and industrial channels discussed in the last chapter, and continue to be highly productive. The predominance of expensive, sophisticated equipment in textile plants also means that these firms operate under a different set of imperatives than those of domestic apparel-makers.

Still, American public and trade policies have linked these industries in the past, in part because of the crucial role textiles play in the classic retail-apparel-textile channel. Much of this chapter will address U.S. trade policy, which has historically protected the domestic textile and apparel industries. The emergence of the General Agreement on Tariffs and Trade (GATT) and the phasing out of the Multi-Fiber Arrangement (MFA) by the year 2005, which is scheduled to eliminate import quotas, make clear that these American industries are likely to face more global challenges soon. But while other commentators predict a dire future for U.S. apparel and textile firms, we believe that other trends and structural developments—many of which have been detailed in earlier chapters—will also shape what these industries become.

The growing regionalization of textile- and apparel-making may mean that skilled processes, such as cutting in apparel manufacturing and finishing operations in textiles, will remain in first-world countries like the United States, Japan, Germany, and Italy; the lower paid occupations of assembly in apparel-making will continue to go to developing countries in Latin America, Asia, Eastern Europe, or North Africa, which can provide lower labor costs—but with a significant twist. Because time-to-market and the exigencies of short-cycle production are beginning to impact competition in retail-apparel-textile channels, three global regions are emerging: the United States plus Mexico and the Caribbean Basin; Japan plus East and Southeast Asia; and Western Europe plus Eastern Europe and North Africa. Each of these regions includes both advanced economies and developing areas that are close to consumer markets. The growth of new product markets in expanding economies like those of the People's Republic of China and Mexico may also affect trade patterns.

What this implies, in a larger sense, is that the classical economic view of comparative labor-cost advantage—in which the lion's share of textile and apparel production would shift to developing countries, where labor rates are much lower—has been modified in some respects by lean retailing practices and short-cycle production strategies. In fact, these two factors are driving global regionalization of the industries, and a realistic assessment of textiles and apparel has to account for a more complicated array of sourcing decisions. As we stressed in Chapter 7, although low labor costs may still be the basis for production planning, speed and proximity to markets are other key factors, especially if a manufacturer uses some production lines or plants that can turn around an order in under two weeks.

The trade policy changes that GATT and the North American Free Trade Agreement (NAFTA) represent are potentially so basic that no one can entirely predict how they will affect textiles and apparel after 2005. But we will emphasize the various trade-offs—low labor rates versus short-cycle production, for example—that can deepen an analysis of what might happen, moving beyond the conventional wisdom about "dying" U.S. industries.

Textiles and Apparel in Economic Development

Many economists have recognized the role textile- and apparel-making play in developing countries. In the late 1940s, T. S. Ashton wrote, "In all parts of the world textiles have been one of the earliest offshoots of a peasant economy."[9] Economic historian Alexander Gerschenkron noted twenty years later that, in England,

> [T]he industrial revolution ushered in the textile age, and the textile industry then looked back upon a long premodern history: single artisans, artisans united in craft guilds, merchant employers, and so on.... The modern factory had to compete against all these preindustrial formations before it could assert itself.[10]

In countries that industrialized early, such as England and the United States, as well as in the developing nations still plagued with what Gerschenkron calls "economic backwardness,"[11] textiles and apparel made outside the household often constitute a significant step in early economic development. These home-grown industries may not necessarily provide the impetus for a major spurt in economic growth, but they often set the stage for increasing industrialization.

As less developed countries adopt industrialization policies, textiles and factory-made apparel often become a focus of government stimulus. For example, following World War II, Japan faced the destruction of much of its manufacturing base and focused on its textile and apparel industries to rebuild that base. In 1950, Japanese textiles accounted for 24 percent of the country's total shipments and 48 percent of exports. But these figures had declined to 5.2 percent and 4.8 percent, respectively, by 1980. In other words, textiles and apparel declined in importance as Japan became more industrialized and wage pressures increased.[12] These industries have also played a significant role in the development process in India and China.

More generally, the past thirty years have seen a significant shift in world exports of textiles and apparel toward developing market economies and away from developed economies. Table 13.1 summarizes these shifts in the percentage of all exports.

It is not hard to understand why textiles and garment-making have so frequently proven to be an early step in the industrialization process. Before countries become industrialized, these activities are performed in the household. The factory workplace initially provides a transition

Table 13.1. Developing and Developed Countries' Share of the World Export Market, 1965–1990

	Textile		Apparel	
	Developing	Developed	Developing	Developed
1965	16.0%	76.4%	14.8%	69.7%
1975	17.6	74.6	32.0	54.5
1985	28.0	62.2	47.9	41.5
1990	39.0	59.1	56.4	41.3

Source: Murray, Lauren A., "Unraveling Employment Trends in Textiles and Apparel," *Monthly Labor Review*, August 1995, p. 68.

from the household workplace. These sectors require very few workers with sophisticated skills. In apparel, skilled employees do cutting or repair sewing machines and probably constitute no more than 3 percent of the workforce. Most sewing work is employee-paced, and supervision is simplified by piece-rate operations. Capital requirements are small, and secondhand sewing machines are cheap and available.

In textiles, skilled workers are loomfixers and some weavers, and probably constitute no more than 5 percent of the workforce. As we have noted, textile labor costs amount to a relatively smaller proportion of total production costs than in apparel-making. Therefore, domestic textile production is relatively less vulnerable to lower labor rates and benefits abroad. According to Lauren Murray, "In 1990, thirty percent more labor was required for every dollar of output in the apparel industry than in textiles."[13]

Most textile operations are machine-paced, and capital requirements are appreciable, particularly by international trade standards. To be sure, secondhand equipment from advanced countries has been available to firms in developing areas—many textile plants in third-world countries got their start this way. However, the increasing importance of finishing operations in creating higher value products—especially items like sheets with proprietary prints that are sold directly to retail outlets—means that high-quality textile operations tend to remain in advanced countries.

U.S. Policies on Apparel and Textile Trade

W. Denney Freeston and Jeffrey Arpan claim, "Probably no other manufactured products receive as much protection as fabric and apparel."[14] Michael Finger and Ann Harrison put it another way: "Although textiles and apparel account for less than 2 percent of total employment in the U.S. economy, protecting them against import competition accounts for 83 percent of the net cost to the U.S. economy of all import restrictions."[15] Before examining how current trade patterns are shifting, we will briefly outline the historical policies governing textiles and apparel.

Beginning in the late 1950s, the national policy of the United States was to restrain the growth of textile and apparel imports through agreements with other governments that specify limitations on imports or on their percentage increase over a previous period. A 1957 agreement with Japan specified an annual aggregate limit on cotton textile exports to the United States and established ceilings for particular products. The Long-Term Arrangement Regarding Trade in Cotton Textiles was negotiated in 1962 and signed by 33 countries. The more comprehensive MFA became effective in 1974. It was renegotiated and ratified four times, most recently in 1986.[16] The MFA expired at the end of 1994, but its provisions are to be gradually phased out by the year 2005 under the interim Agreement on Textiles and Clothing.

The MFA operated outside the emerging regulations of GATT, allowing signatory countries to negotiate bilateral agreements to place import quotas on trade in textiles and apparel, including limitations on rates of increase in exports and imports. In addition to such negotiated limits, the MFA authorized unilateral restraints against imports that disrupted or threatened to disrupt the U.S. market. The MFA was designed to allow the orderly and nondisruptive growth of textile and apparel imports into the United States. In the 1980s, advocates like Stanley Nehmer and Mark Love argued that

> [A] formal managed trade arrangement that replaces the often chaotic, uncoordinated, and widely divergent economic behavior and policies of individual countries could act to reduce uncertainty in world markets, in certain industries, and lead eventually to more efficient, rational and open trading.[17]

The actual growth of the U.S. apparel market, however, has historically been below the rates of increase for imports specified in the various bilateral agreements under the MFA. Consequently, import penetration of the domestic market kept increasing. By the 1980s, the number of products and supplying countries, particularly the People's

Republic of China (PRC), outstripped the rates of growth envisaged in the bilateral agreements and American policymakers, responding to interest group pressures, resorted to unilateral restraints against such imports. In turn, the MFA regime was severely criticized by many economists because of the costs imposed on consumers by quotas restricting imports and by tariffs. William Cline concluded in 1990 that

> [t]he annual consumer costs per direct job preserved by protection amounts to $134,686 in textiles and $81,973 in apparel. These costs are extremely high. Considering that average wages in textiles and apparel are in the range of $12,000 annually, consumers pay nearly seven times as much to sustain job positions through protection as it would cost them to provide permanent vacations at full salary to the workers involved.[18]

The quotas assigned under the MFA for particular products were allocated by agreements to governments rather than to particular producers, and the exporting country's government officials were authorized to distribute the quota among its producers. As might be expected in a large number of countries, this procedure created a secondary market for quotas that was added to the exporter's price. There was also some transfer of quotas among countries that American customs officials were not always able to identify. A 1994 report from the Council of Economic Advisors states, "The most common technique has been to ship goods produced in China to third countries, and from there re-export them to the United States under the third countries' quotas."[19] (Note that as of this writing, China is not a member of GATT.)

In addition to the MFA and bilateral agreements to manage textile and apparel imports by quotas, the United States developed partial-duty exemptions for the importation of articles assembled abroad with American-made components. Although these "Section 807" rules,[20] as originally developed in the Tariff Act of 1930, were for general application, they had a direct impact on textiles and apparel. Under these rules, cutting textiles in the United States and shipping the pieces abroad to be sewn allowed them to be imported back to the United States with duties paid only on the value added by assembly.[21] This arrangement in textiles and apparel favored the use of U.S. textiles and assembly operations in the Caribbean Basin and Mexico.

In 1985, under the new bilateral agreements with Caribbean Basin countries, unlimited access was provided for products of firms that, in addition to using cut fabric from the United States, worked with American-made textiles and other materials. This sourcing agreement was termed "807a." As we will show later in this chapter, such trade preference has contributed to increased apparel imports from Mexico and the Caribbean over the past decade.[22]

The Uruguay Round, Phase-Out of the MFA, and NAFTA

The Uruguay Round of multilateral negotiations under GATT was initiated as early as 1986. A major objective of governments participating in these negotiations was, according to a 1992 report of the Council of Economic Advisors, "to open world textile and apparel markets and reintegrate these products into the normal GATT regime."[23] On January 1, 1995, the Agreement on Textiles and Clothing (ATC) became part of the World Trade Organization agreements and replaced the MFA. The ATC provided for the "integration" of textiles and apparel into the GATT regime in three stages over a ten-year transition period that is to end on January 1, 2005.

As products are integrated into the GATT regime, quotas are eliminated and trade becomes subject to normal GATT rules.[24] By 2005, all quotas on U.S. imports of textiles and apparel are scheduled to be eliminated, and tariffs—which in 1997 on a trade-weighted basis averaged almost 9 percent on textiles and 16.4 percent on apparel[25]—are to be reduced, although not eliminated.[26] Moreover, preferential duties on items assembled from U.S. textiles are not affected. Note that while these sweeping changes in quotas are supposed to be gradually implemented, the agreement has actually been "back-loaded." That means most of the significant changes, such as elimination of import quotas on items with the largest volumes, will not take place until the last several years of the ten-year period.

Another major shift in the trade structure of textiles and apparel began on January 1, 1994, with the implementation of NAFTA. This regional trade agreement among Canada, Mexico, and the United States includes in its provisions the phase-out of most tariffs and non-tariff barriers on industrial products over ten years, including on all textiles and apparel items that have regional content. Among other provisions, NAFTA liberalizes the markets for financial, land transportation, and telecommunications services, which may be expected to affect competition in textiles and apparel as well.

The impact of NAFTA, like that of the MFA's phase-out, should occur incrementally over the years, although many business decisions have anticipated projected trade deregulation. Such developments may arise in unexpected ways. Consider, for instance, the offshore assembly provision of the U.S. Harmonized Tariff Schedule, which permits the duty-free return of domestically manufactured components that have been assembled in Mexico or the Caribbean Basin—items that originally fell under the 807 and 807a rules and are now covered by subheading 9802.00.80.[27] Transportation costs, largely for trucking, give U.S. manufacturers of domestic apparel components an incentive to locate near the border to be closer to the Mexican assembly plants they supply. The 9802.00.80 provisions may affect, as Gordon Hanson notes, "not only the international location of assembly but also the internal location of complementary manufacturing activities in the source country."[28] Simply put, the Texas border area, on both sides, is now gaining activity at the expense of other locations.

The Uruguay Round of GATT agreements, however, instituted an additional change that potentially affects trade in textiles and apparel. New rules are proposed for determining the country of origin for U.S. imports, especially for products that contain components from more than one country. According to the 1995 report of the U.S. International Trade Commission,

> Under the current rules, garments assembled in one country from parts cut from fabric in another are generally considered the product of the country in which the cutting occurs. The new rules will assign origin to the country of assembly. For home textiles like sheets and pillowcases, the current rules generally confer origin in the country in which the goods were cut to size from fabric rolls, hemmed, and otherwise sewn. The new rules will confer origin in the country in which the fabric was woven. For fabrics woven in one country and dyed, printed and otherwise finished in another, the current rules generally confer origin in the country in which the finishing occurs, whereas the new rules will confer origin in the country in which the weaving takes place.[29]

Obviously, these new rules of origin may be expected to impact import and export quotas while they remain, differentially, among countries. The imports most likely to be affected by such changes in definitions of origin are likely to be from Hong Kong, Taiwan, and Korea with more items charged to the quotas of China. But under the provisions of ATC, the United States is obligated to consult with countries affected by the change "with a view to reaching a mutually acceptable solution regarding appropriate and equitable adjustment." As of late 1998, negotiations to reach an "acceptable solution" were still ongoing, and the new rules have not been generally implemented. In the following sections, we will examine the product composition of recent textile and apparel imports and exports as well as the country of origin for imports.

The Product Composition of Trade

The product composition of U.S. apparel imports provides an instructive basis for understanding recent changes in trade flows. In 1997, the $48.4 billion of apparel imports into the United States included the nine product categories or SITC product codes shown in Table 13.2. Each accounted for more than a billion dollars of imported value. These nine product categories together constitute $28.2 billion, or 58 percent of all apparel imports.[30] The remaining $20.2 billion of imports were distributed among eighty-seven other product classifications.

Although aggregate apparel imports increased by almost 98 percent between 1989 and 1997, not all categories of imports increased at this rate over the period. It appears that woven cotton products, rather than knit goods, provided the largest proportion of apparel dollar imports in these billion-dollar categories (with the exception of men's and boys' sweaters). Domestic knit products have shown a lesser decline in employment and a lesser adverse effect from imports than woven products in part as a result of the high productivity of many parts of the U.S. knit good producers (see Chapter 12). The men's apparel items least hit by imports were jeans, tailored clothing, underwear, and knit items like hosiery, sweats, and warm-ups. Among women's garments, jeans, suits, hosiery, and swimwear were the least affected by foreign imports. It is important to note that the product categories least affected are also those with basic or fashion-basic characteristics in which retailers engage in a significant amount of rapid replenishment. We will return to this point.

The U.S. apparel industry exports far fewer products than are

Table 13.2. Total U.S. Apparel Imports by Product Classification, 1997

SITC	Product Classification	Million Dollars
84530	Sweaters, wholly of cashmere, men's and boys' knit	$7,118.8
84140	Trousers and breeches, men's and boys', cotton denim, not knit	4,528.6
84260	Trousers, women's and girls', cotton denim, not knit	4,091.3
84151	Shirts, men's and boy's, not knit	2,246.2
84540	T-shirts, underwear, men's and boy's knit	2,189.7
84270	Blouses of silk, women's and girls', not knit	2,105.7
84119	Anoraks (parkas), men's and boys', woven	1,781.8
84371	Shirts, men's and boys', cotton, knit	1,713.8
84240	Dresses, women's synthetics, not knit	1,286.2
84230	Suit-type jackets, women's, wool, > 30% silk, not knit	1,094.6

Source: U.S. Department of Commerce, Bureau of Census.

imported. In the $8.4 billion of apparel exports in 1997, only two items exceeded one billion dollars—trousers made of cotton denim and men's and boys' cotton T-shirts. Once again, both products are made from textile products in which the United States remains a leader in efficiency and quality. Product branding is also a factor here: U.S. made jeans and other trousers (Levi's 501 jeans are the best known example) have a cachet in many non-U.S. consumer markets.

The textile industry tells a different tale. The U.S. trade in textile-mill products—imports and exports—has remained in relative balance during the years under review. From 1990 to 1994, textile imports averaged $8,159 million and exports $5,700 million, or an average difference of just $2,459 million.[31] As we have already noted, in 1997, aggregate textile imports were $11.9 billion and exports $9.0 billion. The five largest items of textile imports are shown in Table 13.3 (page 232).

Imports are widely diversified among products, with the top five categories comprising about 21 percent of the dollar value of imports of textile-mill products in 1997. In contrast, the top five categories of apparel accounted for 42 percent of all apparel imports in 1997. The five largest textile exports in 1997 are shown in Table 13.4 (page 232). The U.S. Bureau of the Census estimated that in 1989 nearly 10 percent of textile employment was related to direct and indirect exports.[32] By 1994, that figure had grown to about 13 percent.[33]

Table 13.3. Total U.S. Textile Imports by Product Classification, 1997

SITC	Product Classification	Million Dollars
65893	Wall banners, manmade fibers	$869.8
65847	Towels other than dish, cotton	461.4
65163	Synthetic filament yarn, single, not over 50 turns per meter, not for retail	447.7
65842	Pillowcases, cotton, no lace trim	355.5
65243	Cotton woven fabric, denim, not under 85% cotton, over 200 grams/square meter	316.0

Source: U.S. Department of Commerce, Bureau of the Census.

Table 13.4. Textile Exports by Product Classification, 1997

SITC	Product Classification	Million Dollars
65720	Nonwovens, whether or not impregnated	$686.0
65942	Textile floor coverings, tufted, nylon	419.2
65732	Textile fabric, coated with plastic	376.9
65163	Synthetic filament yarn, single, not over 50 turns per meter, not for retail	357.3
65243	Cotton woven fabric, denim, not under 85% cotton, over 200 grams/square meter	270.2

Source: U.S. Department of Commerce, Bureau of the Census.

Countries of Origin and the Changing Patterns of Trade

There are a number of short and longer run factors that influence imports and exports between the United States and other countries. Aside from the economics of particular sectors, relative exchange rates and their variations over time can affect trade significantly in particular periods. During the first half of the 1980s, imports increased rapidly, largely as a result of the overvalued dollar. The multilateral trade-weighted value of the U.S. dollar (March 1973 = 100) was 87.4 in 1980 and rose to 143.0 in 1985; it fell to 89.1 in 1990 and 84.2 in 1995, then rose to 96.4 in 1997. The Japanese yen-to-dollar rate was 210.39 in 1978, 249.6 in 1982—then it dropped to 145.0 in 1990 and 93.96 in 1995, before rising again to 121.06 in 1997.[34]

Volatile exchange rates clearly have an impact on trade in apparel and textiles. From 1980 to 1985, for example, the dollar appreciated in real terms by 35 percent for textile imports and 24 percent for apparel imports.[35] Subsequently, the declining value of the dollar, along with small domestic hourly compensation cost increases relative to overseas producers, made U.S.-based firms more competitive in the late 1980s and early 1990s.

Apparel imports have been highly diversified by country of origin; in 1997 U.S. imports came from more than 175 different countries. For comparative purposes, Table 13.5 shows the countries ranked by the largest value of U.S. apparel imports in 1991 and 1997. In particular, the data for the ten largest sources in 1997 reflect major shifts across the regions that provide imported apparel products to the United States.

The "Big Four" countries for U.S. apparel imports have been the People's Republic of China, Hong Kong, Taiwan, and Korea. China remains the largest source of apparel imports: Imports of apparel from China increased from $2,889.7 million in 1989 to $6,313.4 million in 1994; they declined to $5,853.9 in 1995 and then increased to $7,439.8 million in 1997. Yet despite its continuing significance in absolute terms, China's share of total shipments has remained about constant—15 percent—between 1991 and 1997. The other major Asian countries that historically accounted for a significant share of U.S. imports (Hong Kong, Taiwan, and Korea), declined substantially in their contribution to U.S. apparel imports over this period. Collectively, they went from contributing 38 percent of apparel imports in 1991 to only 16 percent in 1997.

As the traditional Big Four have declined in their relative contribution to U.S. imports, Mexico and the nations that make up the Caribbean Basin have become increasingly important sources of apparel

Table 13.5. Total U.S. Apparel Imports by Country of Origin, 1991, 1997 in Million Dollars (Current)

Country	1991	1997
China, PRC	$3,841.2	$7,439.8
Mexico	909.7	5,349.2
Hong Kong	4,039.2	4,034.6
Dominican Republic	939.7	2,236.4
Taiwan	2,658.4	2,172.3
Indonesia	589.5	1,735.6
Honduras	196.6	1,688.8
Korea, Republic of	2,762.4	1,655.0
Philippines	1,051.2	1,620.0
India	644.5	1,506.0
Total imports (Billions)	25.0	48.4

Source: U.S. Department of Commerce, Bureau of the Census.

products. In percentage terms, Mexico alone accounted for 11 percent of the value of shipments into the United States in 1997, compared with less than 4 percent in 1991. Countries in the Caribbean Basin Initiative (CBI) region like the Dominican Republic, Honduras, and Costa Rica have also dramatically increased their share, with this group as a whole now constituting more than 15.8 percent of imports.[36]

This shift in U.S. apparel imports by country of origin is even more striking when measured in physical units, or millions of square meters of imports. For some purposes, such analysis is useful because it removes the problem of valuing imports that is affected by exchange rates, definitions of landed value, and other issues.[37] The Big Four's share of physical shipments declined from 63 percent in 1984 to only 23 percent of all imports by 1997.[38] At the same time, the share of apparel imports from Mexico and the CBI region—the Dominican Republic, Costa Rica, Jamaica, Guatemala, Honduras, El Salvador, and others—has risen from 7 percent in 1984 to 39 percent in 1997. Mexico's share alone rose from 2 percent to 14 percent during the same period. Thus, in terms of square meters of apparel imports, Mexico and the Caribbean Basin countries now contribute substantially more to the U.S. market than the traditional Big Four, with the former group first surpassing the latter in 1995.[39]

Explaining the causes of such a radical shift in sourcing is complex because numerous factors affect trade flows: exchange rates, international trade agreements and their enforcement, changing international labor costs, and political instability, to name a few.[40] Yet lean retailing and channel integration have contributed to the shift in sources of U.S. apparel.

In fact, one of the principal forces that led to the development of the Big Four region as a major source of apparel imports was the existence of "packagers" in Hong Kong. Packagers provide retailers, manufacturers, and jobbers "one-stop shopping" for the sourcing of goods: An order is placed by the retailer, and the packager fills that order. Hong Kong packagers often draw on networks of contractors that extend into PRC and southeast Asia. By drawing on the very low wages within China, Hong Kong packagers can supply products at extremely low prices.[41]

This model works well, provided the buyer—whether a retailer, manufacturer, or jobber—can tolerate long lead times for delivery. The supply networks that led to the rise of the Big Four over several decades emerged in part because time to delivery was of secondary importance. However, in a world of rapid replenishment, weekly deliveries, and growing retail service requirements, these sourcing arrangements have become increasingly problematic. Some packagers have provided more rapid replenishment from Asia, such as those drawn on by The Limited. However, The Limited's focus on reducing lead times has been the exception rather than the rule. For apparel items in the lower portion of the fashion triangle—basic and fashion-basic products—retailers require suppliers in locations that can operate with lead times measured in weeks rather than months.

Proximity to market therefore becomes a factor in the sourcing of apparel products. Although the shift from the Big Four to Mexico and the CBI region cannot be ascribed entirely to the impact of lean retailing in the 1990s, we believe a significant portion does arise from these changes. Compare the top U.S. apparel items imported from the Big Four with those from Mexico and the CBI region over the critical period of 1991 to 1997, when lean retailing began to spread in the U.S. market. Figure 13.1 shows the principal categories of apparel imported from the Big Four between 1991 and 1997, measured in millions of dollars. Figure 13.2 provides similar figures for Mexico and the Caribbean Basin.

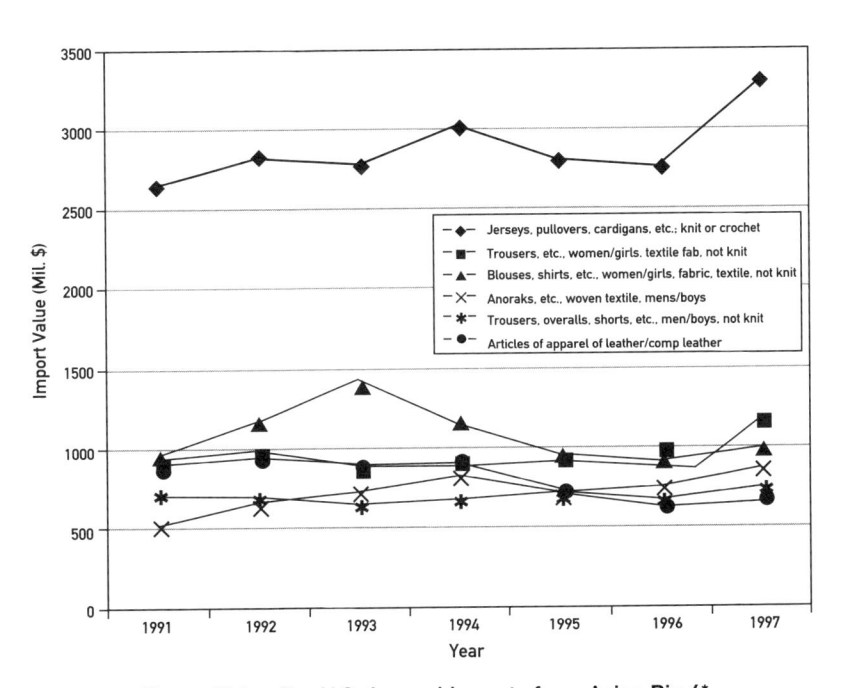

Figure 13.1. Top U.S. Apparel Imports from Asian Big 4*
*Asian Big 4 includes China, Hong Kong, Taiwan, and Korea
Source: U.S. Dept of Commerce data compiled by HCTAR.

The most striking contrast of these figures is the rapid growth in all the major product categories coming from Mexico and the CBI region and the relative stagnation of the major product categories sourced from the Big Four. A review of those product listed on Figure 13.2—trousers, T-shirts, bras, men's and boys' cotton shirts—indicates that they are all prime candidates for rapid replenishment. Although the Big Four also provided some of these products in their major shipments to the United States, they have not experienced such growth over this period of time.

Of the major product types coming from the two regions, nine of the top ten goods imported from Mexico (which account for 70 percent of total apparel imports from Mexico) have been the target of rapid replenishment over the past seven years. In contrast, only three of the top ten goods imported from China (which account for about 64 percent of total Chinese apparel imports) have been the target of rapid replenishment arrangements. The remaining seven product groups from China have fashion elements that make them single season items and therefore (at least until recently) less conducive to rapid replenishment.

These dramatic shifts cannot be ascribed simply to the passage of favorable trade legislation affecting Mexico and the Caribbean Basin

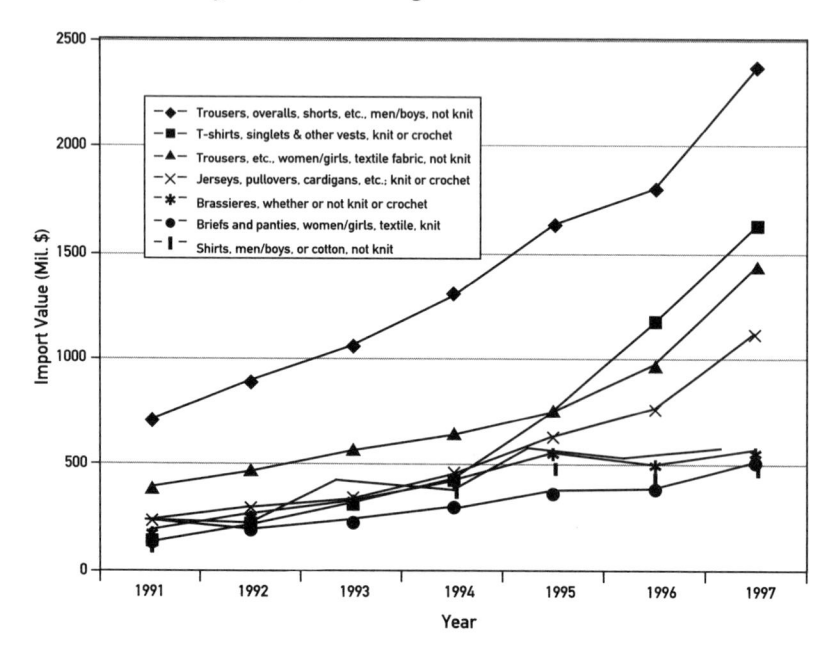

Figure 13.2. Top U.S. Apparel Imports from Mexico and Caribbean
Source: U.S. Dept. of Commerce data compiled by HCTAR.

countries. The preferential treatment under the Caribbean Basin Initiative and the tariffs it establishes for those countries dates back to the Caribbean Basin Economic Recovery Act of 1983 (amended in 1990), well before the onset of the increase in trade flows from the CBI region. Similarly, NAFTA only began to be implemented in 1994, and tariff elimination under its provisions is still being phased into effect.[42] Instead, these trade agreements have further heightened the benefits of proximity that channel integration has made increasingly important.[43]

The change in sourcing patterns discussed here has one other implication. Obviously, apparel imports from the Big Four countries are made from textiles that do not originate in the United States. In contrast, the structure of the trade laws and the preferential treatment given to assembling products in Caribbean nations, combined with the strength of the U.S. textile sector, means that a significant percentage of these products are made from American textiles.

The trade flow figures illustrate this in terms of the volume of textile exports from the United States to China as compared to Mexico. In 1997, total textile exports (SITC 65) to China from the United States equaled $62.4 million, or about 0.8 percent of the value of apparel imports from that country. In the same year, total U.S. exports of textile products to Mexico came to $1.5 billion, or 28 percent of the value of apparel imports from Mexico. This number also understates the impact of the shift on the U.S. textile industry, because it does not include U.S. exports of apparel (SITC 84) to Mexico. In 1997, apparel exports from the United States to Mexico equaled $2.2 billion, while apparel exports to China from the U.S. were a meager $9.2 million.[44]

The emerging patterns of trade, then, are positively affecting the U.S. textile industry, as well as some portions of the U.S. apparel industry. Similar trends may be emerging in other major regions in the world, as the next section will explore.

Regionalization of International Trade

The transformations in the U.S. retail-apparel-textile channel—lean retailing and rapid-replenishment pressures, ever increasing product variety, the need for some short-cycle production—have also spread to the global marketplace, including Europe and Japan. As a consequence, new global patterns of trade and sourcing are evolving to match current competitive demands. Regionalization of textile and apparel production is now coming to the fore. Table 13.6 suggests where different operations in the channel may be located in the coming years.

The left column of the figure lists operations that will probably remain in "advanced" countries like the United States, Japan, and those in Western Europe. For obvious reasons, operations closely related to retailing—design, merchandising, and distribution—stay in the markets for which products are intended. In this schematic, the retail part of the channel encompasses marketing practices employed by either retail outlets or apparel-makers to create or position their own brands. This may involve everything from private-label product lines for mass merchandisers to the recognizable brands of apparel manufacturers like Levi Strauss or "designer" jobbers such as Liz Claiborne and Tommy Hilfiger.

The sourcing issues become more complicated, however, for the apparel and textile links in the channel. Table 13.6 indicates that some sewing, or assembly, will keep going to the developing countries listed in the right column—Mexico and those in the Caribbean Basin, Eastern Europe, and Southeast Asia—that currently offer their advanced regional "partners" both lower labor costs and proximity to market. Even so, some short-cycle assembly, which involves more sophisticated produc-

Table 13.6. Regionalizational of Textile and Apparel Operations

Activities	Europe/Japan U.S.	Eastern Europe/Asia CBI/Mexico
Retail		
Design	√	
Merchandising	√	
Distribution	√	
	Short Cycle	Long Cycle
Apparel		
Cutting	√	√
Sewing	√	√
Press/Package/Finish	√	√
Preparation for Distribution	√	
Textiles		
Finishing	√	
Knitting/Weaving	√	
Spinning	√	

tion lines and planning, may remain in places like the United States or Europe. Meanwhile, the skilled cutting operations that now generally take place in advanced countries may move to developing nations, as industrialization becomes more sophisticated there. As for the packaging and distribution operations that prepare garments for retail distribution, these are likely to stay in the countries where the products will be sold—although, again, regionalization may play a role here, since less developed nations like Mexico are close enough to the United States to offer some of these services at a lower cost for some markets.

In the textile part of the channel, raw materials, such as wool, and synthetics, will be produced in either advanced or developing countries, according to local climate conditions, the ebb and flow of commodity markets, domestic support prices, and capital investments. But the figure makes clear that skilled and capital-intensive operations like spinning, weaving, knitting, and finishing, especially for higher value products, will continue in advanced countries like the United States—unless the textile operations of less developed regional partners, such as Mexico, are raised to more advanced standards. In addition, the U.S. textile industry has become less dependent on the apparel industry in international competition, with expanding markets in household products and industrial textiles for some markets.

These new patterns of trade also have implications for the fashion triangle and the ways its three apparel elements—fashion products, fashion-basics, and basics—will be sourced in the future. For fashion apparel products, in which orders are placed once a season, the practice of sourcing according to lowest labor costs for all operations will likely continue. Much of Asian sourcing has been devoted to fashion items, or those that are ordered once a season, with production shifting away from countries where wage levels have risen (e.g., Japan), and toward lower wage areas in the region (the western PRC, Indonesia, and Thailand). These developments are readily visible in China and East Asia.

But for basic and fashion-basic apparel products, in which frequent replenishment orders are becoming the norm, manufacturers will increasingly source only assembly operations in lower wage countries. In the United States, the growth of the Caribbean Basin and Mexico as locations for assembly in the manufacturing process may be expected to continue. At present, most preassembly operations will stay in the United States, although further shifts to the southern states are likely. Meanwhile, the Japanese and Koreans use China and other low-wage locations for sewing and assembly. France and Germany source assembly operations from Eastern Europe, Turkey, and North Africa.

This view of the global distribution of textile and apparel operations invites questions of labor standards for workers—wages and benefits, hours of work and overtime, occupational health and safety, sanitation, and child labor. The highly competitive structure of apparel, with its jobbers, manufacturers, and contractors, as well as the high proportion of labor costs to total costs, has placed signficant downward pressure almost everywhere on apparel labor costs and standards. A wide range of measures by governments and private groups have sought to ameliorate these conditions by establishing minimum labor standards, and such standards are likely to become increasingly intertwined with trade negotiations in the future. Chapter 15 will return to these fundamental policy matters.

Beyond the MFA: The End of an Era

By the year 2005, the bilateral agreements of the MFA, with their quotas on apparel and textile imports, will be entirely eliminated. The United States will have experienced almost half a century of this specialized means of managing apparel and textile trade. No other major American industries confronted with import competition have been the beneficiary for so long of such bilateral international agreements. Given that fifty years of the quota form of trade protection is about to end, how is one to appraise this experience?

On the one hand, the MFA did not eliminate, as some advocates hoped, the "often chaotic, uncoordinated, and widely divergent economic behavior and policies of individual countries" in apparel and textile markets. The minimum annual growth rates, originally set at 6 percent a year in bilateral agreements, generally exceeded the growth of the domestic market for apparel and textile products, resulting in increasing import penetration despite quotas and tariffs. These divergences in import and domestic-consumption growth rates hit the American apparel industry much harder than textiles.

On the other hand, the system of bilateral agreements under the MFA probably constrained trade only moderately. For textiles, these agreements most likely increased the degree of predictability in the domestic industry, which contributed to the restructuring, reinvestment, and enhanced competitiveness of major U.S. textile producers. Moreover, the extended negotiations necessary to establish these bilateral agreements probably reduced the chances of greater unilateral U.S. action generated by interest groups.

Economists rightly point to the somewhat higher prices American consumers paid for apparel, since the influx of cheaper foreign imports was restrained to some extent during the MFA years. But these effects are easy to exaggerate. As Paul Krugman notes,

> The combined costs of these major restrictions to the U.S. economy [in imports of automobiles, steel, and textiles] are usually estimated at less than three-quarters of 1 percent of U.S. national income....From the point of view of the world as a whole, the negative effects of U.S. import restrictions on efficiency are therefore much smaller—around one-quarter of 1 percent of U.S. GNP.... To take the most extreme example, the cost to taxpayers of the savings and loan bailout alone will be at least five times as large as the annual cost to U.S. consumers of all U.S. import restrictions.[45]

Other considerations need to be evaluated as well. Technical economic analysis alone seldom leads to realistic or even appropriate policy choices. Since the 1950s, for instance, apparel products have represented a declining share in the budget of consumers. Some of this change reflects relatively lower prices, some changing tastes in clothing—the latter being a bit of a wild card when it comes to forecasting. Indeed, the price of apparel and its upkeep has gone up at a lesser rate than the other major components of the Consumer Price Index, such as housing, transportation, or medical care.

Most important, the MFA did manage to dampen and spread out the immediate impact of imports on these American industries and their specialized communities, and spreading the changes over more years has facilitated the adjustment processes in textiles and apparel. Employment declines, substantial in both industries, have occurred more gradually than they would have without a measure of quota protections. During this period, textile employment was concentrated in isolated, rural communities in the southeastern states of North and South Carolina, Georgia, and Alabama, where adjusting to employment changes was often difficult. In the smaller establishments of the apparel industry, adjustments to declining employment rates were harder for rural sites and immigrants in urban communities. In the 1950–1997 period, the textile industry reduced employment by 648,400 and apparel reduced it by 388,700. This amounts to a decline of more than a million workers all together—a major structural change. But with these employment reductions, production has more than doubled in apparel and increased nearly three times in textiles. These data reflect a rapid and productive adjustment process, rather than rigid or inflexible labor and product markets.

A realistic judgment suggests that the MFA era, while not optimal in its restraints on trade, helped to prepare domestic textiles and apparel for a competitive role in global markets in the period ahead. It is also true that current changes in international trade rules and the environment for the U.S. apparel and textile industries are not the only things shaping the near-term future of these sectors. Because so many factors have now come into play, it is hard to disentangle or project the independent effects of quotas, tariffs, trade, technology, logistics, tastes, incomes, or lean retailing practices. The final two chapters will evaluate, as a whole, the many environmental and internal enterprise factors influencing today's transformed retail-apparel-textile channel.

14

Suppliers in a Lean World: Firm and Industry Performance in an Integrated Channel

> The beauty of automatic replenishment is that the buyer is really the customer. She is telling us what she wants and needs in the future. Quite frankly, of all the buying we do, letting our customer make the choice seems to make the most sense.
>
> —*Tom Cole, Chairman and CEO, Federated Logistics and Operations*

> Our goal is to replace the product on the retail shelf as quickly as possible, because that's where the consumer buys it.
>
> —*Jeff Kernodle, Vice President for Replenishment, VF Corp*

Many of the popular accounts of quick response, rapid replenishment, and supply-chain management assume that all parties—consumers, retailers, and suppliers—win as a result of these policies. Consumers have definitely benefited because these practices afford them a greater choice of products at lower average prices.[1] It is safe to say that lean retailers have also come out ahead, given their rapid growth in relation to, and at the expense of, traditional retailers in many different retail channels. But have suppliers benefited from entering into relations with lean retailers? Have such firms improved their competitive position along with the retailers they supply?

The short answer to these questions is "It depends." Although it is certainly true that a supplier gains from successful customers, the degree to which such a company actually benefits has much to do with its internal manufacturing choices. A supplier that has done little to change its internal practices may end up simply "holding the bag" of a retailer's inventory. Alternatively, an adept supplier who uses information for planning, production, and distribution may well share in the competitive advantages derived from better information on the true state of final customer demand.

This chapter examines the reasons that different suppliers win and lose, reviewing many of the innovations we have discussed throughout.[2] Drawing on the HCTAR survey, we first look at the way apparel suppliers adopt combinations of information and manufacturing practices in response to lean retailing.[3] We then show how supplier performance, ranging from the degree of inventory risk to profitability, is changed by their information technology investments and the sequence in which they are adopted. The chapter concludes with a more general discussion of what suppliers in information-integrated channels must do to succeed.

Clusters of Supplier Practices: One Innovation Is Not Enough

Lean retailing allows department stores, mass merchandisers, and other retail outlets to capitalize on information, allowing them to minimize their exposure to demand uncertainty. Retail adoption of these strategies, in turn, means suppliers must invest in a basic set of technologies to provide the information links necessary for rapid replenishment. These investments consist of the capacity to receive and transmit information electronically—the minimum set of practices required for working with lean retailers.

In addition, apparel suppliers must invest in technology and capital improvements to package, label, route, and move products rapidly from their production operations directly to the retailer. Once again, these capital expenditures represent a basic cost of doing business in a lean world. As detailed in Chapter 5, our research indicates that the prevalence of information technologies, advanced distribution and logistics operations, along with the other related services apparel suppliers provide to retailers have grown dramatically since 1988, particularly among business units that supply a large percentage of lean retailers.

Last but not least, responding to lean retailing requirements ultimately necessitates much more sophisticated demand forecasting, production planning, and manufacturing strategies than the practices employed by traditional suppliers. At one extreme, a manufacturer can simply hold inventory for lean retailers and make few changes in its internal practices. At the other end of the spectrum, a manufacturer can alter its internal design, planning, procurement, and manufacturing operations and respond rapidly to demand changes through the use of flexible manufacturing or sourcing practices.

Determining the degree to which a supplier benefits from its technological investments is the real issue. Although there are no easy formulas, it does appear that the specific *combinations* of information technology and assembly methods drawn on by the supplier make a difference in responding to lean retail requirements. In order to study performance we must first examine how different manufacturing practices fit together for suppliers. In this section, we will discuss the interaction of four information and manufacturing practices related to apparel suppliers' ability to provide products in a lean retailing world. These key practices affect how apparel suppliers acquire and use information concerning demand at the SKU level.

Note that the information and manufacturing practices examined here are not specific to the apparel industry—in fact, most were originally introduced in other sectors—but are applicable to a wide variety of consumer product industries. We focus on the retail-apparel channel because HCTAR's surveys provide extensive evidence for the ways in which apparel suppliers are changing. Even if suppliers in other businesses will not make the specific operational changes of an apparelmaker, an increasing number are establishing information links with other channel players and combining information use with technologies and work practices to speed up order processing. For example, textile firms that supply retailers directly with their own products may have to combine equivalent information technologies with manufacturing innovations in finishing lines that shorten production cycles in order to gain competitive advantage. Much of what we have learned about the determinants of success for apparel suppliers can be applied to comparable situations faced by businesses in other retail-driven industries.

Key Practice 1: Bar Codes

The adoption of the Uniform Product Code (UPC) provides unique, optically scannable bar codes for identifying products at the SKU level. The availability of a standardized system of classification gives companies the means to input, store, transmit, and access information concerning demand inexpensively. Use of the UPC bar code system has the potential for significantly decreasing transaction costs with customers. Adopting bar codes, of course, requires a variety of technological investments by business units—in bar code readers and writers, hand scanners, computer hardware and software—and conventions, such as those promulgated by the Uniform Product Council. Even so, use of bar codes has become the norm for apparel-makers and retailers; to date, few channel partners have failed to make this change.

Key Practice 2: Electronic Data Interchange

The second basic practice involves the use of electronic data interchange (EDI) as a means for transmitting data on orders between apparel suppliers and retailers. Like bar codes, the use of EDI requires a set of investments by suppliers and customers in computer technologies capable of sending and receiving data rapidly. It also depends on conventions that standardize the system of data interchange, including payment mechanisms. While many channel players have adopted EDI, it also represents an area of evolving practice; the amount of information that can be transmitted between retailers and suppliers has grown at the same time that the costs of transmission have fallen.

Key Practice 3: Standard Labeling of Shipping Containers

Marking cartons and containers for shipment according to channel-wide standards can speed up distribution. Modern distribution centers are capable of rapidly identifying and sorting incoming shipments from all suppliers—whether apparel-makers, textile producers, or grocery manufacturers—through the use of scanning systems, automated sorting and conveyer systems, and computer controls. At the same time, these systems use the information on container labels to process and reconcile invoice information on incoming and outgoing shipments. This means incoming shipments must adhere to a set of technological and process standards regarding the use of bar codes for labeling cartons in addition to other standards for packing, labeling, placement, shipping, and display of products.

Key Practice 4: Modular Assembly

Finally, apparel manufacturers can make innovations in the assembly stage through modular, or team-based, production. Instead of breaking up sewing into a long series of small steps, modular production entails grouping tasks and assigning them to a team to reduce the elapsed throughput time required for assembling a given product. Adoption of this assembly technique involves altering the physical layout of sewing machines as well as human resource changes in training requirements, compensation systems, and methods of supervision. As Chapter 7 stressed, modular production need not be adopted for all assembly; it makes most sense for products that require rapid replenishment, where the capacity to engage in short-cycle production matters. In particular, retaining some short-cycle capacity may be advantageous for production of SKUs with higher levels of demand variation, whether because of fashion content or uncommon size—that is, for garments that have unique design elements or are in a size few consumers wear.[4]

Combining Key Practices

Firms responding to frequent purchase-order requests from retailers benefit from combining these practices.[5] At the simplest level, the benefits of adopting a uniform system of production identification are reinforced by the presence of EDI transmission of information, which lowers the cost of moving data between channel partners. Business units adopting both bar codes and EDI are therefore able to reduce the transaction costs for processing information about sales and orders.

When bar codes and EDI are combined with advanced shipping practices, the benefit of each practice is enhanced; order processing occurs more rapidly, accurately, and with less paper. The standardized shipping container marker—which is possible only because of the existence of bar codes in the first place—provides a scannable description of a carton that can be electronically associated with data files containing specific information on the individual products shipped to the retailer. This information, sent via EDI, can then be used to check incoming orders against purchase orders and authorize payments to suppliers. It can also rapidly identify discrepancies between invoices and actual shipments, once again lowering the cost of the transaction for both parties.

Meanwhile, modular production allows apparel suppliers to reduce the time required for a given product to move through the assembly process. For instance, by substantially reducing work-in-process buffers in assembly, throughput time on the modular lines of business units in the HCTAR sample dropped to just two days, compared with nine days for standard assembly methods. But the benefits of throughput-time reduction cannot be fully realized unless firms are rewarded for their ability to replenish rapidly. Rapid replenishment, in turn, requires the availability of detailed demand data and its frequent and accurate transmission. Finally, suppliers must be capable of using this data to allocate production capacity between short-cycle (modular) and standard (progressive bundle system) production lines. In this way, modular assembly systems only yield real advantages in the presence of the other three practices.

In particular, advanced practices in distribution and modular production interact with each other because they both reduce throughput time. The time saved in production can be lost if the distribution method is slow, or if there are other impediments to the movement of products from the apparel-maker to the retailer. Alternatively, distribution operations that efficiently process finished products reinforce the benefits of a team-based assembly system. One extreme case illustrates the importance of fit between these performance elements. A men's trousers manufacturer in the early 1990s invested in modular production in some of its lines to reduce throughput times. Yet it left its distribution practices unchanged. The plant required that trucks be filled before making deliveries, which often meant two weeks of production would build up. In other words, the savings created in throughput reduction in assembly were lost on the shipping dock.

What Clustering Looks Like in the Real World

According to the HCTAR survey, apparel suppliers do seem to invest in clusters of practices arising from the joint benefits of adoption. Table 14.1 shows that combinations of practices increased quite dramatically between 1988 and 1992.

For example, in 1988, joint adoption of bar codes and EDI systems was uncommon: Only 25.2 percent of business units had adopted both, while 46.8 percent had adopted neither. By 1992, three-quarters of the business units had implemented both bar codes and EDI technologies, while only 8.0 percent had neither in place. Similar patterns of increased adoption can be seen among other combinations of these practices in Table 14.1.

The mere fact that two practices have been adopted, however, does not tell the whole story. The changing organization of the retail and apparel industries also suggests that there is a particular *sequence* for adopting the four key practices. To begin with, the adoption of bar codes came before rapid replenishment arrangements because retailers required a low-cost means of collecting information at the detailed product level for their own use—that is, they first developed an efficient method for scanning prices at the check-out register and tracking products for internal inventory purposes. Only after a common convention for bar codes had been established and in use for several years

Table 14.1. Frequency of Adopting Technology Pairs, 1988 and 1992

BAR CODE and EDI

1988	EDI		1992	EDI	
BAR CODE	No	Yes	BAR CODE	No	Yes
No	46.8%	8.0%	No	8.0%	8.7%
yes	19.9%	25.2%	Yes	8.7%	74.5%

BAR CODE and SHIPPING CONTAINER MARKERS

1988	SCM		1992	SCM	
BAR CODE	No	Yes	BAR CODE	No	Yes
No	50.5%	4.4%	No	11.4%	5.3%
Yes	30.8%	14.3%	Yes	33.7%	49.5%

EDI and SHIPPING CONTAINER MARKERS

1988	SCM		1992	SCM	
EDI	No	Yes	EDI	No	Yes
No	60.9%	5.8%	No	13.6%	3.1%
Yes	20.4%	12.9%	Yes	31.6%	51.7%

Source: Harvard Center for Textile and Apparel Research.
BAR CODE = Products marked with UPC bar codes at the SKU level.
EDI = Purchase orders received via electronic data interchange.
SCM = Shipments using containers marked with bar codes.

did retailers turn to such systems to transmit and receive data from suppliers.

Indeed, the use of bar codes, followed by implementation of EDI systems, provides the basic foundation for subsequent investments in efficient logistics management in retail distribution centers. Retailers do not get much out of investing in advanced distribution technologies, such as shipping container markers, if they lack a means for electronically identifying and using information concerning the contents of incoming shipments or of connecting that information back to suppliers for invoicing purposes. And suppliers get little return out of providing customers with standardized shipping container markers if neither of these channel players has made previous investments in bar codes and EDI.

As we detailed in Chapter 10, changing the method of production to reduce manufacturing throughput times also makes little sense if a business unit has not first invested in the necessary information links for carrying on rapid replenishment relationships. From an apparel supplier's perspective, the benefits of adopting shipping container markers and modular production are much higher once bar codes and EDI are in place.

In fact, our analysis of the HCTAR data shows that the probability of adopting shipping container markers and modular production significantly increases if both bar codes and EDI have already been implemented.[6] The probability of adopting shipping container markers in 1992, given that bar codes and EDI had been adopted in 1988, was 77 percent compared with only 47 percent if bar codes and EDI were not both present. Similarly, the probability of adopting modular systems in 1992 was 54 percent compared with 30 percent if bar codes and EDI were not both present.[7]

From Supplier Practice to Performance Results

Once these manufacturing and information practices have been adopted, it should come as no surprise that they affect the performance of business units. Based on our survey research, we found that implementing a combination of the four key practices—bar codes, EDI, advanced shipping systems, and modular assembly—increases business-unit performance because these practices interact with and reinforce one another. This is sometimes described as "complementarities" between practices. The specific sequence of adoption should also affect performance outcomes.

Two types of performance measures are of interest in this regard. The first pertains to *operational performance*, or the ability of a supplier to respond to lean retailing replenishment requirements. Successful performance includes providing high levels of order completeness, short lead times for new products, and rapid response to requests for replenishment. However, operational performance measures do not necessarily provide a direct financial return to the supplier beyond allowing that firm to continue supplying a retailer with these service requirements. A second set of outcomes relates to the *financial performance* of the business unit itself. These include impacts on its revenues (prices and sales), cost structures, and profitability. Financial performance encompasses the impact of the supplier's manufacturing investments on its inventory levels, which directly affects the business unit's costs and the degree of risk it bears from holding high finished goods or work-in-process inventories.

From the perspective of operational performance, two business units with different degrees of investment in the four practices may do equally well in the short run. But their financial performance, as measured by inventory levels or profitability, may differ substantially. As we have emphasized in earlier chapters, an apparel manufacturer that meets a lean retailer's replenishment requirements while optimizing the level of inventories it holds per SKU will be exposed to less risk than one that meets retailer requirements by simply holding larger stocks of inventories.

Retail Replenishment Performance

Lean retailers now have much higher standards than they did in earlier years for the accuracy and timeliness of order fulfillment. Our studies of business units with differing levels of the four practices indicate that firms with the complete set of practices achieve similar or slightly better performance in regard to the percentage of goods delivered complete and on time, although these differences between business units are not very dramatic.[8] This is to be expected, given the high penalties faced by suppliers for violation of these standards,[9] and the fact that retail standards may be met without extensive changes to internal apparel production practices.

In contrast, more innovative business units—those that have adopted three or four of the key practices—are able to replenish products more rapidly than less innovative ones. We have observed this in a number of different ways. In 1992, the mean response time for replenishing products that the supplier had agreed to provide on this basis was 2.9 weeks among those business units that had adopted none of the four practices. But the average replenishment interval was only 1.3 weeks for those that had adopted all the key practices. These performance differences persist even after controlling for other characteristics of business units, such as size and product mix, which might also be associated with replenishment speed and technology adoption.[10] The results are particularly striking, given that only the most demanding lean retailers in 1992 required replenishment within two weeks of order placement.

Lead times provide another measure of supplier responsiveness. Lead time is calculated as the number of days required for an apparel manufacturer to procure textiles, manufacture, and deliver a typical product in its collection. The total time includes the number of days it takes a supplier to order and receive fabric, make the marker, cut the fabric, sew the pieces, press and package the product, ship it to a distribution center, and, finally, process it at the center. The shorter the lead time, the more quickly a firm is able to deliver products to retail customers. Based on our 1992 survey, we estimated lead times for two different scenarios: "standard" lead times that represent performance for a typical product in the supplier's selection and "shortest" lead times that indicate a supplier's best practice. Both measures were for products manufactured domestically.

As shown in Figure 14.1, those business units that invested in a more complete set of innovative practices had significantly shorter lead times for standard products. The total elapsed standard lead time for business units with little innovation in practice averaged 172 calendar days compared with only 117 days for those that had invested in bar codes and EDI. Even more striking, lead time dropped to just 66 days among those units that had adopted all four practices.

Figure 14.1 suggests that the most innovative firms are able to produce and deliver their products in less than half the time of the least innovative apparel suppliers. Of course, other firm characteristics, such as business-unit size or product type, might also be correlated with adoption of innovative practices and performance outcomes. Even after we control for these factors using multiple regression techniques, the number of innovative practices adopted by business units have a statistically significant positive effect on lead time.[11]

Inventory Performance

Throughout, we have argued that reducing the substantial risk presented by inventory, particularly in the presence of ever-increasing prod-

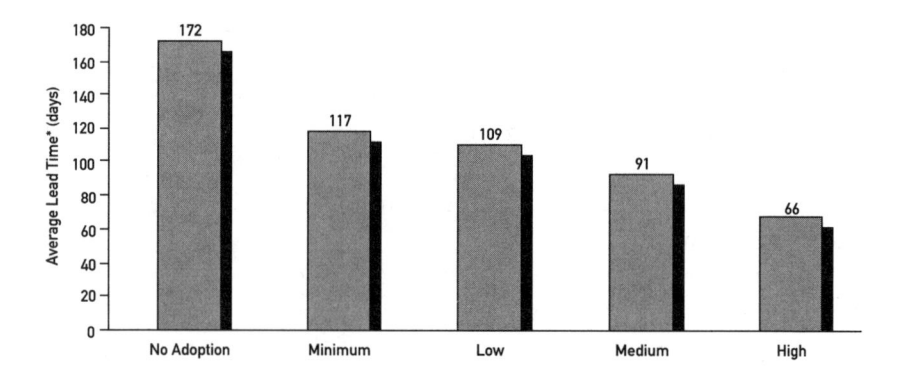

Figure 14.1. Technology Adoption and Lead Time, 1992
Source: Harvard Center for Textile and Apparel Research.
* Lead time is # days from textile procurement to delivery of product

uct proliferation, is essential for improving a manufacturer's performance in integrated retail-apparel-textile channels. That means inventory performance measures are crucial to determining the impact of information technology and flexible manufacturing. In this case, we draw on a unique, matched data set that combines the HCTAR sample results with detailed microdata collected by the U.S. Department of Commerce.[12]

Specifically, we matched data from the HCTAR survey to corresponding establishment-level data from the Department of Commerce's Longitudinal Research Database (LRD). The LRD provides longitudinal data for establishments included in the Bureau of the Census Annual Survey of Manufacturing.[13] To understand the relationship between technology adoption and inventory levels, we matched survey data on adoption decisions in 1988 with inventory observations for the 1988–91 period and adoption decisions in 1992 with inventory observations for the 1992–94 period.

One common way of measuring inventory is to calculate the I/S ratio—that is, the ratio of total finished good inventories to total sales. This measure allows one to compare inventories in firms with different sales volumes. We calculated the I/S ratio for suppliers in our matched sample and then compared those with the ratios of suppliers that used different combinations of the four manufacturing practices. Figure 14.2 illustrates the impact of manufacturing practices on average inventory levels.

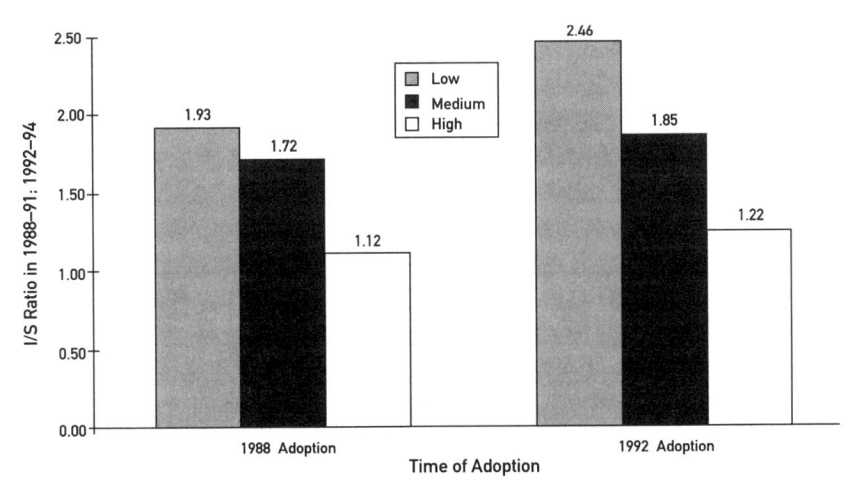

Figure 14.2. Average Inventory/Sales Ratio by Technology Adoption: 1988–91; 1992–94

Source: Harvard Center for Textile and Apparel Research.

The average I/S ratio fell considerably as business units adopted more of the four key technologies during both time periods under study. In the 1988–91 period, firms that adopted none of the four technologies had an average I/S ratio of 1.9, while those that implemented bar codes, EDI, and either advanced shipping container markers or modular assembly—or both—had an average I/S ratio of only 1.1.[14] What is more, these differences between low- and high-level adopters grew dramatically by the 1992–94 period, in which the low-technology firms had more than twice the inventory/sales ratio—2.46 compared with just 1.22 for the high-level adopters.[15]

A reduction in the I/S ratio means that changes in sales will be matched by smaller changes in inventories. Therefore, a lower I/S ratio implies lower inventory volatility or variation.[16] This, in turn, suggests that firms with more of the key technologies in place will have total inventories that are less volatile. One method of capturing volatility is to look at the standard deviation of each establishment's inventory level and I/S ratio for the two time periods.[17] Based on this measure, inventory volatility did not decrease with more technology adoption between 1988 and 1991. However, by the 1992–94 period, firms with all four technologies had lower standard deviations in total inventories compared with less technically innovative ones. This impact on volatility is even more striking when examining variation in I/S ratios for the 1992–1994 period (see Figure 14.3): Standard deviations in the I/S

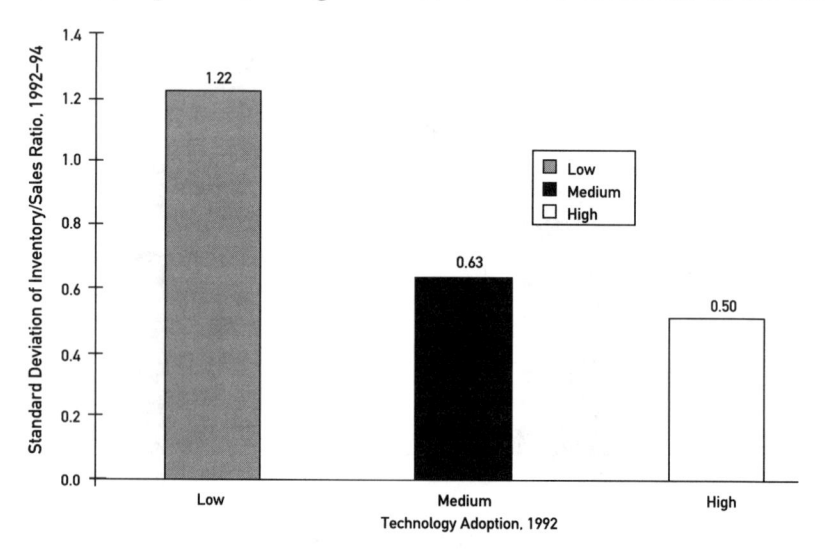

Figure 14.3. Inventory Volatility by Technology Adoption, 1992–94
Source: Harvard Center for Textile and Apparel Research.

ratio of business units with low levels of adoption were 1.22 compared with only .50 for the suppliers that had implemented all the manufacturing practices by 1992. Note that the I/S standard deviations control for differences in firm size. And these results remain even after controlling for other factors, such as product diversity, that may be related to both inventories and the adoption of modern manufacturing practices by suppliers.[18]

Adopting more of these practices also decreases the growth of inventory levels. Figure 14.4 shows the comparative growth rates in inventories from 1992 to 1994 for business units with low, medium, and high technology levels. Adjusting for inflation and other factors that affect inventory growth, we found that establishments with low levels of technology adoption in 1992 experienced far higher annual growth rates in total inventories and I/S ratios than those with a more complete set of innovative practices. This confirms the fact that apparel suppliers investing in both information technology and short-cycle production capacity can move to lower inventory levels more quickly.[19]

The implications of these findings are significant. A supplier attempting to meet the rigorous standards of a lean retailer—whether a shirt manufacturer for Wal-Mart, a pasta-maker for Ralph's Food, or an electronic drill supplier for Home Depot—must hold a far larger amount of inventory if it has not invested in a comprehensive set of

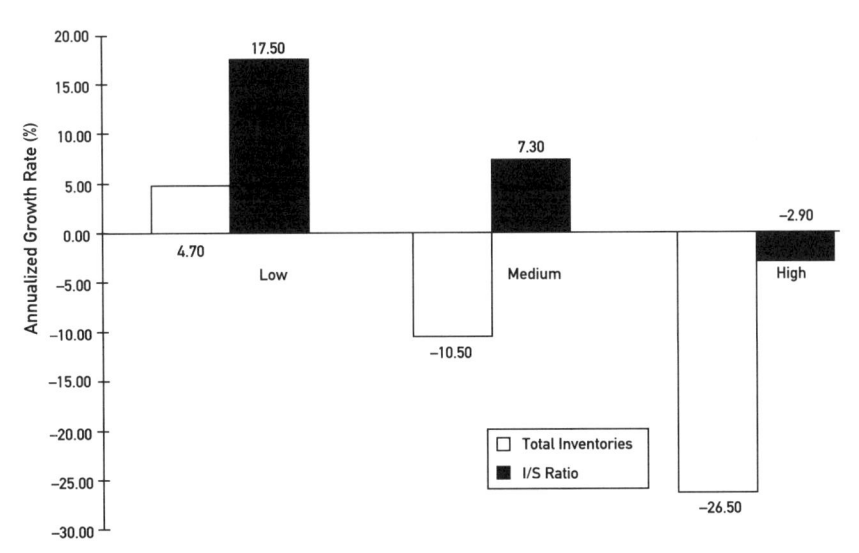

Figure 14.4. Implied Growth Rates in Inventories, 1992–94
Source: Harvard Center for Textile and Apparel Research.

information technology and short-cycle production capacity. As the next section demonstrates, holding larger inventories to service lean retailing demand translates into diminished profitability.

Impact on Profitability

Imagine two men's dress-shirt suppliers. One still operates traditionally, except for the implementation of basic information links to receive orders from lean retailers. The other maintains extensive information systems, which allow it to send, receive, and process information on retail demand, orders, and shipments; advanced information technology also helps it plan manufacturing capacity so that the firm can engage in short-cycle production. Although the first shirt supplier can respond to retailers' weekly orders in a timely manner, its costs for doing so are high, both in terms of the internal expense of transacting frequent orders and its increased exposure to the risk posed by holding inventory. It costs the second supplier less, however, to transact weekly business with retailers because of the electronic systems it has in place. In addition, its capacity to use information on the state of demand allows it to set inventory levels on a SKU basis that balances the benefits of having a product available against the costs of holding work-in-process and finished goods inventories.

As a result of these differences, we expect that the second dress-shirt supplier's financial performance will be decidedly better than that of the first over the long run. Our survey evidence confirms this expectation. Consider the frequency with which suppliers reduce the price of their product for retailers during the selling season. Apparel suppliers in our survey that had adopted all four of the key information and manufacturing practices reported fewer price markdowns by retailers than those with few or none of the practices.[20] Therefore, retailers that work with suppliers employing a more complete set of information, distribution, and manufacturing innovations need not eliminate as many of their unsold products at the end of season via price reductions.

Manufacturing markdowns to retailers provide more direct evidence of the benefits of these innovative practices. Those business units that had adopted all the practices reported an average discount provided to retail customers of just 4.3 percent, compared with an average discount of 22.2 percent among suppliers that had implemented none of them. Although these differences cannot all be directly attributed to the adoption of the practices per se, they do suggest—especially when combined with the significant inventory performance results reported previously—how important it is for manufacturers to be adept at using incoming information from lean retailing customers.[21]

The real question, then, is how do these factors together affect the bottom line? And do business units with the more complete set of innovative technologies have higher profitability? Here the answer is a definite yes. Profitability is measured as operating profit margin—revenue minus costs of goods sold divided by revenue. Figure 14.5 shows our basic results in regard to average profit margin for different levels of technology adoption. Business units that did not adopt any of the four key practices earned the lowest profit margins, about 3 percent in 1992. The most innovative firms were approximately *four times as profitable*, achieving average profit margins of 11.7 percent.

Even after controlling for the independent effects of firm size, product mix, and distribution channel on performance, we found that the most innovative firms were significantly more profitable than those that had adopted fewer of the key practices. In our sample, adding shipping-container markers to established bar code and EDI practices increased operating profits by 2.2 percent—that is, from about 6.2 percent in average profit margins to 8.4 percent; adding some modular assembly capacity to these three practices increased operating profits by about the same amount.[22]

Since HCTAR's 1992 survey, informal case evidence suggests that these disparities in operating and financial performance have only

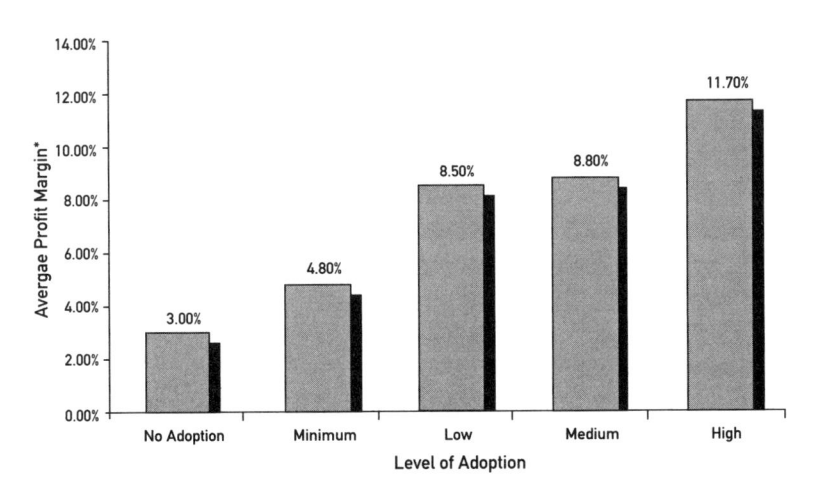

Figure 14.5. Technology Adoption and Profitability, 1992
Source: Harvard Center for Textile and Apparel Research.
*Profit margin is operating profit as a percent of revenue.

grown larger, as lean retailing continues to sweep across distribution channels. The least innovative apparel suppliers are seeing their chances for survival dwindle every year. In contrast, suppliers that have continued to innovate and expand their use of the four practices, as well as other activities described in previous chapters, keep outperforming the industry as a whole.

Management Practice: The Final Ingredient in Enhanced Performance

The upshot of all this is that manufacturers need not hold the bag for lean retailers if they adopt a set of technologies and practices that allow them to collect and process demand information, incorporate it into planning, and use traditional and short-cycle production strategically. Simply doing business with lean retailers in no way confers competitive success. In fact, a supplier that attempts to provide rapid replenishment without any other innovations may end up performing poorly from the perspective of its retail customers. More important, it will sustain higher costs in inventories, face a greater need to mark down the prices of its products, and therefore earn a lower profit margin than those establishments that have invested in comprehensive changes.

Of course, becoming an advanced manufacturer is not just a matter of buying more information technologies or setting up a short-cycle assembly line. The essential force behind the performance impact of these practices is their effective *integration* with one another. Integration does not arise from hardware or software purchases. It comes from successful management.

We have already described some specific ways that managers can think about integration of new information technologies and manufacturing practices. Chapter 7 presented two production planning cases. The first indicated how managers must assess a product line according to the variance in demand for particular SKUs in setting inventory policies. The second case developed how suppliers must use this new perspective on demand to plan production or sourcing strategies. Both cases illustrate the necessity of creating managerial practices that explicitly link the data arising from information technology with changes in manufacturing practices to take full advantage of these innovations.

A contemporary apparel-maker, handling on average 15,000 SKUs in its collection, faces the challenge of replenishing weekly numerous retail customers at high satisfaction levels with a constantly shifting subset of its goods. Managers of such a firm must do so by drawing on information from the past weeks' sales as well as explicitly factoring in the impact of uncertainty. They need real-time information regarding what goods their plants have in finished, work-in-process, and material inventories. They must know the lead-time requirements for procuring textile products and establish relationships with at least some textile suppliers that allow the apparel-maker to procure fabric in smaller quantities and with shorter lead times. This supplier must draw on production lines and sourcing arrangements that provide it with a range of response times, from short-cycle production capacity for products with high demand variability to lines or sourcing arrangements that create larger production runs at lower costs for items with low demand variability. But most important, it must have a managerial system capable of coordinating these elements on an ongoing basis.

Based on our observations of apparel suppliers, coming up with the money for new technologies and practices seems to be less of an impediment than altering basic management conceptions about using these technologies for planning and production. Many of the business units in our sample have adopted specific practices without changing their approach to using them together to compete in an integrated channel. They continue to draw on traditional conceptions of planning, production, and sourcing—in other words, they still think in terms of large orders of their products, placed months before delivery is expected. Needless to say, these business units have not fully benefited from the investments they have made.

Suppliers in most consumer industries now face lean retailing pressures or its equivalent. Many are taking steps to adapt to the changed requirements placed on them. One example is the restructuring beginning to appear in automobile distribution. Traditional auto retailing focuses on selling product lines in production quantities that were largely determined in advance of distribution. The system therefore placed tremendous pressure on auto dealers to sell the enormous finished goods inventory found in a car lot. In contrast to this traditional retailing model, BMW announced in 1997 an effort to restructure its U.S. dealers by allowing consumer customization of car purchases through the use of multimedia computer systems. By allowing customers to design their own cars, BMW dealers hope to reduce their finished goods inventories.[23]

Note that this system poses production questions for BMW similar to those faced by apparel suppliers. The company will need to decide which auto SKU (or subassemblies) to produce using traditional assembly techniques and which to produce with short-cycle production methods. BMW will also need to combine information technologies, planning and forecasting methods, and production techniques to implement such strategies.[24] Similar pressure to innovate automobile distribution and production is also increasing because of the emergence of new retailers like Car Max Auto Superstores and the United Auto Group, which operate under principles more akin to lean retailing.[25]

Two examples from the computer industry further illustrate supplier approaches that integrate information technology and manufacturing decisions. In the early 1990s, facing product proliferation and replenishment requirements for its laser-jet printing products, Hewlett Packard redesigned its manufacturing process for printers. It did so by separating those subassembly processes that were standard across products from those that were distinctive to specific laser-jet products. By using incoming demand information in concert with this subassembly and assembly redesign, Hewlett Packard can now assemble different products with shorter lead times in response to actual information concerning demand; at the same time it continues to take advantage of scale efficiencies in production. The resulting inventory and production policies allow Hewlett Packard to balance the costs of stock-outs with those of unsold inventories.[26]

In 1997, Compaq Computer, the world's largest producer of personal computers, announced a plan to change relations with its distributors. Compaq's main competitors, Dell Computer and Gateway 2000, sell directly to consumers through mail-order and Internet operations. In contrast, Compaq sells its products through computer dealers. Technological advances and rapid diffusion of older technologies make personal computers extremely perishable—much like apparel with a fashion content—and subject to almost constant price markdown pressure. Because Compaq, like other personal computer manufacturers, provides its distributors price guarantees on purchased inventories (i.e., it reimburses the distributor if it must mark down prices in response to falling memory or other costs), its inventory carrying costs are significant.

Rather than continuing to increase inventory, Compaq announced that it would only assemble its new line of personal computers as its retail customers ordered them. And, instead of providing an open-ended guarantee on prices to its distributors, the company would guarantee the price for only two weeks after purchase by the distributor, refusing to take back computers unless they malfunctioned. By changing its method of distributing products, Compaq hopes to reduce the level of dealer inventory across product lines to two weeks' worth and in the process save $1 billion or more a year. These cost savings will be used to reduce prices and compete more aggressively with Dell and Gateway 2000 that do not work through distributors.[27] Therefore, Compaq's competitive strategy arises from its efforts to advance information-integration *forward* in the channels in which it operates.[28] Note also that if Compaq seeks to take full advantage of these changes in distribution, it must also adjust its production strategies to account for differences in demand variability across the computer maker's product lines.

In fact, companies in myriad sectors are grappling with the same managerial challenges and opportunities of those in the American apparel and textile industries. Rethinking how to service stringent retail replenishment requirements for ever broadening product lines in more selling seasons has become a central business challenge.

The implications of these changes do not end here. An economy consisting of lean retailing and corresponding "lean" suppliers operates in a fundamentally different manner from one based on traditional retailing and supply practices. The industrial transformation currently in progress encompasses international trade issues, competitiveness, labor regulation, and macroeconomic policies. Accordingly, the last chapter of this book is devoted to our reflections on the impact of channel integration on certain public policy issues.

15

Information-Integrated Channels: Public Policy Implications and Future Directions

More than a century ago a major wave of innovations in distribution and production led to the modern department store, the mail-order house, and the chain store, and reshaped their suppliers. The present transformation of retail and manufacturing engendered by new information technologies, production methods, and management practices also fundamentally alters the manner in which industries and firms take raw materials, turn them into a profusion of products, and deliver them to consumers. Although these developments are very much a work in progress, information-integrated channels of production and distribution are emerging.

Such channels are not unique to retail-apparel-textile relations but have arisen in a wide variety of consumer product industries in which retailing practices are undergoing similar changes. The developments reported here offer a prototype of the new links among manufacturers, other suppliers, retailers, and consumers.

In fact, the transformation has been gradual and is still under way. Only as recently as the mid-1990s has integration risen to critical levels, providing a clear picture of what channel relations will look like in the future. Information integration has reshaped much of the retail-apparel-textile channel, yet further transformation is likely in the decade ahead, not only for these linked industries, but for consumer product sectors in general.

In this final chapter, we step back to survey the ways in which information-integrated channels will affect the public and private sectors. The pervasive changes arising from lean retailing challenge the conventional wisdom about the future of international trade, labor standards, employment, and even macroeconomic fluctuations. At the same time, these changes alter the nature of competitive strategy for businesses that supply lean retailers in apparel, textile, and other industries.

Trade Issues: The New International Economics

> [W]e estimate that national income would improve if quotas and tariffs were eliminated because the cost to the economy of protecting each worker with import restraints exceeds the wage the worker is paid ... [F]or textiles the cost per job protected is $40,200 while wages are $20,000; for apparel the cost per job is $37,500 while wages are $14,000.[1]

> We want the world to know how strongly we oppose NAFTA expansion and fast track.[2]
>
> —*John J. Sweeney, President, AFL-CIO*

These quotations aptly reflect the continuing controversy over international trade policies. The apparel and textile industries have played a central role in trade discussions since the inception of the United States, just as they have in other developing and developed countries throughout the world. These industries have often been chosen as the means for building manufacturing capacity in the developing world; at the same time they have been the recipient of trade protection in developed economies. More to our point, information integration has added a new dimension to these long-standing controversies.

The textile and apparel industries have often been intertwined in public policy discussions about international trade, the Uruguay round of trade negotiations, the role of World Trade Organization, NAFTA and its labor side-accords, the renewal of fast-track negotiating authority, imports from China and human rights standards, and so on. This stream of general debate, however, is seldom related to a detailed study or analysis of the impact of such developments on the U.S. textile or apparel industries.

From the time of Adam Smith and David Ricardo down through the writings of Hechscher-Ohlin, economic analysis has been devoted to the consequences of trade restraints in the form of quotas, tariffs, and nontariff barriers on output, employment, and prices. Traditional international economics attributes trade to comparative advantage, relative labor costs, and the relative costs of logistics and transportation. A "new international economics" in the past decade has stressed that much global trade actually reflects, as Paul Krugman puts it, "National advantages that are created by historical circumstance" rather than natural resources. "Because comparative advantage is often created, not given, a temporary subsidy can lead to a permanent industry."[3] Note that these economic analyses and policy prescriptions have been applied generally and are not focused on particular industries like textiles or apparel.

In any case, since the 1970s, such debates about the impact of international trade policy have been placed in a new economic context. Increasingly, analysts and public policy makers discuss trade issue in terms of the emergence of a significant and growing inequality in compensation between production and nonsupervisory workers, on the one hand, and managerial, supervisory, or exempt employees and professionals on the other. These differences include a larger disparity in compensation between those highly educated and those who are not, particularly high school dropouts. In addition, there has been an appreciable growth in relatively unskilled immigrants in some localities such as major metropolitan areas around the country.[4] The 1997 *Economic Report of the President*, reporting a colloquium of experts at the Federal Reserve Bank of New York, attributes the growth of inequality to the following: technological change (45 percent), international trade (12 percent), a decline in the real minimum wage (10 percent), rising immigration (8 percent), and other factors (15 percent).[5]

Although such analysis and policy discussions have not singled out specific industries, the nature of the occupational structure and workforce in textiles and apparel—particularly the latter sector—makes the general discussion relevant to these two industries. It would appear that neither the market imports of textiles nor the immigration of low-skilled workers has had an appreciable negative impact on the wages of the textile industry or its major sectors. The average hourly earnings of U.S. employees in textile mill products (SIC 22) went from $4.66 in 1979 to $10.02 in 1997—an increase of 115 percent and more than the increase in all manufacturing or nondurable manufacturing. This relative wage increase in textiles took place despite its concentration in a low-wage region—the southeastern Piedmont states—the low level of collective bargaining, and the higher-than-average percentage of women workers.

But the experience in apparel is less categorical, especially because of the differential impact on various branches of apparel and other textile products (SIC 23). In 1997, the average hourly earnings of apparel workers were $8.25. On the high end, automotive and apparel trimmings (SIC 2396) averaged $11.36; on the low end, women's and misses' blouses and skirts (SIC 2331) averaged $7.01. Correspondingly, employment in automotive and apparel trimmings increased 71.4 percent from 1979 to 1997 while in women's and misses blouses and skirts it declined by 60.6 percent in the same period. Bear in mind, however, that blast furnaces and steel mills (SIC 3312) declined in employment from 478,500 employees in 1979 to 163,300 in 1997. This 65.9 percent decline from 1979 to 1997 compares with a 31.3 percent drop for textile mill products and 37.6 percent for all apparel workers.

Still, there can be little doubt that in a sector like women's and misses blouses and skirts, in which employment is concentrated in small contract shops, import competition from low-wage developing countries and unskilled immigrants have contributed to its deterioration. Moreover, the failure to comply with federal and state employment statutes relating to minimum wages, overtime rates, and child labor, uncovered in periodic enforcement forays, have contributed to the decline of this sector.

The general analysis of the consequences of trade and immigration in the textile and apparel industries clearly requires a much more focused application to detailed sectors to provide reliable conclusions. Moreover, and as this volume indicates, the offsetting influences of lean retailing and short-cycle production in comparison with low foreign labor rates must be evaluated by product demand variability, rather than simply making generalizations about aggregate trade and immigration. For instance, the information-integrated channels in retail-apparel-textile are having some of their most significant impact on sourcing among suppliers, domestic and foreign. The low labor costs for sewing and short time to market from Mexico and the Caribbean countries, and the provisions of the Harmonized Tariff Schedule (formerly Section 807 and 807a, or currently 9802.00.80) that establish duties only on the value added to U.S.-produced materials sent out for assembly, all favor sourcing of apparel from south of the U.S. border rather than Asia. According to the U.S. International Trade Commission, "U.S. imports of textiles and apparel from China and two of the traditional Big Three Asian suppliers—Hong Kong and Korea—continued to decline in 1996, when these countries together with Taiwan, accounted for 23.4 percent of total sector trade, compared with 38.5 percent in 1991."[6]

The information-integrated channels developed in the United States, which are now influencing sourcing patterns from Mexico and the Caribbean Basin, have begun to affect the textile and apparel sectors worldwide. For many fashion apparel products—defined as those planned to last only one season—the practice of sourcing on the basis of lowest labor costs may be expected to continue. Indeed, much of Asian sourcing has been devoted to such items, with production shifting within Asia away from regions where wage levels have risen. But for basic and fashion basic apparel products, for which frequent replenishment orders are becoming the norm, the practice of sourcing some of the assembly and sewing operations from nearby lower wage regions and countries is emerging. At the same time, design, distribution centers, marketing—even cutting—as well as some short-cycle assembly remain in the market region.

As we pointed out in Chapter 13, regionalization of apparel production in three main areas has started to occur. In the U.S. market, most sewing operations take place in Mexico and the Caribbean Basin; in Europe, sewing operations go to North Africa, Turkey, and Eastern Europe; and in Japan, sewing operations go to various East Asian regions. The formal analysis in Chapter 7 specified the factors that determine whether production of items under rapid replenishment policies should be done domestically or outsourced to low wage countries.

For textiles, with their high capital costs, lower labor content, and emphasis on high quality and finishing operations, the concentration in the southeastern United States, Korea and Japan, and industrial Europe may be expected largely to continue. But the longer term viability of American textile centers will depend on the development of infrastructures capable of supporting advanced textile production in countries close to the U.S. market, such as Mexico and elsewhere in Latin America.

Macroeconomic Implications: Inventories, Business Cycles, and Price Levels

In an information-integrated channel, the historic market relationships between buyers and sellers change significantly. It is true that textiles firms still sell to apparel-makers, which in turn sell to retailers, which ultimately sell to consumers. Markets certainly have not disappeared, but these relationships have been transformed. Different channel players now share detailed information on daily sales; investments in technologies mutually benefit both retailers and suppliers; and because of the effective use of information and manufacturing technologies, risk has been reduced across the entire channel. The adoption of standards in the supply channel, such as those that specify packaging, labeling, and marking of products, have reduced further time to market and enhanced efficiencies; this expedites transit and ensures floor-ready merchandise for consumers at the end of the channel from suppliers. As a result, the traditional boundary lines between firms are blurring as the cost of transacting business within and across industries falls dramatically.[7] Note that the technologies and standards that made these information-integrated channels possible were a product of private-sector activities—individual enterprises, trade associations, and consulting firms. The fundamental standards of product identification through bar codes and related technologies have become compatible worldwide without the prescription or regulation of a Bureau of Standards or government regulatory agencies.

Falling transaction costs between sectors allow an economy to increase the total output of goods and services it can produce for a given set of resource inputs.[8] The dramatic decrease in transaction costs across many sectors parallels the wide-scale changes at the end of the last century, which, in the words of Alfred Chandler, reduced "the number of transactions involved in the flow of goods, increased the speed and regularity of the flow, and so lowered costs and improved the productivity of the American distribution system."[9] Yet it often takes time for an economy to reflect the impact of such fundamental shifts. In fact, the current combination of changes in information technology, management practice, and manufacturing strategy may be one of the places where the impact of computers on the economy has been hidden until recently.[10]

The falling costs of conducting business between retailers and their suppliers may also explain why there has been relatively little vertical concentration across industries in the channel—no textile firms have gone into the manufacture of apparel or retail and few apparel firms have set up their own retail outlets.[11] Indeed, an effective information-integrated channel probably works against vertical integration. Sharing information and current knowledge of the market across channel players achieves some of the same objectives—at lower cost—of formally reaching forward or backward into markets. Enterprises in different parts of the channel can therefore concentrate on their business strengths.

Lean retailing and the restructuring of manufacturing supply have also affected the economy as a whole in the area of inventories. Lean retailing itself implies a dramatic reduction in the amount of inventory held by retail enterprises. Chapter 14 documents the large inventory reductions of apparel suppliers that draw fully on information technology in concert with new managerial and manufacturing practices; in some cases they have decreased inventory levels by half.

The impact of these new policies on retailing and manufacturing sectors may have begun to show up in economy-wide measures of inventory. The overall ratio of inventories to final sales of domestic business fell considerably in the past decade, from 2.78 in 1987 to 2.34 in 1997.[12] It has long been known that inventories at the macroeconomic level affect the depth and length of business cycles.[13] The connection between recent changes in inventory policy and the business cycle have only begun to be studied in a systematic fashion.[14] As noted in the 1988 *Economic Report of the President*,

> Adoption of just-in-time inventory management by manufacturers also represents a significant development, since changes in inventories have often been an important source of business-cycle fluctuations. Whether just-in-time inventories will be able to dampen future business cycles, however, remains to be seen.[15]

Our work on apparel supplier adjustments to lean retailing suggests that an economy characterized by an increasing level of modern manufacturing and retailing practices should experience lower levels of inventories relative to sales. Because a reduction in the I/S ratio means that changes in sales will be matched by a smaller change in inventories, a lower ratio also implies lower inventory volatility. This is important because aggregate inventory volatility has historically made up a significant portion of the volatility of Gross Domestic Product (GDP). If the effects documented for retail-apparel-textile channels are more pervasive across other sectors similarly affected by channel integration, these changes could imply lower GDP volatility. This macroeconomic link may prove to be the most profound implication of the adoption of firm-level information technology and manufacturing practices.

Fundamental changes in inventory policies in retail and manufacturing may significantly affect price levels as well. The increased volatility of producer and consumer prices in a number of sectors since 1995 has been attributed in part to the adoption of new inventory polices related to lean retailing.[16] Some have suggested a connection between these policies and price fluctuations.[17] According to one view, an information-integrated channel may lead to increased volatility in aggregate prices because the impact of shifts in supply and demand is more rapidly reflected in consumer prices without the buffering impact of inventory. Competitive information-integrated channels may also reduce aggregate price levels, as expressed by price markup policies that in the past have reflected the incomplete information of channel participants.[18] Whatever the effect, the more widespread adoption of information-integrated channels documented in this book raise a central question for future models of industry- and macroeconomic-price movements.[19]

Labor Standards: The Problem of Sweatshops

> The most effective weapon used by American capital in weakening the power of organized labor has been to hire immigrant workers. . . . [I]mmigrants are cheap and controllable. The conditions they toil under make a mockery of the already low American labor standards—the most regressive among the advanced industrial nations.[20]

For more than a century, the U.S. federal and state governments have investigated sweatshops in the garment industry, including the role of immigrants, and have adopted legislation to ameliorate their impact on workers and consumers. At the turn of the last century, unsanitary conditions, in addition to low wages, long hours, and child labor, were the biggest concerns. State inspectors were authorized to attach a "tenement-made" tag to garments produced by violators. The Consumers' League, organized in 1899, adopted a voluntary label to be attached to garments made by manufacturers that abided by labor standards—that is, they obeyed state factory laws, manufactured on their premises, employed no children under 16, and used no overtime work.[21]

In 1938, the Fair Labor Standards Act (FLSA) for industry generally specified minimum wage rates, overtime after forty hours of work per week, and a prohibition of child labor. The so-called "hot cargo" provisions of the statute, Section 15, made it illegal to transport or sell goods in commerce produced in violation of the provisions of the Act.[22] Despite these strict legislated standards—with wage levels updated from time to time—widespread violations in apparel workplaces have become commonplace in the 1990s. Labor conditions have deteriorated for a number of reasons: the decline in the coverage of collective bargaining agreements with their provisions for regulation of contract shops; the difficulty of policing contributions for health and pension funds from employers in this sector; the increase in immigrants, legal and illegal, concentrated in certain areas; the intense competition from imports; and the sharp drop in employment in apparel in some markets.[23] Sweatshops, it seems, have always been with us.

The El Monte plant in southern California, with immigrants working behind barbed wire, caught the nation's attention in 1996. Federal investigators reported in 1997 that two-thirds of the establishments in New York City's garment industry violated overtime or minimum wage laws.[24] The U.S. Labor Department reports that independent surveys, as well as federal and state compliance data, show minimum wage and overtime violations of the FLSA occurring in 40 to 60 percent of investigated establishments. The policy question is what, if anything, can be done to control or eliminate sweatshops and noncompliance with statutory standards in the United States? And what can be done to ameliorate sweatshop conditions in developing countries that produce and export half of the apparel purchased in this country?

Historically, U.S. governments have employed three general approaches to the problem of sweatshops. First, the federal and state governments used powers of enforcement to seek compliance with labor standards. For the federal government, the Fair Labor Standards Act and its regulations specify the standards and enforcement procedures.[25] But sole reliance on traditional government enforcement activities has serious limitations.[26] The Department of Labor has fewer than 800 investigators to enforce employment statutes for 800,000 apparel industry employees in about 24,000 establishments, not to mention the other 122 million employees in 6.5 million workplaces around the country. Monitoring compliance with wage and hour provisions and pursuing violations is an extremely complicated and time-consuming process.

A second method has involved mobilizing public pressure on consumers, retailers, and manufacturers to raise the incentives for voluntary compliance with labor standards. For example, the Secretary of Labor has used his or her "bully pulpit" to call attention to the problem, urging the public, retailers, and manufacturers to avoid purchasing products made in workplaces that do not meet the standards.[27] Various reports have also publicized government enforcement actions to deter contractors, jobbers, manufacturers, and retailers from violating the standards, such as the release of a series of government reports on the extent of violations and the penalties assessed against violators.[28] In yet another example, Duke University's adoption of a code of conduct to ensure that apparel items bearing the university's name are not made in sweatshops has received public support.[29]

Indeed, efforts to use public concern, and at times outrage, to tackle the sweatshop problem go back to the early part of this century. The most famous case involves public reaction to the fire at the Triangle Shirtwaist Company on March 25, 1911, in which 146 women died. The fire started in a loft of the factory during the workday. The women and girls working in the factory could not escape because the company had locked the doors to the stairs from the outside, ostensibly to prevent theft by employees. The lack of fire extinguishers within the factory and the inability of fire ladders to reach the windows made escape impossible. In this case, public outrage led to early workers' compensation and factory inspection legislation.

But, in general, the effectiveness of focusing public attention on sweatshops and poor labor conditions has been limited by the difficulty of keeping consumers, voters, students, or other groups working on this issue for sustained periods of time. Such avenues are at best a means for focusing the attention of key parties in order to build longer term mechanisms that remain even after public attention wanes.

Finally, voluntary agreements among channel participants to ensure compliance—which sometimes have arisen from efforts to increase public pressure—have been employed at various times. For instance, in 1995, the Labor Department sponsored the Apparel Industry Partnership, in which a number of U.S. apparel manufacturers, UNITE!, the National Consumers League, the Interfaith Center on Corporate Responsibility and others agreed to monitor compliance with labor standards of contractors.[30] Yet these initiatives also have limitations. It is difficult to select an organization to do the monitoring, establish the procedures to be followed, and determine who should serve as outside or independent monitors.[31] Voluntary compliance measures and agreements in the United States, outside of collective bargaining, have thus far had a history of short-term viability and limited effectiveness.

Policies to reduce repugnant workplace conditions—by U.S. standards—in developing nations that export apparel to the U.S. involve an even more complex range of issues. What are the appropriate labor standards? Is one only to apply the standards and regulations of the exporting country or are some higher international standards to be used? How are such standards to be established, recognized, and enforced?[32] One approach would be to extend the conventions and standards established by the International Labour Office (ILO) and to enhance the effectiveness of its enforcement. The ILO held a convention on child labor in June 1998 and is considering a proposal for an annual "global report" on countries that have not ratified certain core workers' rights, such as freedom of association, abolition of forced labor, nondiscrimination and equal remuneration, and minimum age.[33] Even with such international standards adopted by the ILO, the task of enforcement remains daunting.

In the United States a number of programs have been adopted that seek to change labor practices in workplaces overseas. The Department of Labor provided $500,000 to the International Program for the Elimination of Child Labor in a joint effort with the ILO to end the use of children in the manufacture of soccer balls in Pakistan. (In 1994, 35 million soccer balls were produced there, one-quarter by children.)[34] Mattel, Nike, and Kathie Lee Gifford exemplify manufacturers, brand names, and celebrities who have adopted programs for overseas inspections to mitigate criticism of their possible sweatshop imports. The Council on Economic Priorities has established a global, variable "social accountability standard" that companies can follow to prove they adhere to an array of labor standards and pay their workers a sufficient income.[35] The U.S. and European Union, through the Secretary of Labor and Commissioner for Employment and Social Affairs, have sought to develop among labor and management an acceptance of international standards to assure consumers that the products they buy are not made in sweatshops.[36]

In a significant sense, such efforts to deal with labor standards in apparel production simply illustrate the larger issues of trade, labor, and environmental standards that are likely to be a focus of international economic discourse over the decade ahead. In fact, it is doubtful that these issues can be separated to the extent they have been over the past decade. There are sharp differences in the United States between organized labor and business and in the political arena as well. Persistent efforts in the labor standards field indicate that separating trade, labor, and other social issues will no longer be as acceptable in the era ahead. The fact that U.S. Secretary of State Madeleine Albright took up the issue of global sweatshops is a striking example of this reality.[37]

The complexity of sweatshop problems makes any "silver bullet" solution as unlikely now as it has been throughout this century.

Nonetheless, our analysis suggests a number of steps that might be taken to improve compliance with U.S. labor standards in the presence of information-integrated channels. Given the inherent resource limitations in U.S. government enforcement, inspections must be carefully targeted to yield maximum impact. One method for improving targeting would be to require each garment to include a bar code label that shows the place and time of fabrication. This would take advantage of the same technology that has been so fundamental to the changes examined in this book. Information from the bar code could more directly be used by the Wage and Hour inspectors to sample compliance and more rapidly isolate violations. Such requirements could arise either as a result of voluntary agreements among retailers and apparel suppliers or be mandated through regulation.[38] Past experience suggests, however, that in this field voluntary measures need to be reinforced by regulatory authority.

The viability of collective bargaining as a means, once again, to regulate sweatshop conditions largely depends on the ability of UNITE! to rebuild its collective bargaining and membership base in a smaller and more efficient industry responsive to lean retailing.[39] Efforts by the union and apparel employers to link compliance with wage and working condition standards to efforts to improve the competitive viability of the industry offer promise such as through sponsoring training of apparel managers or by helping to build more responsive networks of apparel contractors to deal with retailers. But these initiatives are still at an early stage of development.[40]

Finally, the central role played by retailers in development and operation of the channel points to the fact that any measure—whether taken by the government, through voluntary compliance programs or via collective bargaining—must include their participation and support. The reliance of lean retailing on the promulgation of standards of performance has been well documented in this book. A logical extension of those practices might be the adoption of procedures or systems related to labor standards in domestic or offshore sourcing operations.

The Coming Competitive Landscape

Since the end of World War II, textile-mill products and apparel have both been characterized by substantial reductions in employment; at the same time these sectors show substantial increases in output, including shifts to higher-value products and higher productivity.

Total employment in U.S. textiles is projected to continue its decline, reaching 588,000 workers by 2006, with apparel down to 714,000 at the same date. Meanwhile, outputs are projected to increase 22 and 4 percent, respectively, in the 1996–2006 period.[41]

These are scarcely moribund industries, with inflexible product and labor markets. The textile industry, in particular, has been characterized by rapid technological changes and automation; shifts to large-scale establishments; restructuring and consolidation of enterprises in spinning, weaving, and knitting; substantial capital investments in these activities and finishing operations; and a shift to products with expanding markets. Wages have risen relative to the average of all manufacturing or nondurable manufacturing. Exports have been within a few billion dollars of imports in recent years.

The economics of these channels depend on the costs of the separate steps and transactions—from manufacture, including inventory costs, through distribution costs, retail, and sales, including markdown and stock-out costs. The costs of time to market also matters. This view of costs examined throughout this book yields quite different estimates from the traditional resort to comparative direct labor costs of manufacture as a sole basis for supply-choice decisions. Previous chapters have demonstrated that the lowest purchase price from a supplier does not necessarily yield the lowest costs at the point and time of sale or the largest profit. An established channel in which the various parties focus on time to market results in markedly different supply decisions and dynamics than those dictated by conventional direct labor costs of supplies. Given these crucial changes, the following sections review the competitive "horizon" for each of the industries that make up the channel.

The Retail Horizon

Information-integration is one of the major factors contributing to increasing concentration in the retail sector. Previously, manufacturers and suppliers to a number of retailers were often in a better position, compared with any one retailer, to report on shifting styles and tastes and estimate market direction. In many situations, they chose SKUs and set volumes for retailers. Now point-of-sales information provides retailers with reliable information on market developments and hence gives them more leverage in dealing with direct suppliers and others further from ultimate consumers. In other words, direct measurable information of consumer behavior translates into market power. The lean retailer can also transfer to its suppliers the functions (and costs) of creating floor-ready merchandise, activities that traditional retailers handled in the past. Bear in mind, however, that the information-integrated channel requires substantial investment in technologies by retailers. Although small-scale retailing continues, it is clear that an increasing proportion of retailing will be concentrated among a decreasing number of larger enterprises.[42]

The Internet has been often cited as an alternative to retailing and, presumably, a potential challenge to the dominant role played by lean retailers. In this regard, Tracy Mullin, President of the National Retail Federation (NRF) notes:

> The NRF fields a deluge of calls each week about the Internet's impact on retailing. The most common question we get from reporters: "How long will it take for the Internet to completely replace physical retailing?" We have observed that traditional retailers are taking a cautious approach to the Internet. Yet most understand its great potential, even if they openly admit they don't have all the answers.[43]

A limited number of retailers are currently experimenting with the Internet, although only 9 percent of those surveyed in 1998 indicated that they currently sell products this way.[44] Retailers are currently reluctant to go on-line both because they believe that their products are "ill-suited for Web sales" and are concerned about specific technical limitations, such as the security of electronic financial transactions.[45]

A number of developments, many linked to issues we have discussed, indicate both the potential and limitations of electronic retailing. In one sense, the Internet offers opportunities akin to mail-order retailing for playing a very lean game. For example, Lands' Ends became an early leader in adopting certain lean retailing elements into its catalog operations and has aggressively entered Internet retailing. This retailer launched its Web site in 1995, the first major apparel retailer to do so. Its site incorporates an encryption system to protect customers against credit-card thefts.[46]

The Internet provides some of the advantages of mail-order sales with even lower transaction costs. However, the obstacles to virtual retailing remain formidable. Product offerings are limited in Web retail sites—the Lands' End site, for example, offered only 500 products in 1997. In addition, just as in other areas of modern retailing, a company must have a distribution system capable of getting products out efficiently on an order-by-order basis, either through internal resources or use of third-party consolidators. The economics of distribution for Web retailing, like catalog retailing, are therefore quite different from those developed even by advanced in-store lean retailers.

Finally, measurement, fit, color, and texture remain central components of apparel sales. In apparel—unlike the sale of goods via the Internet such as computers, software, or tools—people want to see, feel, and try on the products. These aspects of selling apparel items do not fit well with "virtual retailing." The mail-order business already contends with this problem, and these retailers cope with returns that sometimes go over one-quarter the value of sales in a given year. Consider Lands' End once more. In 1991 (well before its entrance to the Internet), it was forced to cope with returns of 132,000 shirts. Each return was associated with a processing cost roughly equivalent to 25 percent of its value.[47] Thus, although Internet retailing will certainly grow as a channel of distribution, the most essential longer term developments will involve the expansion of lean retailing principles to a wider and wider variety of goods sold by a decreasing number of major retailers.

The Apparel Industry Horizon

A central feature of information-integrated channels—indeed, the basis for our term "lean retailing"—is the effective management of inventories at the SKU level. Throughout the modern channel, lean inventory management reduces the risk of selling "perishable" products, thus enhancing profits. The capability to compete increasingly depends on an enterprise's ability to manage operations according to the logistics of time and flow of product, reducing time to market and the costs of holding inventory.

We have made clear that holding inventory can be expensive to a supplier, whether it manufactures or sources its products, in several ways. These include capital tied up in work-in-process or finished goods; the costs of facilities used; the risks of failure to sell; and price markdowns to dispose of products. At the same time, the inability to supply product to retailers or customers is another costly risk.

These risks and costs may be minimized and profits enhanced by using a combination of short-cycle and longer-cycle production lines. The short-cycle line turns out products faster but usually at a higher unit cost. The long-cycle line takes longer to produce items, but at lower costs. Balancing these lines by establishing for each SKU the precise pattern of expected variability in demand and point-of-sale information provides the means for maximizing profits. Our research suggests that the cycle time of a fast production line should be no more than a week or two to be an effective alternative for the lower costs of a long-cycle line or plant.

The balancing of short-cycle and long-cycle production alternatives has direct application to the choices manufacturers and retailers face between domestic sources with potential short cycles and foreign sources with longer ones. The future of the domestic apparel industry rests on those items made using short-cycle production, which are often those with high weekly variations in sales. Such short-cycle production necessarily requires methods like modular or UPS assembly rather than the lengthy progressive bundle system. At the same time, it requires an ability to use incoming information on sales in a sophisticated manner to allocate production in this way.

In a related vein, the future of domestic producers also relies on their development of capabilities for supplying fashion products on a replenishment basis. Once again, this requires a combination of practices; by using advanced forecasting methods and innovative production techniques, apparel-makers may be able to respond in very short periods of time to point-of-sale information regarding sale of products with higher fashion content. In addition, as we discussed in Chapter 8, suppliers attempting mass customization of apparel products such as jeans will need similar capabilities.

The Textile Industry Horizon

Textile markets in the United States no longer depend primarily on apparel as they did in the past. Currently, no more than approximately 35 percent of textile shipments are for apparel items. Textile firms now furnish a range of household products (such as sheets, bedding, towels, and rugs) and some knit products (T-shirts) directly to retailers. Such channels have adopted the information-integration described earlier as textile products have been upgraded from greige goods in a brokers' market to those that involve complex finishing operations and extensive product proliferation. A number of integrated channels have therefore been developed among textiles, retailers, and their customers.

Significant markets have also grown for industrial textiles in a wide range of industrial enterprises, such as automobile interiors and tire cord. The range of industrial products is expanding, including knapsacks, tea bags, tents, fishing nets, hammocks, air bags, and parachutes.

Even if textile products flowing to apparel sewn in this country (or in Mexico and the Caribbean Basin, where contractors assemble garments using U.S. textiles) decline, it is realistic to assume that some U.S. textile exports will increase in the near term and that there will be substantial increases in domestic industrial markets.

Still, at least one feature of textile markets warrants attention in their relations to apparel. The size of many orders preferred by the apparel industry is considerably smaller than that preferred by textile firms. Apparel-makers confront frequent changes in styles and new SKUs, while textile manufacturers seek long runs to keep capacity operating round-the-clock. In the retail-apparel-textile channels, there is a need for an information-sharing integrated system—some form of packager—to assist in ameliorating these differences. Once again, the development of Web sites to undertake some of these connections represents an important first step in this direction.

The Future of Information-Integrated Channels

As we have stated throughout, textiles and apparel remain significant sectors of the U.S. economy. In 1997, together they provided more than 1.4 million jobs, and in 2006 they are projected to have combined employment of over 1.3 million—nearly 8 percent of all projected jobs in manufacturing. These sectors are far too vital to their communities and the country, and have proven sufficiently vibrant, to be dismissed by the conventional doctrine of comparative labor costs.

Indeed, rather than turning the future more bleak, the introduction and the widespread adoption of lean retailing by all participants in the retail-apparel-textile channel provides new opportunities for the textile and apparel industries, at least in some segments. We see a viable future for these industries—with a few caveats. These revived opportunities do not apply with equal effect to all branches of apparel or all parts of the fashion triangle. Garments amenable to rapid replenishment principles have the most potential for U.S. production.

Our less pessimistic view of the future of these industries should not be misinterpreted. The textile sector appears more promising because it has become more directly connected to retailers and industrial users. Yet survival in both sectors belongs only to the fittest adopters of the new order of retailing and the channel. Employment levels are not projected to turn around. Instead, employment will gradually decline in both industries, while output and productivity increase—the best that any industrial sector can expect over time in the modern economy. The new order in apparel places more of a premium on scale and size, along with investments in the requisite technologies. The traditional contractor shop and small enterprise will have a smaller and even less secure role unless linked to sophisticated intermediary agents in the channel.

In short, the paths these industries follow will be determined by their interconnection with one another. Providing a stitch—or a package of pasta, a home computer, an automobile—in time requires a growing degree of integration among business enterprises within and across industries. Whether it is Federated Department Stores' or Home Depot's use of point-of-sales information for inventory control; Levi Strauss's or Black and Decker's efforts at customizing products to suit very specific consumer groups; or VF's or Dell Computer's innovations to provide product diversity more efficiently, channel integration is driving the current industrial transformation—and will continue to do so in the period ahead.

Appendix A
List of Acronyms

ACTWU	Amalgamated Clothing and Textile Workers Union
ASN	Advanced Shipping Notice
ATC	Agreement on Textiles and Clothing
BLS	U.S. Bureau of Labor Statistics
CBI	Caribbean Basin Initiative
DAMA	Demand Activated Management Architecture
DOL	U.S. Department of Labor
EDI	Electronic Data Interchange
FLSA	Fair Labor Standards Act of 1938
GATT	General Agreement on Tariffs and Trade
HCTAR	Harvard Center for Textile and Apparel Research
ILGWU	International Ladies' Garment Workers Union
ILO	International Labour Office
I/S	Inventory/Sales Ratio
ITC	U.S. International Trade Commission
ITO	International Trade Organization
JTR	Joint Job Training and Research
LBO	Leveraged Buyout
MFA	Multi-Fiber Arrangement
NAFTA	North American Free Trade Agreement
OTA	Office of Technology Assessment
PBS	Progressive Bundle System
POS	Point-of-Sale
SAM	Standard Allocated Minutes
SCM	Shipping Container Marker
SIC	Standard Industrial Classification
SITC	Standard International Trade Classification

SKU	Stockkeeping Unit
SLS	Straight-line System
TALC	Textile Apparel Linkage Council
[TC]^2	Textile/Clothing Technology Corporation
UCC	Uniform Code Council
UNITE!	Union of Needletrades, Industrial and Textile Employees
UPC	Uniform Product Code
UPS	Unit Production System
VICS	Voluntary Interindustry Communications Standards
VMI	Vendor-Managed Inventory
WTO	World Trade Organization

Appendix B
The HCTAR Survey

One of the early objectives of our study was to assemble detailed information at the business unit level concerning the practices of apparel enterprises operating in the larger retail-apparel-textile channel. This research enterprise required collecting data on a very wide range of apparel supplier practices, including relationships with retailers and textile companies, information systems, distribution arrangements, and production practices. It also required collecting data on characteristics of the product markets for the business involved. To collect such detailed information necessitated the creation of an in-depth survey instrument and an effective method to ensure survey responses.

Survey Development

In the initial phase of development and distribution of the questionnaire in 1992, we targeted a limited set of apparel manufacturers, those that supply Dillard's Inc., a leading practitioner of lean retailing at that time. These discussions culminated in June 1992 in a workshop at Dillard's Little Rock headquarters with a number of the company's major apparel suppliers.

In fall 1992 and winter 1993 we designed a survey instrument and tested it with apparel manufacturers representing a range of products in the men's and women's industries. This process took the questionnaire through four separate iterations. The final questionnaire was divided into eight modules to facilitate the process of distributing the survey section within an apparel company to appropriate divisions and personnel. The sections are (1) Overview; (2) Order Fulfillment Process; (3) Manufacturing; (4) Domestic and International Sourcing;

(5) Human Resources; (6) Supplier Relationship; (7) Sales, Marketing, and Product Line Development; and (8) Distribution. Copies of the questionnaire are available from the HCTAR office on request.

Given the diversity of arrangements within the retail-apparel-textile channels, rather than a random sample of the industry as a whole, we focused on ten specific apparel industry segments, chosen to reflect major branches of both the women's and men's industry. For the men's industry, we chose suits, slacks, jeans, T-shirts, and dress shirts. For the women's sector, we selected outwear (coats and jackets), "bridge" dresses (bridging product price points), intimate apparel, sportswear bottoms, and blouses. While the survey also yielded responses from companies outside this group, the segments provided us with a useful focus in our work with the sponsors.

Sponsorship of the Questionnaire

The size, detail, and confidential information requested in the questionnaire meant that sponsorship and support from industry participants was essential to achieve adequate response rates. Depending on the size and complexity of the business unit, the time required to fill out the entire questionnaire ranged from ten to sixty hours. Sponsorship and intensive follow-up by HCTAR therefore proved crucial to the research effort.

Earlier phases of the research project created a basis for arranging sponsorship of the survey by four key players: Dillard's, Kmart, the Amalgamated Clothing and Textile Workers Union, and the International Ladies Garment Workers Union (the latter two labor unions later merged to form UNITE!). These sponsors provided us with lists of their apparel suppliers, in the case of Dillard's and Kmart, or apparel-makers under collective bargaining agreements in targeted segments in the case of the unions. Executives of those organizations also furnished a letter indicating support of the HCTAR survey as well as assurance that reported results would not be shared with those sponsors, but remain confidential with HCTAR. The letters of support from retail and/or labor union sponsors were sent to the president, CEO, or senior executive of each business unit.

The diversity of the four sponsors provided for broad coverage of the U.S. apparel industry by including companies making products at both high and low price points; small and large manufacturers; companies making men's, women's, and children's clothing; manufacturers that make product in-house and in contract shops; manufacturers that source their production in the United States and abroad; and companies operating under collective bargaining agreements and business units not under such agreements.

Although the sample is limited to U.S.-based business units, it includes business units that source from factories both within and outside the United States. In addition, although the survey was sponsored by specific retailers or unions, each survey requests information from the business unit on its practices, characteristics, and performance for all retail customers. It therefore captures information concerning practices and performance regarding all the business unit's product lines and retail customers.

Response Rates and Survey Representativeness

A total of 435 companies were sent questionnaires. Each company was instructed to answer a separate questionnaire for each of its business units. A business unit was defined as the lowest level of a firm with responsibility for formulating annual policies dealing with merchandising, planning, manufacturing, distribution, and related activities. For some organizations, the business unit was the same entity as the company. For others, several business units operated under a single corporate umbrella.

A total of eighty-four companies completed the survey. Because many of the larger companies had multiple business units, a total of 118 business unit questionnaires were received. Response rates, based on the survey procedure described above, varied among apparel categories. Table B.1 (page 286) provides a breakdown of the number of surveys sent and the response rate by product category. Response rates varied from the 13 to 17 percent in certain women's segments to the mid-60 percent range among pants and jeans manufacturers.

The representativeness of the sample for selected product groups in terms of 1992 dollar shipments is presented in Table B.2 (page 287). Table B.2 compares the total value of shipments for specific product groups as reported by the U.S. Department of Commerce with the sum of total sales per product category of survey respondents. The total volume of apparel shipped by business units (not including other textile products) in the sample equaled $13.8 billion in 1992. The value of total shipments of apparel products in 1991 was $46.4 billion.

Tables B.1 and B.2 indicate that the survey design was particularly successful in assuring responses by apparel business units in the targeted segments (e.g., men's and women's jeans, men's suits, men's shirts). For segments characterized by small manufacturers (e.g., women's dresses, women's blouses), our response rate was lower. As a result, the sample is biased toward larger firms and business units. As a consequence, estimates of manufacturing innovation and performance skewed toward the practices of larger enterprises. Considerable care was taken in all statistical analyses of the data to take into account these potential sources of bias.

Table B.1. HCTAR Survey Response Rate

Product Category[a]	No. of Responses	Total Surveys Sent	Response Rate in Percent
Men's sport	18	51	35%
Women's sport	16	120	13
Intimate apparel	12	39	31
Tailored suits and coats	9	45	20
Shirts	5	19	26
Dresses	10	79	13
Knits	17	39	44
Pants	10	15	67
Jeans	6	10	60
Men's (all categories)	51	143	36
Women's (all categories)	47	273	17
Children's (all categories)	5	22	23
Home	7	33	21
Other	20	110	18

Source: Harvard Center for Textile and Apparel Research.

[a] Some companies are cross-classified.

Appendix B

Table B.2. HCTAR Survey Representativeness

Product Category	Total Dollar Volume in Sample[a] (1992, Millions of Dollars)	Reported Dollar Volume, Commerce Dept.[b]	Sample as Percentage of Commerce Estimate
Men's and women's jeans	3,502	6,443	54%
Men's clothing			
Suits	746	2,450	30
Slacks	1,997	1,499	133
Dress shirts	648	1,173	55
Women's clothing			
Outerwear	488	3,745	13
Dresses	637	5,443	12
Intimate apparel	685	3,660	19
Blouses	226	3,618	6
Apparel and other textile products	14,342	64,115	22
Men's, women's, children's apparel[c]	13,792	46,442	30

[a] Sum of reported shipments in 1992 by business units for stated product categories. The categories in the HCTAR sample do not fully correspond to the SIC groupings used by the Bureau of the Census, leading to some discrepancies as in the case of men's slacks.

[b] Based on 1991 value of product shipments, U.S. Department of Commerce, Bureau of the Census, *Annual Survey of Manufacturers*, Table 1, pp. 2–9, 2–10.

[c] Excluding non-apparel business units and SIC categories from calculations.

Appendix C
Data Sources

The research contained in *A Stitch in Time* arises from a number of data sources in addition to the HCTAR survey described in Appendix B. We drew on data from Standard & Poor's Compustat database regarding retailer performance; the U.S. Department of Commerce for data on imports and exports; and the U.S. Department of Commerce, Bureau of the Census, for detailed microdata on manufacturers for additional information regarding apparel supplier performance. We briefly describe each of these data sources below.

Standard & Poor's Compustat Database

The information regarding the performance of retailers in Chapter 5 is drawn from Standard & Poor's Compustat database for the period 1984 to 1994. The database provides annual balance sheet, income statement, and cash flow information for publicly held companies. Our analyses, which are described in the notes to Chapter 5, used a sample of retailers from four industry segments: department stores, national chains, mass merchants, and specialty stores.

The variables used in the analysis of retail companies in each of the industry segments are drawn directly from Compustat. They are defined as follows:

Sales

This item represents gross sales (the amount of actual billing to customers for regular sales completed during the period) reduced by cash discounts, trade discounts, and returned sales and allowances for which credit is given customers. It includes any revenue source that is expected to continue for the life of the company, other operating revenue, installment sales, and franchise sales (when corresponding expenses are available).

Cost of Goods Sold

This represents all costs directly allocated by the company to production, such as material, labor, and overhead. The total operating costs for nonmanufacturing companies are considered as cost of goods sold if a breakdown is unavailable.

Selling, General, and Administrative Expense

This item represents all commercial expenses (such as expenses not directly related to product production) incurred in the regular course of business pertaining to the securing of operating income. It includes accounting expense, advertising expense, amortization of R&D, bad debt expense, commissions, corporate expense, directors' fees and expenses, foreign currency adjustments, indirect costs when a separate Cost of Goods Sold figure is given, legal expense, marketing expense, and others.

Operating Income Before Depreciation and Taxes

This represents the operating income of a company after deducting expenses for costs of goods sold and selling, general, and administrative expenses.

Import Merchandise Database

The official U.S. import and export statistics used in Chapter 13 are compiled from data extracts taken from the U.S. Department of Commerce, Bureau of the Census, Administrative and Customer Services Division, *U.S. Imports/Exports History, International Harmonized System Commodity Classification by Country by Customs District*, Historical Summary 1991–95 with updates for 1996–97. We gratefully acknowledge the assistance of Everett Ehrlich, then Under Secretary for Economic Affairs of the Department of Commerce, and the staff of its agencies, in understanding the processes of data collection and in their interpretation. We also consulted with the staff of the U.S. Customs Service of the Department of Treasury.

This database is based on information collected by the U.S. Customs Service, specifically in its Customs Service Entry Summary forms that must be filed with the Customs Service at the time the merchandise is released to the importer or exporter. This system—now using both paper filings and computer transmission submissions—receives import data concerning a total of 750,000 shipments each month. We used information for all product classifications relating to apparel and textile categories from this system for the period 1991 to 1997 for purposes of analysis.

The dataset is organized in accordance with the Harmonized Tariff Schedule of the United States Annotated (HTSUSA also known as HS codes) that provides a unique ten-digit reporting number for each product imported into or exported from the United States. Each record in the database represents imports or exports classified at the HS code level, including the value of that shipment for a given time period. It also provides information on the country of origin for imports or export destination.

The data were analyzed at a more aggregated, five-digit product level based on the Standard International Trade Classification (SITC) system. The aggregation was undertaken by using concordance files supplied to us by the U.S. Department of Commerce to identify the appropriate HS codes that correspond with the SITC product codes of concern. Import and export results at the SITC level are reported in the text.

Longitudinal Research Database

Chapter 14 draws on matching the HCTAR sample with a dataset collected by the U.S. Department of Commerce, Bureau of the Census *Longitudinal Research Database (LRD)*. We thank Joyce Cooper and Randy Becker at the Boston Research Data Center of the U.S. Bureau of the Census during 1996–98. The opinions and conclusions expressed here are those of the HCTAR authors and do not necessarily represent the views of the U.S. Bureau of the Census. All these results were screened to ensure that they do not disclose confidential information.

The Bureau of the Census developed the LRD to provide researchers access to the establishment-level data on the manufacturing sector collected for the *Annual Survey of Manufacturers* and the *Census of Manufacturers*. The LRD file consists of a time series of establishment identifiers (used for identification and matching), detailed information on production inputs (labor, material, capital) and outputs (value of shipments), and other basic economic information for each manufacturing plant represented in the LRD. A complete description of LRD can be found in U.S. Department of Commerce, Bureau of the Census, *Longitudinal Research Database Technical Documentation Manual*, Washington, D.C.: Bureau of the Census, 1992.

Using a matching procedure developed at the U.S. Department of Commerce's Boston Research Data Center, we were able to match sixty-two of the business units in the HCTAR sample with establishment-level, longitudinal data in the LRD sample. This allowed us to create the panel of data for the time period 1984–94. Matching the HCTAR and LRD databases was particularly advantageous for our research project in that it allowed us to measure the impact of business unit practices adopted by the end of 1992 on the inventory performance of apparel manufacturing establishments several years after that adoption.

Survey representativeness for the matched dataset can be assessed by comparing the total value of shipments for SIC categories as a whole with the total value of shipments for the matched sample. These results are provided in Table C.1. The matched sample constitute 60 percent of the HCTAR sample of business units because some business units do not directly manufacture (assemble) goods sold by them. Assuming the same size distribution across matched and unmatched business units, we divided the 1992 percent of total by .6 to obtain an estimate of 20 percent representation for the merged LRD/HCTAR sample.

Table C.1. LRD/HCTAR Merged Sample Representativeness

		Total Value of Shipments in Thousands of Dollars (Nominal)			
Year	SIC	Sample	Total	%Total	Product Description
1988	231	$391,495	$3,169,400	12.4%	Men's and boys' suits and coats
1988	232	$3,077,187	$15,293,800	20.1%	Men's and boys' furnishings
1988	233,234,236	$1,037,450	$27,308,600	3.8%	Women's and children's outerwear and undergarments
1988	238,239	$101,503	$18,181,600	0.6%	Miscellaneous, accessories, and fabricated textile products
1988	Total	$4,607,635	$63,953,400	7.2%	
1992	231	$410,247	$2,426,000	16.9%	Men's and boys' suits and coats
1992	232	$5,312,654	$17,933,900	29.6%	Men's and boys' furnishings
1992	233,234,236	$2,102,884	$29,569,800	7.4%	Women's and children's outerwear and undergarments
1992	238,239	$424,350	$21,433,100	2.0%	Miscellaneous, accessories, and fabricated textile products
1992	Total	$8,250,135	$71,362,800	11.7%	

Source: U.S. Department of Commerce, Bureau of the Census, *Annual Survey of Manufacturers, 1988 and 1992 Statistics for Industry Groups and Industries*, M88(AS)-1 and M93(AS)-1, Washington, D.C.: Government Printing Office; U.S. Department of Commerce, Bureau of the Census, *Longitudinal Research Database*.

Appendix D
Companies Visited or Interviewed by HCTAR

U.S. Companies and Associations Visited or Interviewed

American Apparel Manufacturers Association
American Textile Manufacturers Institute
Anne Klein
Arrow Shirt Company
Associated Merchandising Corporation
Bali
Bayer Clothing Group
Biltwell Clothing Company
Bradlees, Inc.
British Home Stores
Brooks Brothers
Burlington Industries
Capital Mercury Shirt Company
Cluett, Peabody & Company
Cliftex Corporation
Cone Mills
Dan Rivers, Inc.
Dillard's Inc.
E. I. Dupont de Nemours & Company
Frederated Department Stores
Frederick Atkins, Inc.
Fruit of the Loom
Garland Shirt Company
Gerber Garment Technology, Inc.
Greif Companies
Haggar Apparel Company

Hampton Industries
Hartmarx Corporation
Hathaway/Warnaco
Hoechst Celanese Fibers
J. C. Penney Corporation
J. P. Stevens & Company
Jet Sew
Kendridge Apparel Group
KGR Inc.
Kmart Corporation
Lands' End
Lee Jeans
Leslie Fay Corporation
Levi Strauss & Company
The Limited
Mademoiselle Inc.
Malden Mills
Manhattan Menswear Group
MAST Industries
May Company
Milliken & Company
Monsanto
Morgan Shirt Corporation
Mothers Work, Inc.
Nautica Sportswear Company
Noah Enterprises
Palm Beach Company
Pendleton Woolen Mills
Phillips-Van Heusen Corporation
Plaid Industries
Procter & Gamble
Reebok Corporation
Russell Corporation
Salant
Sara Lee
Satkin Mills
Shaw's Supermarkets, Inc.
Sport Obermeyer
Springs Industries
Talbot Japan Company, Ltd.

Tama Manufacturing (Anne Klein II and Carole Wren)
Textile/Clothing Technology Corporation [TC]^2
Tommy Hilfiger
Trans-Apparel Group
Uniform Code Council
UNITE!
Vanity Fair Corporation
Warren Featherbone
West Point Pepperell
York Shirt Company

Asian Companies Visited or Interviewed

Alpine Limited
Asahi Chemical Industry Company Inc.
Burringtex Company Limited
China Textile University
Chun Tat Trading Company
Crystal Apparel Limited
Dianshan Lake Fashionable Dress Factory
Good Top Trading Limited
Kojima Fashion Studio
Li & Fung Limited
Obersport, Limited
Riches Knitting & Garment Factory Limited
Shanghai Ai Li Kang Textiles Company Limited
Shanghai Ailuan Fashion Company
Shanghai Donghai Garment Factory
Shanghai DSL Fashion Corporation
Shanghai Easeon Clothing Company Limited
Shanghai Silk Import & Export & Company
Shui Ying Knitting & Garment Factory Limited

European Companies Visited or Interviewed

Benetton S.p.A
CITER (Centro Informazione Tessile dell'Emilia-Romagna)
Coin S.p.A
Courtaulds Automotive Products
Descamps

Dim SA
Doré-Doré
E. Pecci & C. Capalle
Faliero Sarti & Figli S.p.A
Groupe Devanlay, Division Lacoste
Gruppo Finanziaro Tessile S.p.A
Gruppo GFT
Lanificio E. Zegna
Lanificio Guabello
Max Mara S.p.A
NOMISMA, Societ di Studi Economici, S.p.A
Oscar Jacobson
Poron Diffusion
TEXILIA (Textile Tradition and Technology Institute)
Unione Industriale Pratese

Notes

Chapter 1

1. "Bond's Strategy," *Business Week*, July 20, 1946, pp. 83–84.

2. American Apparel Manufacturers Association, *1996 Focus, An Economic Profile of the Apparel Industry*. Arlington, VA: American Apparel Manufacturers Association, 1996, p. 7.

3. The experience of the Textile/Clothing Technology Corporation ([TC]^2)—a major initiative in the early 1980s undertaken by a coalition of apparel and textile manufacturers, apparel labor unions, and the U.S. Department of Commerce—reflects the limitations of the focus on the sewing room. [TC]^2 first sought to introduce automation into the garment assembly room as the means to improve industry competitiveness. There are enormous difficulties in applying automation to clothing. [TC]^2 has recently abandoned its research program on sewing because of its limited impact and more recently concentrated its research program on other aspects of the apparel industry.

4. Casual days also seem to have positive performance impacts: eight out of the ten companies with dress-down days reported "great improvement" or "moderate improvement" in workers' attitudes. These figures are taken from Bureau of National Affairs, *Dress Policies and Casual Dress Days*, Personnel Policies Forum Survey No. 155. Washington, DC: Bureau of National Affairs, January 1998, pp. 1–3.

5. Murray, Lauren, "Unraveling Employment Trends in Textiles and Apparel." *Monthly Labor Review*, August 1995, pp. 64, 65.

6. U.S. Department of Labor, Bureau of Labor Statistics, *BLS Handbook of Methods*, Bulletin 1910. Washington, DC: Government Printing Office, 1976, pp. 91–92.

7. Boskin, Michael J., Ellen R. Dulberger, Robert J. Gordon, Zvi Griliches, and Dale Jorgenson, *Toward a More Accurate Measure of the Cost of Living, Final Report to the Senate Finance Committee from the Advisory Commission to Study the Consumer Price Index*. Washington, DC, December 4, 1996, pp. 62–63. According to this report, little deterioration in quality from 1965 to 1996 was found. Also see

"Symposia, Measuring the CPI," *The Journal of Economic Perspectives*, Winter 1998, pp. 3–78.

8. Joint Center for Housing Studies, Harvard University, *The State of the Nation's Housing*, 1995. Cambridge, MA: Harvard University, 1995, p. 4. Suburbs in metropolitan areas (outside the central cities) grew in population from 41.5 percent to 59.5 percent of the population in the period 1950–90. Inner cities declined from 58.5 percent to 40.4 percent in the same period.

Martin Bucksbaum, who helped to build one of the first shopping centers in 1956, notes "[P]eople did not want to go down-town and fight traffic and parking ramps," in Goldberger, Paul, "Settling the Suburban Frontier," *The New York Times Magazine*, December 31, 1995, pp. 34–35.

9. American Apparel Manufacturers Association, *1996 Focus, An Economic Profile of the Apparel Industry*. Arlington, VA: American Apparel Manufacturers Association, 1996, p. 7.

10. The fact that production of apparel goods (in physical units) remained constant in the face of decreasing employment also reflects the decline in labor content in those goods produced domestically. This in turn relates to the casualization of wardrobes: a men's dress shirt may contain 10 to 25 minutes of assembly labor, yet a knit polo shirt has only 1.5 to 8 minutes of direct labor.

11. Nehmer, Stanley, and Mark W. Love, "Textiles and Apparel: A Negotiated Approach to International Competition," in Scott, Bruce R. and George C. Lodge, eds., *U.S. Competitiveness in the World Economy*. Boston: Harvard Business School Press, 1985, p. 234.

12. The measurement of the extent of import penetration depends on how one values imports as compared to domestic production. By one method, import penetration is the landed value of imports as a percentage of the aggregate of U.S. production (measured in value of shipments) plus imports less exports. This method applied to 1986, when total apparel imports were $14,087 million and domestic production (value of shipments) equaled $57,917, yields an estimated import share of about 20 percent. By 1995, apparel imports hit $34,651 million compared with U.S. production of $78,097—or an import penetration of 30.7 percent of U.S. consumption. (Import figures: U.S. Department of Commerce, Office of Textile and Apparel. Production figures: U.S. Department of Commerce, Bureau of the Census, *Annual Survey of Manufacturers*. Figures for various years are compiled in American Apparel Manufacturers Association, loc. cit.) Although this definition of import penetration uses wholesale prices, an alternative method of import penetration values imports at retail prices as a percentage of U.S. domestic consumption, which requires converting import values to comparable retail levels. The trends in import penetration are similar using this method, but the levels of penetration are higher. In 1977, imports came to 13.3 percent of domestic consumption; by 1993, import penetration by this method had risen to 42.1 percent. These estimates are based on the National Income Accounts and reported in Pfleeger, Janet, "U.S. Consumers: Which Jobs Are They Creating?"*Monthly Labor Review*, June 1996, p. 16.

13. Imports of men's and boys' trousers went from 12 percent in 1973 to 50

percent in 1996. For women's and girls' dresses, import share rose from 6 percent in 1973 to 43 percent in 1996. Imports of women's slacks and shorts increased from 29 percent in 1973 to 55 percent by 1996. These figures are taken from the U.S. Department of Commerce, Office of Textile and Apparel and compiled in American Apparel Manufacturers Association, loc. cit., 1989 and 1997. See Tables 26 (1989) and 25 (1997), "U.S. Apparel Production, Imports and Import/Production Ratios for Selected Apparel Lines."

14. By 1997, business failures had decreased to 364. Based on figures from Dun & Bradstreet, Inc. reported in American Apparel Manufacturers Association, *1998 Focus*, loc. cit., 1998, Table 19.

15. Franklin, James C., "Industry Output and Employment Projections to 2006," *Monthly Labor Review*, November 1997, p. 46.

16. U.S. Department of Labor, Bureau of Labor Statistics, *Employment, Hours and Earnings, United States, 1909–94*, Bulletin 2445. Washington, DC: Government Printing Office, September 1994, Vol. 1, p. 583.

17. In 1994, an average apparel manufacturing establishment employed 38 employees; the average in men's and boys' wear establishments was 113 and in women's wear it was 28 employees. U.S. Department of Commerce, *County Business Patterns*. Washington, DC: Government Printing Office, 1994. The average size of establishments in both sectors declined considerably between 1986 and 1994, although the percentage of establishments with more than a hundred employees increased during the same period.

18. For example, in 1995 labor costs (measured as total compensation) constituted 20 percent of the value of shipments for men's and boys' trousers and slacks; 25 percent for men's and boys' shirts; and 34 percent for men's and boys' suits and coats. U.S. Department of Commerce, Bureau of the Census, *Annual Survey of Manufacturers*. Washington, DC: Government Printing Office, 1995.

19. For example, in 1992 hourly compensation costs for production workers in apparel and other textile products [Standard Industrial Classification, (SIC) 23] were $9.00 for the U.S.; $1.40 for Mexico; $3.60 for Hong Kong; and $3.20 for Korea. See International Labour Office, *Globalization of the Footwear, Textiles, and Clothing Industries*. Geneva, Switzerland: International Labour Office, Sectoral Activities Programme, 1996, Table 2.1.

20. The market share of white shirts as a percent of all dress shirts fell from 72 percent in 1962 to 52 percent in 1967 to about 21 percent by 1986. See Pashigian, Peter B., "Demand Uncertainty and Sales: A Study of Fashion and Markdown Pricing," *American Economic Review*, December 1988, pp. 936–53.

21. This contrasts with the women's industry, where there is greater diversity of products, a large number of fashion seasons, and greater volatility in consumer preference. The women's industry is characterized by small firms, contractor shops, and few examples of large producers, except for a few products like hosiery.

22. Import and production figures for men's and boys' woven shirts, of cotton and man-made fiber, based on U.S. Department of Commerce, Office of Textiles and Apparel, 1996 and reported in American Apparel Manufacturers Association, *1997 Focus,* loc. cit., Table 25. Employment estimates from Bureau of Labor Sta-

tistics, Employment and Earnings. The men's dress shirt industry was the first industry segment studied as a channel by the authors. See Abernathy, Frederick H., John T. Dunlop, Janice H. Hammond, and David Weil, *Improving the Performance of the Men's Dress Shirt Industry: A Channel Perspective*, Report on the Men's Dress Shirt Workshop, Harvard University, August 1991. (This report is available through HCTAR.)

23. Pashigian, Peter, loc. cit.

24. In the late 1960s and early 1970s, labor costs of the typical supermarket were approximately 50 percent of total operating expenses, exclusive of cost of goods sold, and the front-end labor costs (the checkout and cashier functions) were 40 percent of all labor costs. Average hourly earnings in food stores, moreover, were increasing at a rate of 6 percent or more a year. Labor productivity remained almost static during this period. See Dunlop, John T., and Kenneth J. Fedor, *The Lessons of Wage and Price Controls—The Food Sector*. Cambridge, MA: Harvard University Press, 1977, pp. 184–87; see also Brown, Stephen A., *Revolution at the Checkout Counter: The Explosion of the Bar Code*. Cambridge, MA: Harvard University Press, 1997.

25. Similar industry-wide standards originated by private parties emerged over this time period with the aim of coordinating the flow of product information among retailers, manufacturers, and other suppliers, including the Textile and Apparel Linkage Council (TALC) and the Voluntary Interindustry Communication Standard (VICS) Committee.

26. U.S. Congress, House of Representatives, 98th Congress, Second Session, *Hearings Before the Subcommittee on Trade of the Committee on Ways and Means*, March 29, 1984, p. 71. The average hourly earnings of production workers in the U.S. apparel industry in March 1984 were $5.50.

27. U.S. Department of Commerce, Bureau of the Census, *1995 Annual Survey of Manufacturers, Men's and Boys' Apparel*, MC87–I–23A. Washington, DC: Government Printing Office, 1995.

28. For example, in the men's shirt industry, 73 percent of all production workers are found in the sewing department versus 6 percent in the cutting room and 14 percent in the finishing department. See U.S. Department of Labor, Bureau of Labor Statistics, *Industry Wage Survey: Men's and Boys' Shirts*, September 1990, Bulletin 2405. Washington, DC: Government Printing Office, April 1992, Table 1.

29. U.S. Department of Commerce, International Trade Administration, *U.S. Industrial Outlook*. Washington, DC: Government Printing Office, 1990, p. 35.

30. These estimates are provided by our colleagues at the MIT International Motor Vehicle Program. The estimates vary widely by manufacturer, model, and assembly date. A separate estimate of the costs associated with distribution of BMW automobiles in the United States puts the percentage at about 29 percent of the sales price in 1997. See Christian, Nichole, "BMW Starting an Overhaul of U.S. Dealers," *Wall Street Journal*, June 12, 1997, p. A6.

31. Dertouzos, Michael L., Richard K. Lester, Robert M. Solow, and the MIT Commission on Industrial Productivity, *Made in America: Regaining the Productive Edge*. Cambridge, MA: MIT Press, 1990, p. 301.

32. Estimate based on HCTAR survey of apparel business units.

33. Much of the "high-fashion" segment, however, which is driven by designers and caters to a very high income (and small market) will remain in the United States given its very different market dynamics. We do not address this small segment of the industry in this book.

34. Murray, Lauren, loc. cit., p. 68.

35. Mexico and the Caribbean provided negligible imports to the United States through the mid-1980s (6 percent in 1984), but by 1996 their share had grown to 31 percent, thereby surpassing the Asian "Big Four" in square meters. Note that the Big four still constituted a larger share of all U.S. imports as measured by dollar value, providing 30 percent of the $36.4 billion of apparel imports versus the 23 percent originating in Mexico and Caribbean countries. Nonetheless, as Chapter 13 will show, Mexico and the Caribbean surpassed the Asian Big Four in a growing number of major product categories measured in dollar and physical quantities beginning in 1995. These data are taken from the U.S. Department of Commerce, Office of Textiles and Apparel. The data source is discussed in greater detail in Appendix C. In fact, these figures may underestimate the extent of imports contributed by Mexico because a growing proportion of Mexican imports under NAFTA enter duty-free and are therefore not included in import estimates. See United States International Trade Commission, *The Year in Trade, 1995: Operation of the Trade Agreements Program During 1995, 47th Report, August 1996, USITC Publication 2971*. Washington, DC: United States International Trade Commission, August 1996, p. 43, note 28.

Chapter 2

1. Among the works consulted for this story are the following: Tucker, Barbara May, *Samuel Slater and Sons: The Emergence of an American Factory System, 1790–1860*, University of California, Davis, Ph.D. dissertation, 1974; White, George, S., *Memoir of Samuel Slater, The Father of American Manufactures, Connected with a History of the Cotton Manufacture in England and America, with Remarks on the Moral Influence of Manufactures in the United States*, Second Edition. Philadelphia, printed at Number 46 Carpenter Street, 1836; Syrett, Harold C., ed., *The Papers of Alexander Hamilton*, Volume IX, August 1791–December 1791. New York: Columbia University Press, 1965, pp. 432–41. Also see the Slater Collection, Harvard Business School, Baker Library.

2. Letter of December 10, 1789, from Moses Brown to Samuel Slater, in White, George S., loc. cit., pp. 9–10.

3. Williamson, Harold F., *The Growth of the American Economy*, Second Edition. New York: Prentice-Hall, 1951, p. 300.

4. Chandler, Alfred D., Jr., *The Visible Hand: The Managerial Revolution in American Business*. Cambridge, MA: Harvard University Press, 1977, p. 209. The discussion draws on Chapter 7 of this volume.

5. Ibid., p. 209.

6. Ibid., p. 224.
7. Ibid., p. 228.
8. Ibid., p. 231.
9. Apparel and accessory stores have in fact doubled in employment since 1950, particularly in women's and family clothing stores. Department stores, as broadly defined by the U.S. Census, increased from 920,000 employees in 1960 to over two million in the early 1990s. In addition, in the 1980s, nonsupervisory hourly earnings were slightly lower than those in textiles or apparel, but by the early 1990s they had outpaced apparel (although they were still below the wages paid to textile workers). However, the average weekly hours of retail employees, a field traditionally dominated by women in part-time positions, have been lower than in either the apparel or textile industry and have become relatively much lower in the past two decades—only 29 hours in the early 1990s compared with 37 hours in apparel and 41 hours in textiles. See U.S. Department of Labor, Bureau of Labor Statistics, *Employment, Hours, and Earnings, United States, 1909–1994*, Volumes I and II, Bulletin 2495, September 1994; data for SIC 22, 23, and 531.
10. Zaretz, Charles Elbert, *The Amalgamated Clothing Workers of America*. New York: Ancon Publishing Company, 1934, p. 16.
11. Ibid., p. 17.
12. Some product lines today still use home work; others send the sewing to Latin America under Section 807 and 807a trade laws.
13. Stone, N. I., "Systems of Shop Management in the Cotton Garment Industry," *Monthly Labor Review*, June 1938, pp. 1–22.
14. Note that even before the 1930s, the longer runs and the greater degree of specialized sewing operations in men's apparel (such as in woven shirts and pants) tended to result in a faster pace of operations than in women's apparel (such as in dresses and coats), in which an operator often performs a wider range of operations on shorter runs of a specified style.
15. See Gomberg, William, *A Trade Union Analysis of Time Study*, Second Edition. New York: Prentice-Hall, 1955. The union perspective is summarized by Gomberg: "[M]odern industrial time study techniques can make no claim to scientific accuracy. . . . They are at best empirical guides to setting up a range within which collective bargaining over production rates can take place" (p. 246). Also see Abruzzi, Adam, *Work, Workers, and Work Measurement*. New York: Columbia University Press, 1956.
16. U.S. Department of Labor, Bureau of Labor Statistics, *Industry Wage Survey: Men's and Boys' Shirts (Except Work Shirts) and Nightwear, May–June 1961*, Bulletin 1323, March 1962, p. 7; *Industry Wage Survey: Men's and Boys' Shirts, September 1990*, Bulletin 2405, April 1992, p. 4.
17. The target buffers between different steps will vary within an assembly line in order to achieve overall line balance.
18. Hungarian, German, and Austrian Jews entered the trade as early as 1873, followed in the late 1880s by Russian and Polish Jews. See Adams, Thomas Sewell, and Helen Sumner, *Labor Problems: A Text Book*, Eighth Edition. London:

The Macmillan Co., 1915, pp. 119–20; Myers, Robert J., and Joseph W. Bloch, "Men's Clothing," in *How Collective Bargaining Works*. New York: The Twentieth Century Fund, 1942, pp. 393, 403.

19. New York Department of Labor, State Factory Investigating Commission, *Manufacturing in Tenements*, Vol. 1. Albany, NY: New York Department of Labor, 1914, pp. 90–123.

20. In New York City, at the time the largest center for the women's apparel industry, an estimated 80 percent of production originated in sweatshop production. See U.S. Congress, House of Representatives, Committee on Manufactures, "The Sweating System," *House Reports*, 52nd Congress, 2nd Session, Vol. 1, no. 2309, 1893, pp. iv–viii.

21. The United Garment Workers of America represented workers in the work clothes branch of the industry.

22. There is an extensive literature on this subject. For example, see Zaretz, loc. cit.; Slichter, Sumner H., *Union Policies and Industrial Management*. Washington, DC: The Brookings Institution, 1941, pp. 393–436; Braun, Kurt, *Union-Management Cooperation: Experience in the Clothing Industry*. Washington, DC: The Brookings Institution, 1947; Carpenter, Jesse, *Competition and Collective Bargaining in the Needle Trades*. Ithaca, NY: New York State School of Labor and Industrial Relations, 1972.

23. In 1900, the median weekly wage of a cutter was $17 versus $7 for sewing workers and $25 for a shop foreman. New York Bureau of Labor Statistics, "Wages in the Clothing Trade," in *Twentieth Annual Report of the Bureau of Labor Statistics*. New York: Bureau of Labor Statistics, 1902, pp. 1–28.

24. Galenson, Walter, *The CIO Challenge to the AFL: A History of the American Labor Movement, 1935–41*. Cambridge, MA: Harvard University Press, 1960, pp. 283–324. For an account of an early history of the two unions, see Perlman, Selig, and Philip Taft, *History of Labor in the United States, 1896–1932*, Vol. IV. New York: The Macmillan Company, 1935, pp. 289–317.

25. Dubinsky, David, and Abe H. Raskin, *David Dubinsky: A Life with Labor*. New York: Simon & Schuster, 1977, p. 118.

26. For example, the 1935–37 agreement between the ILGWU and employers from the cloak, suit, and skirt industry stated: "Every member of the Association who employs or deals with contractors or sub-manufacturers shall confine his production to his inside shop if he maintains one, and to the contractors or sub-manufacturers heretofore designated by him. He shall distribute his work equitably to and among his inside shop and the said contractors or sub-manufacturers with due regard to the ability of the contractor or sub-manufacturer to produce and perform." Use of non-union contractors, or contractors not designated under the agreement, was expressly forbidden. Signatories who used them were subject to steep fines and the possibility of expulsion from the association. See *Agreement of Merchants Ladies Garment Association, Inc. with International Ladies Garment Workers Union and Joint Board of Cloak, Suit, Skirt, and Reefer Makers Union of the International Ladies Garment Workers Union*, 1935–37, Section 6(a). Later agreements of the ILGWU with other employer associations describe in more detail the meth-

ods of designating contractors, enforcing compliance, and handling disputes on these matters.

27. The Amalgamated Clothing Workers of America and its employers undertook in the mid-1930s and early 1940s an ambitious plan to standardize labor costs across geographical markets in the men's suit sector, which was largely under collective bargaining agreements. Wage costs could not be standardized by creating a uniform system of piece rates because of differences in product specification and local piece rates in each plant and market. With the cooperation of manufacturers, stabilization plan garments were classified into six grades, with grade 1 being the cheapest. The parties established uniform minimum wage costs for an entire garment beginning with grades 1 and 2 and later extended by 1941 to grades 3 and 4. The wage cost established for each grade was then divided among the job classifications that made the respective garment grades, with appropriate piece rates filed with the Union's Stabilization Department. The program on an industry-wide basis did not survive as such, because of shifts in product competition and geographical market, although union concern with the standardization of labor costs by garment price lines continued. See Braun, Kurt, loc. cit., pp. 103–107. Also see Dunlop, John T., "Trade Union Interest in Related Markets," in *Wage Determination Under Trade Unions*. New York: Macmillan and Co., 1944, pp. 95–121.

28. Gomberg, loc. cit.

29. Hillman, in particular, embraced the idea of scientific management as a means of improving the efficiency of the men's clothing industry and conditions for his members. In this effort, he worked closely not only with large employers like Hart, Schaffner, and Marx, but also exchanged ideas with leading retailers of his day, including Lincoln and Edward Filene, founders of the retailing complex headquartered in Boston. See Fraser, Steven, "Sidney Hillman: Labor's Machiavelli," in Dubofsky, Melvyn, and Warren Van Tine, eds., *Labor Leaders in America*. Urbana: University of Illinois Press, 1987, pp. 211–12.

30. See Dunlop, John T., and Arnold M. Zack, *Mediation and Arbitration of Employment Disputes*. San Francisco: Jossey-Bass Publishers, 1997, pp. 7–9.

31. Dalzell, Robert F., Jr., *Enterprising Elite: The Boston Associates and the World They Made*. Cambridge, MA: Harvard University Press, 1987, pp. 5–6.

32. Waterpower in New England was abundant, nearly free, and located close to major seaports to allow economic shipment of cotton to the mills and finished cloth to the major markets along the seacoast. On the other hand, it was expensive to operate steam power. Steam-driven water pumps installed in the Fairmount Waterworks of the City of Philadelphia in 1815 cost $200 a day to operate, mostly because of the ten cords of wood consumed daily. The steam pumps were replaced by water-powered pumps in 1822, reducing daily operating costs to $4.11. See Hunter, Louis C., *A History of Industrial Power in the United States 1780–1930; Volume Two: Steam Power*. Richmond: University Press of Virginia, 1985, pp. 55–59.

33. Dalzell, loc. cit., p. 27.

34. Although companies manufacturing textile machinery were at one time a

significant element of the American industry, few such firms have survived except in the parts business. American textile firms largely rely on German, Swiss, Japanese, and Italian equipment manufacturers for new machinery and important innovations.

35. For the early history of one segment of knit products, see Taylor, George W., *Significant Post-War Changes in the Full-Fashioned Hosiery Industry*. Philadelphia: University of Pennsylvania Press, 1929.

36. Office of Technology Assessment, *The U.S. Textile and Apparel Industry: A Revolution in Progress, Special Report*. Washington, DC: Office of Technology Assessment, 1987, pp. 30–31.

37. Ibid.

38. In an industry sector, large establishments and enterprises generally tend to pay higher average earnings than smaller establishments. Further, because apparel employees generally work fewer hours a week than those in textiles, the weekly pay differences are even more striking. In 1950, average weekly earnings in textiles amounted to $48.59 compared with $44.60 in apparel. By 1980, textile weekly earnings had risen to $203.31 compared with $161.40; in 1997, textile workers earned $414.83 a week compared with $308.55 for those in apparel. See U.S. Department of Labor, Bureau of Labor Statistics, 1994, loc. cit. and *Employment and Earnings*, March 1998, p. 107.

39. In the past several decades, however, an increasing percentage of nonwhites has been employed. See Chaykowski, Richard P., Terry Thomason, and Harris L. Zwerling, "Labor Relations in American Textiles," in Voos, Paula B., ed., *Contemporary Bargaining in the Private Sector*. Madison, WI: Industrial Relations Research Association, 1994, p. 400.

40. Chaykowski et al., pp. 388–94.

41. "Bruce Raynor: On UNITE's Front Lines," *Women's Wear Daily*, February 17, 1998, p. 11.

42. For information on the experience of Burlington Mills with converters and forward integration, see Wright, Annette C., "Strategy and Structure in the Textile Industry: Spencer Love and Burlington Mills, 1923–1962," *Business History Review*, 69, Spring 1995, pp. 63–70.

43. Chandler, Alfred D., Jr., *Scale and Scope: The Dynamics of Industrial Capitalism*. Cambridge, MA: The Belknap Press of Harvard University Press, 1990, pp. 45–46.

Chapter 3

1. This account is based on Klein, Maury, "The Gospel of Wanamaker." *Audacity*, Summer 1996, pp. 27–40.

2. For apparel products, an SKU is a unique product with a specified manufacturer, color, fabric, style, and size. An example of an SKU is a white, men's button-down dress shirt, size 16" (collar) and 35" (sleeve) made of pin-point oxford cloth manufactured by a specific company.

3. Compensation for buyers was tied to their success in achieving this task. The majority of a successful buyer's pay in a given year came from bonuses pegged to the retailer's gross margins in the particular department. For a historical study of the compensation of sales clerks, see Bezanson, Anne, and Miriam Hussey, *Wage Methods and Selling Costs: Compensation of Sales Clerks in Four Major Departments in 31 Stores*. Philadelphia: University of Pennsylvania Press, 1930.

4. Retailers developed a variety of auditing tools to monitor inventories periodically. These manual techniques provided the retailer with a method of counting, checking, and comparing actual inventory from reported inventory (the difference between retail purchases from suppliers and sales to consumers). The high cost of storing information at a detailed level either in inventory counts or in order/sales information made this process even more difficult and costly. See McNair, Malcom, Charles Gragg, and Stanley Teele, *Problems in Retailing*. New York: McGraw-Hill, 1937. In the 1940s, J. C. Penney used manual methods to audit frequently its inventory of approximately 25,000 different items. However, the high cost of undertaking frequent manual audits led a leading scholar on inventory control, Thomson Whitin, to conclude, "The advisability of reviewing and ordering (on a frequent basis) is doubtful. . . .It would seem very likely that reductions in ordering costs brought about by ordering at less frequent intervals would be greater than the additional carrying charges incurred by the necessary concomitant increases in inventory, particularly in the case of the more staple items such as sheets, denims, etc." Whitin, Thomson, M., *The Theory of Inventory Management*. Princeton, NJ: Princeton University Press, 1953, p. 21.

5. Steinhauer, Jennifer, "Sorry, We're All Out of Great Merchants," *New York Times*, August 30, 1996, pp. D1, D16.

6. Klein, loc. cit., p. 30.

7. Steinhauer, Jennifer, "Squeezing into the Jeans Market," *New York Times*, March 14, 1997, pp. C1, C15. Retail analysts have ascribed part of Sears's revitalization in recent years to its aggressive introduction of private-label lines, including Canyon River Blues, Fieldmaster, and Trader Bay.

8. Standard & Poor's, "Retailing: Basic Analysis," *Industry Surveys*, 159, no. 17, May 2, 1991, p. R77.

9. Growing use of international sources of apparel did create a niche for companies like Frederick Atkins and American Merchandising Company which serve as intermediaries between U.S. retailers and international apparel and textile manufacturers.

10. Only a very limited number of basic items (such as men's and women's hosiery) were replenished by manufacturers through periodic visits by a manufacturer representative, who would take inventory on site and "fill in" the retailer's stock.

11. Department stores also faced threats from the growth of specialty stores that grew in popularity during the 1980s.

12. The market share of white shirts as a percent of all dress shirts has fallen from 72 percent in 1962 to 52 percent in 1967 to about 21 percent by 1986, with the remaining 79 percent made up of a wide variety of products. From Pashigian,

Peter B., "Demand Uncertainty and Sales: A Study of Fashion and Markdown Pricing," *American Economic Review*, December 1988, pp. 936–53. A recent example of the variable nature of demand within the dress shirt industry is the rise and rapid fall of black shirts in 1992 and deep blue shirts in 1996. See Kirkpatrick, David, "Faddish Shirt Tale: Buyers' Blue Mood Has Retailers Smiling," *Wall Street Journal*, July 19, 1996, pp. A1, A4.

13. Similar trends are occurring in other "basic" apparel lines. For example, a typical jeans manufacturer's product line contains 10,000 to 20,000 different SKUs.

14. The connection between product proliferation in apparel and personal computers (PCs) has been vividly made by Todd Flaming, a columnist on technology policy. "In the future, I think planned obsolescence will become a regular part of [PC] purchasing decisions. Computers will become in a lot of ways like clothing." Flaming quoted in Burrows, Peter, "Uh-Oh, They're Going Like Hotcakes," *Business Week*, October 13, 1997, p. 56.

15. See Standard & Poor's, "Retailing: Basic Analysis," *Industry Surveys*, 161, no. 19, May 13, 1993, p. R76.

16. The trend in food retailing is illustrative. The size of the typical new supermarket remained relatively constant between 1955 and 1973 (about 22,000 square feet). Beginning in 1973, however, store size began to increase, almost doubling to 40,000 square feet by 1989 and reaching 52,000 square feet for the median store in 1996. These numbers are based on annual data on new supermarket stores reported by the Supermarket Institute, 1954–72, and its successor, the Food Marketing Institute. See Food Marketing Institute, *Facts About Development 1997*. Washington, DC: Food Marketing Institute, 1997, Tables 5 and 23. See also Food Marketing Institute, *Food Marketing Institute Speaks 1998*. Washington, DC: Food Marketing Institute 1998, pp. 8–9.

17. The size of shopping malls also increased in this time period. Indicative is the emergence of "mega-malls," such as the Mall of America in Bloomington, Minnesota (4.2 million square feet), the Del Amo Fashion Center in Torrance, California (3.0 million square feet), and the South Coast Plaza/Crystal Coast mall in Costa Mesa, California (2.9 million square feet). Size figures from International Council of Shopping Centers, quoted in *Business Week*, July 28, 1997, p. 4.

18. Annual retail center space per capita figures from Deloitte Touche reported in Silverman, Dick, "Has Expansion Boom Finally Brought Retail to Saturation Point?," *Women's Wear Daily*, October 30, 1997, p. 10.

19. Bureau of National Affairs, *Daily Labor Report*, No. 232, December 4, 1995, p. D–5.

20. American Apparel Manufacturers Association, *1996 Focus: An Economic Profile of the Apparel Industry, 1996*. Arlington, VA: American Apparel Manufacturers Association, 1996, p. 7.

21. Indicative of this trend, retail sales per square feet (in 1992 dollars for all goods) fell from $235 per square foot in 1972 to $170 by 1996. See Kuntz, Mary, "Reinventing the Store," *Business Week*, November 27, 1995, p. 88 and Silverman, loc. cit., p. 10.

22. In 1980, Walter Salmon noted, "The 1980s will be a particularly critical decade for multi-unit traditional department stores. Well into maturity, these full-line retailers face a combination of external and internal challenges that will maintain pressure on their market position." See Salmon, Walter, "Organizational Barriers to Department Store Success," Harvard Business School Case, 9–581–027. Boston, MA: Harvard Business School, 1980.

23. From Market Research Corporation of America, *Soft Goods Consumer Panel*, based on household surveys of men age sixteen and older, 1986–90.

24. In addition, the family department store, typically a privately held, single-site enterprise providing a department-store collection of goods, declined rapidly.

25. Frazier, Robert M., "Quick Response in Soft Lines," *Discount Merchandiser*, January 1986, p. 42.

26. Pashigian, Peter B., and Brian Bowen, "Why Are Products Sold on Sale?: Explanation of Pricing Regularities," *Quarterly Journal of Economics*, 1991, pp. 1015–38.

27. Quoted in Ives, Blake, and Sirkka Jarvenpaa, "J. C. Penney: Fashioning a Retailing Nervous System for the Future," Harvard Business School Case, 9–996–011. Boston, MA: Harvard Business School, 1995, p. 2.

28. The largely unforeseen rise of lean retailing is reflected in press accounts of the late 1980s. Commenting on the falling margins, overcapacity of retail space, and slow growth in sales, an article in 1989 noted, "Only merchants with low prices, good service or a specialty will survive." No mention, however, was made of the need to improve management of the costs associated with inventory, markdowns, or stock-outs. See Wayne, Leslie, "Rewriting the Rules of Retailing," *New York Times*, October 15, 1989, pp. D1–D6.

29. For a history of Wal-Mart, see Vance, Sandra, and Roy Scott, *Wal-Mart: A History of Sam Walton's Retail Phenomenon*. New York: Twayne Publishers, 1994; and Walton, Sam with John Huey, *Sam Walton: Made in America*. New York: Doubleday, 1992.

30. Although Kmart preceded Wal-Mart in adopting scanning and bar codes, Wal-Mart successfully integrated these information technologies with its modern distribution centers, creating a more efficient retailing system. Unlike the more established Kmart, which had in place a distribution system built on the traditional model, Wal-Mart started its system essentially from scratch.

31. "Change at the Check-Out," *The Economist: A Survey of Retailing*, March 4, 1995, pp. 5–6.

32. Lou Pritchett quoted in Seideman, Tony, "What Sam Walton Learned from the Berlin Airlift," *Audacity*, Spring 1996, p. 60.

33. This account is drawn from Ives and Jarvenpaa, loc. cit. .

34. More recently, these efforts to improve its ability to move apparel to store floors rapidly led the company to further centralize buying decisions. See Haber, Holly, "New Buying Strategy at Penney Aims to Cut Delivery Time, Costs," *Women's Wear Daily*, November 24, 1997, pp. 1,15.

35. For a history of Dillard's, see Rosenberg, Leon Joseph, *Dillard's: The First*

Fifty Years. Fayetteville: University of Arkansas Press, 1988. For more recent accounts, see Ortmeyer, Gwendolyn, and Walter Salmon, "Dillard's Department Stores." Harvard Business School Case, 9–593–040, 1992; Ortega, Bob, "Nearing 80, Founder of Dillard Stores Seeks to Keep on Growing," *Wall Street Journal*, May 11, 1994, pp. A1, A6.

36. In their early growth period, Wal-Mart and Dillard's intentionally avoided head-to-head competition with established retailers and built stores in "one-horse towns." Sam Walton did this by opening stores in towns where there were no other major retailers, while Dillard's grew by buying out the main retailer (usually single-site and family-owned stores) in smaller towns.

37. Cole, Tom, "Remarks to the National Governors Association," Committee on Economic Development and Commerce, National Governors Association, February 2, 1997.

38. A Federated executive described the tension between selecting new items for sale (merchandising) and figuring out how to respond to incoming information once you have sales data (logistics) as the difference between art and science.

39. The exceptions to this general rule, aside from Procter & Gamble in grocery retailing, are several major apparel suppliers including Levi Strauss, VF Corporation, and Haggar, which advocated using electronic links to improve supply relations for many years. Many of the early experiments with elements of lean retailing began with these large suppliers before they were extended more generally.

Chapter 4

1. Quoted in "Clout," *Business Week*, December 21, 1992, p. 66.

2. Investments in improved logistics also can lower direct costs of material handling for a retailer. One major retailer we studied believed that the full implementation of its logistics program in its distribution centers could reduce the direct cost of processing goods by about $135 million annually, leading to a full point increase in the company's earnings before interest and taxes.

3. See Brown, Stephen A., *Revolution at the Checkout Counter: The Explosion of the Bar Code*. Cambridge, MA.: Harvard University Press, 1997. For an analysis of the circumstances creating bar codes and their economic consequences, see the introduction by Dunlop, John T., and Jan Rivkin, pp. 1–38. For background information see, *Hearings before the Subcommittee for Consumers of the Committee on Commerce, United States Senate*, 93 Cong. 2d. Sess., "Symposium on the Universal Product Coding System," December 11, 1974, pp. 1–78; Harvard Business School Case, 9–676–087, *Grocery Industry in the U.S.A.: Choice of a Universal Product Code*. Cambridge, MA.: Harvard Business School, 1975; Harvard Business School Case, 9–677–045, *Grocery Industry in the U.S.A.: Choice of a Standard Symbol*. Cambridge, MA: Harvard Business School, 1976.

4. The UCC provided this research project with a record of all bar codes

issued to enterprises since the outset through 1994, including date of issue, an industry classification, and sales volume at the time of the issuance of the bar code.

5. These were mainly margin controls on prices, which began on August 15, 1971, and ran until April 15, 1974.

6. The consulting firm McKinsey & Company assisted the committee.

7. See Brown, loc. cit., pp. 20–22.

8. The bar code includes an eleventh digit for verification purposes.

9. Manufacturers and retailers could have potentially saved even more by not placing price stickers or labels on individual items, but such omission was strongly opposed in legislative actions in states and localities by labor unions and consumer groups.

10. Brown, loc. cit., p. 5.

11. See Food Marketing Institute, loc. cit., p. 9. In 1997 the median number of items carried in conventional stores was 27,102, while large combination stores carried a median number of 97,536 items. The size of new supermarkets rose from approximately 22,000 square feet in the early 1970s to almost 52,000 square feet in 1996.

12. Brown, loc. cit., p. 5.

13. At the time, food chains created the Efficient Consumer Response Program, which sought to gain further advantage in inventory reduction and replenishment efficiency through improved lean retailing practices in the grocery industry.

14. Based on analysis of annual UCC registration data provided to HCTAR by Peter Fisher, Harvard Center for Textile and Apparel Research, June 1994.

15. Voluntary Interindustry Communications Standards Committee, *Voluntary Guidelines for Floor-Ready Merchandise*, November 1994.

16. Based on analysis of annual UCC registration data by Peter Fisher, Harvard Center for Textile and Apparel Research, June 1994.

17. See Baum, Michael S., and Henry H. Perrit, Jr., *Electronic Contracting, Publishing and EDI Law*. New York: John Wiley & Sons, Inc., 1991, p. 6: "*Electronic contracting* involves the exchange of messages between buyers and sellers, structured according to a prearranged format so that the contents can be processed by machine and automatically give rise to contractual obligations."

18. Joint Industry Project on Efficient Consumer Response, *ECR 1994, Progress Report*, 1995, p. 86.

19. See Voluntary Interindustry Communication Standards Committee, "VICS Retail Industry Conventions and Implementation Guidelines for Electronic Data Interchange," undated manuscript.

20. For example, using a "data warehouse," Target (a division of Dayton/Hudson) is attempting to identify merchandise that appeals to specific shoppers on a store level. As a result, the retailer hopes to go from 15 to 20 percent of its merchandise tailored to a specific store up to 30 percent. See Tosh, Mark, "Data Warehousing: Retailing's New Weapon," *Women's Wear Daily*, July 23, 1996, p. 23.

21. The information and data contained in this section arise from field visits

with retailers in department stores, mass merchants, and national chains collected by the authors.

22. Wal-Mart operates thirty regional distribution centers to support its nearly $100 billion in annual sales revenue operation. The average size of these distribution centers is one million square feet. An average center shipped about 32 million cases of merchandise in 1995. See Gill, Penny, and Jules Abend, "Wal-Mart: The Supply Chain Heavyweight Champion," *Supply Chain Management Review*, Summer 1996, p. 14.

23. These figures are based on estimates of regional distribution center costs of a major department store in 1997. A somewhat smaller distribution center built by L. L. Bean to service its mail-order business, which handles approximately twelve million packages annually, cost $38 million to build and bring on line. See Kane, Kate, "L. L. Bean Delivers the Goods," *Fast Company*, August/September 1997, pp. 104–13.

24. This figure is based on information on capital investment and average employment from a major department store and assumes twenty-year depreciation of capital equipment at a 10 percent discount rate.

25. Figures from Foley, Sharon, and Takia Mahmood, "Wal-Mart Stores, Inc.," Harvard Business School Case, 9–794–024. Boston, MA: Harvard Business School, 1996, p. 7; Gill and Abend, loc. cit., p. 13.

26. The trend among many retailers is to increase the percentage of shipments arriving direct from suppliers via full truckload carriers. To increase efficiency in handling the flow of incoming goods (particularly from overseas sources), retailers often use consolidators. Consolidators build full truckloads for distribution center delivery—that is, from manufacturers to consolidators to distribution center. Vendors pay the transportation costs from their facilities to the consolidator, while typically the retailer pays transportation costs from consolidator to distribution center.

27. A major exception to this trend is Wal-Mart, which still owns and operates its own truck fleet, including 3,000 tractors and close to 10,000 trailers. Wal-Mart uses its fleet both for picking up shipments from vendors and deliveries among Wal-Mart's distribution centers and its stores. See Gill and Abend, loc. cit., pp. 13–14.

28. In certain areas of retailing (e.g., grocery), outsourcing transportation also reflects the need for specialized equipment and procedures for shipping perishable products like meat or fruit.

29. As with product bar codes, standardization of scannable shipping containers was undertaken under the auspices of the UCC, which promulgated the UCC–128 Serial Shipping Container Code bar code.

30. Retailers also have auditing procedures to monitor vendor accuracy and assess penalties for discrepancies. Many retailers are moving from 100 percent inspections to randomized audits of a small percentage (2 to 10 percent) of shipments of incoming materials. To be approved for participation in a cross-docking program in both cases, vendors must submit to a 100 percent audit as well as

demonstrate they are using a number of other practices, such as "scans and packs" of shipments.

31. Such activities are particularly common for goods that have come from foreign producers and will be sold on a single-season basis.

32. Although current technology could support direct store shipments, the yields do not justify it in the minds of many apparel retailers. One logistics executive from a major retailer notes: "What makes more sense, 1 truck per day or 179 trucks with small loads?" Other retailing segments rely on direct store shipments for certain product types, such as perishable food or bulky items.

33. The highly publicized luggage system at Denver International Airport is a famous example of advanced materials handling technology that is similar to the central package conveyance systems used in retail distribution centers.

34. The downside of this is that disruptions are quickly engendered by a breakdown in the central conveyer system. Although such breakdowns are infrequent, a distribution center is like an airport: If the main system goes down, shipments rapidly pile up. A major distribution center we visited could physically accommodate about four days of goods if the main conveyer line broke down.

35. Because the distribution center described here runs two shifts of workers, it does batch processing of data between 2 A.M. and 6 A.M. to prepare for the next day of incoming and outgoing shipments.

36. This is described by the VICS Committee as "Receipt-Ready Shipments." Such shipments "provide for a consistent flow of information between trading partners relative to the movement of merchandise. . . . This reduces both the time and processing required to move the merchandise from the supplier to the retail receiving location." Voluntary Interindustry Communications Standards Committee, *Voluntary Guidelines for Floor-Ready Merchandise*, November 1994, p. 33.

37. Each truck carries an electronic manifest of the order as a whole, but the specific information about which products are being delivered will have already been transferred electronically via an advanced shipping notice (ASN) as the truck leaves the distribution center bound for the individual store.

38. Arguing that both retailers and manufacturers gain by standardizing the preparation of garments for store delivery, VICS commissioned a group of retailers and apparel suppliers in June 1992 to study how common standards in the area of floor-ready merchandise could reduce product lead time. The report concluded, "Merchandise should be floor-ready when received at retail selling locations; standardized, voluntary guidelines are necessary in order to develop efficient mechanisms for shipping and/or receiving floor-ready merchandise; pipeline benefits can be substantial depending on individual trading partner circumstances." See Voluntary Interindustry Communications Standards Committee, loc. cit., p. 5.

39. There are VICS standards regarding price-marking procedures, as well as for retailer communication of prices using EDI documents that comply with VICS EDI standards. These appear in the *VICS Retail Industry Conventions and Implementation Guidelines for Electronic Data Interchange* (1994) and the *UPC Marking Guidelines for General Merchandise and Apparel* (1994). In regard to the transmission of retail price information, the VICS guidelines note, "It is important that

trading partners fully understand the timing involved in the ticketing process to determine when it is necessary to supply the retail price or appropriate to modify the price. In general, the retail price must be known prior to the earliest time the price can be applied. In some cases, where an adhesive sticker is applied as part of the packing process, this may be a few days prior to the ship date. If the price is printed on the product label during manufacturing, it must be known when the manufacturing order is issued." Voluntary Interindustry Communications Standards Committee, loc. cit., p. 11.

40. The "hanger application guidelines" include specifications for the color, shape, strength, and dimensions for a variety of hangers, arranged by product category. See Voluntary Interindustry Communications Standards Committee, loc. cit., pp. 16–28.

41. The retailers involved in this agreement include J. C. Penney, Sears, Kmart, and The Home Depot. See Power, Denise, "Retailers Push Plans for POS Systems Standards," *Daily News Record*, January 28, 1998, p. 7; Power, Denise, "Retail Blueprint for '98: Mix and Match Technology," *Women's Wear Daily*, December 10, 1997, p. 13.

42. The penalties for noncompliance also cover a variety of other areas including charges for failure to use electronic invoicing, sending merchandise that was not ordered, and various transportation problems caused by the vendor. See Federated Department Stores, Inc., *The FASST Plan Vendor Standards Manual*, Cincinnati, OH: Federated Department Stores, 1996, pp. 39–41.

43. For other examples, see Bird, Laura, and Wendy Bounds, "Stores' Demands Squeeze Apparel Companies," *Wall Street Journal*, July 15, 1997, pp. B1, B3; Zimmerman, Kim Ann, "Saks Plans Expansion of Vendor Accreditation Program," *Daily News Record*, November 12, 1997, p. 27; Duff, Christina, "Big Stores' Outlandish Demands Alienate Small Suppliers," *Wall Street Journal*, October 27, 1995, pp. B1, B5.

Chapter 5

1. Quoted in Schiller, Zachary, and Wendy Zellner, "Clout," *Business Week*, December 21, 1992, p. 66.

2. Markell, Cliff, "Bar Code Scanning and EDI Are in Fashion at KGR," *ID Systems*, August 1996, pp. 10–17.

3. Standard & Poor's, "Retailing: Basic Analysis," *Industry Surveys*, May 13, 1993, p. R77.

4. Standard & Poor's Compustat database provides annual balance sheet, income statement, and cash flow information for publicly held companies. In order to undertake the comparison between lean retailers and their retail channel competitors, data for 1984–94 were used for the lean retailer and a group of retail channel competitors. (The panel data includes missing observations for the period under study.) We have categorized retailers based on definitions used by

Standard & Poor's, Dun & Bradstreet, and apparel industry sources. The variables used in the analysis, taken directly from Compustat, are defined in Appendix C.

In addition to Dillard's Inc., J. C. Penney, and Wal-Mart Stores, the companies used in the analysis are:

Department Stores: Federated Department Stores, May Department Stores, Neiman-Marcus, Nordstrom Inc., Younkers Inc., Bon-Ton Stores, Broadway Stores, Carson Pirie Scott, Kohl's Corporation, Mercantile Stores, Macy (R. H.) & Company, Marshall Fields.

National Chains: Montgomery Wards, Sears Roebuck and Co.

Mass Merchants: Ames Department Stores, Bradlees Inc., Brendles Inc., Caldor Corp., Dayton Hudson, Hills Stores, Jamesway Co., Kmart Corporation, Roses Store, Shopko Store, Solo Serve Company, Stuarts Department Store, Value City, Venture Stores, Brauns Fashion.

Specialty Stores: Ann Taylor Stores Corp., A Pea in the Pod Inc., Bankers Note Inc., Cache Inc., Catherines Stores Corp., Charming Shoppes, Chicos Fashion Inc., Clothestime Inc., Deb Shops Inc., Dress Barn Inc., Evans Inc., Gantos Inc., Paul Harris Stores, Petrie Stores Corp., Talbots Inc., United Retail Group, Inc., Wet Seal Inc.

Methodologically, reported comparison group averages are based on sales-weighted averages of the variables under study to capture the relative importance of different retailers in the sample. The comparison group averages do not include data for lean retailers.

5. A second type of comparison would look at inventory levels for lean retailers and their competitors. At first blush, one would predict that lean practices would reduce inventory (or the ratio of inventory to sales, cost of inventories to cost of goods sold, and so on). In fact, lean retailers like Dillard's hope to hold larger total inventories, reflecting a wider product mix, while holding *less* of a given SKU at a point of time. In addition, as we document, the number of SKUs held by retailers dramatically increased over the time period we were studying. Thus, in order to measure the true effect of lean retailing practices, one must also hold constant the number of SKUs handled by retailers that independently increase this ratio. That makes using the aggregate inventory numbers reported in Compustat for comparative purposes difficult. We use a different data set on establishment-level inventories in Chapter 14 to examine related issues in regard to apparel suppliers.

6. Financial reporting changes by retailers in the "national chain" group make this type of comparison impossible.

7. The comparable SGA expense as a percent of sales for competing mass merchants was 22.2 percent for Kmart, 24.4 percent for Caldor, and 29.4 percent for Bradlees. Caldor and Bradlees filed for bankruptcy in 1995.

8. This is not to imply that lean retailing constituted the only source of growth over this period. For example, Nordstrom also grew rapidly during these years, based on its strategy of service and quality directed at affluent consumers.

9. McNair, Malcom, Charles Gragg, and Stanley Teele, *Problems in Retailing*. New York: McGraw-Hill, 1937, pp. 22, 30.

10. See Steinhauer, Jennifer, "Woolworth Gives Up on the Five-and-Dime,"

New York Times, July 18, 1997, pp. A1, C4. Lean retailing has also moved across the U.S./Canadian border, placing competitive pressure on venerable retailers in that country, most notably the department store T. Eaton Company. See DePalma, Anthony, "Canadian Retailer Imperiled as U.S. Rivals Move In," *New York Times*, March 11, 1997, pp. D1, D7.

11. U.S. Department of Commerce, Bureau of the Census, *Census of Retail Industries*. Washington, DC: Government Printing Office, 1977 and 1992.

12. A study by Kurt Salmon Associates concluded that the top ten retailers would account for 60 percent of public company sales by the year 2000. See Kurt Salmon Associates, "Dancing with Juggernauts," *The KSA Perspective*, January 1992. A separate study by Consultants Management Horizons predicted similar levels of concentration. See Schiller and Zellner, loc. cit.

13. This is not limited to apparel. Other examples include Toys "R" Us (children's toys); Home Depot (building supplies); Circuit City (consumer electronics); and Costco (warehouse club).

14. These are unweighted percentages of shipments for business units in the HCTAR sample.

15. The percentage of sales going to five segments of retail distribution (mass merchants, national chains, department stores, specialty stores, and mail order) shifted little between 1988 and 1992. For a discussion of this issue, see Hwang, Margaret Y., and David Weil, "The Diffusion of Modern Manufacturing Practices: Evidence from the U.S. Retail and Apparel Sectors," *Center for Economic Studies, Bureau of the Census, Discussion Paper Series* 97–11, 1997, p. 18.

16. This information is based on our observations of department store distribution centers in 1996 through 1997.

17. Federated Department Stores, Inc., *Technology for Today and Tomorrow*, Cincinnati, OH, 1996.

18. Haggar Apparel Company, "Service Strategy," June 1993, p. 19.

19. Comparisons are made on the basis of unweighted means for specific business unit practices in 1988 and 1992. When business unit operations are weighted by sales volume, the results are similar, implying even larger estimated changes in business unit practice than those presented here. This arises because the large apparel suppliers in the HCTAR sample adopted innovative practices at a higher rate than others.

20. Other factors can potentially confound such comparisons, however. For example, product mix of a given business unit is correlated with both information technology adoption and with the degree to which its goods are subject to replenishment requirements. Similarly, the degree to which apparel suppliers invest in "innovative" practices may be a function of business unit size as well as its degree of replenishment pressure. Still, the influence of retail pressure remains, even when both factors are held constant by statistical methods. A full presentation of this analysis can be found in Abernathy, Frederick, John T. Dunlop, Janice Hammond, and David Weil, "The Information Integrated Channel: A Study of the U.S. Apparel Industry," *Brookings Papers on Economic Activity: Microeconomics*, 1995, pp. 175–246; Hwang and Weil, loc. cit.

21. These investments are often portrayed in the industry press, however, as inherently mutually advantageous investments.

22. See, for example, D'Innocenzio, Anne, "Fighting Mark-down Money," *Women's Wear Daily*, January 28, 1998, p. 12.

Chapter 6

1. Quote taken from Rosenberg, Leon Joseph, *Dillard's: The First Fifty Years*. Fayetteville: University of Arkansas Press, 1988, p. 95.

2. Strom, Stephanie, *New York Times*, June 2, 1994, p. D–4. Specifically, the article reported that 46 percent of the customers who shopped at Macy's entered the store and left without making a purchase. Of those who left, 56 percent did not purchase anything because the product they wanted was not available in the store.

3. See for example, Hadley, G., and T. M. Whitin, *Analysis of Inventory Systems*. Englewood Cliffs, NJ: Prentice-Hall, Inc., 1963; Kurawarwala, Abbas, A., and Hirofumi Matsuo, "Forecasting and Inventory Management of Short Life-Cycle Products," *Operations Research*, January–February 1996, pp. 131–50. There is also an extensive economics literature on inventory management. See, for example, Arrow, Kenneth, T. Harris, and J. Marschak, "Optimal Inventory Policy," *Econometrica*, 1951, pp. 250–72; Blinder, Alan S., and Louis J. Maccini, "Taking Stock: A Critical Assessment of Recent Research on Inventories," *Journal of Economic Perspectives*, 1991, pp. 73–96; Blinder, Alan S., and Louis J. Maccini, "The Resurgence of Inventory Investment: What Have We Learned?" Cambridge, MA: National Bureau of Economic Research Working Paper No. 3408, August 1990; Chikan, A., and Michael C. Lovell, eds., *The Economics of Inventory Management*. Amsterdam: Elsevier, 1988.

4. In theory, retailers should also consider products that customers return after the purchase, although this can be a somewhat complicated analysis depending on the length of time between the purchase and return. Direct-mail firms are particularly vulnerable to high rates of product return—one mail-order firm told us that 30 percent of its apparel products were returned by customers.

5. The type of data analysis described in this section can be performed using a variety of methods. Winter's model is a well-known exponential smoothing method that can be used to decompose a time-series into the four components described here. Regression analysis can also be used to analyze the relationship between historical demand and various explanatory variables. See Winters, P., "Forecasting Sales by Exponentially Weighted Moving Averages," *Management Science*, April 1960, pp. 324–42; Heath, David C., and Peter L. Jackson, "Modeling the Evolution of Demand Forecasts with Application to Safety Stock Analysis in Production/Distribution System," *IIE Transactions*, May 1994, pp. 17–30; or Silver, Edward A., David F. Pyke, and Rein Peterson, *Inventory Management and Production Planning and Scheduling*, Third Edition. New York: John Wiley and Sons, 1998, p. 98.

6. In general, a buyer would be responsible for purchasing a product category for many stores. In this chapter, we simplify the exposition by assuming that the buyer is making purchasing decisions for only one store.

7. Fisher, Marshall L., Janice H. Hammond, Walter R. Obermeyer, and Ananth Raman, "Making Supply Meet Demand in an Uncertain World," *Harvard Business Review*, May/June 1994, pp. 83–93.

8. Fisher, Marshall L., Walter R. Obermeyer, Janice H. Hammond, and Ananth Raman, "Accurate Response: The Key to Profiting from QR," *Bobbin Magazine*, February 1994, pp. 48–62.

9. To illustrate how increasing variety raises demand uncertainty, consider a situation in which a retailer offers N products in a category, each with independent, identically distributed demand distributions. Let $E[D_i]$, σ_i, and $C_v[D_i]$ denote the expected value, standard deviation, and coefficient of variation, respectively, of D_i, the demand for SKU_i. Then by definition, $C_v[D_i] = \sigma_i / E[Di]$.

Because the demand variables for the individual SKUs are identically distributed, the moments of the demand for each SKU are the same. Thus, if we let $\bar{D} = E[D_i]$ and $\sigma = \sigma_i$ for $i = 1, \ldots, n$, and define the total demand $T = \sum_{i=1}^{N} D_i$, then $E[T] = N \cdot \bar{D}$, $\sigma_T = \sigma\sqrt{N}$ (since the D_i's are independent), and the coefficient of variation of T is $C_v[T] = \sigma\sqrt{N}/\bar{D} = C_v [D_i]/\sqrt{N}$.

Thus, if we hold the moments of the distribution for total demand constant, we find that $C_v [D_i] = C_v [T] \cdot \sqrt{N}$, that is, the coefficient of variation of each individual SKU increases as the square root of the number of SKUs. (This logic follows the standard "risk pooling" argument; in this case, increasing product variety decreases the ability to pool customer demand for specific products.)

10. For a discussion of related issues, see Irvine, F. Owen, Jr., "Retail Inventory Investment and the Cost of Capital," *American Economic Review*, September 1981, pp. 633–48.

11. See, for example, Silver, Pyke, Peterson, loc. cit., p. 385.

12. Ibid., p. 244.

13. The literature on (R, s, S) models is extensive. See, for example, Silver, Pike, and Peterson, ibid., p. 240.

14. Ibid., p. 282.

15. Some retailers do have overnight shipments. For example, the maternity-wear retailer Mothers' Work places orders each evening to replenish items that sold in its stores during that day; the small replenishment shipments are sent to each store using overnight mail. (Information based on interviews with Mothers' Work CEO Rebecca Mathieson in August 1995).

16. Many retailers impose a minimum order quantity for the number of units ordered from a particular manufacturer. For example, if the minimum quantity for Levi jeans is twelve units, the retailer would replenish the Levi inventory only if the total number of units sold the previous week of Levi jeans in all sizes and styles was at least twelve.

17. Even "two-bin" policies, often used in manufacturing situations to implement continuous review policies, are difficult to implement in retailing, especially when customers have access to stock and can thereby move products from their

original stocking locations. See, for example, Silver, Pike, and Peterson, loc. cit., p. 363.

18. Clark, Theodore, and Janice H. Hammond, "Reengineering Channel Reordering Processes to Improve Total Supply Chain Performance," *Journal of Production and Operations Management*, 6, No. 3, Fall 1997, p. 248.

19. For further discussion of the benefits of channel coordination, see Hammond, Janice H., "Coordination and Quick Response in Manufacturing and Retail Channels: A Case for 'Virtual' Integration," Harvard Business School Working Paper 92–007.

20. Note, however, that even having the manufacturer hold finished goods inventory reduces the amount of inventory that is needed in the entire channel to meet consumer demand, since demand across multiple retail outlets is "pooled" at the manufacturer.

21. See, for example, King, Russell E., and N. Alan Hunter, "Quick Response Beats Importing in Retail Sourcing Analysis," *Bobbin Magazine*, March 1997, pp. 22–29.

Chapter 7

1. McDonald quote from Lewis, Robin, "Consumers at Apex of VF Vision," *Women's Wear Daily*, February 12, 1998, pp. 8–9.

2. Demand variation estimates are often difficult to make because of the way historical sales information is stored in company records. For a discussion of other problems in the storage and transmission of information that affect production planning, see Lee, Hau L., V. Padmanabhan, and Seungjin Whang, "The Bullwhip Effect in Supply Chains," *Sloan Management Review*, 1997, pp. 93–102.

3. Silver, Edward A., David F. Pyke, and Rein Peterson, *Inventory Management and Production Planning and Scheduling,* Third Edition. New York: John Wiley and Sons, 1998, p. 515.

4. The coat manufacturer described in the case study used a modified form of the standard (R, s, S) policy. Specifically, it considered both work-in-process and finished goods inventories when computing inventory levels. Thus, for example, the company placed a production order whenever the *total* inventory level dropped below ten weeks. Use of this unusual form of the (R, s, S) model explains why the factory chose such high values for the parameters S and s.

5. The details of this approach appear in Diehl, Gregory, Frederick H. Abernathy, and Janice H. Hammond, "Customer Demand and Scheduling for Clothing Manufacturers," HCTAR Working Paper Series, November 1996.

6. A number of companies currently sell planning software for decision support in production. These decision tools, however, are not capable of formulating robust production plans to deal with problems involving rapid replenishment demand, large numbers of SKUs with different C_ys, and several plants with different costs and cycle times.

7. For this manufacturer, the weekly orders were so large for each SKU that

there was no need to consider minimum production order quantities. In addition, to simplify the case, no seasonal variation in demand was considered.

8. Markdown estimates are based on unweighted volume of sales in the HCTAR sample. Although we use a single markdown level here, ideally, inventory carrying cost should also vary by SKU. Some products face a higher probability of being marked down, for example, because of their fashion content. In this way, the level of markdown is associated once again with variability in demand.

9. Lee, Loo Hay, "Ordinal Optimization and Its Application in Apparel Manufacturing Systems," Ph.D. Dissertation. Cambridge, MA: Harvard University, 1997.

10. To calculate maximum profit, we computed:

{ (Wholesale selling price − Cost of goods sold) x (Units sold)

− (Units of work-in-process and finished goods inventory) x (Cost of goods sold) x

(Annual inventory carrying cost) − Penalty }

where the penalty was sufficient to assure that the service level or satisfaction rate was 95 percent or greater in all cases. In only one or two cases in Figure 7.6 was it necessary to invoke a small penalty to assure the 95 percent service level to the retailer.

11. It is important to remember that the target inventory level S for each SKU depends on the fraction of the total product made in the short-cycle plant.

12. Textbooks on operations management suggest figures of 25 percent or more for annual inventory carrying costs. For the hard goods, the texts indicate that any operation that does not add value to the product (e.g., storage racks and the floor area that goods occupy) should be considered as part of inventory carrying cost. There are also costs associated with insurance, taxes, handling, and the cost of capital tied up in the inventory. See, for example, Hadley, G., and T. M. Whitin, *Analysis of Inventory Systems*. Englewood Cliffs, NJ: Prentice-Hall, Inc., 1963.

13. The target inventory level does depend on the gross manufacturing margin and the work-in-process inventory carrying cost. But in this case, without revealing any of the manufacturer's cost figures, it is fair to say that the data in Table 7.1 are not strongly dependent on the exact values of the work-in-process carrying cost actually used.

14. In both cases, we have assumed that final product quality is not an issue.

Chapter 8

1. [TC]^2 was created to explore the possibility of automating sewing. The original target was to automate the sewing of a sleeve of a men's suit coat. The assembly involves joining the two sleeve panels, folding the cuff to construct a mitered vent, and then closing the sleeve. A fully automatic sewing system was built but it could not achieve the yield and quality of trained sewing operators. Nor could the sleeve be produced at a low enough cost to provide the paybacks perceived as acceptable by the apparel industry. For a history of [TC]^2 see Dunlop,

John T., *Dispute Resolution: Negotiation and Consensus Building*. Dover, MA: Auburn House, 1984, pp. 247–52. The automation study is contained in Charles Stark Draper Laboratories, *Final Report of the First-Year R&D Program for the Men's Tailored Clothing Industry*. Cambridge, MA: Draper Laboratories, May 1982.

2. Much of the discussion contained in this chapter is based on the authors' observations of manufacturing facilities and assembly operations in this country and abroad, and from the HCTAR survey. Appendix B describes the HCTAR survey data.

3. The relation of different tiers in apparel design gives rise to the separate problem of "knockoffs" in which other designers copy the leading designers in the industry. See, for example, Agin, Teri, "Fashion Knockoffs Hit Stores Before Originals as Designers Seethe," *Wall Street Journal*, August 8, 1994, pp. A1, A4.

4. A large front and back panel make up each leg of a pair of pants. Pockets have facing pieces, and the waistband is made of two separate pieces of the basic shell fabric of the pants.

5. The software is called the UltraMark *Optimizer* System and is now commercially available from Gerber Garment Technology.

6. Because of their key position in preassembly phases of manufacturing, cutters historically have been "strategic" workers in the apparel industry. The implications of this role on human resource policies are discussed in Chapter 10.

7. Worldwide, there are an estimated 3,500 Gerber cutting systems in operation, and an additional 4,500 from other manufacturers.

8. These tags are supposed to be removed during the final inspection, but customers who buy inexpensive casual pants will occasionally find the stickers on the inside of each pant leg.

9. There are other preassembly operations as well, generally carried out near the cutting room, before the garment parts are sent out for sewing. Stiffening material may be heat-fused to the shell fabric to add body and strengthen some parts of the final garment. (The cuffs of most suits have a "wigan" of nonwoven material fused to the sleeve material.) Fabric wigans are still used in the most expensive suits and are sewn to the sleeve before the cuff is turned. Fusing material is added in many places in coat and shirt cuffs and collars. Most retail customers are not aware of these details, and they are unlikely to know if the wigans were fabric and sewn (to give a softer feel) or nonwoven material heat-fused to the shell fabric (generally stiffer than a cloth wigan).

10. Retail shops that cater to the big, tall, athletic, and small and specialized catalogs that offer a wide range of sizes of some items with some small final adjustments have offered a limited alternative to fill part of this demand. Product selection among this group of retailers is usually quite limited, however.

11. Several of the largest jeans manufacturers make over 25,000 different SKUs of jeans. This number includes children's, men's, and women's product categories.

12. For most women, there is a question of where on the hip they want the waist to be. For men of a certain shape, the question becomes whether the waist is above or below the stomach bulge, or perhaps balanced in the middle at the

largest diameter, with the pants held up by suspenders. The inseam length is also somewhat a matter of personal preference. Some customers want the jeans to just touch their shoes; others like them either above or below that level, depending on current styles.

13. The actual process is a bit more complicated because the standard jeans pattern has to be modified to reflect the customer's measurement. The computer and cutting systems that support mass customization were developed by Sung Park. Park modified a machine developed originally to cut sails for sailboards. See Montgomery, M.R., "The Genie of Jeans," *Boston Globe*, January 4, 1995, pp. 53, 57.

14. An overview of the opportunities for mass customization offered by [TC]^2 is contained in Kurt Salmon Associates, *Mass Customization: A Key Initiative of Quick Response*, Cary, NC: Kurt Salmon Associates, August 1997. For more information regarding this project, contact [TC]^2 at 211 Greyson Drive, Cary, North Carolina 27511–7909.

15. Eisenberg, Anne, "If the Shoe Fits, Click It: The Promise of Body Scans," *The New York Times*, August 13, 1998, pp. E1, E6.

Chapter 9

1. American Apparel Manufacturers Association, *1996 Focus: An Economic Profile of the Apparel Industry*. Arlington, VA: American Apparel Manufacturers Association, 1996, p. 4.

2. See U.S. Department of Labor, Bureau of Labor Statistics, *Employment, Hours, and Earnings, United States, 1909–94*, vol.1, Bulletin 2445. Washington, DC: Government Printing Office, September 1994, pp. 583–84.

3. When the raw edges of the two pattern pieces to be joined are folded back from the edge, interlocked, and then stitched together through two rows of stitching, this is called a felled seam. Other felling operations involve simply turning under the raw edge of one piece of fabric and stitching it down, as in the bottom seam of a dress shirt, or a more complicated process in the lining of a coat. Note that felling operations in factories are derived from hand-sewing and older forms of garment assembly. Books describing home sewing will list dozens of different types of seams and many more types of stitching patterns to decorate or to cover the raw fabric edge, such as in the stitching around a buttonhole.

4. Much of the discussion contained in this chapter is based on the authors' observations of manufacturing facilities and assembly operations in this country and abroad and from the HCTAR survey. Appendix B describes the HCTAR survey data.

5. The terminology used in home sewing and the factory vary, as well as from factory, to factory depending on the type of garments being sewn.

6. Sewing also involves the force with which the presser foot pushes down on the cloth around the needle during stitching. The presser foot can be lifted to allow the cloth to be delivered to the needle, but it must press down and hold the

fabric during sewing. The presser foot is a tool with a spring-loaded plate having two fingers that come down on both sides of the needle, pressing the two plies of cloth onto the serrated teeth of the feed-dog. The feed-dog is a cam-driven plate with raised rows of teeth that come up through slots in the stitch plate. At the appropriate point in the stitch cycle, after the needle has withdrawn from the cloth, the feed-dog advances the cloth one stitch length. The teeth then drop below the surface and cycle back to begin the next stitch while the presser foot holds the cloth in place.

7. The proportion of total employees that were women in this industry (SIC 2321) in 1993 was 86 percent, as compared to 77 percent for all apparel (SIC 23). See U.S. Department of Labor, Bureau of Labor Statistics, loc. cit., p. 593.

8. A number of these steps can be automated. Some machines have an automatic needle-positioning feature that will leave the needle up or down as programmed. Others have a programmable feature to backstitch automatically at the beginning and end of the seam. And some sewing operations involve automatic unloading devices, activated by the sewing operator using a foot pedal, which take the finished parts and stack them in preparation for the next operation.

9. Our survey results indicate that the average business unit operated multiple cutting plants, and that each plant serviced 4.5 sewing rooms.

10. The "ideal" number of minutes required to make a men's dress shirt can vary from ten minutes to twenty-five minutes or more, depending on the desired stitch patterns, the details of the collar, cuffs, and pockets, and the equipment available in the sewing room. For a given style of shirt and a particular factory, the time to make a shirt will depend on the average skill of the operators and the average level of effort.

11. U.S. Department of Labor, Bureau of Labor Statistics, *Monthly Labor Review*, March 1998, Table 13, p. 105.

Chapter 10

1. To take another example, in 1995, 45 percent of the value of shipments for men's trousers was composed of material costs, while 23 percent arose from compensation costs. Compensation costs include payroll, fringe benefits, social security, other legally required payments, and other employer payments and programs (e.g., pension, health, and welfare). U.S. Department of Commerce, Bureau of the Census, 1995 *Annual Survey of Manufactures, Men's and Boys' Apparel*, MC95–I–23A. Washington, DC: U.S. Government Printing Office, 1995.

2. Given the high turnover among garment workers in the sewing room, training for new workers has been a long-term concern of industry and the government. In response to these concerns, the Amalgamated Clothing and Textile Workers Union, the Clothing Manufacturers Association, and the U.S. Department of Labor together created the Joint Job Training and Research Corporation in 1978 to improve U.S. apparel competitiveness. The corporation's goal was to address training deficiencies in the industry. See Dunlop, John T., "The Work of

Labor-Management Committees," in *Dispute Resolution: Negotiation and Consensus Building*. Dover, MA: Auburn Publishing Company, 1984, pp. 247–51.

3. Based on estimated SAMs for particular clothing items multiplied by average hourly earnings for those sectors. SAM figures collected by the authors; average hourly earnings are based on U.S. Department of Labor, Bureau of Labor Statistics, *Employment and Earnings, 1995*.

4. U.S. Department of Labor, Bureau of Labor Statistics, *Productivity Measures for Selected Industries and Government Services*, Bulletin 2379. Washington, DC: U.S. Department of Labor, May 1991, p. 44; *Monthly Labor Review*, March 1998, Table 42, p. 132. Output per hour increased 4.3 percent in the year 1995–96. U.S. Department of Labor, Bureau of Labor Statistics, USDL 98–310, July 23, 1998.

5. This approach has and continues to be common in the women's industry, where subcontractors are given small discrete operations to complete. Note that the use of subcontractors constitutes the area most prone to employment abuses (i.e., home work, child labor, and sweatshops).

6. Manager descriptions of modular activities from our sample indicate that workers in modules focus primarily on those matters directly related to production, as well as on scheduling hours, breaks, and planned absenteeism for team members. Modules had, on average, "some or little" influence on the selection of team leaders and members, training, performance evaluation, and dispute resolution; they had "little or no" influence on the introduction of new technologies and capital investments.

7. See, for example, American Apparel Manufacturers Association, *Flexible Apparel Manufacturing: The Coming Revolution*. Report to the AAMA Technical Advisory Committee. Arlington, VA: American Apparel Manufacturers Association, 1992; Hill, Ed, "Flexible Manufacturing Systems," *Bobbin Magazine*, April 1992, pp. 48–50.

8. American Apparel Manufacturers Association, "Survey of Apparel Manufacturing," Technical Advisory Committee Report. Arlington, VA: American Apparel Manufacturers Association, 1992. Note, however, that there are several methodological problems with the AAMA results. First, the AAMA surveys do not track the same firms over time. Survey results are based on the aggregated responses of responding firms in the individual years. Second, the survey results combine men's and women's and knit and woven apparel producers. Third, the AAMA survey tends to be biased toward larger firms. Taken together, these factors probably lead to an overestimation of the prevalence of modular and non-bundle systems in the men's industry as a whole.

9. See Lowder, Robert, "Balance: A Delicate Word in Modular Manufacturing," *Bobbin Magazine*, November 1991, pp. 132–38.

10. One study found that modular systems have a *negative* effect on various measures of worker satisfaction. See Berg, Peter, Eileen Appelbaum, Thomas Bailey, and Arne Kalleberg, "The Performance Effects of Modular Production in the Apparel Industry," *Industrial Relations*, July 1996, pp. 356–73.

11. In fact, a feature of the U.S. tariff system promoted such offshore assem-

bly by only assessing tariffs on the value-added from assembly operations on U.S. produced textiles, not on the value of the garment as a whole.

12. This section is taken from a more detailed paper by Dunlop, John T., and David Weil, "Diffusion and Performance of Modular Production in the U.S. Apparel Industry," *Industrial Relations,* July 1996, pp. 334–55.

13. The analysis of this chapter applies to a subsample of forty-two business units in the men's shirt, suit, and pants segments, and in men's and women's jeans and undergarments. These product categories rely on in-house manufacturing and have relatively large production runs. The survey response rate for these product categories was about 50 percent, resulting in a sample that represents 30 percent of the total volume shipped by U.S. producers in the five product categories studied.

14. These factors were cited by all eight of the business units that had dropped modular assembly. Only two business units cited other factors, such as workforce or management disruptions, as reasons that modules were dropped.

15. All business units in the HCTAR sample that had modules in 1992 had adopted them after 1988.

16. Of the ten business units in the adopter group, one introduced modules in 1989, six in 1991, and three in 1992.

17. See Dunlop and Weil, loc. cit., Table 4, p. 345.

18. For a more technical analysis of this issue, see Hwang, Margaret, and David Weil, "The Diffusion of Modern Manufacturing Practices: Evidence from the Retail-Apparel Sectors," *Center for Economic Studies*, Discussion Paper 97–11, 1997.

19. Since our concern is with performance at the business-unit level, we do not consider here the direct impact of modules on unit labor costs in the sewing room per se. A comparison of labor costs in the sample reveals that business units with modular lines have average unit labor costs that are about 4 to 5 percent lower than those with only PBS lines. Berg, Appelbaum, Bailey, and Kalleberg, loc. cit., found that modules outperformed PBS lines in quality, costs, and responsiveness based on a case study of three apparel companies. A detailed study by Catherine George that includes direct comparisons of modular and nonmodular lines in a single company indicates that modular lines have more difficulty adapting to changing product variety, whereas PBS and UPS lines more readily absorb changes in production operations. She more generally shows that the choice of assembly systems should take into account the impacts of product variety and production scheduling. See George, Catherine M., "The Impact of Product Variety on Production Efficiency: A Comparison of Alternate Production Systems in the Apparel Industry," Ph.D. Dissertation, Harvard University, June 1998.

20. See Hammond, Janice, "Coordination in Textile and Apparel Channels: A Case for 'Virtual Integration,'" Working Paper 92–007, Graduate School of Business Administration, Harvard University, 1992.

21. See "Partnership Agreement Levi Strauss & Co./Amalgamated Clothing and Textile Workers Union," October 1994. For accounts in the press, see Uchitelle, Louis, "A New Labor Design at Levi Strauss," *New York Times*, October

13, 1994, pp. D1,D6; Bureau of National Affairs, "Levi Strauss, ACTWU Announce New Partnership Arrangement," *Daily Labor Report*, October 14, 1994, pp. A10–A11. Our understanding of the agreement has also benefited from discussion with Jerry Erlenbach, Director of Industrial Relations, Levi Strauss & Co., and Jack Sheinkman, UNITE!.

22. See Sherman, Stratford, "Levi's: As Ye Sew, So Shall Ye Reap," *Fortune*, May 12, 1997, pp. 104–116. Haas undertook an even larger buyout from company shareholders and family members in April 1996, when the company paid out $4.3 billion in an LBO recapitalization.

23. "Injured Workers Sue Levi's Over Re-Entry Program," *Wall Street Journal*, May 20, 1998, p. A6.

24. Elections are held by card recognition and through an expedited process.

25. See Rutberg, Sid, and Miles Socha, "Levi's Cutting Back Production; 11 Plants to Shut," *Women's Wear Daily*, November 4, 1997, p. 2. The company announced further cuts in 1998. For a critical account of Levi's efforts in the areas of distribution and retail relations, see Sherman, loc. cit., pp. 114–16.

26. One of the problems involves workers who receive high earnings under individually based piece rates and often see those earnings go down when placed in teams. See King, Ralph T., "Jeans Therapy: Levi's Factory Workers Are Assigned to Teams, and Morale Takes a Hit," *Wall Street Journal*, May 20, 1998, pp. A1, A6.

27. In the textile industry, historically, there was no similar strategic job classification, although the loomfixer and certain weavers' classifications were critical in some respects.

28. Lean retailing has also severely diminished the role of traditional retail buyers, whose feel for the market—and the compensation and career paths associated with that "art"—are being replaced by the merchandise manager's analysis of real-time sales data, advanced forecasting methods, and replenishment partnerships.

29. See "UNITE Gains Voluntary Recognition for 600 Marshall Workers in Virginia," *Daily Labor Report*, Washington DC: Bureau of National Affairs, Inc., May 9, 1997, pp. A1–A3; "UNITE Gains Recognition at Marshall's Distribution Center; Bargaining to Start Soon," *Daily Labor Report*, May 6, 1998, pp. A3–A4. "Recognition at the Woburn (Massachusetts) center marked the completion of UNITE's organizing effort at all the Marshall's and TJMaxx distribution facilities in the United States." *Daily Labor Report*, September 23, 1998, p. A–7.

30. *Reports of the Industrial Commission on Immigration and on Education*. Washington, DC: Government Printing Office, 1901, Vol. XV, pp. 319–20. Professor John R. Commons was the author of Part III, "Immigration and Its Economic Effects," pp. 293–743.

31. Ibid., pp. 321–22.

32. Ibid., p. xi.

33. 29 U.S.C. 201, et seq. The 1938 Act was signed June 25, 1938.

34. These collective bargaining agreements between clothing unions and contractors, jobbers, and manufacturers were exempted from the National Labor

Relations Act strictures against secondary boycotts. After the Taft-Hartley Act (1947) outlawed the secondary boycott in industry generally, Congress authorized the continued use of the boycott and the enforcement of agreements to regulate the relations among manufacturers, jobbers, and contractors in the clothing industry. This authorization was included in Section 8 (e) of the 1959 amendments to the National Labor Relations Act.

35. "A Great and Good Union Points the Way for America's Labor Movement," *Life Magazine*, August 1, 1938.

36. In a case cited by the Department of Labor, a Chinese immigrant worker was paid the equivalent of $2.14 an hour for 84 hours of work—less than half the 1998 minimum wage of $5.15 an hour. See Greenhouse, Steven, "Two-Thirds of Garment Shops Break Wage Laws, U.S. Says," *New York Times*, October 17, 1997, p. A37.

37. Also indicative of renewed concern over sweatshops—and the controversy the issue continues to raise—is a 1998 exhibit mounted by The National Museum of American History, Smithsonian Institution, in Washington, DC, entitled "Between a Rock and a Hard Place: A History of American Sweatshops, 1820–Present." Liebhold, Peter, and Harry R. Rubenstein, "Between a Rock and a Hard Place, The National Museum of American History's Exhibition on Sweatshops, 1820–Present," *Labor's Heritage*, Spring 1998, pp. 4–25.

Chapter 11

1. Dalzell, Robert F., Jr., *Enterprising Elite: The Boston Associates and the World They Made*. Cambridge, MA: Harvard University Press, 1987, p. 6.

2. Ibid., pp. 32–34.

3. In contrast, the labor system developed in the southern cotton textile industry focused on bringing the entire family into the life of the mill. With the textile mill as the centerpiece of housing for workers, basic education of younger family members, on-the-job training for those entering into mill work, and employment, the system effectively limited labor mobility, enhanced the benefits arising from training, and lowered turnover of adult operatives. For a discussion of the family labor system, see McHugh, Cathy L., *Mill Family: The Labor System in the Southern Cotton Textile Industry 1880–1915*. New York: Oxford University Press, 1988.

4. Landes, David S., *The Wealth and Poverty of Nations: Why Some Are So Rich and Some So Poor*. New York: W.W. Norton and Company, 1998, p. 299.

5. The tying-in machine arranges and clamps warp thread from a full-loom beam to ends of warp from an exhausted loom beam to continue weaving.

6. Lahne, Herbert J., *The Cotton Mill Worker*. New York: Farrar & Rinehart, 1944, p. 153.

7. Ibid., p. 154.

8. Ibid., p. 156.

9. For a case study, see Slichter, Summer H., *Union Policies and Industrial*

Management. Washington, DC: The Brookings Institution, 1941. Chapter XVIII describes "The Naumkeag Co-operative Experiment," pp. 532–59.

10. Murray, Lauren A., "Unraveling Employment Trends in Textiles and Apparel," *Monthly Labor Review*, August 1995, p. 63.

11. American Textile Manufacturers Institute, *The U.S. Textile Industry, Scope and Importance*. Washington, DC: American Textile Manufacturers Institute, 1998, pp. 24–26.

Between 1987 and 1997 shuttle loom hours operated declined from 505 million to 45 million while shuttleless loom hours operated stayed in the vicinity of 455 million. In the period 1991 to 1997 ring spindle hours declined from 55 billion to 29 billion, while open end spindle hours increased from 5 billion to 7.3 billion. American Textile Manufacturers Institute, *Textile Highlights*, June 1998, p. 5.

12. For occupational job descriptions, see U.S. Department of Labor, Bureau of Labor Statistics, *Industry Wage Structure: Textile Plants, August 1990*, Bulletin 2386, September 1991, pp. 100–107.

13. U. S. Department of Labor, Bureau of Labor Statistics, *Industry Wage Survey: Textile Mills, June 1985*, Bulletin 2265. Washington, DC: U.S. Department of Labor, February 1987; U.S. Department of Labor, Bureau of Labor Statistics, 1991, loc. cit.

14. Women workers currently constitute approximately 47 percent of textile-mill-products employees compared with a little less than a third for all manufacturing.

15. Cline, William R., *The Future of World Trade in Textiles and Apparel*, Revised Edition. Washington, DC: Institute for International Economics, 1990, p. 85.

16. Based on analysis of data from U.S. Department of Commerce, Bureau of the Census, *U.S. Total Imports/Exports*. See Appendix C for a description of this dataset.

17. American Apparel Manufacturers Association, *1998 Focus, An Economic Profile of the Apparel Industry*. Arlington, VA: American Apparel Manufacturers Association, 1998, p. 11.

18. Based on a private conversation with executives of the Russell Corporation, Alexander City, Alabama.

19. Specifically, 80s denotes yarn of such diameter that 80 x 840 yard, or 67,200 yards of yarn, weighs one pound; a 1's yarn would be 840 yards long and weigh one pound.

20. See Adanur, Sabit, *Wellington Sears Handbook of Industrial Textiles*. Lancaster, PA: Technomic Publishing Co., 1995, p. 75.

21. Actual production data from one major textile firm suggest that a 37s, 100-percent cotton yarn would be produced at only about twenty meters a minute, and an 80s yarn would be produced at a still lower rate. It might take nearly three days to produce a pound of 80s yarn.

22. This equipment would consist of 960 spindles and 18 winders. Data supplied to us by a large U.S.-based textile firm.

23. The U.S. annual consumption of domestically manufactured apparel is twelve items of outerwear per capita. Assuming that the weight of the average item of outerwear is between a half and one pound, this yields an apparel consumption of between 1.6 and 3.2 billion pounds of fiber a year. Using an average cost figure of $500,000 (assuming more open-end-spun than ring-spun yarn is produced) for the production of 70 pounds of 18s yarn an hour, the capital cost of the yearly production can be between 9 and 18 billion dollars, after allowing for the fact that apparel accounts for only one-third of yearly textile production. The weighted average yarn size of eighteen is a reasonable number. Typical oxford shirting is made from 40s; quality household sheets are made with 37s; T-shirts are made with 19s to 22s; fleece uses 10s to 27s; and denim is made with 4s, 6s, or 8s, depending on the weight.

24. Data on textile machinery imports from U.S. Department of Commerce, Bureau of the Census, U.S. Total Imports/Exports. See Appendix C for details.

25. The Bureau of Labor Statistics, for wage survey purposes, defines a slasher operator as a worker who: "[O]perates a machine that combines the warp yarn of a number of section beams onto a single loom beam and coats threads of warp yarn with sizing solution to give the yarn strength and to make the fibers adhere closely. Work involves most of the following: Positioning section beams of warp yarn in creel; drawing warp through slasher by tying ends from new section beams to ends from exhausted beams, or by threading warp through starch pot, around heated cylinders and onto loom beams; observing that yarn is properly sized; connecting broken ends; doffing full loom beams and replacing section beams; washing and cleaning the rollers and size box." U.S. Department of Labor, Bureau of Labor Statistics, *Industry Wage Survey: Textile Plants, August 1990*, Bulletin 2386. Washington, DC: Government Printing Office, September 1991, p. 103.

26. Dalzell, loc. cit., p. 31.

27. Adanur, loc. cit., p. 118.

28. Ibid., p. 118.

29. Data supplied to us by a large U.S.-based textile firm.

30. Espen, Hal, "Fleeced," *New York Times Magazine*, February 15, 1998, pp. 20–23.

31. Ibid., p. 22.

Chapter 12

1. Executive Office of the President, *Standard Industrial Classification Manual*. Washington, DC: Government Printing Office, 1987.

2. "The major group includes establishments engaged in performing any of the following operations: (1) preparation of fiber and subsequent manufacturing of yarn, thread, braids, twine, and cordage; (2) manufacturing broadwoven fabrics, narrow woven fabrics, knit fabrics, and carpets and rugs from yarn; (3) dyeing and finishing fiber, yarn, fabrics, and knit apparel; (4) coating, waterproofing, or oth-

erwise treating fabrics; (5) the integrated manufacture of knit apparel and other finished articles from yarn; and (6) the manufacture of felt goods, lace goods, nonwoven fabrics, and miscellaneous textiles." See Executive Office of the President, ibid., p. 85.

3. Under the new 1997 North American Industry Classification System, textile-mill products (SIC 22) appears to have been subdivided into two major categories: textile mills (313) and textile product mills (314), each with a number of four-, five-, and six-digit headings. Apparel and other textile products (SIC 23) has been replaced with apparel manufacturing (315) and a number of four-, five-, and six-digit headings. See Office of Management and Budget, Federal Register, Part II. Washington, DC: Office of Management and Budget, April 9, 1997.

4. Similarly, there are a number of codes in SIC 23 (apparel and other finished products made from fabrics and similar materials) such as miscellaneous fabricated textile products (SIC 239), that include the direct products of textile operations rather than output from garment establishments. These codes include housefurnishings (SIC 2392), textile bags (SIC 2393), canvas and related products (SIC 2394), and automotive trimmings (SIC 2396). Note that a 1995 draft report by the Office of Technology Policy treats SIC 239 as a part of the textile industry for the purposes of its analysis. See U.S. Department of Commerce, Office of Technology Policy, *Meeting the Challenge: U.S. Industry Faces the twenty-first Century, The U.S. Textile Industry, manuscript*, Washington, DC: U.S. Department of Commerce, August 1995, p. 28.

5. For example, miscellaneous fabricated textile products (SIC 239) constituted 11.3 percent of apparel (SIC 23) employment in 1960, and 24.9 percent in 1996; the average hourly earnings of production workers in fabricated textile products (SIC 239) were 1.9 percent above the apparel average in 1960 but 15.9 percent higher in 1996. The average hourly earnings data for apparel thus currently exaggerate the wage level for apparel, if that is interpreted as sewn woven or knit products from apparel plants only.

6. As the National Bureau of Economic Research stated many decades ago, "The markets in which gray [sic] goods prices are made are thus essentially brokers' markets." See National Bureau of Economic Research, *Textile Markets: Their Structure in Relation to Price Research, Report of the Committee on Textile Price Research to the Conference on Price Research*. New York: National Bureau of Economic Research, 1939, p. 98.

7. Murray, Lauren A., "Unraveling Employment Trends in Textiles and Apparel," *Monthly Labor Review*, August 1995, p. 66. Also see Ghadar, Fariborz, William H. Davidson, and Charles S. Feigenoff, *U.S. Industrial Competitiveness: The Case of the Textile and Apparel Industries*. Lexington, MA: Lexington Books, DC Heath and Co., 1987, pp. 16–17.

8. See World Bank, World Development Report, *Workers in an Integrating World*. New York: Oxford University Press, 1995. Also see Audet, Denis, "Globalization in the Clothing Industry," in *Globalization of Industry, Overview and Sector Reports*. Washington, DC: O.E.C.D., 1997, pp. 323–55.

9. International Labour Office, *Globalization of the Footwear, Textile and Clothing Industries*. Geneva, Switzerland: International Labour Office, 1996, p. 5.

10. Ibid., p. 5.

11. U.S. Department of Commerce, Office of Technology Policy, Draft, loc. cit., p. 28.

12. U.S. Department of Commerce, *News*, CB–97–26. Washington, DC: U.S. Department of Commerce, February 19, 1997, pp. 21–22 and updates.

13. The comparative average annual rates of increases in multifactor productivity for textile mill products and total manufacturing in various subperiods were as follows: 1949–73, 2.2 percent for textiles and 1.5 for manufacturing; 1973–79, 3.3 percent for textiles and .4 for manufacturing; 1979–90, 2.0 percent for textiles and 1.0 for manufacturing; and 1990–96, 1.4 percent for textiles and 1.9 percent for manufacturing. These estimates are from U.S. Department of Labor, Bureau of Labor Statistics, *Multifactor Productivity Trends, 1995 and 1996* (USDL 98–187). Washington, DC: U.S. Department of Labor, May 6, 1998. Also see Gullickson, William, "Multifactor Productivity in Manufacturing Industries," *Monthly Labor Review*, October 1992, p. 24.

14. "Annual Indexes of Output Per Hour for Selected Industries," *Monthly Labor Review*, November 1997, pp. 130–31; U.S. Department of Labor, Bureau of Labor Statistics, *Productivity Measure for Selected Industries and Government Services*, Bulletin 2379. Washington, DC: U.S. Department of Labor, May 1991, pp. 41–43. Also see U.S. Department of Labor, *Productivity by Industry, 1995* (USDL 97–132). Washington, DC: U.S. Department of Labor, April 23, 1997. For 1995–96 output per hour, see U.S. Department of Labor, Bureau of Labor Statistics, *Productivity by Industry, 1987–1996,* (USDL 98–310), Washington, DC, July 23, 1998. The 1995–96 increase in output per hour for SIC 221,2 was 3.5 percent; for SIC 2251,2 was 14.1 percent; and for SIC 2281 was 11.9 percent.

15. See Critchlow, Robert, "Productivity Growth Improves in Housefurnishings Industry," *Monthly Labor Review*, March 1996, pp. 23–28. The data are for SIC 2392 and indicate an annual rate of increase of just 1.2 percent a year for 1972–91, but the 1973–79 period showed an annual decrease of 2.3 percent.

16. Franklin, James C., "Employment Outlook: 1996–2006, Industry Output and Employment Projections to 2006," *Monthly Labor Review*, November 1997, p. 46.

17. Although great strides have been made by the U.S. textile industry in increasing productivity through automation and capital investments in modern spinning and weaving technologies, textile labor costs are still a significant part of the final product. If we break down the production costs of lightweight cotton and 50/50 cotton-blended fabrics into just three categories—labor, materials, and all other costs—then the three contribute nearly equally to production costs of both fabrics. The blended fabric costs roughly two-thirds as much to make as the pure cotton fabric does, and the labor materials costs are proportionally lower. Data supplied to us by a large U.S. textile firm.

18. See U.S. Department of the Treasury, U.S. Custom Service, *Foreign Assem-*

bly of U.S. Components: Qualifying Imported Goods for Partial Duty Exemption. Washington, DC: Department of the Treasury, December 1996, pp. 10–17.

19. Congress of the United States, Office of Technology Assessment, *The U.S. Textile and Apparel Industry: A Revolution in Progress.* Washington, DC: 1987, p. 61.

20. American Apparel Manufacturers Association, *1998 Focus: An Economic Profile of the Apparel Industry.* Arlington, VA: American Apparel Manufacturers Association, 1998, p. 11.

21. For an allocation of the value of total industry, see the 1995 U.S. Department of Commerce, Office of Technology Policy draft, loc. cit., p. 2.

22. In particular, a group of "factors" acted as arbitragers who bought greige goods and piece-dyed them into more varied fabric products closer to the season and in smaller lot sizes.

23. In fact, the variance in lead times of our business units reveals that some units under high replenishment waited as long as eight to nine months for textile orders to arrive in 1992. For more detail on these comparative results, see Abernathy, Frederick H., John T. Dunlop, Janice H. Hammond, and David Weil, "The Information-Integrated Channel: A Study of the U.S. Apparel Industry in Transition," *Brookings Papers: Microeconomics*, 1995, pp. 218–19 and Table 4.

24. See Goldberg, Carey, "A Promise Is Kept: Mill Reopens," *New York Times*, September 16, 1997, p. A14; Teal, Thomas, "Not a Fool, Not a Saint," *Fortune*, November 11, 1996, pp. 201–4; Uchitelle, Louis, "The Risks of Keeping a Promise," *New York Times*, July 4, 1996, pp. D1, D3.

25. Cole, Caroline Louise, "Fabric of Life, Then and Now," *Boston Sunday Globe*, Northwest Weekly, April 13, 1997, pp. 1, 6.

26. HCTAR appreciates the visits to plants and headquarters of a few of these textile companies and the detailed data that was furnished to us. The text preserves the confidentiality of proprietary data and information.

27. Abernathy, Dunlop, Hammond, and Weil, loc. cit., pp. 175–246.

28. Adanur, Sabit, *Wellington Sears Handbook of Industrial Textiles.* Lancaster, PA: Technomic Publishing Company, 1995, p. 757.

29. Piore, Michael J., and Charles F. Sabel, *The Second Industrial Divide: Possibilities for Prosperity.* New York: Basic Books, 1984, pp. 213–16.

30. The success of this region in terms of exporting textile and apparel products continued into the 1990s. See Tagliabue, John, "Where Small Is Molto Bello: For Italy's Family-Owned Weavers, Life Is Good," *New York Times*, February 3, 1996, pp. 35–36.

31. This type of coordinating function is of particular importance for New York City, which has a concentration of manufacturers and contractors in the women's industry and is also the headquarters of many major retail firms. Providing replenishment of fashion products by drawing on a network of textile suppliers could play a critical role in the future of apparel there. For an account of some efforts in this regard, see Foderaro, Lisa, "Apparel Making Regains Lost Ground," *New York Times*, January 13, 1998, p. A19.

Chapter 13

1. World Bank, *Workers in an Integrating World: World Development Report, 1995*. New York: Oxford University Press, 1995, p. 51.

2. Council of Economic Advisors, *Economic Report of the President, Transmitted to the Congress February 1998, Together with the Annual Report of the Council of Economic Advisors*. Washington, DC: Government Printing Office, 1998, p. 216.

3. World Bank, loc. cit., p. 51.

4. From U.S. Department of Commerce, Bureau of the Census. *U.S. Total Imports, Apparel*. This data series provides detailed import and export information by SITC product category and country of origin. References to U.S. Department of Commerce, Bureau of the Census in this chapter refer to analysis of this data set, including the data presented in Tables 13.2 to 13.7. See Appendix C for a description of the dataset.

5. Cline, William R., *The Future of World Trade in Textiles and Apparel*, Revised Edition. Washington, DC: Institute for International Economics, 1990, p. 40.

6. These numbers come from several sources. See Murray, Lauren A., "Unraveling Employment Trends in Textiles and Apparel," *Monthly Labor Review*, August 1995, p. 67; American Apparel Manufacturers Association, *1998 Focus: An Economic Profile of the Apparel Industry*. Arlington, VA: American Apparel Manufacturers Association, 1998, p. 4. Also note that the 1996 *Apparel Market Monitor* reports that the aggregate apparel market in the United States was $161 billion, of which $49 billion was men's apparel, $85 billion was women's apparel, and $27 billion was divided among boys', girls', and infants' and toddlers' apparel. In each broad category, the import share of the dollar volume was approximately 50 percent. American Apparel Manufacturers Association, AAMA Marketing Committee, *Apparel Market Monitor, Annual 1996*. Based on data provided by the NPD Group. Arlington, VA: American Apparel Manufacturers Association, 1996.

7. U.S. Department of Commerce, Bureau of the Census loc. cit.; Cline, loc. cit., p. 40.

8. Specifically, from 1979 to 1981, the value of exports exceeded that of imports, c.i.f. value (i.e., cost plus insurance and freight). See Cline, loc. cit., p. 309; U.S. Department of Commerce, Office of Technology Policy, *Meeting the Challenge: U.S. Industry Faces the Twenty-first Century, The U.S. Textile Industry*, manuscript. Washington, DC: U.S. Department of Commerce, August 1995, p. 104.

9. Ashton, T. S., *The Industrial Revolution, 1760–1830*. London: Oxford University Press, 1948, p. 28.

10. Gerschenkron, Alexander, *Continuity in History and Other Essays*. Cambridge, MA: The Belknap Press of Harvard University Press, 1968, p. 117.

11. Gerschenkron, Alexander, *Economic Backwardness in Historical Perspective: A Book of Essays*. Cambridge, MA: The Belknap Press of Harvard University Press, 1962. Gerschenkron further notes, "In fact, one is almost tempted to argue that the more backward a country, the more appropriate it is to define its spurt of

industrial development as a process during which the textile industry was divested of its dominant position" (p. 209).

12. Murray, loc. cit., p. 66.

13. Ibid., p. 65.

14. Freeston, W. Denney, Jr., Chairman, and Jeffrey S. Arpan, Rapporteur, *The Competitive Status of the U.S. Fibers, Textiles, and Apparel Complex: A Study of the Influences of Technology in Determining International Competitive Advantage.* Washington, DC: National Academy Press, 1983, p. 50.

15. Finger, J. Michael, and Ann Harrison, "Import Protection for U.S. Textiles and Apparel: Viewed from the Domestic Perspective," in Krueger, Anne O., ed., *The Political Economy of Trade Protection.* Chicago: University of Chicago Press, 1996, p. 48. Also see Hufbauer, Gary Clyde, Diane T. Berliner, and Kimberly Ann Elliott, *Trade Protection in the United States: 31 Case Studies.* Washington, DC: Institute for International Economics, 1986, pp. 117–53.

16. The MFA actually expired in 1991, by which time most nations had agreed on its elimination. But the arrangement was extended until negotiations for its elimination could be completed in 1994.

17. Nehmer, Stanley, and Mark W. Love, "Textiles and Apparel: A Negotiated Approach to International Competition," in Scott, Bruce R., and George C. Lodge, eds., *U.S. Competitiveness in the World Economy.* Boston: Harvard Business School Press, 1985, p. 258.

18. Cline, loc. cit., p. 194. Also see Metzger, Michael R., Randi Boorstein, Morris E. Morkre, and James D. Reitzes, *The Regional Welfare Effect of U.S. Import Restraints on Apparel, Petroleum, Steel and Textiles.* Brookfield, VT: Ashgate Publishing Company, 1996. Based on Cline's aggregate estimates, Chapter 4 of the latter volume examines the regional costs and benefits of import restrictions on textiles and apparel: "Our results indicate that between three and seven states realize net gains from existing textile restrictions and that as many as seven states— but perhaps none—realize net gains from apparel restrictions" (p. 65).

19. Council of Economic Advisors, *Economic Report of the President, Transmitted to the Congress February 1994, Together with the Annual Report of the Council of Economic Advisors.* Washington, DC: Government Printing Office, 1994, p. 222. Also see United States International Trade Commission, *The Year in Trade: Operation of the Trade Agreements Program During 1996, 48th Report*, USITC Publication 3024. Washington, DC: United States International Trade Commission, April 1997, p. 149; and Trade Statistics Subgroup, Trade and Investment Working Group, Joint Commission on Commerce and Trade, *Report of the Trade Statistical Subgroup*, Presented October 17, 1995. This latter report deals with the differences between the published trade statistics of the People's Republic of China and the U.S. and develops an explanation of possible causes for the discrepancies.

20. The Harmonized Tariff Schedules of the United States. The section has been renumbered 9802.00.80. See Mittelhauser, Mark, "Employment Trends in Textile and Apparel, 1973–2005," *Monthly Labor Review*, August 1997.

21. The U.S. Tariff Code defined the covered articles as follows: "Articles assembled abroad in whole or in part of fabricated components, the product of the

United States, which (a) were exported in condition ready for assembly without further fabrication, (b) have not lost their physical identity in such articles by change in form, shape, or otherwise, and (c) have not been advanced in value or improved in condition abroad accept by being assembled and except by operations incidental to the assembly process such as cleaning, lubricating and painting." See Murray, Lauren, loc. cit.

22. American Apparel Manufacturers Association, loc. cit., p. 3; U.S. Department of Commerce, Bureau of Census, loc. cit.

23. Council of Economic Advisors, *Economic Report of the President, Transmitted to the Congress February 1992, Together with the Annual Report of The Council of Economic Advisors.* Washington, DC: Government Printing Office, 1992, p. 213.

24. United States International Trade Commission, *The Year in Trade: Operation of the Trade Agreements Program During 1995, 47th Report,* USITC Publication 2971. Washington, DC: United States International Trade Commission, August 1996, pp. 81–82.

25. These trade-weighted averages reflect average tariffs for all imported apparel and textile products, which includes some that have no tariffs and others with very high tariffs. There is a wide range of actual duties on specific products. For instance, men's and boys' overcoats, capes, and related garments made of wool (6201.11.00)—a category that has been historically protected—have a duty rate of 19.1 percent of the value of shipments. In contrast, the rate for women's and girls' overcoats, capes, and related garments containing 70 percent or more by weight of silk (6202.99.10) is only 1.8 percent.

26. Mittelhauser, loc. cit., p. 29.

27. U.S. Department of the Treasury, U.S. Customs Service, *Foreign Assembly of U.S. Components: Qualifying Imported Goods for Partial Duty Exemption.* Washington, DC: U.S. Department of the Treasury, December 1996. The guide explains partial duty exemption under subheading 9802.00.80, Harmonized Tariff Schedule of the United States (HTSUS), for the importation of articles assembled abroad from U.S.components.

28. Hanson, Gordon H., "The Effects of Offshore Assembly on Industry Location: Evidence from U.S. Border Cities," Cambridge, MA: National Bureau of Economic Research, Working Paper Series 5400, December 1995, p. 1. Hanson argues, "The most likely scenario is that NAFTA will cause Mexican assembly plants and U.S. component producers to expand, in which case one can expect manufacturing activities in the United States to continue to relocate to the U.S. border region" (p. 18).

29. United States International Trade Commission, 1995, loc. cit., p. 87.

30. U.S. Department of Commerce, Bureau of the Census, loc. cit.

31. U.S. Department of Commerce, Office of Technology Policy, loc. cit., p. 104.

32. U.S. Department of Commerce, Bureau of the Census, *Exports from Manufacturing Establishments, 1988 and 1989,* AR 89–1. Washington, DC: U.S. Department of Commerce, November 1992, p. 30.

33. Davis, Lester A., *U.S. Jobs Supported by Goods and Services Exports, 1953–94,*

a staff research report. Washington, DC: U.S. Department of Commerce, Economics and Statistics Administration, November 1996, p. 30.

34. Council of Economic Advisors, loc. cit., p. 406.

35. Cline, loc. cit., p. 60.

36. Unless otherwise noted, estimates in this section derive from analysis of data from the U.S. Department of Commerce, Bureau of the Census, loc. cit., described in Appendix C.

37. Comparisons using physical units do not, however, adequately reflect relative dollar value of imports because not all square meters of products are valued at the same price.

38. The share of all Asian countries, including the Philippines, Indonesia, Thailand, Singapore, and Malaysia, has in aggregate remained unchanged. Yet if we isolate the Southeast Asian countries—Bangladesh, India, Sri Lanka, Pakistan, and Malaysia—this group's share of imports has increased by roughly the same extent as the Asian countries as a whole.

39. 1984 figures for these regions are from American Apparel Manufacturer's Association, *1995 Focus*, loc. cit., p. 5. 1997 data for these regions are presented in American Apparel Manufacturer's Association, *1998 Focus*, loc. cit., p. 6.

40. Part of the ongoing work of HCTAR is to examine the comparative significance of each of these factors in determining trade flows into and out of the United States as well as other regions in the world.

41. For a discussion of the development of packagers in Asia, see Gereffi, Gary, "The Organization of Buyer-Driven Global Commodity Chains: How U.S. Retailers Shape Overseas Production Networks," in Gereffi, Gary, and Miguel Korzeniewicz, eds., *Commodity Chains and Global Capitalism*. Westport, CN: Greenwood Press, 1994, pp. 95–123; Bonanich, Edna, and David Waller, "The Role of U.S. Apparel Manufacturers in the Globalization of the Industry in the Pacific Rim," in Bonanich, Edna, ed., *Global Production: The Apparel Industry in the Pacific Rim*. Philadelphia, PA: Temple University Press, 1994, pp. 21–41.

42. In fact, trade with Mexico is still governed in part by the preexisting provisions of the Harmonized Tariff Schedule as well as the provisions of NAFTA. According to the International Trade Commission, "Prior to the implementation of NAFTA, almost all U.S. imports from assembly plants in Mexico entered under Harmonized Tariff Schedule provision 9802.00.80. In the two years since the implementation of NAFTA, a growing portion of production-sharing imports has been entering duty free under NAFTA exclusively rather than under 9802.00.80 or under both provisions." As a result of the gradual phase in under NAFTA, even by 1999, 20 percent of the tariffs and quotas (classified as those pertaining to "non-originating goods") will remain in effect. Only by 2004 will all tariffs and quotas affecting trade between the United States and Mexico be removed. See United States International Trade Commission, 1995, loc. cit., p. 43.

43. In order to disentangle these effects, continuing research at HCTAR is examining trade flows for rapid replenishment products where tariffs remained in place throughout this time period.

44. U.S. Department of Commerce, Bureau of the Census, loc. cit.

45. Krugman, Paul, *The Age of Diminished Expectations: U.S. Policy in the 1990s.* Cambridge, MA: MIT Press, 1991, p. 104.

Chapter 14

Epigraphs from Ryan, Thomas J., "Federated VF Corp. Laud Quick Response as Vital Cost-Center," *Women's Wear Daily*, November 17, 1997, pp. 1, 22.

1. The notion of "everyday low prices" implies that consumers benefit in the long run from reduction in the price of goods through more efficient distribution practices. The flip side is that consumers will purchase a smaller percentage of "on sale" items, which carry a reduced price in response to retailers' need to clear unsold merchandise. The aggregate effect on everyday low pricing (and lean retailing) nonetheless remains an open question, with important implications for retail price levels and inflation.

2. The results reported in this chapter are taken from three primary sources: Abernathy, Frederick H., John T. Dunlop, Janice Hammond, and David Weil, "The Information-Integrated Channel: A Study of the U.S. Apparel Industry in Transition," *Brookings Papers on Economic Activity: Microeconomics*, 1995, pp. 175–246; Hwang, Margaret, and David Weil, "The Diffusion of Modern Manufacturing Practices: Evidence from the U.S. Retail and Apparel Sectors," *Center for Economic Studies, Bureau of the Census Discussion Paper Series*, 97–11, 1997; and Hwang, Margaret, and David Weil, "Who Holds the Bag? The Impact of Workplace Practices and Information Technologies on Inventories," in *Proceedings of the 50th Annual Meeting of the Industrial Relations Research Association*. Madison, WI: Industrial Relations Research Association, 1998, pp. 68–77.

3. We use data from the HCTAR survey of apparel business units (see Appendix B), as well as a matched sample consisting of the HCTAR dataset and a microdata set maintained by the U.S. Department of Commerce that is described later in the text and in Appendix C.

4. Methods for throughput reduction differ markedly between apparel and textile industries. Throughput reduction in apparel assembly results largely from work flow redesign, whether via introduction of modular, UPS, or modified PBS lines. In contrast, given the capital intensity of all three major stages of textile production, throughput reductions arise from changes in machinery and production processes.

5. There is a growing theoretical and empirical literature regarding the economics of complementary practices. These include Milgrom, Paul, and John Roberts, "The Economics of Modern Manufacturing," *American Economic Review*, June 1990, pp. 511–528; Milgrom, Paul, and John Roberts, "Complementarities and Fit: Strategy, Structure, and Organizational Change in Manufacturing," *Journal of Accounting and Economics*, 1995, pp. 179–208. Empirical studies include Ichniowski, Casey, Kathryn Shaw, and Giovanna Prennushi, "The Effects of Human Resource Management Practices on Productivity," *American Economic Review*, June

1997, pp. 291–313; and MacDuffie, John Paul, "Human Resource Bundles and Manufacturing Performance: Organizational Logic and Flexible Production Systems in the World Auto Industry," *Industrial and Labor Relations Review*, January 1995, pp. 197–221.

6. An alternative way of showing that business units have tended to introduce these practices in a common sequence can be found in the following. There are sixteen possible permutations for adopting the four key practices examined here. Of the sixteen possible combinations, five conform to the expected sequence implied by the above description: bar code adoption as the base practice, followed only then by EDI, and then the two practices in concert with advanced shipping practices and/or with modular production. When we compare frequency of business units adopting any of the sixteen possible patterns in 1992, we find that the vast majority followed the expected sequencing pattern: 80 percent of the HCTAR sample business units adopted the four technologies in one of the five expected sequences.

7. See Hwang and Weil, 1997, loc. cit., Tables 11 and 12 for details. These adoption results remain even after explicitly controlling for other factors—such as business unit size, labor costs, and replenishment requirements—that also affect adoption decisions.

8. Abernathy, Dunlop, Hammond, and Weil, loc. cit., Table 6 and related discussion, pp. 223–25.

9. See, for example, Bird, Laura, and Wendy Bounds, "Stores' Demands Squeeze Apparel Companies," *Wall Street Journal*, July 15, 1997, pp. B1, B3; and Duff, Christina, "Big Stores' Outlandish Demands Alienate Small Suppliers," *Wall Street Journal*, October 27, 1995, pp. B1, B5.

10. See Abernathy, Dunlop, Hammond, and Weil, 1995, loc. cit., Tables 6 and 7, pp. 223, 225.

11. See Hwang and Weil, loc. cit., pp. 25–27.

12. We thank Joyce Cooper and Randy Becker at the Boston Research Data Center of the U.S. Census Bureau for their help with the Longitudinal Research Database. Work on this topic was carried out at the Boston Research Data Center of the U.S. Bureau of the Census during 1996–98. The opinions and conclusions expressed herein are those of the HCTAR authors and do not necessarily represent the views of the U.S. Bureau of the Census. All these results were screened to ensure that they do not disclose confidential information.

13. For a complete description, see Davis, Steve, and John Haltiwanger, "Wage Dispersion Between and Within U.S. Manufacturing Plants: 1963–1986," *Brookings Papers on Economic Activity: Microeconomics*, 1991, pp. 115–200.

14. We use somewhat different definitions for technology-adoption combinations in the 1988–91 and 1992–94 periods, because of confidentiality restrictions (minimum cell sizes) required by the U.S. Department of Commerce in using the Longitudinal Research Database.

15. The overall pattern of inventory/sales ratios for the sample of business units shows little change over the time period under study. The I/S ratios for three periods, 1984–87, 1988–91, and 1992–94, do not vary much from a mean of 1.5.

The lack of trend in these I/S ratios is consistent with the reported I/S ratios for the category "other nondurable goods" reported by the Bureau of the Census over the same time period. U.S. Department of Commerce, Bureau of the Census, "Real Inventories, Sales, and Inventory-Sales Ratios for Manufacturing and Trade," *Survey of Current Business*, May 1996, pp. 62–72.

16. See Filardo, Andrew, "Recent Evidence on the Muted Inventory Cycle," *Economic Review*, Federal Reserve Bank of Kansas City, vol. 80, no.2, 1995, pp. 27–43.

17. Volatility was measured by calculating the standard deviation of total inventories and I/S ratio for each establishment over the relevant time period. The average of these establishment-based standard deviations are presented in Figure 14.3.

18. One could argue that the relationship between technology adoption and inventory is an artifact of some other unmeasured variable. Product diversity, for example, is a particularly confounding factor. A business unit's absolute and relative level of inventory will be affected by the number of different products provided by the supplier. If units with higher levels of technology adoption also tend to have more limited product mixes than those units that have adopted few or none of the four key technologies, the results reported above may be more directly attributed to this factor than to information technology/workplace practices. In another analysis, however, we controlled for product diversity explicitly by including the log number of individual SKUs provided by the apparel supplier in 1988 and 1992. No matter which technology variable is used, and even holding constant product diversity, we found that information technology results in significantly lower I/S ratios. See Hwang and Weil (1998), loc. cit., pp. 73–74.

19. These estimates are based on regression models of the determinants of inventory growth rates, including controls for changes in business unit size and the product diversity offered by the supplier, both of which also impact inventory growth. For complete results, see Hwang and Weil (1998), ibid., pp. 74–76.

20. This encompasses all retail markdowns, including those occurring at the end of the season. When suppliers were separately asked the same question regarding the frequency of retail markdowns *excluding* end-of-season markdowns, the "innovative" business units differed little from suppliers that had adopted few or none of the four practices. This is not surprising, since much of the markdown activity arising from ordering too much of a product relative to demand occurs at the end of the season.

21. Estimated retail and manufacturer markdowns are based on business unit responses to the HCTAR survey. Unpublished results are available from the authors.

22. However, note that this test for the impact of practice on profitability suffers from potential multicollinearity and selection-bias problems. If the supplier practices are complementary, then single and interactive terms will tend to be highly correlated. Firms that adopt more "innovative" activities may do so because managers expect benefits from adoption to be greater or costs to be lower than those of other comparable business units. If this is the case, then higher produc-

tivity effects attributed to the most "innovative" clusters may be due not to complementarities between the activities per se but to differences in underlying adoption incentives. For a comprehensive discussion of these issues, see Athey, Susan, and Scott Stern, "An Empirical Framework for Testing Theories About Complementarities," MIT Sloan School of Management, manuscript, May 1996. An analysis of pair-wise correlation coefficients between the various explanatory variables (available from the authors) reveals low correlations among them, which implies that results do not suffer from multicollinearity problems. But it is difficult to argue that potential endogeneity biases do not exist, and therefore the estimates can be regarded as supporting other evidence that is consistent with the hypothesis.

23. See Christian, Nichole M., "BMW Starting an Overhaul of U.S. Dealers," *Wall Street Journal*, June 12, 1997, p. A6.

24. BMW reports that it is able to deliver customized versions to U.S. consumers of several product lines in as little as two weeks from its Spartanburg, South Carolina, plant. See Christian, ibid., p. A6.

25. See Henderson, Angelo, and Valerie Reitman, "Detroit Strikes Back in Dealership Revolution," *Wall Street Journal*, August 27, 1997, pp. B1, B8.

26. See Lee, Hau L., and Corey Billington, "Managing Supply Chain Inventory: Pitfalls and Opportunities," *Sloan Management Review*, Spring 1992, pp. 65–73. For a formal treatment of this problem, see Lee, Hau L., "Effective Inventory and Service Management through Product and Process Redesign," *Operations Research*, January–February 1996, pp. 151–59.

27. See Zuckerman, Laurence, "Sure It's No. 1, But It's Trying to Change," *New York Times*, June 16, 1997, pp. D1, D9.

28. It is interesting to contrast this case with the typical situation in apparel. In apparel and textile, and many consumer sectors, retailers have driven channel integration. In Compaq's case, a manufacturer with significant market power has instituted policies within its distribution channel resulting in shifting inventory risk forward to *computer retailers*—unless these retailers are adept at using consumer demand information in placing orders with Compaq.

Chapter 15

1. The wages quoted are mid-1980 levels. From Metzger, Michael R., Randi Boorstein, Morris E. Morkre, and James D. Reitzes, *The Regional Welfare Effect of U.S. Import Restraints on Apparel, Petroleum, Steel and Textiles*. Brookfield, VT: Ashgate Publishing Company, 1996, p. xviii.

2. The quote from John Sweeney appears in "Clinton Defends Fast-Track Proposal, But Union Leaders Remain Opposed," *Daily Labor Report*. Washington, DC: Bureau of National Affairs, Inc., September 25, 1997, p. A–1.

3. Krugman, Paul, *The Age of Diminished Expectations: U.S. Economy in the 1990s*. Cambridge, MA: MIT Press, 1991, p. 110.

4. For a discussion of the inequality of compensation and the role of trade

and immigration, see Freeman, Richard B., *When Earnings Diverge: Causes, Consequences, and Cures of the New Inequality in the U.S.* Washington, DC: National Policy Association, 1997. Freeman assigns 15 to 20 percent of the rise in wage inequality to trade and immigration. Also see Cline, William R., *Trade and Income Distribution*. Washington, DC: Institute for International Economics, November 1997; Borjas, George J., Richard B. Freeman, and Lawrence F. Katz, "How Much Do Immigration and Trade Affect Labor Market Outcomes?," *Brookings Papers on Economic Activity*, 1997, pp. 1–67; Lerman, Robert I., "Reassessing Trends in U.S. Earnings Inequality,"*Monthly Labor Review*, December 1997, pp. 17–25; Burtless, Gary, Robert Z. Lawrence, Robert E. Litan, and Robert J. Shapiro, *Globaphobia: Confronting Fears About Open Trade*. Washington, DC: Brookings Institution, Progressive Policy Institute, Twentieth Century Fund, 1998, pp. 44–88; Feenstra, Robert C., Gordon H. Hanson, and Deborah L. Swenson, "Offshore Assembly from the United States: Production Characteristics of the 9802 Program," Conference on the Impact of International Trade on Wages, National Bureau of Economic Research, February 27–28, 1998; "Policy Forum: Trade and Labour Market Adjustment," *Economic Journal*, September 1998, pp. 1,450–1,510.

5. Council of Economic Advisors, *Economic Report of the President*, Transmitted to the Congress, Along with the Annual Report of the Council of Economics Advisors, February 1997. Washington, DC: U.S. Government Printing Office, 1997, p. 175.

6. U.S. International Trade Commission, *The Year in Trade: Operation of the Trade Agreement Program During 1996, 48th Report, USITC Publication 3024*. Washington, DC: U.S. International Trade Commission, April 1997, p. 150.

7. See Hart, Oliver, *Firms, Contracts, and Financial Structure*. Oxford: Clarendon Press, 1995.

8. In more formal terms, falling transaction costs within and across industries shift out the production possibilities frontier for the economy as a whole, meaning that more goods of all varieties can be produced with the same resources.

9. Chandler, Alfred D., Jr., *The Visible Hand: The Management Revolution in American Business*. Cambridge, MA: Harvard University Press, 1977, p. 209.

10. See, for example, Krueger, Alan B., "How Computers Have Changed the Wage Structure: Evidence from Microdata, 1984–1989," *Quarterly Journal of Economics*, February 1993, pp. 33–60; McGuckin, Robert H., and Kevin Stiroh, *Computers, Productivity, and Growth: Explaining the Computer Productivity Paradox*. Economic Research Report 1213–98–RB. Washington, DC: The Conference Board, 1998.

11. It is true that Hartmarx operated retail chains in the past, but it has curtailed these outlets; currently Levi Strauss has established a retail presence. Yet aside from the traditional factory outlet store, these instances are exceptions to vertical integration. For a discussion of the literature regarding the boundary of the firm, see Milgrom, Paul, and John Roberts, *Economics, Organization, and Management*. Englewood Cliffs, NJ: Prentice-Hall, 1992, Chapter 16, pp. 538–84; and Hart, loc. cit.

12. Council of Economic Advisors, *Economic Report of the President, Transmitted to the Congress, Along with the Annual Report of the Council of Economics Advisors*, February 1998. Washington, DC: U.S. Government Printing Office, 1998, p. 306.

13. See Abramowitz, Moses, *Inventories and Business Cycles*. New York: National Bureau of Economic Research, 1950; Blinder, Alan, "Inventories and Sticky Prices: More on the Microfoundations of Macroeconomics," *The American Economic Review*, June 1982, pp. 334–48; Blinder, Alan, and Stanley Fischer, "Inventories, Rational Expectations, and the Business Cycle," *Journal of Monetary Economics*, November 1981, pp. 277–304. For a discussion of the effects of retail inventory policy on the business cycle, see Blinder, Alan, "Retail Inventory Behavior and Business Fluctuations," *Brookings Papers on Economic Activity*, 1981, pp. 443–505; Caplin, Andrew, "The Variability of Aggregate Demand with (S,s) Inventory Policies," *Econometrica*, November 1985, pp. 1,395–1,409.

14. See, for example, Filardo, Andrew, "Recent Evidence on the Muted Inventory Cycle," *Economic Review*, Federal Reserve Bank of Kansas, Second Quarter 1995, pp. 27–43; Huh, Chan, "Just-in-Time Inventory Management: Has It Made a Difference?" *FRBSF Weekly Letter*, Federal Reserve Bank of San Francisco, May 1994; Little, Jane S., "Changes in Inventory Management: Implications for the U.S. Recovery," *New England Economic Review*, November/December 1992, pp. 37–65.

15. Council of Economic Advisors, *Economic Report of the President*, Transmitted to the Congress, Along with the Annual Report of the Council of Economics Advisors, February 1988. Washington, DC: U.S. Government Printing Office, 1988, p. 63.

16. See, for example, Lucchetti, Aaron, "Low Inventories Aggravate Price Spikes," *Wall Street Journal*, March 11, 1997, pp. C1, C12; Hershey, Robert D., Jr., "The Law of Supply on Demand: New Technology Helps Keep Inventories Just Lean Enough," *New York Times*, December 28, 1996, pp. 1, 40; Salpukas, Agis, "Wild Price Swings at the Pump: Refiners Gamble on Low Inventories, Insuring Volatility," *New York Times*, December 16, 1996, pp. D1, D6.

17. For recent theoretical treatments of price effects of inventory policy, see Deneckere, Raymond, Howard Marvel, and James Peck, "Demand Uncertainty, Inventories, and Resale Price Maintenance," *The Quarterly Journal of Economics*, August 1996, pp. 885–913; Bental, Benjamin, and Benjamin Eden, "Inventories in a Competitive Environment," *Journal of Political Economy*, 1993, pp. 863–86.

18. Note that these two views need not be contradictory: The effect of information integration might be to reduce growth in average retail price levels while increasing volatility around that mean.

19. A separate consumer price effect related to our findings concerns the construction of measures of consumer price level itself. Large-scale product proliferation and an increasing number of selling seasons complicate the measurement of the consumer price index, particularly for apparel components. The complexities of separating rapid changes in style, quality, taste, and quantities make measurements of price changes from one period to another extraordinarily difficult. In fact, similar difficulties have arisen generally in consumer products and services.

20. Kwong, Peter, *Forbidden Workers: Illegal Chinese Immigrants and American Labor*. New York: The New Press, 1997, p. 207.

21. Industrial Commission on Immigration and Education, *Report of the Industrial Commission on Immigration and Education*. Washington, DC: Government Printing Office, 1901, vol. XV, p. xxxii.

22. Consider the following example from 1998: "The Labor Department has convinced a federal judge in New York to sanction a manufacturer of women's garments for transporting goods made by its contractor in violation of the Fair Labor Standards Act's minimum wage and overtime requirements." From *Daily Labor Report*, Washington, DC, Bureau of National Affairs, Inc., February 12, 1998, pp. A2–A3.

23. For instance, employment in apparel in New York City dropped from 267,400 in 1960 to 72,400 in 1996. Some branches of the industry, such as men's and boys' suits and coats and women's and children's undergarments, have almost been eliminated in the area.

24. Greenhouse, Steven, "Two-Thirds of Garment Shops Break Wage Laws, U.S. Says," *New York Times*, October 17, 1997, p. A–37.

25. In addition, the National Labor Relations Act, as amended in 1959, provides in Section 8 (e) that the secondary boycott provisions of the statute "... shall not include persons in the relation of a jobber, manufacturer, contractor, or subcontractor working on the goods or premises of the jobber or manufacturer or performing parts of an integrated process of production in the apparel and clothing industry: *Provided further*, That nothing in this Act shall prohibit the enforcement of any agreement which is within the foregoing exception." See Chapters 2 and 10. In New York state, Governor Pataki on August 10, 1998, signed into law Bill S07628 that holds manufacturers liable for the unpaid wages of contractors' employees in the garment industry.

26. For discussions of the general problem of enforcement, see Dunlop, John T., "The Limits of Legal Compulsion," *Labor Law Journal*, January 1976, pp. 67–74; Weil, David, "Implementing Employment Regulations: Insights on the Determinants of Regulatory Performance," in Bruce E. Kaufman, ed., *Government Regulation of the Employment Relationship*. Madison, WI: Industrial Relationship Research Association, 1997, pp. 429–74.

27. The "Educational Forum of the U.S. Department of Labor's No Sweat Initiative" with Secretary Robert B. Reich—together with Kathie Lee Gifford—at Marymount University on July 16, 1996, provides an illustration of this approach.

28. See the quarterly *Garment Enforcement Report*. The April through June 1997 report shows that the Labor Department conducted 268 investigations, found violations in 107 of them, and assessed fines of $260,423. "DOL's Sweatshop Initiative Nets $1.2 Million in Back Wages for 2,443 Garment Workers,"*Daily Labor Report*, Washington, DC, Bureau of National Affairs, Inc., August 29, 1997, pp. A1–A2.

29. Students, religious groups, labor unions, and other organizations (including coalitions such as the National Labor Committee) are pressing for the adop-

tion of similar pledges at a number of other major universities. See "Duke Opposes Sweatshop Merchandise," *Atlanta Journal and Constitution*, March 9, 1998, pp. A1–A3.

30. U.S. Department of Labor, "Labor Secretary Robert B. Reich, Apparel Manufacturers Announce Major Breakthrough in Effort to Eradicate U.S. Sweatshops" (USDL 95–421), Washington, DC: U.S. Department of Labor, October 17, 1995; "Report on Apparel Industry Partnership to President Clinton," *Daily Labor Report*, Washington, DC:Bureau of National Affairs Inc., April 15, 1997, pp. E5–E7; Cushman, John H., "Nike Pledges to End Child Labor and Apply U.S. Rules Abroad," *New York Times*, May 13, 1998, pp. D1,D5; "Labor Secretary Herman's Remarks at Marymount University's Conference on Sweatshops in the Garment Industry," *Daily Labor Report*, Washington, DC: Bureau of National Affairs, June 2, 1997, pp. E5–E7.

31. See U.S. Department of Labor, *Augmented Compliance Program Agreement*, February 5, 1996, DOL Form ACPA (AM), p. 5.

32. See Nichols, Martha, "Third-World Families at Work: Child Labor or Child Care?," *Harvard Business Review*, January–February 1993, pp. 12–23, including commentary by John T. Dunlop, pp. 16–19.

33. "Fighting Child Labour: From Dream to Reality," *World of Work, The Magazine of the ILO*, December 1997, pp. 18–24; "ILO Expects 'Hard Nose Negotiations' to Yield Declaration in Core Worker Rights," *Daily Labor Report*, Washington, DC: Bureau of National Affairs, Inc., May 19, 1998, pp. C1–C3; "Text of the ILO Declaration on Fundamental Principles And Follow-up Mechanism," *Daily Labor Report*, Washington, DC: Bureau of National Affairs, Inc., June 18, 1998, pp. E1–E2.

34. "Labor Department Funds Project to End Child Labor in Production of Soccer Balls," *Daily Labor Report*, Washington, DC: Bureau of National Affairs, Inc., February 18, 1997, p. A6.

35. "Nonprofit's 'Social Accountability' Standard Would Verify Firms Pay, Treat Workers Well," *Daily Labor Report*, Washington, DC: Bureau of National Affairs, Inc., March 23, 1998, pp. A2–A3.

36. "Herman to Co-Host Symposium in Brussels Focusing on Codes of Conduct, Monitoring," *Daily Labor Report*, Washington, DC: Bureau of National Affairs, Inc., February 19, 1998, pp. A9–A10; February 23, 1998, pp. A9–A10.

37. Secretary of State Madeleine K. Albright stated in a May 22 commencement speech at the University of Maryland that as long as she was secretary, the United States would employ diplomacy to help build a world where "global norms of worker rights and environmental protection rise so that profits increasingly result from inspiration and perspiration, not exploitation." See "Secretary of State Highlights Worker Rights, Child Labor During Commencement Address," *Daily Labor Report*, Washington, DC: Bureau of National Affairs, Inc., May 27, 1998, p. A–3.

38. A related approach is adopting labels on apparel items that indicate to consumers that the product has been made in a workplace in compliance with labor standards, as has been done recently in the rug industry regarding compli-

ance with child labor laws. However, such methods do not ensure compliance with standards in those workplaces without a separate monitoring and enforcement procedure, nor would they provide the detailed information that could be attached to a bar code. See Iovine, Julie, "Must-Have Label: Rug Makers and Sellers Seeking Ways to Trumpet Compliance with Child-labor Law," *New York Times*, October 16, 1997, pp. C1, C10.

39. See Friedman, Arthur, "UNITE's Bruce Raynor: Heir Apparent Moves to Step Up Organizing," *Women's Wear Daily*, February 17, 1998, pp. 1, 10.

40. These efforts include the Garment Industry Development Corporation in New York City and Project 2000 in San Francisco. Both are not-for-profit organizations funded and led by labor, management, and government participants who seek to improve the competitiveness of the apparel industry (primarily the women's sector) in those cities.

41. Franklin, James C., "Employment Outlook: 1996–2006, Industry Output and Employment Projections to 2006," *Monthly Labor Review*, November 1997, p. 46.

42. See Brown, Stephen A., *Revolution at the Checkout Counter: The Explosion of the Bar Code*. Cambridge, MA: Harvard University Press, 1997, Table 1, pp. 14–15.

43. Tracy Mullin quoted in Ernst & Young, *Internet Shopping*, Ernst & Young Special Report for the National Retail Federation, January 1998, p. 3.

44. See Ernst & Young, loc. cit., p. 10. The Ernst & Young report notes that "the current list of online sellers is far from a who's who of retailing." The list of retailers that have Internet sites includes J. C. Penney, Lands' End, Eddie Bauer, J. Crew, and Wal-Mart.

45. For detailed results of a survey of retailers concerning Internet shopping, see Ernst & Young, ibid., pp. 10–14.

46. See Span, Paula, "The Catalogue: 1–800–SHIRT," *Washington Post Magazine*, November 16, 1997, pp. 31–32.

47. Return levels are from Harvard Center for Textile and Apparel Research, "Improving the Performance of the Men's Dress Shirt Industry: A Channel Perspective," report on the Men's Dress Shirt Workshop, August 6–7, 1991. See also Ferguson, Tim, "Shrink Inventory? Lands' End Likes it Loose," *Wall Street Journal*, January 18, 1994, p. A17.

Subject Index

"Accurate Response" forecasting, 95
Advanced shipping notice (ASN), 81, 82, 83, 314n37, 339n6
Agreement on Textiles and Clothing (ATC), 226, 228, 230
Air-jet looms, 189, 190
Air-jet spinning, 195, 196, 199
Amalgamated Clothing and Textile Workers Union (ACTWU), 179, 180, 325n2
Amalgamated Clothing Workers of America, 30–32, 35–36, 306n27. *See also* UNITE!
American Apparel Manufacturers Association, 168, 171, 325n8
Analogy forecasting, 95
Annual Survey of Manufacturing (Bureau of the Census), 253
Apparel industry
   capital costs in, 35, 244
   channel perspective about, 10–17
   competition in, 1–20, 27, 31, 32, 165, 173, 175, 179, 225–28, 239, 240, 242, 266, 274–78
   in developing nations, 223, 224–25, 239
   expenditures in, 4
   future of, 6–8, 15–17, 264–67, 270–80
   in Great Britain, 26
   history of, 26–32, 36–38
   human resources in, 27–29, 35, 165–84, 299n4
   impact of lean retail on, 40, 76–84
   and information-integrated channels, 264–67, 270–75, 277–78, 279–80
   profitability in, 256
   regulation in, 32
   safety in, 32
   suppliers for, 244–50, 259
   and traditional retail, 42, 44
   transformation of, 1–2, 264–80
   See also Apparel-retail channel; Apparel-textile channel; *specific topic, especially* Assembly operations and Preassembly operations
Apparel Industry Partnership, 271
Apparel-retail channel, 245, 269
Apparel-textile channel, 38, 179, 187, 203, 208–13, 217–19, 279
Asia, 239, 266, 267. *See also* Southeast Asia; *specific nation*
ASN (advanced shipping notice), 81, 82, 83, 314n37, 339n6
Assembly operations
   buffers for, 167, 169, 171, 247
   capital costs for, 149, 163, 172
   and competition, 3, 5, 12–14, 173, 175, 179, 278, 279
   customization in, 164, 169, 181
   decentralization of, 162–63
   and demands of rapid replenishment, 164
   flow of goods for, 159–63
   and globalization, 5, 223, 229, 237, 238, 239, 240
   and history of apparel industry, 32
   human resources for, 168–82
   impact of lean retail on, 172–75
   and information-integrated channels, 267, 278, 279
   inspection in, 155, 322n8
   and labor costs, 12–14, 163, 164, 166–68, 172, 326n14
   and location of facilities, 149

Assembly operations *(continued)*
  for men's apparel, 116–17, 131, 152, 154, 159–63, 177, 302*n*28, 304*n*14, 324*n*10, 325*n*8
  organization of, 164
  preassembly operations to, 149–50, 158–59
  and productivity, 151, 166–68, 172
  propositions about, 12–14
  and suppliers, 245, 246–47, 250, 254
  technology in, 13, 149–50, 168
  in textile industry, 279
  and trade, 237, 238, 239, 240, 267, 326*n*11, 336*n*21
  traditional, 164
  wages in, 12–13, 168–69, 172, 181, 247, 327*n*26
  of women's apparel, 131
  See also Contracting out; Cutters/Cutting; Cycle times; Modular assembly; Offshore manufacturers; Progressive bundle system; Sewing; Sewing operators; Sourcing
ATC. *See* Agreement on Textiles and Clothing
Automated checkout counter, 60. *See also* Bar codes; Scanning systems
Automobiles, 13–14, 259–60

Bankruptcies, 47, 301*n*14, 316*n*7
Bar codes
  benefits/purposes of, 61, 69
  as building blocks of lean retail, 56, 57–62, 65–67, 69
  capital costs for, 61
  and channel coordination, 10
  for distribution, 65–67, 310*n*30
  early usage of, 10, 58–60
  and future directions, 268
  and impact of lean retail, 81, 82–83, 84
  and information-integrated channels, 268, 274
  and inventory, 61, 104, 108
  and lean retail as alternative to traditional retail, 40, 50
  and modular assembly, 175, 178
  and profitability, 166, 178
  and suppliers, 245–46, 247, 248–49, 250, 251–52, 254, 256–58, 339*n*6
  and sweatshops, 274, 346*n*38
  and textile industry, 216
Basic products
  and competition, 12–14, 15–16
  design and patterns for, 132
  and future of apparel industry, 14–15

  and inventory, 99, 106, 108, 109–10, 308*n*10, 309*n*13
  and lean retail as alternative to traditional retail, 51–52
  propositions about, 14–15
  and textile industry, 211, 214
  and trade, 230, 235, 239–40, 267
  See also Fashion triangle
"Big Four," 16, 233–35, 236, 237, 303*n*35
Bleaching, 200–201
Blending, 193–94
Boycotts, 328*n*34, 344*n*25
Brand names, 43–44, 231, 273
Bundle system, 12–13, 131, 144–45. *See also* Progressive bundle system (PBS)
Bureau of the Census, U.S., 231, 253
Bureau of Labor Statistics, U.S., 330*n*25
Bureau of Standards, U.S., 268
Buyers, 25–26, 42, 43, 308*n*3, 319*n*6, 327*n*28

CAD (Computer-Aided-Design (CAD) systems), 133–34, 148
Canada, 228, 317*n*10
Capital costs
  in apparel industry, 31, 35, 244
  for assembly operations, 149, 163, 172
  for bar code system, 61
  and inventory, 96, 123
  and preassembly operations, 142, 143, 149, 150
  and supplier practices, 244
  in textile industry, 33–35, 187, 189, 190, 192–93, 196, 199, 200, 202, 208, 211, 213, 215, 216, 225, 267, 275, 330*n*23, 338*n*4
Carding, 193–94
Caribbean Basin, 16, 223, 227–29, 234–39, 266–67, 279, 303*n*35, 304*n*12
Caribbean Basin Economic Recovery Act (1983), 237
Caribbean Basin Initiative, 234, 235, 236–37
Carrying costs, inventory, 55, 118, 119, 120, 123–24, 164, 260, 321*n*8, 321*n*12, 321*n*13
Casual clothing, 4, 151
Catalog stores, 47. *See also* Mail-order houses
Category management, 63
Census of Manufacturers, 190, 203
Chain stores, 23, 38, 50–52, 58, 74, 77, 81. *See also* Food chain stores; *specific store*
Chain-stitch sewing machines, 154–55
Channels
  definition of, 2

for industrial products, 213–16
propositions concerning, 10–17
See also Information-integrated channels; Integrated channels; *specific channel*
Child labor, 22, 32, 183, 240, 266, 270, 273, 325n5, 346n38
China, People's Republic of
consumers in, 2
economic development in, 223, 224
and future/viability of apparel industry, 7, 15, 16
and globalization, 223, 224, 226–27, 230, 233, 234, 236, 237, 239, 240
and sourcing decisions, 17
and trade, 15, 16, 223, 226–27, 230, 233, 234, 236, 237, 239, 240, 264, 266, 335n19
and viability of textile industry, 205, 206, 215
wages in, 7, 16
See also "Big Four"
CIO (Congress of Industrial Organizations), 35–36
Cleaning, for spinning, 193–94
Clinton Administration, 182
Clothing Manufacturers Association, 325n2
Coefficient of variation, 96, 101, 113, 117, 120, 122–23
Combing, 194
Commerce Department, U.S., 253, 299n3
Commodity dealers, rise of, 23
Compensation. *See* Wages
Competition
in apparel industry, 1–20, 27, 31, 32, 165, 173, 175, 179, 225–28, 239, 240, 242, 266, 274–78
and assembly operations, 3, 5, 12–14, 173, 175, 179, 278, 279
and bundle system, 12–13, 27
and customization, 278
and cycle times, 277–78
and delivery time, 164
and distribution, 1, 8, 277
and employment, 5, 6, 7
and fashion triangle, 12–16
and forecasting, 11, 278
future directions of, 264, 270, 274–79
and globalization, 5–6, 223, 225–28, 239, 240, 242
and human resources, 165, 173, 175, 179
and impact of lean retail, 71, 72–76, 165, 173
and information systems, 1, 3, 8, 14–15

and information-integrated channels, 264, 266, 270, 271, 274–79
and inventory, 8, 126, 277–78, 316n5
and labor costs, 7, 8, 12–14, 275
and management practices, 16
and product proliferation, 278, 309n14
and productivity, 13, 275
and public policy implications, 274–79
and quality, 131
in retail sector, 275–77, 311n36, 317n10
and retail-apparel-textile channel, 3, 212
and sourcing, 16
and suppliers, 244, 245, 261, 275
and sweatshops, 271
and technology, 1, 5
in textile industry, 15–16, 36, 202, 212, 217, 219, 225–28, 239, 240, 242, 245, 274–75, 278–79
and trade, 5–6, 239, 240, 266
and traditional retailing, 47
Compustat database (Standard & Poor's), 315–16n4
Computer industry, 260–61, 341n28
Computer systems
and assembly operations, 149–50
and building blocks of lean retail, 56, 57, 66, 67
and competition, 1
and distribution, 66, 67
and industrial revolution, 22
and information-integrated channels, 268
and inventory, 117, 123, 126
and preassembly operations, 129–30, 133–34, 136–38, 140, 141–43, 147–48, 149, 150
supplier performance, 260
in textile industry, 211, 218
Computer-Aided-Design (CAD) systems, 133–34, 148
Consolidators, 313n26
Consumers, 2, 47, 270, 271, 338n1
Consumers' League, 270, 271
Continuous Product Replenishment (CPR). *See* Vendor-managed inventory
Continuous production, 192, 202, 215
Continuous Replenishment Programs (CRP). *See* Vendor-managed inventory
Contracting, electronic, 312n17
Contracting out
of assembly operations, 130–31, 152, 163
See also Offshore manufacturers; Sourcing
Contractors/subcontractors, 26–27, 30, 271, 325n5, 328n34, 344n25

Conveyer systems, 66, 67, 246, 314*n*33, 314*n*34
Cotton Textile Work Assignment Board, 188
Council of Economic Advisors, 227, 228
Council on Economic Priorities, 273
Cross-docking facility, 64–66, 82, 314*n*30
Customization
　and assembly operations, 164, 169, 181
　and competition, 278
　and human resources, 169, 181
　and information-integrated channels, 278
　and labor costs, 169
　mass, 130, 145–49, 164, 169, 181, 278, 322–23*n*11, 323*n*12, 323*n*13
　and preassembly operations, 130, 145–49
Cutters/Cutting
　and assembly operations, 157, 158, 159, 324*n*9
　automated, 129, 140, 141–43, 149, 150
　errors in, 157
　and globalization, 223, 225, 239
　and history of apparel industry, 26, 30–31
　and human resources, 172, 179, 182, 302*n*28, 305*n*23
　and information systems, 179
　labor organization of, 30–31, 182
　and mass customization, 146–47, 149
　and operating profits, 179
　as preassembly operation, 129, 131, 140–44, 146–47, 149, 150, 158, 159, 322*n*6
　sourcing of, 172
　and trade, 267
C_v. *See* Coefficient of variation
Cycle stock, 100–101
Cycle times
　and assembly operations, 149, 164, 173, 181, 247
　challenges of, 9
　and competition, 277–78
　and globalization, 223, 237, 239
　and human resources, 173, 181
　and information-integrated channels, 266, 267–70, 277–78
　macroeconomic implications of, 267–70
　and management practices, 259–60
　and manufacturers' inventory, 108, 109, 117, 119, 123–27
　for mass customization, 164
　and preassembly to assembly operations, 149
　and suppliers, 247–48, 255–56, 258

　in textile industry, 214, 216
　and trade, 237, 239, 266, 267
Cyclicality, and demand forecasting, 92–93

DAMA (Demand Activated Manufacturing Architecture), 218
Data processing, 62–63, 67, 315–16*n*4. *See also* Information systems
Demand Activated Manufacturing Architecture. *See* DAMA
Demand. *See* Forecasting, demand; Uncertainty, demand
Demand variability, 100, 109–19, 320*n*2, 321*n*8
Department stores
　challenges facing, 310*n*22
　competition for, 308*n*11, 317*n*10
　decline in number of, 46, 47, 310*n*24
　design and patterns from, 132
　distribution for, 64–65, 68–69
　employment in, 304*n*9
　family-owned, 75, 310*n*24
　and history of retail, 23, 24–25
　impact of lean retail on, 72–73, 74, 75, 77–78
　and information systems, 244
　and integration among apparel, retail, and textile industries, 38
　lean retail as alternative for, 52–54
　and overstoring of America, 46
　regional, 75
　replenishment in, 77–78
　and retail challenge, 40
　and textile industry, 214
　in traditional retail, 23, 24–25, 46, 47, 52–54
　See also specific store
Design, apparel, 132–34, 149, 238, 267, 322*n*3. *See also* Patterns
Desizing, 200–201
Developing nations
　apparel industry in, 223, 224–25, 239
　and assembly operations, 131, 163
　and globalization, 223, 224–25, 239
　industrialization of, 222, 224, 335*n*11
　and information-integrated channels, 266, 271, 272–73
　and preassembly operations, 138–39
　sweatshops in, 271, 272–73
　textile industry in, 186, 205, 223, 224–25, 239
　and trade, 239, 266
　wages in, 266

See also Globalization; Offshore manufacturers; Sourcing; *specific nation*
Display/hangers, 69–70, 79, 80, 84, 315n40
Distribution
 in apparel industry, 8, 11–12, 179, 181, 182, 244
 and assembly operations, 179, 181
 auditing of, 313–14n30
 automated, 10
 of automobiles, 259–60
 bar codes for, 65–67, 310n30
 as building block of lean retail, 56, 57, 63–69
 and channel coordination, 10
 and competition, 1, 8, 277
 consolidators for, 313n26
 for department stores, 64–65, 68–69
 history of, 22, 23–24
 and human resources, 63–64, 179, 181, 182
 impact of lean retail on, 75, 76–77, 82
 and information systems, 1, 48–54, 314n37
 and information-integrated channels, 263, 267, 268, 277
 and Internet, 277
 and inventory, 88
 and labor unions, 182
 lean retail as alternative in, 40, 48–54
 macroeconomic implications of, 268
 and management practices, 260–61
 for mass merchant, 65
 and profitability, 179, 311n2
 in retail sector, 25–26, 68–69, 75, 277
 and retail-apparel-textile channel, 10–11
 to sales floor, 68–69, 310n34
 scanning for, 65–66, 67, 68, 310n30
 and size of distribution center, 63
 and standardization, 67–68
 and suppliers, 243–44, 246, 248, 249, 259–60, 261
 technology for, 66–68, 314n32, 314n33, 314n34
 in textile industry, 215, 216
 and trade, 238, 239, 267
 for traditional retail, 42, 68, 310n30
 warehousing compared with, 63
 wholesale-jobber, 23–24, 25
 See also Advanced shipping notice (ASN); Flow of goods
Duke University, 271
Dyeing, 154, 189, 197, 200–201, 209, 214

Eastern Europe, 223, 238, 240, 266, 267
Economic Report of the President (1988), 269
Economic Report of the President (1997), 265
Economics, 264–70
Economies of scale, 7, 33–35, 36, 49, 51, 53, 210
EDI (electronic data interchange)
 benefits/purposes of, 62
 as building block of lean retail, 62–63, 70
 and channel coordination, 10
 early usage of, 62
 failure to comply with, 70
 and future of apparel industry, 8
 and impact of lean retail, 71, 79, 80, 81–82, 83, 314–15n39
 and inventory, 108
 and lead times, 178
 and lean retail as alternative to traditional retail, 50, 51
 and modular assembly, 175, 178
 and profitability, 178
 and suppliers, 246, 247, 248, 249, 250, 251–52, 254, 256–58, 339n6
 in textile industry, 214, 216
Efficient Consumer Response Program, 312n13
Electronic contracting, 312n17
Electronic data interchange. *See* EDI
Embroidery machines, 192
Employment
 in apparel industry, 5, 6, 7, 151, 157, 241–42, 265–66, 270–75, 279–80, 300n10, 301n17, 304n9, 324n7, 344n23
 and competition, 5, 6, 7
 and future directions, 266, 270–75, 279–80
 and globalization, 241–42
 and technology, 5
 in textile industry, 5, 36, 205–10, 215, 241–42, 265, 266, 274–75, 279–80, 328n2, 329n14
Energy Department, U.S., 218
Equipment. *See* Machinery/equipment; *specific equipment*
Europe, 223, 238, 239, 240, 266, 267
European Union, 273
Exchange rates, 7, 232
Expenditures, 4, 47

Fair Labor Standards Act (1938), 183, 270, 271, 344n22
Fall River (Massachusetts) strike (1904), 188

Family labor, 22, 328*n*3
Fashion products
  and competition, 278
  and future of apparel industry, 14–15, 303*n*33
  and inventory, 106, 125
  propositions about, 14–15
  and retail-apparel-textile channel, 211, 212
  sourcing for, 125
  and textile industry, 211, 212, 218
  and trade, 239, 267
  See also Fashion triangle
Fashion triangle
  and competition, 12–16
  components of, 8–9
  and future directions, 279
  and lean retail as alternative to traditional retail, 52
  and trade, 235, 239–40
  and traditional retailing, 45
  See also Basic products; Fashion product; Fashion-basic products
Fashion-basic products
  and competition, 12–14, 15–16
  design and patterns for, 132
  and future of apparel industry, 14–15
  and inventory, 99, 106
  propositions about, 14
  and textile industry, 214
  and trade, 230, 235, 239–40, 267
  See also Fashion triangle
Federal Reserve Bank of New York, 265
Felling operations, 323*n*3
Financial performance
  of suppliers, 250, 251, 256–58
  See also Profitability
Finished goods inventory
  carrying costs of, 277
  and demands of rapid replenishment, 164
  and inventory models, 101, 320*n*4, 320*n*20
  and manufacturers' inventory, 108, 110, 112, 115, 117, 119, 123, 125–26, 320*n*4, 320*n*20
  and preassembly to assembly operations, 149
  and supplier performance, 250, 256, 259
  traditional, 210
Finishing operations
  and competition, 275, 278
  and economic viability of textile industry, 208, 209 211, 213, 214
  employment in, 302*n*28

  and globalization, 223, 225, 239
  historical background of, 33–34
  and information systems, 245
  and information-integrated channels, 267, 275, 278
  and location of facilities, 149
  and preassembly to assembly operations, 149
  steps in, 199–202
  and supplier practices, 245
  and technology, 189
  and trade, 266
Flow of goods
  and assembly operations, 159–63
  and building blocks of lean retail, 64–66
  and manufacturers' inventory, 116–17, 121–22
Food chain stores, 58–60, 302*n*24, 309*n*16, 312*n*11, 312*n*13
Forecasting, demand
  "Accurate Response," 95
  by analogy, 95
  building, 93–94
  caveats about, 90–92
  challenges of, 9, 88, 89
  and channel propositions, 11
  and competition, 11, 278
  and demand data, 90–91
  and historical data, 90, 92–93, 318*n*5
  and information-integrated channels, 278
  and management practices, 103, 260
  for new products, 95–96
  and "point forecast," 91–92
  probabilistic, 91–92, 95
  and product proliferation, 95–96
  for products with selling history, 90–94
  purpose of, 91
  and retail-apparel-textile channel, 213
  and sales data, 90, 106
  and supplier practices, 244–45
  and uncertainty, 92, 94, 95–96, 319*n*9
Fusing, 322*n*9

General Agreement on Tariffs and Trade (GATT), 6, 15, 222, 223, 226, 227, 264
  Uruguay Round of, 6, 228–30, 264
General stores, 23–26
Gerbers automated cutting equipment, 129, 141–42, 322*n*5
Germany, 223
Globalization
  in apparel industry, 221–42, 304*n*12, 308*n*9

and competition, 5–6, 223, 225–28, 239, 240, 242
  effects on U.S. of, 5–6
  and employment, 241–42
  and labor costs, 205, 223, 225, 238, 240
  and lean retail, 221, 234, 235, 237
  and quality, 225
  of textile industry, 204–6, 221–42
  See also Developing nations; Offshore manufacturers; Sourcing; Trade
The Grange (farmers' organization), 25
Great Britain
  apparel industry in, 26
  Industrial Revolution in, 224
  textile industry in, 21, 22, 32–33, 185, 186
Greige goods, 200, 204, 214, 215, 278, 333n22
Grocery Industry Ad Hoc Committee on Universal Product Coding, 59–60

Hangers, items on, 69–70, 79, 80, 315n40
Harmonized Tariff Schedule of the United States (HTSUS), 229, 266, 336n27, 337n42
HCTAR survey
  and economic viability of textile industry, 214
  and EDI, 63
  and human resources in apparel industry, 168, 171, 173, 175, 177, 178
  and impact of lean retail, 71, 77, 80
  and inventory, 105, 123
  and modular assembly, 168, 171, 173, 175, 177, 178
  and preassembly operations, 138, 143
  and supplier performance, 252, 253, 257–58
  and supplier practices, 244, 245, 247, 248, 339n6
  and team-based assembly operations, 168, 171, 173, 175, 177–78
  and trade, 337n40, 338n43
Historical data, 90, 92–93, 318n5, 320n2
Home furnishings, 5, 24, 37, 203, 208, 210, 214–16, 229
Home as workplace, 26–32, 224–25, 304n12, 325n5
Hong Kong, 7, 16, 230, 233, 234–35, 266, 301n19. *See also* "Big Four"
"Hot cargo" provisions, 270
Household products, 239, 278
HTSUS. *See* Harmonized Tariff Schedule of the United States

Human resources
  in apparel industry, 27–29, 35, 165–84, 299n4
  for assembly operations, 168–82, 324–25n2
  and competition, 165, 173, 175, 179
  and distribution, 63–64, 179, 181, 182
  and integration among apparel, retail, and textile industries, 38
  and new strategic workers, 182
  and PBS, 27–29
  and supplier practices, 246
  in textile industry, 35–36, 186, 216
  See also Productivity; Sweatshops

Immigrants, 30, 183, 184, 241, 265, 266, 270, 271, 305n18, 328n36, 328n36
Impannatore, 217–18
Imports/exports
  and apparel industry, 5–6, 16, 32, 225–28, 229, 231, 233–34, 240, 241, 300n12, 300–301n 13, 334n6
  and assembly operations, 151
  and competition, 5–6
  countries of origin of, 233–34, 303n35
  and definition of import penetration, 300n12
  and globalization, 225–28, 229, 231, 233–34, 240, 241
  product composition of, 231
  shifting flow of U.S., 222
  and textile industry, 5–6, 36, 191–92, 206, 209, 219, 225–28, 229, 231, 233–34, 240, 241, 275, 279
India, 17, 224
Industrial Commission, 183
Industrial products, in textile industry, 37, 203, 205, 208–10, 213–16, 219, 239, 278–79
Industrial Revolution, 32, 33–34, 186, 224
Information systems
  in apparel industry, 8, 11–12, 166, 175–77, 178–79, 181, 182, 244, 245
  and apparel-textile relationship, 38, 187
  and assembly operations, 175–77, 178–79, 181
  as basis of lean retail, 40, 48–54
  and building blocks of lean retail, 55–56
  and competition, 1, 3, 8, 14–15
  and cutting, 179
  and distribution, 1, 48–54, 314n37
  growing adoption of, 79–84, 175

Information systems *(continued)*
  and human resources, 166, 175–77, 178–79, 181, 182
  and impact of lean retail, 79–84
  and Industrial Revolution, 22
  and inventory, 8, 48–54, 63, 104, 340n18
  and lead times, 178, 218
  and management practices, 258–61
  and mass merchandising, 49–50
  performance impact of, 3
  and preassembly operations, 129–30, 133, 134
  and profitability, 166, 178–79
  and retail sector, 11–12, 13, 311n38
  and retail-apparel-textile channel, 10–11, 38, 211, 212
  for sewing, 129–30, 179
  and standardization, 302n25
  and suppliers, 1, 243–50, 253, 255–56
  in textile industry, 36, 211, 212, 214–18, 245
  for traditional manufacturers, 107
  See also Bar codes; Data processing; Scanning systems
Information-integrated channels
  and apparel industry, 264–67, 270–75, 277–78, 279–80
  and competition, 264, 266, 270, 271, 274–79
  and future directions, 263–80
  and inventory, 269, 270, 277–78, 280
  and lean retail, 263–64, 266, 269, 274, 275–78, 279
  macroeconomic implications of, 267–70
  and manufacturing, 263–80
  and public policy implications, 263–80
  and retail sector, 263–80
  and retail-apparel channel, 269
  and sourcing, 266, 267, 278
  and technology, 265, 268, 274, 275, 276, 280
  and textile industry, 264–67, 274–75, 278–80
  and trade, 264–67
  and wages, 264, 265–66, 267, 270–74, 275
Injuries, from PBS, 173, 179–80
Inspection, 149, 155, 322n8
Integrated channels
  as challenge, 216–19
  of information systems and manufacturing practices, 258–61, 341n28
  and suppliers, 243–62
  and trade, 234

  See also Information-integrated channels; *specific channels*
Interfaith Center on Corporate Responsibility, 271
International Brotherhood of Teamsters, 182
International Labour Office (ILO), 273
International Ladies' Garment Workers Union (ILGWU), 30–32, 183–84, 305–6n26
  See also UNITE!
International operations. *See* Developing nations; Globalization; Offshore manufacturers; Sourcing
International Program for the Elimination of Child Labor, 273
International Trade Administration, 13
International Trade Commission, U.S., 229, 266, 337n42
Internet, 218, 276–77, 346n44
Inventory
  in apparel industry, 8, 29, 277–78
  and bar codes, 61, 104, 108
  and basic products, 99, 106, 108, 109–10, 308n10, 309n13
  and capital costs, 96, 123
  carrying costs of, 55, 118, 119, 120, 123–24, 164, 260, 321n8, 321n12, 321n13
  case studies about, 115–26
  challenges of, 41, 88
  and competition, 8, 126, 277–78, 316n5
  and computer systems, 117, 123, 126
  and cycle time, 108, 109, 117, 119, 123–27
  and demand uncertainty, 92, 94, 95–96, 101, 109, 120
  and demand variability, 100, 109–19
  determining optimal allocations for, 123–26
  errors in, 97–98
  and flow of goods, 116–17, 121–22
  in food chains, 60
  and future directions, 8, 269, 270, 280
  goal of, 87
  impact of lean retail on, 107, 316n5
  and information systems, 8, 48–54, 63, 104, 340n18
  and information-integrated channels, 269, 270, 277–78, 280
  and lead times, 100–103, 106, 108–10, 112, 119, 120, 124, 125
  and lean retail as alternative to traditional retail, 48–54

in lean retail environment, 105–6
macroeconomic implications of, 267–70
for mail-order houses, 90
for manufacturers, 107–27, 320n2, 320n4, 320–21n6, 320n20, 321n7, 321n13
and multiple plants, 119–26
and nonreplenishables, 97–99
and offshore manufacturers, 109
periodic versus continuous review of, 103–4, 308n4, 320n17
and product availability, 96, 103
and product proliferation, 87, 95–96, 114–15, 340n18
and product variability, 109–15
and production planning, 119–26
and production process, 116–18
and profitability, 256, 321n10
and replenishables, 96, 97–98, 101–3, 105–6, 107, 108–9, 112
for retail sector, 41, 87–106, 308n4, 308n10, 319–20n17
and retail-apparel-textile channel, 38
and sales ratios, 340n15
and setting levels in store, 96–105
and sourcing, 120–26
steps in, 88
of suppliers, 244–45, 250–61, 269, 340n15, 340n18
and technology, 253–56, 340n18
in textile industry, 214, 215–16
traditional policy for, 101–3, 107
in traditional retail, 42, 44, 48, 68, 91, 101–3, 120, 122
of unwanted products, 44
vendor-managed, 63, 104–5
See also Forecasting, demand; *type of inventory*
Inventory model
for nonreplenishable products, 98–99
(R, s, S), 101–3, 104, 320n4
for replenishable products, 99–103
Italian Prato region, 217–18
Italy, 217–18, 223

Japan, 223, 224, 226, 237, 239, 240, 266, 267
Job classifications, in textile industry, 189–90, 327n27
Jobber-contractors, 26–27, 30
Jobbers, 26, 31, 131, 234, 238, 240, 271, 328n34, 344n25
Just-in-time inventory, 269

Knitted goods, 143, 144, 149–50, 199, 201, 210, 230, 278
Knitting, 196–99, 208, 209, 239, 275
Knitting machines, 34, 198–99
Knitting mills, 209
Knockoffs, 322n3
Korea, 16, 230, 233, 240, 266, 267, 301n19. *See also* "Big Four"

Labor costs
in apparel industry, 7, 16, 27, 29, 30, 31–32, 166–68, 169, 172, 223, 225, 301n18, 324n1
and assembly operations, 12–14, 163, 164, 166–68, 172, 326n14
and bar codes, 58
and building blocks of lean retail, 58, 60
and competition, 7, 8, 12–14, 275
and customization, 169
and future directions, 7, 279
and globalization, 205, 223, 225, 238, 240
and human resources, 166–68, 169, 172
and information-integrated channel, 266, 267, 275, 279
and labor unions, 30
and offshore sourcing, 16
propositions about, 12–14
standardization of, 306n27
in textile industry, 36, 186, 205, 223, 225, 332–33n17
and trade, 36, 186, 205, 223, 225, 238, 240, 266, 267
Labor Department, U.S., 271, 273, 325n2
Labor standards, 240, 266, 270–74. *See also* Sweatshops
Labor unions
and apparel industry, 27, 29–32, 182
and cutting, 182
decline of, 184
and distribution workers, 182
and labor standards, 270, 273, 274
and lean retail, 274
and manufacturers, 31, 328n34
and standardization, 31, 306n27
and sweatshops, 183, 270, 273, 274
and textile industry, 35–36, 188, 190
See also specific organization
Laser technology, 59, 143–44. *See also* Scanning systems
Lead times
and competition, 177
and human resources, 177, 178

Lead times *(continued)*
  and information systems, 178, 218
  and inventory, 100–103, 106, 108–10, 112, 119, 120, 124, 125
  and retail-apparel-textile channel, 211–12
  and supplier performance, 251–52, 259
  and team-based assembly operations, 177, 178
  and textile industry, 210, 211–12, 218, 333n23
  and trade, 234–35
Lean retail/world
  as alternative to traditional retail, 48–54
  in apparel industry, 76–84
  building blocks of, 55–70
  and buyers, 26
  characteristics of, 3, 49–70
  and future directions, 263–64, 269, 275–77, 279
  and globalization, 221, 234, 235, 237
  and human resources, 165, 167, 172–79
  impact of, 3, 71–85, 211, 216, 259–60, 310n28
  and information-integrated channels, 263–64, 266, 269, 274, 275–78, 279
  and integration, 243–62
  and inventory, 105–6, 277–78
  and management practices, 258, 261
  manufacturer's dilemma with, 126–27
  and modular assembly, 172–79
  and performance among retailers, 72–76
  and productivity, 167
  and retail-apparel-textile channel, 211
  and sourcing, 235
  suppliers in, 71–72, 77–79, 82, 84–85, 243–62, 311n39, 317n20
  and sweatshops, 274
  in textile industry, 3, 187, 202, 211, 216, 217
  and trade, 234, 237, 266
  traditional versus, 39–48
Lockstitch sewing machines, 153–54
Long-Term Arrangement Regarding Trade in Cotton Textiles, 226
Longitudinal Research Database (LRD), 253
Looms, 189, 190, 198–99, 328n5, 329n11

Machinery/equipment
  for textile industry, 185–86, 189, 190–92, 198–99, 215, 307n34, 328n5.
  See also specific type of machinery
Macroeconomics, 267–70

Mail-order houses, 23, 24, 25, 38, 90, 277, 318n4
Management, category, 63
Management practices, 3, 11–12, 16, 258–61, 263, 268. *See also specific practice*
Manufacturers' coupons, 60
Manufacturers/manufacturing
  changing functions of, 108
  dilemma of, 126–27
  and history of apparel industry, 26–32
  and history of textile industry, 34
  impact of lean retail on, 84–85, 108, 145, 149
  inside, 26, 27
  integration of information systems and, 258–61
  inventory for, 107–27, 320n2, 320n4, 320–21n6, 320n20, 321n7, 321n13
  and labor standards, 271
  and labor unions, 31, 328n34
  and "packagers," 234
  propositions about, 11–12
  transformation of, 263–80
  See also Offshore manufacturers; Suppliers
Markdowns, 8, 55, 87, 97, 123, 256, 258, 275, 277, 310n28, 321n8, 340n20
Markers, 131, 134–39, 141, 146, 149, 150, 159
Mass customization, 130, 145–49, 164, 169, 181, 278, 322–23n11, 323n12, 323n13
Mass merchandisers
  distribution for, 65
  history of, 23–26
  impact of lean retail on, 72–73, 77
  and information systems, 49–50, 244
  replenishment of, 77
  and textile industry, 214
  and trade, 238
  and traditional retailing, 47
  See also specific merchant
Men's apparel
  assembly of, 116–17, 131, 152, 154, 159–63, 177, 302n28, 304n14, 324n10, 325n8
  and future of apparel industry, 7–8
  and history of apparel industry, 29, 30, 306n29
  and human resources, 166, 167, 177, 301n17
  inventory for, 115–19
  labor costs of, 301n17, 324n1
  and labor unions, 30
  preassembly of, 141, 144–45, 302n28

and productivity, 167
profitability in, 256
and retail-apparel-textile channel, 210
shirts as, 7–8, 29, 45, 154, 159–63, 166, 192, 256, 301n18, 302n28, 309n12, 324n10
suits as, 141, 144–45, 163, 301n18, 306n27
and textile industry, 192
and trade, 300–301n13, 336n25
and traditional retailing, 45
Merchandisers/merchandising
impact of lean retail on, 72, 314n38
and information systems, 244, 311n38
and lean retail as alternative, 53
mass, 23–26, 47, 49–50, 65, 72–73, 77, 214, 238, 244
and retail-apparel-textile integration, 38
and textile industry, 214
and trade, 238
and traditional retail, 43, 53
Merchants Ladies Garment Association, Inc., 305–6n26
Mexico
and future directions, 7, 266, 267, 279
and globalization, 223, 227–29, 233–39
retail space in, 47
and trade, 15, 16, 223, 227–29, 233–39, 303n35, 336n28, 337n42
and viability of apparel industry, 15, 16
wages in, 7, 301n19
MFA. *See* Multi-Fiber Arrangement
MIT Commission on Industrial Productivity, 14
Modular assembly, 162, 216, 246–47, 250, 278, 325n6, 326n10, 326n14, 338n4, 339n6
benefits of, 172–75
and information systems, 175–77
in lean retail, 172–79
PBS compared with, 168–72, 174–75, 177–78, 179–80, 181, 326n19
performance effects of, 175–79, 254, 256–58, 326n19
and wages/compensation, 172, 247
Multi-Fiber Arrangement (MFA), 5–6, 36, 222–23, 226–27, 228–30, 240–42, 335n16
Multiple plants, 119–26, 214, 324n9

NAFTA. *See* North American Free Trade Agreement
National Bureau of Economic Research, 331n6

National Consumers League, 270, 271
National Drug Code, 59
National Labor Committee, 345n29
National Labor Relations Act, 328n34, 344n25
National Museum of American History (Smithsonian Institution), 328n37
National Recovery Administration, 188
National Retail Federation (NRF), 182, 276
National Sourcing Data Base (NSDB), 218
"New international economics," 264–67
New products, forecasting demand for, 95–96
New strategic workers, 182
New York City, 14, 15, 204, 217, 271, 305n20, 333–34n31, 344n23
"News-vendor" problem, 98
Nonreplenishable products, inventory models for, 97–99
North Africa, 223, 240, 266, 267
North American Free Trade Agreement (NAFTA), 16, 223, 228–30, 237, 264, 303n35, 336n28, 337n42
North American Industry Classification System, 331n3

Occupational Safety and Health Administration (OSHA), 34
Office of Technology Assessment, U.S., 210
Offshore manufacturers
and future of apparel industry, 7
and globalization, 229
and human resources, 172
and inventory, 109
and labor costs, 16
and retail-apparel-textile channel, 213
and sweatshops, 274
and team-based assembly operations, 172
and traditional retail, 44
and U.S. trade policies, 326n11
See also Developing nations; Sourcing; *specific nation*
"One-price" policy, 39, 40
"One-stop" shopping, 59, 234
Open-end spinning, 189, 195, 199, 329n11
Operating profits, 177, 178–79
Operational performance, of suppliers, 250–56
Order-fulfillment rate, 112, 116, 117, 120, 123
Out-of-stock items, 60
Over-edge sewing machines, 155–56
Overcapacity, in retail sector, 46–48, 310n28

Overlocking sewing machines, 155–56
Overstocking of inventory, 97–98, 101
Overstoring of America, 44, 46–48, 309n16, 309n17, 309n18, 309–10n21, 310n28

Pacific Rim countries, 125. *See also* Developing nations; *specific nation*
Packagers, 234–35, 279
Packaging, 149, 239
Pakistan, 273
Patterns, 130, 131–34, 146, 148. *See also* Markers; Sewing
PBS. *See* Progressive bundle system
Performance
   financial, 250, 251, 256–58
   and innovations, 13
   and lean retail, 72–76
   and managerial practices, 258–61
   and modular assembly, 175–79, 254, 256–58, 326n19
   operational, 250–56
   of suppliers, 250–61, 340–41n22
   traditional, 3
   in U.S. textile industry, 206–8
"Point forecast," 91–92
Point-of-sales (POS) information
   and bar codes, 56, 57, 61
   and building blocks of lean retail, 56, 57, 61, 62, 70
   and competition, 1, 275, 278
   and demand forecasting, 106
   and future directions, 275, 278, 280
   and impact of lean retail, 82
   and information-integrated channels, 275, 278, 280
   and inventory, 106, 112, 115
   and lean retail as alternative to traditional retail, 49–54
   and modular assembly, 172
   and standardization, 70
Pooling, 113, 319n9, 320n20
Power looms, 32–33, 185, 198
Prato textile region (Italy), 217
Preassembly operations
   to assembly operations, 149–50, 158–59
   average time necessary for, 150
   and bundling the parts, 131, 144–45
   as capital intensive, 142, 143, 149, 150
   centralization of, 149–50
   and computers, 129–30, 133–34, 136–38, 140, 141–43, 147–48, 149, 150
   and customization, 130, 145–49
   and demand uncertainty, 130

   design and patterns for, 130, 132–34, 146, 148
   and fusing, 322n9
   imperfection of, 157
   and information systems, 129–30, 133, 134
   and location of facilities, 149
   markers in, 131, 134–39, 141, 146, 149, 150, 159
   and product proliferation, 149
   and quality, 131, 139, 141
   and scanning, 133, 147, 148–49
   and sourcing alternatives, 130, 138–39
   spreading as, 131, 139–40, 149, 157, 159
   and trade, 239
   See also Cutters/Cutting
Pressing machines, 26
Pricing, 11, 69, 79, 241, 269–70, 312n9, 314–15n39, 338n1, 343–44n19
Private labels, 43–44, 129, 132, 238, 308n7
Probabilistic forecasting, 91–92, 95
Product development, 215
Product labeling, 40
Product life cycle, 87. *See also* Seasonality
Product proliferation
   challenges of, 8, 9, 40–41
   and competition, 278, 309n14
   and forecasting, 95–96
   and globalization, 221
   and history of apparel industry, 31
   impact on manufacturers of, 149
   and inventory, 87, 95–96, 114–15, 340n18
   and lean retail as alternative, 52–54
   and preassembly operations, 149
   and retail-apparel-textile integration, 38
   and sourcing, 17
   and supplier performance, 252–53
   in textile industry, 36, 202, 214, 215, 278
   and traditional retail, 39, 44, 45–46, 47–48, 52–54
   for women's apparel, 301n21
   See also Fashion triangle
Product variability, 109–15, 326n19
Production planning, 9, 119–26, 320n2, 320–21n6
Production processes, 38, 116–18, 188–89
Productivity
   and assembly operations, 151, 166–68, 172
   and building blocks of lean retail, 59, 60
   and competition, 13, 275
   in food stores, 302n24

and future directions, 280
and history of apparel industry, 27, 29
and history of textile industry, 34, 35–36
and human resources, 166–68, 172, 300n10
and information-integrated channels, 275, 280
and technology, 12–13
in textile industry, 187, 189, 190, 191, 205, 206–8, 219, 332n13, 332n14, 332n15, 332–33n17
traditional ways to increase, 166
in U.S. textile industry, 206–8
and wages, 12
See also Performance
Products
"churning" of, 46
See also type of product
Profitability
in apparel industry, 256
and bar codes, 166, 178
and distribution, 179, 311n2
and human resources i, 166
and inventory, 256, 321n10
operating, 177, 178–79
and supplier performance, 251, 256–58, 340–41n22
and technology, 257
Progressive bundle system (PBS)
and competition, 278
and customization, 147
and demands of rapid replenishment, 164
dominance of, 171
and economic viability of textile industry, 216
efficiency of, 165
and future directions, 278
and history of apparel industry, 27–29
and human resources, 165, 166, 167, 168–72, 173, 174–75, 177–78, 179–80, 181
injuries from, 173, 179–80
and Levi Strauss-UNITE! partnership, 179–80, 181
modular assembly compared with, 168–72, 173, 174–75, 177–78, 179–80, 181, 326n19
and productivity, 166, 167
and sewing operations, 159, 160, 166, 167
and suppliers, 248
and team-based assembly, 168–72, 173, 174–75, 177–78, 179–80, 181
throughput time for, 177–78, 338n4

Project 2000 (San Francisco, California), 346n40
Projectile looms, 198
Public policy, future directions of, 263–80

Quality
and competition, 131
and globalization, 225
and human resources, 173
and preassembly operations, 131, 139, 141
and retail-apparel-textile channel, 212–13
in textile industry, 191, 196–97, 267
Quick Response Program, 14–15

(R, s, S) inventory model, 101–3, 104, 115, 320n4
Random fluctuation, 93
Ready-made clothing, 24, 26
"Receipt-Ready Shipments," 314n36
Regionalization of trade, 223, 237–40, 267
Regulation, 32
Replenishable products
and impact of lean retail, 76, 77–79, 82
and inventory, 96, 97–98, 99–103, 105–6
Replenishment
and assembly operations, 164
of chain stores, 77
challenges of, 164, 261
and future directions, 267, 279
and information-integrated channels, 267, 279
and management practices, 258–59, 261
and profitability, 258
in retail sector, 251–52
in textile industry, 216
and trade, 236, 237
See also Inventory; Replenishable products; *type of product*
Respiratory diseases, 192
Retail fallout, 47–48
Retail sector
challenges facing, 40–41
competition in, 275–77, 311n36, 317n10
concentration in, 75–76
and distribution, 277
and economic viability of textile industry, 213–16
expansion/overcapacity in, 46–48, 309n16, 309n17, 309n18, 309–10n21, 310n28
future directions of, 275–77, 279
history of, 23–26, 36–38

Retail sector *(continued)*
  and information systems, 11–12, 13
  and information-integrated channels, 263–80
  and Internet, 276–77
  inventory for, 41, 87–106, 308*n*4, 308*n*10, 319–20*n*17
  keys to effective, 55
  replenishment performance in, 251–52
  structural changes in, 4–5
  suppliers for, 275
  and sweatshops, 274
  and technology, 268, 276
  and trade, 238
  transformation of, 3–6, 11, 13, 263–80
  wages in, 304*n*9
  See also Lean retail/world; Mass merchandisers; Retail-apparel-textile channel; Retail-textile channel; Traditional retail
Retail-apparel-textile channel
  and competition, 3, 212
  definition of, 2
  distribution in, 10–11
  and economic viability of textiles, 203, 208, 210–13
  and fashion triangle, 211, 212
  and forecasting, 213
  future directions of, 279–80
  history of, 36–38
  and human resources, 38
  and information systems, 10–11, 38, 211, 212
  and inventory, 38
  and lead times, 211–12
  and lean retail, 211
  and offshore manufacturers, 213
  and operating costs, 213
  propositions about, 10–17
  relationships within, 2–3, 10–11
  and trade, 16
Retail-textile channel, 203, 208, 209, 210, 213–16, 219
Returns, 277, 318*n*4
Ring spinning, 189, 195, 329*n*11
Robots, 130, 193

Safety issues, 32, 173
Safety stock, 100–101, 102
Sales, 41, 340*n*15. *See also* Point-of-sales (POS) information
Sales floor, distribution center to, 68–69, 310*n*34

SAM (Standard Allocated Minutes), 28, 167, 325*n*3
Scanning systems
  and building blocks of lean retail, 57, 60, 61–62, 65–66, 67, 68
  and distribution, 65–66, 67, 68, 310*n*30
  errors in, 88
  and inventory, 88
  and lean retail as alternative to traditional retail, 40, 51, 52
  and preassembly operations, 133, 147, 148–49
  and supplier practices, 246, 248
  See also ASN; Bar codes; EDI; Shipping container markers
Scientific management, 28, 306*n*29
SCM. *See* Shipping container markers
Seasonality, 92, 93, 112, 239
Sewing, 12–13, 152–63, 164, 302*n*28, 323*n*3, 326*n*19
  automated, 130, 149–50, 299*n*3, 321–22*n*1
  and capital costs, 150
  and competition, 13
  and globalization, 225, 238, 240, 304*n*12
  information systems for, 129–30
  and information-integrated channels, 266, 267, 279
  and location of facilities, 149
  and mass customization, 147
  and operating profits, 179
  and preassembly operations, 145, 147, 150
  productivity in, 166–68
  reasons for, 152
  in textile industry, 279
  and trade, 238, 240, 267
  See also Sewing machines; Sewing operators
Sewing machines, 26, 28, 152, 153–56, 157, 163, 225, 246, 323*n*3, 324*n*6, 324*n*8
Sewing operators
  and bundling, 145
  and human resources, 169, 172, 179–80, 324–25*n*2
  injuries among, 173, 179–80
  operations of, 156–57, 159, 304*n*14
  and production standards, 152–53
  and sewing machines, 152–53, 154
  team-based, 162, 164, 172
  wages for, 159, 169, 172, 305*n*23

Subject Index 361

Shipping container markers (SCMs)
  and building blocks of lean retail, 65–66, 67, 68
  and distribution, 65–66, 67, 68
  and impact of lean retail, 79, 80, 82, 83, 84
  standardization of, 313n29
  and suppliers, 246, 247, 249, 250, 254, 256–58
Shopping centers, 46, 300n8, 309n17
Shuttleless looms, 189, 190
SIC. *See* Standard Industrial Classification (SIC)
Singeing, 200–201
Sizing, 197
SKUs. *See* Stockkeeping units (SKUs)
Slashing, 197–98, 199, 330n25
Sourcing
  of assembly operations, 5, 44
  and competition, 16
  of cutting, 172
  and information-integrated channels, 266, 267, 278
  and inventory, 120–26
  and lean retail, 235
  and multiple plants, 119–26
  and "packagers," 234–35
  parameters for deciding, 164
  and preassembly operations, 130, 138–39
  and product proliferation, 17
  and regionalization of trade, 238
  in textile industry, 215, 216, 219
  and traditional operations, 44
  of transportation, 313n28
  and uncertain demand, 17
  See also Developing nations; Globalization; Imports/exports; Offshore manufacturers; Trade; *specific agreement or nation*
Southeast Asia, 205, 215, 223, 234, 238, 239, 337n38
Special orders, 162
Specialty stores, 24–25, 47, 74, 308n11
Speculative stock, 106
Spinning, 189, 192–96, 199, 202, 203, 208, 209, 214, 239, 275, 329n11
Spreading, 131, 139–40, 149, 157, 159
Standard Allocated Minutes (SAM), 28, 167, 325n3
Standard Industrial Classification (SIC), 203–4, 331n3, 331n4, 331n5
Standardization
  benefits of, 67–68, 314n38
  as building block of lean retail, 56, 57, 59, 60, 61, 67, 69–70

  compliance with, 70, 79, 315n42
  and distribution, 67–68
  and history of apparel industry, 31–32
  and impact of lean retail, 76–77, 79, 314n38
  and information systems, 302n25
  of labor costs, 306n27
  and labor unions, 31
  and pricing, 69
  and suppliers, 246, 247
  of wages, 31–32, 306n27
  See also ASN; Bar codes; EDI; Shipping container markers
Stock-outs, 48, 55, 97, 119, 275, 310n28
Stockkeeping units (SKUs)
  and bar codes, 10, 58, 60
  and building blocks of lean retail, 56
  and economic viability of textile industry, 214
  example of, 307–8n2
  and finishing operations, 200, 202
  in food chain stores, 58–59
  and forecasting demand, 89
  and inventory, 107, 110, 111, 113, 115–17, 119–23, 125–26, 316n5, 321n6, 321n7
  and lean retail as alternative, 52
  and modular assembly, 247
  and product proliferation, 45–46
  and retail-apparel-textile channel, 211
  and suppliers, 245, 247, 251, 258–59
  and traditional retail, 41, 45–46, 52
Straight-line system (SLS), 27, 28–29
Stretch out, 188–89
Suppliers
  for apparel industry, 244–50, 259
  and assembly operations, 245, 246–47, 250, 254
  and capital costs, 244
  and competition, 244, 245, 261, 275
  and cycle times, 247–48, 255–56, 258
  and distribution, 243–44, 246, 248, 249, 259–60, 261
  and EDI, 246, 247, 248, 249, 250, 251–52, 254, 256–58
  impact of lean retail on, 71–72, 77–79, 82, 84–85, 243–62, 311n39, 317n20
  and information systems, 1, 243–50, 253, 255–56
  and information-integrated channel, 268, 269, 275
  in integrated channels, 243–62

Suppliers *(continued)*
   inventory of, 244–45, 250–61, 269, 340n15, 340n18
   performance results of, 250–61
   practices of, 243–50, 258–61, 269, 317n20, 339n6
   profitability of, 251, 256–58, 340–41n22
   and retail sector, 275
   and standardization, 246, 247
   and technology, 244, 245, 253–56, 268
   for textile industry, 245
   See also Contractors/subcontractors; Manufacturers
Sweatshops, 30, 32, 183–84, 270–74, 305n20, 325n5, 328n36, 328n37, 344n28, 345n37, 345–46n38

Taft-Hartley Act, 328n34
Taiwan, 16, 230, 233, 266. *See also* "Big Four"
Tariff Act (1930), 227
Taylorism, 28, 306n29
[TC]^2, 321–22n1, 323n14
Team buying, 53
Team-based assembly operations, 162, 164, 168–79, 182
Technology
   in apparel industry, 29, 168, 244
   and assembly operations, 13, 168
   and channels, 10
   and competition, 5
   for distribution, 66–68, 314n32, 314n33, 314n34
   and employment/human resources, 5, 168
   and future directions, 265, 268, 280
   and information-integrated channel, 265, 268, 274, 275, 276, 280
   and inventory, 253–56, 340n18
   and labor standards, 274
   and PBS, 29
   and productivity, 12–13
   and profitability, 257
   and retail sector, 268, 276
   and suppliers, 244, 245, 253–56, 268
   in textile industry, 189–90, 191, 198, 202, 208, 214, 216, 219, 275
   and trade, 221, 265
   and traditional retail, 42
   See also type of technology
Textile and Apparel Linkage Council (TALC), 302n25
Textile industry
   assembly operations in, 216, 279
   automation in, 188, 189, 208
   capital costs in, 33–35, 187, 189, 190, 192–93, 196, 199, 200, 202, 208, 211, 213, 215, 216, 225, 267, 275, 330n23, 338n4
   challenges to, 202, 216–19
   channels for, 203–19
   competition in, 15–16, 36, 202, 212, 217, 219, 225–28, 239, 240, 242, 245, 274–75, 278–79
   computers in, 211, 218
   continuous operations in, 192, 202
   cycle times in, 214, 216
   decline in U.S. of, 206
   definition of, 203–4
   in developing nations, 186, 205, 223, 224–25, 239
   distribution in, 215, 216
   economic viability of, 203–19
   employment in, 5, 36, 205–10, 215, 241–42, 265, 266, 274–75, 279–80, 328n2, 329n14
   establishments in, 34–35, 190, 330–31n2
   and future of apparel industry, 15–16
   future of, 6–8, 264, 267, 278–79
   globalization of, 204–6, 221–42
   in Great Britain, 21, 22, 32–33, 185, 186
   history of, 21–22, 32–38, 185–86, 306n32
   human resources in, 35–36, 186, 216
   impact of different channels on, 208–11
   importance of, 186
   industrial products in, 37, 203, 205, 208–10, 213–16, 219, 239, 278–79
   information systems for, 36, 211, 212, 214–18, 245
   and information-integrated channels, 264–67, 274–75, 278–80
   inspection and repair in, 139
   inventory in, 214, 215–16
   job classifications in, 189–90, 327n27
   labor costs in, 36, 186, 205, 223, 225, 332–33n17
   labor unions in, 35–36, 188, 190
   lead times in, 210, 211–12, 218, 333n23
   lean retail's impact on, 3, 36, 40, 187, 202, 216, 217
   machinery/equipment for, 185–86, 189, 190–92, 198–99, 215, 307n34, 328n5
   management practices in, 259
   multiplants in, 214
   outlets for, 37–38
   performance in U.S., 206–8

product development in, 215
product proliferation in, 36, 202, 214, 215, 278
production processes in, 188–89
productivity in, 187, 189, 190, 191, 205, 206–8, 219, 332n13, 332n14, 332n15, 332–33n17
propositions about, 12–14
proprietary techniques in, 200
and quality, 191, 196–97
restructuring of, 34–35
sourcing in, 215, 216, 219
and supplier practices, 245
technology for, 189–90, 191, 198, 202, 208, 214, 216, 219, 275
and trade, 5–6, 15–16, 191–92, 206, 209, 219, 225–31, 232–42, 264–67, 275, 279
and traditional retail, 40
transformation of, 1–2
vertical and horizontal integration in, 34, 36–38
wages/compensation in, 35, 188, 189–90, 216, 217, 265, 275, 301n19, 304n9, 307n38, 331n5
work assignments in, 188–89
See also Apparel-textile channel; Finishing operations; Retail-apparel-textile channel; Retail-textile channel; Spinning; Weaving
Textile mills, development of modern, 187–92
Textile Workers Union of America, 35–36
Theft, 68
Threading, 197–98
Throughputs, 167, 169, 172–73, 176–78, 211, 246–49, 338n4
Trade
 and apparel industry, 15–16, 225–31, 232–42, 264–67, 300n12, 300–301n13, 336n25
 and assembly operations, 237, 238, 239, 240, 267, 326n11, 336n21
 changing patterns of, 232–37
 and channel integration, 234
 and competition, 5–6, 239, 240, 266
 countries of origin of, 229–30, 232–37
 and cycle times, 237, 239, 266, 267
 future directions of, 264–67
 growth in U.S., 221
 and information-integrated channels, 264–67
 international economics of, 264–67

 and labor costs, 36, 186, 205, 223, 225, 266, 267
 and labor standards, 266
 and lean retail, 234, 237, 266
 product composition of, 230–31
 regionalization of, 223, 237–40, 267
 and textile industry, 5–6, 15–16, 36, 191–92, 206, 209, 219, 225–31, 232–42, 264–67, 275, 279
 U.S. policies on, 225–28, 264–67
 and wages, 16, 239, 240, 264, 265, 267
 See also Developing nations; Imports/exports; specific agreement or nation
Traditional retail
 distribution for, 42, 68, 310n30
 elements of, 41–44
 fallout in, 47–48
 growing costs of, 44–48
 and inventory, 68, 91, 101–3, 120, 122
 lean retail as alternative to, 48–54
 lean versus, 39–48
 overcapacity in, 46–47
 and product proliferation, 45–46
Training, 169–70, 172, 181, 246, 274, 324–25n2
Transportation, 38, 42, 313n28. See also Distribution
Trends, 92
"Two-bin" policies, 319–20n17
Two-plant sourcing model, 121–23

UCC. See Uniform Code Council
UltraMark Optimizer System, 322n5
Uncertainty, demand, 17, 55, 92, 94, 95–96, 101, 109, 120, 130, 309n12, 319n9
Understocking, 97–98, 101
Unfinished goods. See Greige goods
Uniform Code Council (UCC), 58, 59, 60–62, 69, 313n29. See also Bar codes
Uniform/Universal Product Code (UPC), 59, 60, 61, 70, 71, 79, 81, 246. See also Bar codes; Uniform Code Council
Unit Production System (UPS), 162, 164, 278, 338n4
UNITE! (Union of Needletrades, Industrial and Textile Employees), 166, 168, 179–81, 182, 271, 274, 326n19, 327n29
United Garment Workers of America, 305n21
Unsold goods, 48
Unwanted goods, 44, 87

UPS. *See* Unit Production System
Uruguay Round (GATT), 6, 228–30, 264
U.S. Tariff Code, 336*n*21

Vendor-managed inventory, 63, 104–5
VICS committee (Voluntary Interindustry Communications Standards (VICS) committee), 61, 62, 70, 80, 302*n*25, 314*n*38, 314–15*n*39
VMI programs, 104–5

Wages
  in apparel industry, 7, 31–32, 35, 168–69, 172, 181, 183, 184, 265–66, 301*n*19, 302*n*26, 304*n*9, 307*n*38, 331*n*5
  in assembly operations, 12–13, 168–69, 172, 181, 247, 327*n*26
  and building blocks of lean retail, 59
  and bundle system, 12
  and competition, 7
  of cutters, 305*n*23
  in developing nations, 266
  in food stores, 302*n*24
  and future directions, 7, 264
  and information-integrated channels, 264, 265–66, 267, 270–74, 275
  and "packagers," 234
  and productivity, 12
  in retail sector, 304*n*9, 308*n*3
  for sewing operators, 159, 169, 172, 305*n*23
  standardization of, 31–32, 306*n*27
  and supplier practices, 247
  and sweatshops, 183, 184, 270–74, 328*n*36
  in textile industry, 35, 188, 189–90, 216, 217, 265, 275, 301*n*19, 304*n*9, 307*n*38, 331*n*5

and trade, 16, 239, 240, 264, 265, 267
Warehouses, 63
Weavers/weaving
  and competition, 202, 275
  and economic viability of textile industry, 203, 208, 209, 211, 214, 215
  and globalization, 225, 229, 239
  and history of textile industry, 185, 188–89, 192
  looms and machines for, 189, 190, 198–99
  preparations for, 197–98
Web sites, 279. *See also* Internet
WebPDM software, 134
Wholesale-jobbers, 23–24, 25
Wigans, 322*n*9
WIP. *See* Work-in-process inventory
Women workers, 190, 304*n*9, 324*n*7, 329*n*14, 329*n*14
Women's apparel, 7, 30, 31, 131, 163, 183, 210, 301*n*13, 301*n*17, 301*n*21, 336*n*25
Work-in-process inventory
  and assembly operations, 161, 169, 173
  and future of apparel industry, 277
  and human resources, 167, 169, 173, 181
  and manufacturers' inventory, 117, 123, 125, 181, 320*n*4, 321*n*13
  and productivity, 167
  and supplier performance, 181, 250, 256, 259
  and traditional system, 167, 210
Working conditions, 31–32, 274. *See also* Child labor; Labor standards; Sweatshops
World Bank, 221
World Trade Organization, 228, 264
World War II, apparel industry in, 1
Write-offs, 55

Name Index

Adanur, Sabit, 216
Albright, Madeleine K., 273, 345n37
Arpan, Jeffrey, 225
Ashton, T. S., 224
Atkins, Frederick, 308n9

Best, Ronald, 71
Brown, Moses, 21
Bucksbaum, Martin, 300n8

Cartwright, Edmund, 185
Chandler, Alfred, 22, 23, 24, 25, 38, 268
Cline, William, 190–91, 227
Cole, Tom, 243

Dalzell, Robert, 32–33, 185
Dillard, William T., 87
Drexler, Millard S., 43
Dubinsky, David, 31

Feldstein, Martin, 11
Field, Marshall, 43
Filene, Edward, 306n29
Filene, Lincoln, 306n29
Finger, Michael, 226
Flaming, Todd, 309n14
Freeston, W. Denny, 225

George, Catherine, 326n19
Gerber, Joseph, 129, 141
Gerschenkron, Alexander, 334–35n11
Gifford, Kathie Lee, 273
Gomberg, William A., 304n15
Gookin, R. Burt, 59
Guido, David, 71

Haas, Robert, 179, 180, 327n22
Hanson, George, 229
Harrison, Ann, 226

Herman, Alexis, 184
Hillman, Sidney, 31, 306n29
Howell, William, 48

Kernodle, Jeff, 243
Krugman, Paul, 241, 265

Lahne, Herbert, 187–88
Landes, David, 186
Love, Mark, 226
Lowell, Francis Cabot, 32–33, 185–86, 198

McDonald, Mackey, 109
Macy, Rowland, 40
Marcus, Stanley, 43
Mullin, Tracy, 276
Murray, Lauren, 225

Nehmer, Stanley, 226

Park, Sung, 323n13
Pataki, George, 344n25
Piore, Michael, 217
Pritchett, Lou, 50

Reich, Robert, 184

Sabel, Charles, 217
Salmon, Walter, 310n22
Sheinkman, Jack, 180
Sidell, Chet, 71
Slater, Samuel, 21–22, 32, 185
Sweeney, John J., 264

Tappan, Arthur, 40

Walton, Sam, 3, 39–40, 50, 311n36
Wanamaker, John, 39, 43
Whitin, Thomson, 308n4
Winters, P., 318–19n5

Levi Strauss *(continued)*
   information systems at, 181
   as lean retailer, 311*n*39
   mass customization by, 146, 147
   modular production at, 176–77, 179–81
   PBS at, 179–80, 181
   private label at, 43
   and retail-apparel-textile integration, 37
   as retailer, 217, 342*n*11
   and trade, 231, 238
   UNITE! partnership with, 166, 179–81
The Limited, 71, 72, 74, 125, 235
Liz Claiborne, 131, 238
L.L. Bean, 211, 313*n*23
Lord & Taylor, 40

Macy's, 5, 25, 47, 49, 79, 87, 318*n*2
Malden Mills, 200, 202, 211
Mall of America (Bloomington, Minnesota), 309*n*17
Marshall Field and Company, 5, 24, 25, 43
Marshall's, 182, 327*n*29
MAST Industries, 131
Mattel, 273
Mercantile, 37
Milliken, 34, 37
Montgomery Ward, 25, 75
Mothers' Work, 319*n*15

Nieman Marcus, 43
Nike, 273
Nordstrom, 91, 316*n*8
North Face, 211

Patagonia, 211
Procter & Gamble, 50, 311*n*39

Saks Fifth Avenue, 47, 49
Sears Roebuck and Co., 25, 39, 43, 49, 62, 71, 308*n*7, 315*n*41

South Coast Plaza/Crystal Coast Mall (Costa Mesa, California), 309*n*17
Springs Textile Company, 37

T. Eaton Company, 317*n*10
Target, 312–13*n*20
Textile and Clothing Technology Corporation, 299*n*3
TJMaxx, 327*n*29
TJX Company, 182
Tommy Hilfiger, 43, 238
Toys "R" Us, 317*n*13
Trader Joe's, 81
Triangle Shirtwaist Company, 271

United Parcel Service, 182

VF Corporation, 43, 84, 280, 311*n*39

Wal-Mart
   bar codes/EDI in, 60–61, 62
   and competition, 5, 311*n*36
   distribution for, 65, 313*n*22, 313*n*27
   impact of lean retail on, 71, 72, 73, 74–75
   information technologies at, 310*n*30
   as innovator, 3, 39
   and interaction with suppliers, 50
   as lean retail, 40, 49–50, 51, 52, 53
   as mass merchant, 5, 49–50
   as on-line seller, 346*n*44
   performance of, 72, 73, 74–75
   Procter & Gamble partnership with, 50
Wanamaker's
   bankruptcy of, 47
   and building blocks of lean retail, 57
   buyers at, 43
   and history of retail, 25
   and keys to effective retailing, 55
   as traditional retail, 39, 40, 41–42, 43

Business Index

Almy and Brown, 21–22
Almy, Brown and Slater, 22
American Merchandising Company, 308n9
Arkwright and Strutt, 21, 22
Arrow Shirt Company, 7

Black and Decker, 280
Bloomingdale's, 79
BMW cars, 259–60, 302n30, 341n24
Bond Stores, 1–2, 4, 20, 37
Boston Manufacturing Company, 185–86
Bradlees, 316n7
Burlington Industries, 34, 37, 307n42

Caldor, 316n7
Circuit City, 317n13
Compaq Computer, 260–61, 341n28
Costco, 41, 317n13

Dayton/Hudson, 312–13n20
Del Amo Fashion Center (Torrance, California), 309n17
Dell Computer, 15, 260, 261, 280
Denver International Airport, 314n33
Dillard's Inc., 3, 40, 52, 62, 71, 72, 73, 74, 107–8, 311n36, 316n5

Eddie Bauer, 346n44
El monte (California) plant, 271

Federated Department Stores, 40, 47, 52–53, 62, 71, 79, 280, 315n42 *See also* Bloomingdale's; Macy's
Field, Leiter and Company, 24
Fruit of the Loom, 7
F.W. Woolworth, 75

The Gap, 43, 72, 74
Garment Industry Development Corporation, 346n40
Gateway 2000, 260, 261
Gerber Garment Technology Company, 129, 134, 322n5
Gimbel's, 47

Haggar Apparel Co., 7, 80, 84, 176–77, 311n39
Hart, Schaffner, and Marx, 7, 26, 37, 306n29, 342n11
Hathaway Shirt Company, 7
Hewlett Packard, 260
The Home Depot, 15, 280, 315n41, 317n13

IBM, 62, 63

J. Crew, 346n44
J.C. Penney, 40, 43, 50–52, 71, 72, 74, 308n4, 315n41, 346n44

KGR, 71
Kmart Corporation, 3, 39, 40, 50, 51, 52, 60–61, 62, 310n30, 315n41, 316n7
Kroger Co., 39

Lands' End, 71, 193, 211, 276–77, 346n44
Levi Strauss
  customization at, 181
  distribution for, 181
  and economic viability of textile industry, 217
  future directions for, 280
  human resource development at, 166, 176–77, 179–81